Margaret Mead and Samoa

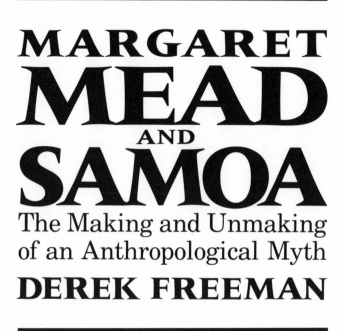

MARGARET MEAD AND SAMOA

The Making and Unmaking
of an Anthropological Myth

DEREK FREEMAN

Harvard University Press • Cambridge, Massachusetts
and London, England   1983

Library of Congress Cataloging in Publication Data

Freeman, Derek.
Margaret Mead and Samoa.

Includes bibliographical references and index.
1. Ethnology—Samoan Islands.
2. Mead, Margaret, 1901–   .   3. Adolescence.
4. Nature and nurture. I.   Title
GN671.S2F73   1983   306'.0996   82-15620
ISBN 0-674-54830-2

To Karl R. Popper

Contents

II Mead's Samoan Research

III A Refutation of Mead's Conclusions

IV Margaret Mead and the Boasian Paradigm

Illustrations

Preface

BY FAR the most widely known of Margaret Mead's numerous books is *Coming of Age in Samoa,* based on fieldwork on which she embarked in 1925 at the instigation of Franz Boas, her professor at Columbia University. Boas had sent the 23-year-old Mead to Samoa to study adolescence, and she returned with a startling conclusion. Adolescence was known in America and Europe as a time of emotional stresses and conflicts. If, Mead argued, these problems were caused by the biological processes of maturation, then they would necessarily be found in all human societies. But in Samoa, she reported, life was easy and casual, and adolescence was the easiest and most pleasant time of life. Thus in anthropological terms, according to Mead, Samoa was a "negative instance"—and the existence of this one counterexample demonstrated that the disturbances associated with adolescence in the United States and elsewhere had cultural and not biological causes. In the controversy between the adherents of biological determinism and those of cultural determinism, a controversy that was at its height in the 1920s, Mead's negative instance appeared to be a triumphant outcome for believers in the sovereignty of culture.

When *Coming of Age in Samoa* was published in 1928 it attracted immense attention, and its apparently conclusive finding swiftly entered anthropological lore as a jewel of a case. Since that time Mead's finding has been recounted in scores of textbooks, and through the vast popularity of *Coming of Age in Samoa,* the best-selling of all anthropological books, it has influenced the thinking of millions of people throughout the world. It is with the critical examination of this very widely accepted conclusion that I am concerned in this book.

Scientific knowledge, as Karl Popper has shown, is principally advanced through the conscious adoption of "the critical method of error elimination." In other words, within science, propositions and theories are systematically tested by attempts to refute them, and they remain acceptable only as long as they withstand these attempts at refutation. In Popper's view, "in so far as a scientific statement speaks about reality it must be falsifiable," and rational criticism entails the testing of any particular statement in terms of its correspondence with the facts. Mead's classing of Samoa as a negative instance obviously depends on the adequacy of the account of Samoan culture on which it is based. It is thus very much a scientific proposition, for it is fully open to testing against the relevant empirical evidence.[1]

While the systematic testing of the conclusions of a science is always desirable, this testing is plainly imperative when serious doubts have been expressed about some particular finding. Students of Samoan culture have long voiced such doubts about Mead's findings of 1928. In this book I adduce detailed empirical evidence to demonstrate that Mead's account of Samoan culture and character is fundamentally in error. I would emphasize that I am not intent on constructing an alternative ethnography of Samoa. Rather, the evidence I shall present has the specific

purpose of scientifically refuting the proposition that Samoa is a
negative instance by demonstrating that the depictions on
which Mead based this assertion are, in varying degree, mistaken.

In undertaking this refutation I shall limit my scrutiny to
those sections of Mead's writings which have stemmed from, or
refer to, her researches on Samoa. My concern, moreover, is
with the scientific import of these actual researches and *not*
with Margaret Mead personally, or with any aspect of her ideas
or activities that lies beyond the ambit of her writings on
Samoa. I would emphasize also that I hold in high regard many
of the personal achievements of Margaret Mead, Franz Boas,
and the other individuals certain of whose assertions and ideas I
necessarily must question in the pages that follow.

According to Mead, the making of her study of adolescence
in Samoa was an accident of history. It is also by an accident of
history that I have come to write this book. In the late 1930s, at
Victoria University College in Wellington, New Zealand, I
chanced to become a student of Ernest Beaglehole, who had
studied anthropology at Yale under Edward Sapir, a former
student of Franz Boas. Beaglehole's anthropology was very similar to Mead's, and it was this approach, stemming from the
teaching of Boas, that I had adopted when, with Beaglehole's
encouragement, I decided to do ethnographic research in the
Samoan islands. When I reached Western Samoa in April 1940,
I was very much a cultural determinist. *Coming of Age in
Samoa* had been unreservedly commended to me by Beaglehole, and my credence in Mead's findings was complete.

After two years of study, during which I came to know all the
islands of Western Samoa, I could speak Samoan well enough to
converse in the company of chiefs with the punctilio that Samoan etiquette demands, and the time had come to select a
local polity for intensive investigation. My choice was Sa'anapu,
a settlement of 400 inhabitants on the south coast of Upolu. On
my first visit to Sa'anapu I had become friendly with Lauvi
Vainu'u, a senior talking chief. When I arrived to begin my researches I learned of the death of Lauvi's youngest son,
Fa'imoto. Lauvi had been deeply attached to Fa'imoto, and he

experienced my return as reparation for his loss. He had decided, he told me, that I was to become his adopted son. From that time onward I lived as one of the Lauvi family whenever I was in Sa'anapu.

In my early work I had, in my unquestioning acceptance of Mead's writings, tended to dismiss all evidence that ran counter to her findings. By the end of 1942, however, it had become apparent to me that much of what she had written about the inhabitants of Manu'a in eastern Samoa did not apply to the people of western Samoa. After I had been assured by Samoans who had lived in Manu'a that life there was essentially the same as in the western islands, I realized that I would have to make one of the objectives of my research the systematic testing of Mead's depiction of Samoan culture.

Soon after I returned to Sa'anapu its chiefs forgathered one morning at Lauvi's house to confer on me one of the chiefly titles of their polity. I was thus able to attend all *fono,* or chiefly assemblies, as of right, and I soon came to be accepted by the community at large. From this time onward I was in an exceptionally favorable position to pursue my researches into the realities of Samoan life.

By the time I left Samoa in November 1943 I knew that I would one day face the responsibility of writing a refutation of Mead's Samoan findings. This would involve much research into the history of early Samoa. This task I began in 1945 in the manuscript holdings of the Mitchell Library in Sydney and later continued in England, where I thoroughly studied the Samoan archives of the London Missionary Society.

During 1946–1948, while studying anthropology at the University of London, I wrote a dissertation on Samoan social organization, and my intention was to return to Polynesia. There then came, however, the opportunity to spend some years among the Iban of Borneo. With this diversion, which later took me to Cambridge University to complete my doctoral studies and then in new anthropological directions, the continuation of my Samoan researches was long delayed.

I finally returned to Western Samoa, accompanied by my wife and daughters, at the end of 1965. Sa'anapu, now linked to

Apia by road, was once again my center of research. The chiefs
of Sa'anapu immediately recognized the title they had conferred on me in 1943, and I became once again an active member of the Sa'anapu *fono*. My family and I remained in Samoa
for just over two years, making frequent visits elsewhere in the
district to which Sa'anapu belongs, as also to numerous other
parts of the archipelago, from Saua in the east to Falealupo in
the west.

Many educated Samoans, especially those who had attended
college in New Zealand, had become familiar with Mead's writings about their culture. A number of them entreated me, as an
anthropologist, to correct her mistaken depiction of the Samoan
ethos. Accordingly, early in 1966 I set about the systematic examination of the entire range of Mead's writings on Samoa,
seeking to test her assertions by detailed investigation of the
particulars of the behavior or custom to which they referred. I
also investigated, with the permission of the prime minister of
Western Samoa, confidential court and police records, an inval-
uable source of data on crucial aspects of the aggressive and
sexual behavior of Samoans, including that of adolescents.

Sa'anapu, it so happens, was founded in ancient times by
migrants from the island of Ta'ū, the main site of Mead's researches in 1925–1926. Taking advantage of this fact, in 1967 I
organized a formal traveling party to Ta'ū. We visitors were received as long-lost kinsmen, and in the company of chiefs from
both Ta'ū and Sa'anapu I was able to review all those facets of
Mead's depiction of Samoa which were then still at issue. In
Ta'ū I also recorded the testimony of men and women who remembered the period to which Mead's writings refer. In many
instances these recollections were vivid and specific; as one of
my informants remarked, the happenings of the mid 1920s were
still fresh in their memories.

As my inquiries progressed it became evident that my critical scrutiny of Mead's conclusions would have to extend to the
anthropological paradigm of which *Coming of Age in Samoa*
was a part. In order to comprehend the circumstances that had
prompted Boas to send Mead to Samoa I would have to investigate not only the history of anthropology but that of biology as

well, and in particular the interaction of biological and anthropological ideas from the time of Darwin's *Origin of Species* onward. Because it was imperative to consult the relevant primary
sources, this investigation occupied me intermittently for more
than a decade.

The account of the interrelated histories of biological and
anthropological ideas that I give in Chapters 1–4 of this book
provides a background essential for understanding the way the
ideology and projects of Francis Galton and his followers in the
eugenics movement produced a reaction by anthropologists and
others that culminated in the frenetic nature-nurture controversy of the mid 1920s. A knowledge of these ideological developments of the late nineteenth and early twentieth centuries is
also necessary for understanding the pivotal significance of
Mead's Samoan researches for the school of American anthropologists led by Franz Boas and Alfred Kroeber, which from
1917 onward was committed to a doctrine of extreme cultural
determinism. This book, then, while primarily given to the refutation of the general conclusion that Mead drew from her
Samoan researches, is also concerned with examining related
aspects of the wider myth of absolute cultural determinism, and
with arguing that this now antiquated doctrine should be abandoned in favor of a more scientific anthropological paradigm.

My researches were not completed until 1981, when I finally
gained access to the archives of the High Court of American
Samoa for the 1920s. Thus my refutation of Mead's depiction of
Samoa appears some years after her death. In November 1964,
however, when Dr. Mead visited the Australian National University, I informed her very fully, during a long private conversation, of the empirical basis of my disagreement with her depiction of Samoa. From that time onward we were in
correspondence, and in August 1978, upon its first completion, I
offered to send her an early draft of my refutation of the conclusions she had reached in *Coming of Age in Samoa*. I received
no reply to this offer before Dr. Mead's death in November of
that year.

In September 1981 I returned to Western Samoa with the
specific purpose of submitting a draft of this book to the critical

scrutiny of Samoan scholars. Chapters 5 to 19 were meticulously checked by Le Tagaloa Leota Pita of the University of Samoa. From Western Samoa I traveled to Tutuila and Manu'a for discussions with other knowledgeable Samoans, whose comments I have also taken fully into account. In the course of the refutation of Mead's misleading account of their culture, which many Samoans encouraged me to undertake, I have had to deal realistically with the darker side of Samoan life. During my visit of 1981 I found among contemporary Samoans both a mature appreciation of the need to face these realities and a clear-headed pride in the virtues and strengths of the Samoan way of life.

The chapters that follow, then, are based on investigations that have extended, off and on, over some forty years, including six years spent in Samoa and even longer in the research libraries of Australia, New Zealand, England, and the United States. My work in Samoa during the years 1965–1968 and again in 1981 was carried out from the Research School of Pacific Studies of the Institute of Advanced Studies of the Australian National University; it is the exceptional opportunity for research provided by this institute that has enabled me to explore the history of both anthropology and biology, and to bring to fruition this study of a major twentieth-century myth. It is a study that bears on problems of the greatest anthropological importance and that will, I hope, contribute constructively to their solution.

I

THE EMERGENCE
OF CULTURAL
DETERMINISM

1

Galton, Eugenics, and Biological Determinism

MARGARET MEAD began work on *Coming of Age in Samoa,* the book that was to become the most widely known of all her writings, in the autumn of 1926. A newly appointed assistant curator of ethnology at the American Museum of Natural History in New York, she had just returned from the South Seas, where she had gone in 1925 at the behest of Franz Boas, the celebrated professor of anthropology at Columbia University, to try to establish for the Samoans of Western Polynesia to what extent adolescent behavior was physiologically determined and to what extent culturally determined.[1]

In the mid 1920s the nature-nurture controversy, which had begun in earnest in about 1910, was still very much alive. "No subject of sociological inquiry within recent years," Stuart Rice wrote in 1924, "has proved to be more controversial than the effort to determine the relative importance of biological and of purely social factors in the development of human society." On the one hand biologists like H. M. Parshley were maintaining that the child was "a rigid complex of inherited proclivities," while on the other J. B. Watson and his supporters were fervently proclaiming that "nurture—not nature" was responsible "for what the child becomes." It was onto this confused and hectic battlefield that the young Margaret Mead sallied.[2]

The question uppermost in the minds of the scientific world at this time was, as Mead records, "What is human nature?" It was to answering this and related questions that Mead turned in *Coming of Age in Samoa.* She swept into the fray armed with the results of a special inquiry devised by Boas, based on evidence she had collected during field research in a remote Polynesian society very different indeed from the America of the 1920s, and the conclusion she announced, to the discomfort of biological determinists and the delight of their opponents, was the complete dominance of nurture over nature. The difficulties and unrest associated with adolescence in the United States and elsewhere had long been regarded as the concomitants of a natural process. Among Samoans, however, according to Mead, such disturbances did not occur. This demonstrated, she concluded, that adolescent behavior had to be explained in purely cultural terms.[3]

Coming of Age in Samoa appeared in 1928, accompanied by an appreciative foreword by Boas. Later that same year, in his *Anthropology and Modern Life,* Boas made specific mention of Mead's momentous finding that in Samoa "the adolescent crisis disappears." Boas' ready acceptance of this finding and of Mead's sweeping view that social pressure exercises an "absolute determination in shaping the individuals within its bounds" is understandable, for these conclusions strikingly confirmed his own most cherished beliefs. In 1916 he had launched an attack on the "ambitious theory" that for some years had been "preached" by the "apostles of eugenics." His own belief, in sharp contrast to that of the eugenicists, was that "the social stimulus is infinitely more potent than the biological mechanism." It was precisely this view that his own student, Margaret Mead, had validated in Samoa.[4]

Boas' chief complaint in 1916 was that the battle-cry of the eugenicists, "nature not nurture," had been raised to the rank of a dogma, and that in consequence "the environmental conditions that make and unmake man, physically and mentally," had been relegated to the background. Boas was well justified in this complaint. In 1915, for example, Paul Popenoe, editor of *The Journal of Heredity,* had affirmed his faith (based, he claimed, on incontrovertible fact) that "heredity is not only much stronger than any single factor of the environment, in producing important human differences, but is stronger than any possible number of them put together." That same year, Karl Pearson, the first Galton Professor of Eugenics at the University of London, had declared that the assertion that "nature is five to ten times as influential as nurture" was free from any exaggeration and formed a solid ground upon which to base reforms to "accelerate racial progress." By the time Boas delivered his broadside against eugenics, assertions like these had become commonplace. Moreover, they were directly linked with racist views like those contained in Madison Grant's *The Passing of the Great Race.*[5]

In a lecture at Columbia University in December 1907, Boas had given it as his view that a separation of anthropological methods from the methods of biology and psychology was impossible, and then gone on to express the hope that "the safe methods of biological and psychological anthropometry and anthropology" would help to remove the problems of "race-mixture" and eugenics from heated political discussion and make them subjects of calm scientific investigation. By 1916, however, his attitude had decisively changed. During the intervening years the eugenics movement had effloresced into a pseudo-scientific cult, and Boas had come to see both eugenics and the racial interpretation of history as irremediably dangerous. The extreme doctrines of the hereditarians, Boas pointed out, had set anthropologists and biologists at odds, and so much so that a "parting of the ways" had been reached.[6]

These were portentous words. Within the space of a few months, two of the most able and active of Boas' former students, Alfred Kroeber and Robert Lowie, had published intellectual manifestos that conceptually dissociated cultural anthropology from biology. Their solution was the propounding of a doctrine of absolute cultural determinism that totally excluded biological variables. This turning point in the history of twentieth-century anthropology was the culmination of processes, especially within biology, that had begun during the second half of the nineteenth century. It is to a consideration of these momentous events that I turn in this first chapter, beginning in 1859, the year of publication of Charles Darwin's *The Origin of Species by Means of Natural Selection,* and ending in 1911, the year of the death of Francis Galton, "the father of Eugenics," who more than anyone else was responsible for the extreme hereditarian doctrines against which Boas, Kroeber, and Lowie so categorically reacted.[7]

In his preface to Grant's *The Passing of the Great Race,* written in July 1916, Henry Fairfield Osborn explicitly linked both eugenics and the racial interpretation of history to the "great biological movement" which went back to the teachings of Francis Galton and August Weismann in the last third of the nineteenth century. These teachings were primarily concerned with the phenomenon of natural selection, and both stemmed from the theory advanced in *The Origin of Species,* with which had commenced, in Weismann's words, "a new era in biology." Although Darwin had been convinced from September 1838, when he first conceived of the way in which natural selection operated in animal populations, "that man must come under the same law," he elected to include in *The Origin of Species* no more than the terse words: "Light will be thrown on the origin of man and his history." Yet from the outset the bearing of Darwin's theory on the human species became the center of passionate debate, as in the confrontation between T. H. Huxley and Samuel Wilberforce in June 1860 at the Oxford meeting of the British Association for the Advancement of Science. One of those present at this famous debate was Francis Galton, the half first cousin of Charles Darwin.[8]

In 1860 Francis Galton was thirty-eight years of age, a Fellow of the Royal Society, and a gentleman of independent means. After taking his degree at Trinity College, Cambridge, he had traveled in Egypt and the Sudan and made a major journey of exploration in South-West Africa, before becoming in 1857 the honorary general secretary of the Royal Geographical Society. By 1859 he had already begun to interest himself in "the human side of Geography," and being in this way "prepared to appreciate" Darwin's theory, absorbed it "almost at once." It was an experience that he likened to baptism, and he came to think of Darwin "in the same way as converts from barbarism think of the teacher who first relieved them from the intolerable burden of their superstition." From his study of *The Origin of Species* Galton became deeply convinced that "a great power was at hand wherewith man could transform his nature and destiny." Imbued with intense enthusiasm for this idea, he turned his powerful intellect to the possibilities of applying selection to the human species. As early as 1865 he published a general statement of the extreme hereditarian doctrines to which he staunchly adhered for the rest of his days.[9]

At the time of the publication of Darwin's theory of evolution by means of natural selection, there was no understanding of human cultures as socially inherited systems of information. Instead, it was generally supposed that the differences that existed among human societies had come into being, in the course of their separate histories, through the inheritance of acquired characters. Moreover, credence in the inheritance of "functionally-produced modifications" (to use Herbert Spencer's term) persisted throughout Darwin's lifetime, for it was not until 1883 that Weismann first advanced convincing evidence for the rejection of Lamarckian doctrine. It was in this setting that Galton began, in the early 1860s, to develop his own far-reaching ideas about the power of hereditary influence in human affairs.

Although in *The Origin of Species* Darwin explicitly recognized "use and disuse" as ancillary agents in evolutionary change, it was his view that natural selection had given rise to "all the more important modifications of structure." He was closely followed in this by Galton, who from the outset of his own theorizing was even more dubious about the inheritance of acquired characters, giving it as his opinion in 1865 that "if the habits of an individual are transmitted to his descendants, it is, as Darwin says, in a very small degree, and is hardly, if at all, traceable." Accordingly, in the formulation of his own views Galton gave complete predominance to natural selection, ruling out Lamarckian mechanisms and giving no effective recognition to the existence of cultural processes.[10]

Galton's doctrines stemmed from the basic assumption that natural selection, as a pervasively determinative force, applied to all aspects of human character and history. In 1865 he proclaimed "the enormous power of hereditary influence," and presented, according to Karl Pearson, such a clear epitome of the whole doctrine of eugenics that "it might almost have been written as a résumé of his labours after they were completed." He roundly asserted that Darwin's law of natural selection, which acted with "unimpassioned, merciless severity" in the case of physical qualities, also operated in the case of moral character, religious sentiments, and the like, and that mental characters were the direct products of natural selection just as were physical characters. This extreme conclusion that the law of natural selection resulted in "the like inheritance" of mental and physical characters became, in Pearson's words, the foundation stone of Galton's life's work, and the most fixed principle of his teaching.[11]

From Galton's fixed principle that natural selection results in the like inheritance of the mental and physical, and so adequately accounts for human character and history, various related doctrines stemmed, all of them directly impinging on the nascent science of anthropology. Foremostly, Galton's fixed principle was essential to his view of the past evolution of man and his estimation of "the comparative worth of different races." Galton was convinced that all of the differences between "savage" and "civilized" societies could be explained by the "innate character of different races." "Every long-established race," he asserted in 1869, "has necessarily its peculiar fitness for the conditions under which it has lived, owing to the sure operation of Darwin's law of natural selection."[12]

Giving natural selection this totally determinative power, and lacking any appreciation of cultural values and processes, Galton was swiftly led to overweening conclusions, many of them, in the light of present knowledge, markedly racist. The white residents of North America, he claimed in 1865, having been "bred from the most restless and combative class of Europe," had, under the influence of natural selection, become "enterprising, defiant and touchy; impatient of authority; furious politicians; very tolerant of fraud and violence; possessing much high and generous spirit, and some true religious feeling, but strongly addicted to cant." While in the case of Negroes "the sure operation of Darwin's law of natural selection" had resulted in the number of those "whom we should call half-witted men" being very large. "Every book alluding to negro servants in America" was, according to Galton, "full of instances." Moreover, he had been much impressed by this characteristic of Negroes during his travels in Africa, the mistakes that they made being "so childish, stupid and simpleton-like" as frequently to make him ashamed of his own species. As he was the first evolutionist to apply natural selection to human races and cultures in this naive and sweeping manner, we may trace back to Galton in particular, as did Osborn, the racial interpretation of human history that became popular among eugenicists and others from about 1916 onward, and to which Boas and other anthropologists were so rootedly opposed.[13]

Combined with this belief in major innate differences in character and intellect between human races was the closely related doctrine that nature is ever dominant over nurture. In Galton's early papers the opposition was between "race" and "nurture." In 1873, for example, he wrote of race being far more important than nurture. But from 1874 onward he adopted the "antithetic terms of Shakespearean origin," nature and nurture. "The phrase 'nature and nurture,' " he wrote, "is a convenient jingle of words, for it separates under two distinct heads the innumerable elements of which personality is composed. Nature is all that a man brings with him into the world; nurture is every influence from without that affects him after birth."[14]

As early as 1873 it was Galton's fixed belief that "when nature and nurture compete for supremacy on equal terms" it is always nature that proves the stronger. In 1883, after completing an inquiry into the life history of twins, he greatly expanded his claims, declaring that he had succeeded in "proving the vastly preponderating effects of nature over nurture." This sweeping conclusion became, in Lowie's words, the "cornerstone of Galton's biological philosophy," and the basic doctrine of the eugenics movement he launched during the early years of the twentieth century.[15]

Convinced that nature was preponderatingly important in the formation of human character and civilization, Galton was impelled to develop elaborate schemes for "hereditary improvement." "What an extraordinary effect might be produced on our race," he wrote in 1865, if it were the practice to "unite in marriage those who possessed the finest and most suitable natures, mental, moral and physical." In this way, he surmised, for "a twentieth part of the cost and pains" spent on the improvement of the breed of horses and cattle, a "galaxy of genius" might be created. He went on in 1873 to envisage a future in which "a perfect enthusiasm for improving the race might develop itself among the educated classes," who would avow it as their "paramount duty, to anticipate the slow and stubborn processes of natural selection, by endeavouring to breed out feeble constitutions and petty and ignoble instincts, and to breed in those which are vigorous and noble and social." For Francis Galton such "race improvement," to which in 1883 he gave the name *eugenics,* was the grandest of all objects, and from 1901 onward, during the last ten years of his long life, he succeeded in arousing in numerous others something closely akin to a perfect enthusiasm for his utopian schemes.[16]

Although Darwin was impressed by Galton's work (when *Hereditary Genius* appeared in 1869, Darwin remarked to its author, "I do not think I have ever in all my life read anything more interesting and original") he never became a proponent of his cousin's scheme for hereditary improvement, and in his overall view of human evolution, as Karl Pearson has observed, Darwin differed essentially from Galton. Thus, while always affirming the fundamental importance of natural selection and believing that it did have some bearing on social questions, Darwin gave decidedly more recognition than did Galton to the significance of cultural processes in human evolution. He summarized his general position in *The Descent of Man* in 1871: "Important as the struggle for existence has been and even still is, yet as far as the highest part of man's nature is concerned there are other agencies more important. For the moral qualities are advanced, either directly or indirectly, much more through the effects of habit, the reasoning powers, instruction, religion, &c., than through natural selection; though to this latter agency may be safely attributed the social instincts, which afforded the basis for the development of the moral sense."[17]

In this formulation the way is open for recognition of the coexistence of biological and cultural factors, and of their complex interaction in human evolution. There were within evolutionism, however, a number of less enlightened trends, and unfortunately for the infant science of anthropology, by the early twentieth century the doctrines of hereditarians like Galton held sway within human biology.

By about 1871, with the publication of E. B. Tylor's *Primitive Culture,* evolutionism had become the dominant force in anthropology. Its main characteristic (as Boas pointed out in 1911) was the "application to mental phenomena of the theory of biological evolution." At this time all evolutionists, including Darwin to some extent, gave credence not only to evolution by means of natural selection but also to relatively rapid evolutionary change through the inheritance of acquired characters. Indeed, not a few evolutionists, most notably Herbert Spencer, were convinced that the inheritance of "functionally-produced modifications" ranked as the chief cause of evolutionary change in human societies. This mistaken credence in Lamarckian principles persisted, without serious challenge, until 1883 when August Weismann, in a lecture at the University of Freiburg, rejected the assumption of the transmission of acquired characters and propounded in its stead his theory of "the continuity of the substance of the germ-cells, or germ-plasm."[18]

By the mid-1880s Weismann's views had excited widespread interest among biologists, and in 1887, when he attended the fifty-seventh meeting of the British Association for the Advancement of Science in Manchester to lecture on his theory of heredity, a special symposium was arranged devoted to the question: "Are Acquired Characters Hereditary?" This symposium and the dissemination of Weismann's ideas elsewhere made the theory of the noninheritance of acquired characters, in the words of George John Romanes, the most important question that had been raised in biology "since the promulgation of Mr. Darwin's great doctrine"; and in mid 1889 Romanes ranked the widespread abandonment of Lamarckian principles that had been brought about by Weismann and others as "a most extraordinary revolution of biological thought" and "the turning of a tide of scientific opinion."[19]

By about 1889, then, Weismann, with the aid of other experimental biologists, had brought about a "sea change" in evolutionary thought. The leading evolutionists of the day were quick to explore the theoretical consequences of this fundamental reorientation, and two opposing trends soon emerged. The first of these was a marked accentuation, in the writings of the Social Darwinists in particular, of the significance of natural selection in human societies, without any corresponding recognition of cultural processes. The second was the dawning of a realization that for the understanding of human societies it was vitally important to recognize cultural processes as being essentially different from those of evolution by means of natural selection.[20]

With his demonstration that acquired characters were not inherited, Weismann had placed Darwin's original hypothesis on apparently unshakable foundations, and in the eyes of Benjamin Kidd and other Social Darwinists of the 1890s (who in their enthusiasm went far beyond the views of Darwin himself), this left natural selection as "the immutable law of progress" in human societies as among other forms of life within the cosmos.

"Not only is the cosmic process everywhere triumphant," Kidd proclaimed, "but our ethical and moral progress have no meaning apart from it; they are mere phases of it, developed, as every phase of life from the beginning has been, on the strictest and sternest conditions of Natural Selection." Again, soon after the collapse of the theory of the inheritance of acquired characters, A. R. Wallace expressed the opinion that some form of selection now remained "the only possible means of improving the race."[21]

These developments created a favorable atmosphere for Galton's doctrine of the vastly preponderating effects of nature over nurture as also for his schemes for "hereditary improvement." A further major development was the rediscovery in 1900 of Mendel's laws of heredity. In the following year, in his Huxley Lecture to the Anthropological Institute of Great Britain and Ireland, Galton initiated what he called, and what during the next decade rapidly became, a "crusade" for "race improvement." The eugenics movement was under way.[22]

That Galton should have launched this crusade in a Huxley Lecture was ironic, for in his *Evolution and Ethics and other Essays,* published in 1894, T. H. Huxley had remarked that eugenics hardly came "within the region of practical politics." In this same volume there also appeared Huxley's remarkable Romanes Lecture of 1893, in which he adumbrated an anthropological paradigm in which cultural as well as biological processes were explicitly recognized. "The history of civilization," he declared, detailed the steps by which men had succeeded in "building up an artificial world within the cosmos," and he gave it as his view that the "progressive modification which passes by the name of the 'evolution of society' " was in fact "a process essentially different from that which brought about the evolution of species, in the state of nature."[23]

This same quite fundamental point was taken up a few years later by another distinguished Darwinian, E. Ray Lankester. In a historically important paper, Lankester (who was at this time Director of the British Museum of Natural History) drew special attention to the educability of the human species as compared with apes. "The character that we describe as 'educability,' " Lankester noted, "can be transmitted, it is a congenital character. But the *results* of education can *not* be transmitted. In each generation they have to be acquired afresh." In later writings on this same theme, Lankester made it clear that in 1899 he had used the phrase "the results of education" to refer to "the enormous mass of accumulated experience, knowledge, tradition, custom and law, which pervades and envelopes ... the mere physical generations of this or that pullulating crowd of human individuals" and that this constituted a peculiarity of man that affected his manifestation of qualities "in a way unknown to any other living thing." The general term that Lankester applied to the results of education was "tradition." From his accounts of what he meant by tradition it is clear that Lankester was discussing what Boas and others were by this time calling culture.[24]

By the beginning of the twentieth century, then, there were within biology two sharply contrasting views of man's place in nature. On the one hand stood thinkers like Huxley and Lankester, who believed that in the case of the human species there existed two relatively autonomous but closely interacting evolutionary systems, one genetic and the other exogenetic. On the other hand stood scientists like Galton for whom the hereditary nature of man was of vastly preponderating importance. As the twentieth century unfolded the doctrine of the vastly preponderating importance of heredity gained the ascendancy, and it eventually provoked the misconceived nature-nurture controversy of the second and third decades of the century, during which the enlightened views of Huxley and Lankester were almost wholly ignored.

In his account of Galton's efforts to bring eugenics to the attention of the general public, Karl Pearson (who was Galton's fervent collaborator) describes Galton seeking "proselytes" to his "faith." Galton, according to Pearson, was teaching a new morality with a definite plan of eugenics propagandism, and his cry of "Awake my people," was "like that of a religious prophet of olden time." The use of such language by so rigorous a methodologist of science as Karl Pearson may seem odd, but it was appropriate, for Galton made it plain that he conceived of eugenics as an expression of "the religious significance of the doctrine of evolution." In his Huxley Lecture of 1901 he talked of "an enthusiasm to improve the race" being so noble an aim as to give rise to the sense of a religious obligation, and of the founding of a great society which in its crusade for race improvement would be "like a missionary society with its missionaries."[25]

In 1905, by endowing a research fellowship, Galton was able to have eugenics recognized by the University of London, and in 1907 the Eugenics Education Society was established to popularize the results and methods of eugenics. By this time, according to Galton, the once feeble flame of eugenics had become "a brisk fire, burning freely by itself."[26]

As the eugenics movement grew in popularity in England, its leaders lost none of their fervor. At Oxford in 1907 Pearson extolled eugenics as the virile "creed of action" which "alone can make a reality of statecraft," and spoke approvingly of countries where "race betterment" had already "assumed the form of a religious cult." Galton, in his Spencer Lecture of that same year, looked forward to a time when, with the desired fullness of information, it would be possible to "proclaim a 'Jehad' or Holy War against customs and prejudices that impair the physical and moral qualities of our race." As these and other solemn expressions of zeal indicate, the eugenics movement was (in C. W. Saleeby's words) "at once a science and a religion." Its great popularity and marked influence have to be understood in these terms.[27]

A comparable zeal characterized the eugenics movement in the United States. Galton's Huxley Lecture was republished in the Annual Report of the Smithsonian Institution for 1901, and, according to Pearson, "attracted more attention and bore ampler fruit" in America than in England. In 1906 the American Breeders Association set up a Committee on Eugenics, with David S. Jordan, a prominent biologist and chancellor of Stanford University, as its chairman, to "investigate and report on heredity in the human race" and to "emphasize the value of superior blood and the menace to society of inferior blood." At this time research in genetics was very active, and a high percentage of geneticists, especially in America, were attracted to, and became proponents of, Galton's ideas.[28]

The principal enthusiast was Charles B. Davenport, a geneticist who became the secretary of the Committee on Eugenics of the American Breeders Association. Like Galton, Davenport was convinced of the imperative need for race improvement, as he argued in 1910 in his book *Eugenics: The Science of Human Improvement by Better Breeding*. Davenport's fervor matched that of Galton himself. Eugenics was seen as biology's panacea for the social ills of mankind. There was, Davenport declared, an urgent need both to set forth "the way to secure sound progeny" and to "annihilate the hideous serpent of hopelessly vicious protoplasm." Ten million dollars spent on eugenics would, he believed, be vastly more effective than ten million dollars devoted to charity, and the giver of such a gift to "redeem mankind from vice, imbecility and suffering" would be the world's wisest philanthropist. In response to this appeal a benefactor did in fact appear with sufficient funds to set up, toward the end of 1910, a Eugenics Record Office, with Davenport as its director. Devoted to "the advancement of the science and practice of Eugenics" through investigating "the laws of inheritance of traits in human beings" and proffering advice as to the consequences of proposed marriage matings, this office, on Long Island, New York, became the center of the movement in America.[29]

By the end of the first decade of the twentieth century, then, eugenics was thriving in both England and the United States and had become a major social movement vouched for, with both scientific and philanthropic zeal, by many of the leading biological pundits of the day. In contrast, the first decade of the twentieth century was a period of mounting confusion in evolutionary biology during which, principally as a result of Hugo De Vries' theory of saltatory mutation, doubt was cast on the efficacy of natural selection. Indeed, by 1909, Emanuel Rádl had declared that Darwinism was dead. During these same years, however, there were fundamental advances in genetics (as this science came to be known in 1905) resulting, as Raymond Pearl later remarked, in a broader comprehension of the meaning of heredity and a deeper insight into the laws of inheritance than had been gained from all the previous investigation and speculation about these basic problems. By 1909 J. A. Thomson could claim that geneticists, having formed a picture of what was going on "in the hidden world of the germ cells" were "reaching towards *a control of life.*"[30]

These developments added greatly to the appeal of eugenics, especially in America, for it seemed to many that biological knowledge had advanced to a stage that made feasible, as Pearl put it, "the conscious and deliberate *control* and *direction* of human evolution, physical, mental and moral." We now know that these hopes were illusory, that Huxley was right about the impracticality of Galtonian race improvement. By the 1930s, as M. H. Haller has documented, the eugenics crusade "lay in wreckage." In 1910, however, enthusiasm for eugenics was still rapidly mounting.[31]

In the judgment of Karl Pearson it was Galton's conviction that nature was indefinitely stronger than nurture that had driven him to his "eugenetic solution of the national welfare problem," and so given rise to the eugenics movement. In 1910, in a publication of the Galton Laboratory for National Eugenics entitled *Nature and Nurture: The Problem of the Future,* Pearson essayed (as befitted a statistician) to quantify Galton's conviction. There was, according to Pearson, no real comparison between nature and nurture, and he thought it "quite safe to say" that the influence of the environment was "not one fifth that of heredity, and quite possibly not one tenth of it." With this trenchant pronouncement, the nature-nurture controversy entered upon a new and more contentious phase.[32]

In his *The Mind of Primitive Man,* which appeared in 1911, Boas observed that no subject was attracting wider attention among both scientists and the general public than the phenomenon of heredity. The importance of heredity, he added, was, through the influence of Francis Galton and his followers, being expressed in the formula "Nature not nurture." By this time Galton was dead, but the movement he had founded was flourishing as never before. Pearson had become the Galton Professor of Eugenics in the University of London, and as a writer in the *Eugenics Review* put it, the fire that Galton had kindled in the breasts of his followers, far from being extinguished, was growing day by day. During the next few years the ardent followers of Galton's doctrines were to promote the formula "nature not nurture" even more insistently, until the point was reached at which Boas, whose principal concern for the previous twenty years had been to free the concept of culture from hereditarian assumptions, was moved to call a halt.[33]

2

Boas and the Distinction between Culture and Heredity

OF THE POTENCY of the sway that Franz Boas exercised over American cultural anthropology during its formative years, his leading students have provided eloquent testimony. To Alfred Kroeber, Boas was a Promethean genius of massive and acute intelligence who became the *"facile princeps* of his profession, irrespective of generation," and who, in both theory and method, was of "transcendent importance." In Robert Lowie's estimation Boas was the founder of the American anthropological school and perfected the methodology of every division of the vast subject of anthropology. For Lowie he became the great exemplar of the anthropological science of his time, who, "driven by a sacred thirst to ever new Pierian springs," gained ever deeper insights into the nature of man. And in Alexander Goldenweiser's opinion Boas had come from nineteenth-century Germany, like some theomorphic culture-hero, to bestow clarification and scientific fiber upon American anthropology.[1]

This clarification was most clearly evinced in *The Mind of Primitive Man,* the most influential of all Boas' books, which, as the title of its German edition, *Kultur und Rasse,* indicates, was concerned above all else with the relationship between culture and biology. It was on the nature of this relationship that Boas' whole anthropological career turned. In December 1900, in his presidential address to the American Folk-Lore Society, he emphasized the need to clearly distinguish between the influences of culture and race. A decade later in *The Mind of Primitive Man* he laid the foundation of the then emerging paradigm of American cultural anthropology by affirming—in direct contradiction to Galtonian doctrine—"the independence of cultural achievement from race." Boas had come to this conclusion from an intellectual background very different from that of Francis Galton.[2]

Following the publication of *The Origin of Species* in 1859, natural selection, as we have seen, was directly applied by Galton and others to the entire range of human character and history. In September 1882, a few months after Darwin's death, Ernst Haeckēl, pointing to "the irrefragable fact of the unexampled success of Darwin's reform of science," declared that never before in the history of human thought had any new theory penetrated so deeply to the foundation of the whole domain of knowledge, or so deeply affected the most cherished personal convictions of individual students. In Haeckel's opinion, Darwin's work (together with that of Lamarck) had made possible a "monistic explanation of the whole" in which "every phenomenon appears as but efflux of one and the same all comprehensive law of nature." Moreover, Haeckel, like other evolutionists, unhesitatingly applied this law of nature to the whole of human history, arguing that the theory of evolution, together with the monistic philosophy based on it, formed the "best criterion for the degree of man's mental development." In a similar vein, Pitt-Rivers maintained in 1875 that, the principles of variation and natural selection having established an unbreakable bond between "the physical and cultural sciences," history was but "another name for evolution."[3]

This naturalistic theory prompted, in Boas' words, "the idea of a general, uniform evolution of culture in which all parts of mankind participated." The most prominent of those who embraced this notion was E. B. Tylor. In his *Primitive Culture,* published in 1871, Tylor adopted the view that the history of mankind was part and parcel of the history of nature and that "our thoughts, will and actions" accorded with "laws as definite as those which govern the motion of waves, the combination of acids and bases, and the growth of plants and animals." The phenomena of culture, so Tylor believed, were subordinate to the laws of evolution, and it was the operation of these natural laws, beyond the reach of human agency, that determined the course of culture and produced a "movement along a measured line from grade to grade of actual savagery, barbarism and civilization." Evolutionism and monistic theory thus dealt with the age-old question of the relationship between culture and nature by pronouncing that culture was an entirely natural process, like the growth of plants and animals, and not to be differentiated from other natural phenomena. It was against this facile application of the principles of biological evolution to the highly complex phenomena of cultural history by Galton, Tylor, and others that Boas was opposed from the outset of his anthropological career.[4]

While Francis Galton was a right-minded member of the secure and wealthy upper middle class of Victorian England, and interested in the cultivation, by selective breeding, of "natural nobility," Franz Boas grew up in a home in which, as he put it, "the ideals of the revolution of 1848 were a living force." One of Boas' uncles, Abraham Jacobi, a physician, was imprisoned for his participation in the 1848 revolution, before escaping to the United States. To Abraham Jacobi and many others, the uprisings of 1848 symbolized (in Wittke's words) "a triumph of the rationalism of the Enlightenment and a realization of the dreams of poets and intellectuals who championed a cosmopolitan humanitarianism, based on natural law and the inalienable

rights of man which transcended all national and racial boundaries."[5]

These revolutionary ideals the young Boas took to heart.
Convinced that "all that man can do for humanity is to further
the truth," he yearned to "live and die" for "equal rights for all,
for equal possibilities to learn and work for poor and rich alike."
These values had also been shaped by his study of the thought
of such leaders of the German Enlightenment as J. G. Herder,
who believed that we live in a world that we ourselves create,
and Schiller, who wrote of how strong custom rends us from
each other. Another major formative influence was Kant, in
whose ideas Boas became keenly interested at the University of
Kiel when he attended the lectures of Benno Erdmann, a leading student of Kantian philosophy. During Boas' Arctic ex-
plorations in 1883, when the temperature outside his igloo was
below −40° C. and he was suffering acutely from hunger, his so-
lace during the long evenings was a copy of Kant.[6]

Nature, as conceived of by Kant, is "the existence of things
in so far as that existence is determined by universal laws."
Man, as a creature of nature, is entirely subject to these laws.
But given the historical fact of civilizations with ethical systems, man, Kant postulated, is also a being with the capacity to
make choices, in whose life reason and values have a determining influence. Because of this, human beings are able to a significant extent to construct their own characters and those of their
societies—and this prepotency differentiates humans from the
rest of animate (and inanimate) nature. So it was that Kant advanced as the watchword of the Enlightenment the inspiring
exhortation *Sapere aude!*—"Dare to be wise!"[7]

When Boas began the study of philosophy under Erdmann
in the early 1880s, the neo-Kantian movement was in a flourishing state. The most notable of its illuminati was Wilhelm
Dilthey. Dilthey had declared himself Kant's disciple, and
much of his life was devoted to an attempt to liberate the
human or moral sciences from the domination of the natural
sciences by demonstrating that human studies "cannot be a
continuation of the hierarchy of the natural sciences, because
they rest upon a different foundation." Again, Dilthey was re-

sponsible for the philosophical analysis and subsequent popularity of the concept of *Weltanschauung,* and made a prime distinction between naturalism, which takes a mechanistic view of the world, and what he termed the idealism of freedom, which was based on Kant's postulate of man as "a being in whose life reason can have a determining influence."[8]

Although Boas' university course was predominantly in the natural sciences, and especially in physics (his doctoral dissertation was an analysis, using photometric methods, of the color of sea water), his philosophical studies and his involvement with neo-Kantian thought were crucially significant. By April 1882, as he reported in a letter to his uncle Abraham Jacobi, he had decided that the "materialistic *Weltanschauung*" that he had held as a physicist was no longer tenable. The shift that the twenty-three-year-old Boas made was toward a world view that had much in common with Dilthey's idealism of freedom. His previous interests, Boas later recounted, had, through his reading of the writings of philosophers, become "overshadowed by a desire to understand the relation between the objective and the subjective world." In 1882 this desire prompted Boas to propose, as his life's task, investigation of the question: "How far may we consider the phenomena of organic life, and especially those of the psychic life, from a mechanistic point of view, and what conclusion can be drawn from such a consideration?"[9]

From about this same time, Boas became greatly interested in the relation between traditional and individual action. As a youth he had been shocked when one of his fellow students had "declared his belief in the authority of tradition and his conviction that one had not the right to doubt what the past had transmitted to us." Such implicit belief in the authority of tradition was foreign to Boas' mind. In 1888, in discussing the aims of ethnology, he emphasized how important it is "to observe the fight of individuals against tribal customs" and to see "how far the strong individual is able to free himself from the fetters of convention." Like William Blake, Boas was keenly aware of man's "mind forg'd manacles." In his anthropological credo (published when he was eighty) he recorded that he had been stimulated to action in his own life by cultural conditions that ran counter to his ideals, and confessed that his whole outlook upon social life had been "determined by the question: How can we recognize the shackles that tradition has laid upon us?" He added that once these shackles had been recognized, we were able to break them.[10]

When, after the radical reorientation of his scientific interests in 1882, the opportunity to pursue psychological investigations did not present itself in Germany, Boas decided to make a journey to the Arctic for the purpose of adding to knowledge of unknown regions, and of developing his understanding of the reaction of the human mind to the natural environment. From August 1883 to August 1884, in addition to surveying hundreds of miles of unexplored coastline in the Cumberland Sound region of Baffin Island, he lived among the Eskimo "as one of them." Having learned their language, he was able (as he reported in 1884) to understand the old songs and tales that had been handed down from their ancestors, and he quickly realized the prime importance for his study of the Eskimo of their "habits and traditions." In his field notebook for December 1883, for example, he dwelt with great sympathy on both the "beautiful" customs and the "superstitions" of the Eskimo with whom he was living, and after noting that among these Eskimo, as among the rest of mankind, the fear of traditions and old customs was deeply implanted, he added the revealing comment that it was "a difficult struggle for every individual and every people to give up tradition and follow the path of truth."[11]

In his discussion of tradition, as in his account of implements, houses, clothing, laws, religious ideas, and the like in his monograph *The Central Eskimo,* Boas is clearly dealing with "that complex whole ... acquired by man as a member of society," to which Tylor had given the name culture. Tylor and other evolutionists, as we have seen, looked on culture as resulting from the operation of immutable laws beyond the reach of human agency. In contrast, Boas, whose mind was informed by the German Enlightenment, and who himself had recently undergone a major reorientation in his thinking, perceived from the beginning of his anthropological studies that tradition was something that an individual or a people could "give up." In other words, cultures, in contradistinction to those natural phenomena which have evolved entirely independently of human agency, are, in fact, man-made, or *exogenetic,* and so susceptible to modification by human action.[12]

Prior to his departure for the Arctic, Boas had made contact with Rudolf Virchow, the undisputed leader of German anthropology, and with Adolf Bastian, Virchow's close collaborator. On his return to Germany in 1885, Boas became an assistant to Bastian in the Royal Ethnographical Museum in Berlin, and renewed his association with Virchow. Virchow had gained his formidable scientific reputation in the field of cellular pathology, in particular from having established, in the mid 1850s, the fundamentally important biological generalization that all cells necessarily derive from preexisting cells. At first Virchow had been inclined to accept Darwin's theory of natural selection, but, with the extension of evolutionary principles to the human species, particularly by his former student Ernst Haeckel, who became the outspoken leader of the evolutionary movement in Germany, his attitude changed. At Munich in 1877 (the year in which Boas began his university studies) Virchow launched a caustic attack on Haeckel in particular and on evolutionary theory in general.

Virchow began his denunciation of the theory of evolution by issuing a grave warning that if carried through to its extremely dangerous consequences by the socialists it might bring to Germany all those horrors which "similar theories had brought to France"—a reference to the murderous excesses of the Paris Commune of 1871. He expressed his strong disagreement with Haeckel's evolutionary monism, asserted that fossils of "lower human development" were "entirely wanting," and contested vigorously, on the basis of his own inquiries in the domain of prehistoric anthropology, the evolutionists' conclusion that man was phylogenetically allied to the rest of the animal world. Virchow's opinions carried great weight. He was widely extolled as a public-spirited hero who had turned the dangerous tide of Darwinism, and Bastian jubilantly recorded in the *Zeitschrift für Ethnologie* that Virchow had freed science from a nightmare by banishing "the incubus called Descent." From the late 1870s onward, then, a principal sector of German anthropology was inveterately opposed to Darwinian theory, and in Berlin in particular there was, as Haeckel noted, a "sovereign disdain" for evolutionary thinking.[13]

For Boas, Virchow was one of the great leaders of science for whom he had a profound admiration. In Kroeber's judgment Virchow probably influenced Boas more than any other scientist. Boas called Virchow a cautious master, with a "cold enthusiasm for truth," who had been right in rejecting the far-reaching conclusions of Haeckel and other evolutionists. It is evident that much of the disdain that Virchow had for evolutionary thought was communicated to Boas, for, as Boas' student Paul Radin has noted, Boas "always took a prevailingly antagonistic position" to the theory of evolution. This antagonism was undoubtedly Boas' great shortcoming as an anthropologist, for while it spurred him to oppose the unwarranted application of biological principles to cultural phenomena, it also caused him to underestimate the importance of biology in human life, and to impede the emergence of a scientifically adequate anthropological paradigm based on recognition of the pervasive interaction of biological and cultural processes.[14]

Another major influence on Boas was the thought of Theodor Waitz, author of the many-volumed *Anthropologie der Naturvolker* and a celebrated professor at the University of Marburg from 1848 until his death at the age of forty-three in 1864. The first volume of Waitz's opus, entitled *Über die Einheit des Menschengeschlechtes und den Naturzustand des Menschen* [Concerning the Unity of Mankind and Man's Natural State], appeared in the same year as Darwin's *Origin of Species,* and the nature-nurture controversy of the early twentieth century largely stemmed from these two books. Whereas Galton and those who championed nature based their extreme views on their extension to man of Darwinian natural selection, it was to Waitz that Boas, the equally extreme vindicator of nurture, traced his view of culture. In 1934, for example, after the publication of Mead's findings from Samoa, Boas proclaimed genetic elements to be "altogether irrelevant" as compared with "the powerful influence of the cultural environment," and he noted that this conclusion had been expressed by Waitz as early as 1859 and was "the basis of all serious studies of culture." In Boas' estimation Waitz was one of the "great minds" who had "laid the foundation of modern anthropology."[15]

The anthropological theories of Waitz sprang from his studies of human development and pedagogy, in which he was much influenced by the Kantian thinker J. F. Herbart, a philosopher and educationist who in 1809 was appointed to Kant's former chair at Königsberg. Defining anthropology as the science of the nature of man, Waitz argued in 1859 that while cultures had become differentiated in the course of history, the whole of mankind nonetheless possessed a fundamental "psychic unity." All humans, he believed, had followed the same general course of psychic development, the particular state of any given group being determined by "the degree of cultivation" it had reached in the course of its history. When Waitz was formulating these doctrines, Darwin's discovery of the process of natural selection was as yet unpublished, and in company with Herbert Spencer and other thinkers of the 1850s Waitz was an out-and-out Lamarckian. Early in the first volume of *Anthropologie der Naturvolker* (which, under the title *Introduction to Anthropology,* appeared in an English translation in 1863), there is an unqualified avowal of the inheritance of acquired characters, both psychical and physical, in man (as in animals), and numerous examples, such as the inheritance of battle scars, which now seem most droll, are solemnly given.[16]

Improved "mental culture," Waitz believed, promoted this kind of inheritance in man, with the result that human progeny inherited "better predispositions than those possessed by their progenitors." These better predispositions then produced (especially if aided by good pedagogy) a further improvement in mental culture, in an unending process in which, through the inheritance of acquired characters, there was a steady development of mankind with a gradually improving civilization as its universal destination. Waitz also believed in what he called "the metamorphosis of the physical type by altered conditions of civilization," and claimed that "the shape of the skull is everywhere essentially dependent on mental culture and changes with it." Finally, Waitz took a decided stance on the nature-nurture issue, declaring that it had been proved that "the various degrees of culture in various peoples" depended to a much greater extent on "mode of life" than on "original mental endowment." Above all else Waitz wanted, as Ernest Becker has observed, "no physical determinism that would limit human freedom in creating a better world."[17]

All of these doctrines of Waitz are reflected in the anthropology of Boas. As others have shown, while Boas remained throughout his career quite skeptical of natural selection and suspicious of Mendelian heredity, he went on believing as long as he lived that "Lamarck was still to be reckoned with," and not a few of his theories were Lamarckian. He supposed, for example, that man was a domesticated form and believed that in the process of domestication the "changes brought about by external conditions" were "undoubtedly hereditary." Following Waitz he placed great emphasis on "the plasticity of human types." He thought that "no event in the life of a people passes without having its effect on later generations" and was utterly convinced that environment has an important effect upon the anatomical structure and physiological functions of man. In interpreting apparent changes in the bodily form (including the cephalic index) of immigrants to the United States he was "inclined to believe" that these changes had been "directly affected by financial panics."[18]

Conjointly with these beliefs, Boas, who accepted Waitz's conclusion that "the mental characteristics of man are the same all over the world," was especially impressed by Waitz's perspective on cultural development. In 1894 when he made his first major contribution to discussion of the relation between race and culture, he based his argument on this perspective, claiming that "the true point of view" had been expressed most happily by Waitz: "The faculty of man does not designate anything but how much and what he is able to achieve in the immediate future and depends upon the stages of culture through which he has passed and the one which he has reached."[19]

In their original context in the first volume of *Anthropologie*

der Naturvolker, these words were part of Waitz's unequivocally Lamarckian theory of human development. When Boas
quoted them in 1894 their Lamarckian connotations went unre-
marked and they became the basis for a theory of explicitly cultural, as opposed to biological, determinism. For Boas they
epitomized Waitz's viewpoint, which he deemed to be basic to
all serious studies of culture, and he cited them on two subsequent occasions in his long campaign against the hereditarians:
in 1911 in *The Mind of Primitive Man,* and in 1924 in an article
in the *American Mercury,* written at the very height of the
nature-nurture debate, just prior to his planning of Margaret
Mead's Samoan researches.[20]

As we have seen, Boas first became aware of the nature of
culture in 1883 during his intimate participation in the lives of
the highly traditional Eskimo of Baffin Island. He retained this
awareness when he returned to North America in 1886 to survey the coastal tribes of British Columbia. In his preliminary
report (of March 1887) on these inquiries he noted that the
common culture of these tribes was deserving of thorough
study. Again, in a lecture in 1888, he advocated the study of
"the gradual development of the manifestations of culture" for
"the whole of mankind, from its earliest traces . . . up to modern
times." This study, as he emphasized on numerous subsequent
occasions, had to be pursued "by strict historical methods." By
this time Boas' appreciation of the phenomenon of culture had
become both deeper and more acute. In 1889 he published in
the newly founded *American Anthropologist* a short article,
"On Alternating Sounds," in which, as Stocking has observed,
he saw "cultural phenomena in terms of the imposition of conventional meaning on the flux of experience" and so "as historically conditioned and transmitted by the learning process." In
Stocking's judgment "it is impossible to exaggerate the significance of this article for the history of anthropological thought."
Here, for the first time in the history of post-Darwinian anthropology, there is full recognition of the exogenetic nature of culture.[21]

At about this time Boas began his penetrating critique of
evolutionist anthropology. In 1896 he called on anthropologists

to "renounce the vain endeavour to construct a uniform systematic history of the evolution of culture," arguing that the changes that occurred in human cultures did not take place in a single line, but in a multiplicity of converging and diverging trends. In 1899 he was appointed professor of anthropology at Columbia, and the following year, in a major address entitled "The Mind of Primitive Man," he developed further his vision of cultural anthropology. Culture, he argued, "is an expression of the achievements of the mind, and shows the cumulative effects of the activities of many minds." It is created by human agency; the whole domain of art and of ethics rests on the mind's "power of choosing between perceptions and actions according to their value." Here, as in "On Alternating Sounds," Boas conceived of culture as referring to phenomena to which the laws of biology do not apply.[22]

In this same address, in dealing with the question "Do differences exist in the organization of the human mind?" Boas stipulated that "we must clearly distinguish between the influences of civilization and race." A similar distinction, as we have seen, was being argued for at this same time by the evolutionary biologist E. R. Lankester. This dichotomy between nature and culture is of great antiquity, dating from at least the fifth century B.C., when Protagoras established in Greek thought the categories of *physis,* or nature, and *nomos,* or usages based on tradition. Usages based on tradition, resulting as they do from the human capacity to conceive of and enact alternatives, are man-made and, as such, according to Protagoras, must be distinguished clearly from natural phenomena that are entirely unconnected with human agency. Since then many other anthropological thinkers have stressed the significance of this dichotomy. Rousseau, in the judgment of Lévi-Strauss, founded modern anthropology when in his *Discourse on the Origins and Foundations of Inequality among Men* he posed the question of the relationship between nature and culture.[23]

In the heyday of evolutionism, and especially during the decades when the Lamarckian suppositions of Herbert Spencer held sway, this distinction between nature and culture was largely ignored, for it was widely believed that human history in all its aspects had resulted from the operation of biological laws. In the 1890s, however, with the collapse of Lamarckism, it became apparent to some thinkers that cultural phenomena, in their extraordinary diversity, could not possibly be explained by the simple evocation of natural selection. Another set of factors was plainly involved, as Huxley, Lankester, Boas, and others realized, and so, by the beginning of the twentieth century, the nature of the relationship between culture and biology, or to use Galton's terms, between nurture and nature, had become a scientific and intellectual issue of fundamental significance.

Boas' principal concern from this time onward was to foster the study of culture. During the first quarter of the twentieth century this project unfortunately involved a mounting confrontation with hereditarians, who were intent on applying their assumptions to cultural phenomena. As late as 1907 (the year in which Galton was envisaging a Holy War against customs and prejudices that impaired "the physical and moral qualities" that were dependent on "race") Boas was still hoping that the claims of eugenics might be subjected to calm scientific discussion. The claims of the more extreme eugenicists soon became so overweening, however, as to make this impossible, and by about 1910, as Boas noted, the issue of what among humans was genetically inherited was attracting wider attention than any other topic.

It was in direct response to this situation that Boas wrote *The Mind of Primitive Man,* just as Waitz, in the late 1850s, had written his *Anthropologie der Naturvolker* in opposition to the racist doctrines of the Count de Gobineau's *Essai sur l'inégalité des races humaines. The Mind of Primitive Man,* as Lowie has noted, closely parallels the argument of the first volume of *Anthropologie der Naturvolker,* and like that work has as its objective the establishment of "the independence of cultural achievement from race." Having noted in his introduction that it was still "very generally assumed . . . that racial descent determines cultural life," Boas quickly moved to a definition of culture as exogenetic, and to the claim that "the psychological basis of cultural traits is identical in all races." Culture, he argued, reiterating his finding of 1894, is "not an expression of innate mental qualities" but "a result of varied external conditions acting upon general human characteristics." This view, Boas emphasized, was that of Herder and of Waitz, to whose central conclusion regarding the cultural conditioning of human behavior he again referred.[24]

Boas went on to examine the assumption that "racial descent determines cultural life" and to conclude that not the slightest successful attempt had been made "to establish causes for the behavior of a people other than historical and social conditions." An unbiased review of the facts, he asserted, showed that "belief in hereditary racial characteristics and the jealous care for purity of race is based on the assumption of non-existing conditions." To the eugenicists of the day, who with the rise of genetics felt certain of the factualness of their beliefs, these were defiant and challenging words. And so they were intended, for from 1894 onward, and especially in *The Mind of Primitive Man,* the whole thrust of Boas' thought, as Stocking has observed, was "to distinguish the concepts of race and culture, to separate biological and cultural heredity, to focus attention on cultural process, to free the concept of culture from its heritage of evolutionary and racial assumption, so that it could subsequently become ... completely independent of biological determinism."[25]

When *The Mind of Primitive Man* first appeared, the hereditarian cause was strongly ascendant. In 1911 Charles Davenport, the leading spokesman of the eugenics movement in the United States, published his *Heredity in Relation to Eugenics* and other papers, propounding with certainty and fervor "the fundamental fact that all men are created *bound* by their protoplasmic makeup and *unequal* in their powers and responsibilities" and proclaiming that "heredity stands as the one great hope of the human race; its savior from imbecility, poverty, disease, immorality."[26]

Here, then, in 1911, were two antithetical intellectual and scientific schools—that of Boas and that of Davenport—with neither disposed to explore, in a constructive way, the coexistence and interaction of genetic and exogenetic processes. Instead, the two schools, in Davenport's words, stood opposed, "each viewing the other unkindly." The stage was set for an unrelenting struggle between two doctrines, each insufficient in scientific terms, which had originated amid the theoretical confusions of the late nineteenth century, the one overestimating biology and the other overvaluing culture.[27]

3

The Launching of Cultural Determinism

WHEN FRANCIS GALTON died in 1911, the eugenics movement, which he had founded, was in a flourishing state. This was especially so in the United States, where as Raymond Pearl observed, eugenics had by 1911 risen to a position "certainly very respectable," and was by the following year " 'catching on' to an extraordinary degree, with radical and conservative alike." Indeed, with the guidance of genetics, eugenics gave promise, so Pearl thought, of some day becoming the crowning one of all the biological sciences. In a similar vein Karl Pearson, who by the terms of Galton's will had become the Foundation Professor of Eugenics at the University of London, was proclaiming that "the science of eugenics" formed "the coping-stone to the science of life" and supplied the groundwork for future national progress. In this atmosphere of certitude and high-flown enthusiasm the First International Eugenics Congress was held in London in July 1912.[1]

One of those who had, under the direct influence of Galton and Pearson, become enamored of hereditarian ideas was Cyril Burt, then a lecturer in experimental psychology in the University of Liverpool. In 1912 Burt published a paper in which he avowed the belief, which in later life he was to support with quite unprincipled eristic fervor, that "mental inheritance ... moulds the character of individuals" and "rules the destiny of nations." It was against this very doctrine that Boas had been struggling since 1894, and that Margaret Mead, beginning in 1928 with the publication of *Coming of Age in Samoa,* was, as a leading Boasian, to fight with the "whole battery" at her command. By the second decade of the twentieth century, then, the nature-nurture controversy, in which two fervently held half-truths contended vainly for outright mastery, was about to enter upon the most active phase of its existence.[2]

Prominent among the American delegation to the Eugenics Congress was Charles Davenport, who by this time had been elected to the National Academy of Sciences and was recognized as the leader in the study of eugenics in the United States. Absolute in his conviction that the only hope for "the real betterment of the human race" lay in "better matings," Davenport, on his return to Long Island, with financial support from John D. Rockefeller and others, extended the activities of the Eugenics Record Office with the explicit objective of securing the preponderance of "America's most effective blood lines" and the restricting of the "defective and delinquent." Davenport was a fervent Mendelian whose thinking was based on the assumption that human nature was constituted entirely of traits that were "discrete, unit characters determined by pairs of distinct immutable factors," the one dominant over the other. The research to which the Eugenics Record Office under Davenport's direction gave principal attention was the inheritance of particular traits. From about 1912 onward Davenport's research activity in this field was assiduous, and especially into those traits which, following Galton, he believed to be determinants of social behavior. Working with family histories collected by the Eugenics

Record Office, he produced, with immense seriousness and apparent certitude, lists of behavioral traits that were, he pronounced, genetically determined. In a paper presented in 1914, for example, he listed a tendency to tantrums and violent eroticism as dominant traits, depressions with impulsions to suicide as recessive, and dipsomania and nomadism as sex-linked characters. In his analysis of the heredity of naval officers, he identified an inborn love of the sea as a trait almost certainly caused (as it was males and not females who ran away to sea) by a sex-linked recessive factor. In another study, insincerity, stinginess, seclusiveness, and untruthfulness were among negative traits said to be inherited as unit characters.[3]

In these conclusions Davenport was, in the eyes of the ardent eugenicists of the time, giving substance in the most specific and scientific way to Galton's fundamental assumption that "mental qualities are inherited in the same way as bodily characteristics." Equally, Davenport's conclusions gave potent support to their conviction that nature was more important than nurture, which, as Karl Pearson reemphasized in 1915, was the very basis of Galton's lifework. Indeed, Davenport's application of Mendelian principles to all aspects of human character went beyond Galton's extreme view of "the vastly preponderating effects of nature over nurture" to a doctrine of absolute biological determinism. As Charles Rosenberg has documented, in Davenport's view criminals, prostitutes, tramps, and other "defective" individuals lacked the gene or genes the appearance of which "through mutation in man's distant past had allowed him to control his more primitive asocial instincts and thus develop civilization." The criminal was a criminal, the prostitute a prostitute, because their genetic makeup had not provided them with the neurological or physiological means for circumventing their brutish urges. Similarly, feeblemindedness resulted from the persistence of primitive genes, and was, Davenport declared, not a reversion but a direct inheritance, an "uninterrupted transmission from our animal ancestry." For Davenport then, as Rosenberg has pointed out, "social and physical evolution were one" and "cultural change merely reflected underlying physical developments."[4]

During these same years, largely because of Davenport's activities, there was a rapid growth in the general popularity of eugenics and an associated upsurge in racial theory and sentiment, which in Henry Fairfield Osborn's opinion was in strong accord with the true spirit of the eugenics movement. There was talk of a eugenics millennium, and Helen Baker, whose *Race Improvement or Eugenics* appeared in 1912, assured her readers that American eugenicists would never rest until the American race became "the fittest on earth." In these popular writings there was (as an onlooker remarked in 1914) "a fervour of moral enthusiasm," and the eugenics movement in the United States came to resemble the crusade for race improvement of which Galton had dreamed a decade or so before. By 1914 forty-four U.S. colleges, including Harvard and Cornell, the Universities of California and Chicago, and the Massachusetts Institute of Technology, were offering lectures or courses about eugenics. G. H. Parker, of Harvard, in the influential journal *Science* pointed in 1915 to "the elimination of the strikingly defective members of society" as "a reasonable and a humane possibility," and advocated enforced sterilization. A number of states adopted such policies. In 1915 a translation of the Count de Gobineau's *The Inequality of Human Races* was published in New York, and in the following year appeared Madison Grant's *The Passing of the Great Race,* in which, as M. H. Haller has shown, "eugenics and racism united in a scientific doctrine of an elite about to be swamped by the incompetence of those whose inheritance placed them among the enemies of civilization." In Grant's opinion, democracy was "not favourable to the preservation of superior strains" and the only solution was "a thorough campaign of eugenics." In halls and Chautauqua tents throughout America, itinerant lecturers were, in Margaret Mead's words, "insisting raucously that 'you can't change human nature,'" and proclaiming their faith in race betterment through the science of eugenics, which as Davenport had remarked in an earlier lecture was all that could save the people from "perdition."[5]

By 1916 the situation for those opposed to these fanatical developments had become insufferable, and in that year both

Boas and his former student Robert Lowie launched incisive attacks on the eugenics movement. In an article in *The New Republic* on Alfred Russel Wallace, the discoverer, with Darwin, of natural selection, Lowie warmly commended Wallace's distrust of eugenics and his pointed deprecation of "the meddlesome interference of an arrogant scientific priestcraft" in human affairs. That Wallace should have taken this attitude is understandable, for as early as 1864 (when Galton was formulating the extreme hereditarian doctrines that gave rise to the eugenics movement), Wallace had questioned the extent to which natural selection applied to the later stages of human evolution. He had pointed out that man had long been able to modify his life by "putting himself into certain conditions, instead of leaving nature to select those conditions for him." Wallace was thus the first biologist (of the epoch that began in 1859) to draw attention to the crucial significance of exogenetic processes in human evolution. In 1916 he was eagerly claimed as an ally by Lowie, who concluded his article with the barbed comment that the "half-baked biologists" who dabble in social reform and "their still less amiable little brothers, the practical eugenists with their legislative tinkerings" might well pay heed to the social philosophy and noble spirit of that great evolutionary biologist, A. R. Wallace.[6]

Boas' condemnation of eugenics in the November 1916 issue of *The Scientific Monthly* was more direct and substantial. The doctrines of the apostles of eugenics, Boas lamented, had taken hold of the public mind to such an extent that eugenic measures had found a place in the statute books of a number of states and there was disapproval of marriages thought bound to produce unhealthy offspring. While it was the first duty of the eugenicist to determine empirically and without bias what features were hereditary and what not, this they had conspicuously failed to do. Instead, their battle-cry "nature not nurture" had been raised to the rank of a dogma, and environmental conditions had been ignored. The eugenicist's policy of eliminating the unfit, and of the deliberate selection of superior strains, rested on the overestimation of conventional standards, and was, to Boas' mind, intolerable. Eugenics, he warned with remarkable prescience, was not a panacea that would cure human ills, but rather a dangerous sword that might well turn its edge against those who relied on its strength. This expedient of eliminating "the unfit" would soon reach a terrible culmination in National Socialist Germany, beginning with Hitler's decreeing of a Eugenic Sterilization Law in 1933.

In contrast to the eugenicist, declared Boas, the anthropologist was convinced that many different anatomical forms could be adapted to the same social functions; further, because of the observed fact that the most diverse types of man could adapt themselves to the same forms of life, it had to be assumed (unless the contrary could be proved) that "all complex activities are socially determined." Indeed, Boas asserted, "in the great mass of a healthy population, the social stimulus is infinitely more potent than the biological mechanism." This was an anthropological doctrine wholly antithetical to that of Davenport and the more extreme of his fellow eugenicists. To say, as did Boas, that the anthropologist and biologist were "at odds" was to understate the situation: they were implacably opposed, with no prospect of reconciliation between their markedly divergent anthropological doctrines.[7]

Boas' strong feelings about the "apostles of eugenics" were shared by another of his students, Alfred Kroeber. Eugenics, Kroeber declared in the *American Anthropologist* in 1917, was a fallacy, a mirage, like the philosophers' stone, and a dangerous snare. Galton was, Kroeber conceded, one of the most truly imaginative intellects produced by England, and his close collaborator Pearson possessed one of the keenest minds of his generation; yet together with their followers they had been beguiled by a simple fallacy, set in an envelope of enticing complications. If social phenomena were only organic, then eugenics was right, but if the social was something more than the organic, then eugenics was an outright error, at the childlikeness of which the future would surely smile.[8]

Kroeber has confessed that "almost as a boy" he had a strong intuition that "all search for 'origins' is vain." This belief he carried with him when, in 1896, he began his studies with Boas, and it was given great prominence in his first major anthropological study. In 1901 Kroeber asserted that any search for origins in anthropology could lead to "nothing but false results." The phenomena studied by anthropologists, he declared, had no origin; all arts and all institutions were as old as man; every word was as old as speech; culture was "beginningless."[9]

This odd intuition from his boyhood remained basic to Kroeber's subsequent anthropological thought. In 1910 he dwelt on the differences between man and the highest animals, among whom there was, he asserted (incorrectly, as we now know), "nothing homologous to the rudest culture or civilization," and he gave it as his opinion that the members of the human species were "apparently exempt from the operation of the laws of biological evolution." Kroeber, then, had not the slightest difficulty in accepting Boas' affirmation of the independence of cultural achievement from race. From 1900 onward Boas had stressed the importance of making a clear distinction between culture and biology, and by 1911, in his statement that culture was "not an expression of innate mental qualities" but "a result of varied external conditions acting upon general human characteristics," had adumbrated the central tenet of what was to become, during the next decade, the ruling dogma of American anthropology. As the struggle against hereditarian ideologies intensified from 1916 onward, it was Boas' students Kroeber and Lowie who gave this tenet its definitive form by pressing to its logical limit Boas' emphasis on the independence of culture.[10]

Kroeber, from 1914 onward, made adroit use of dissension within biology. During the first twenty years of the century, evolutionary studies and theories were in a state of chaos and confusion. Until 1915, when T. H. Morgan and his associates established chromosome theory, genetics was torn by a feud between the Mendelians and the biometricians; and there was talk (as A. R. Wallace lamented) of Darwinism being played out. Again, there was a marked recrudescence of belief in the inheritance of acquired characters. In 1914, addresses by Hugo De Vries (in Brussels) and William Bateson (in Melbourne and Sydney) extolling Mendelism and highly critical of Darwinian theory, were republished in *Science*. In his paper "Inheritance by Magic," on which he was working at the time of August

Weismann's death in November 1914, Kroeber wryly remarked that some Mendelians seemed to think that the greatest accomplishment of their science had been "the superseding of Darwinism." He went on to observe that although Weismann, in the 1880s, had proved Lamarckian doctrine to be "absolutely hollow," biology was still very much of two minds about the inheritance of acquired characters. This, Kroeber argued, was because the majority of biologists failed to recognize that in addition to the evolution of organic life there was, in the case of man, a quite distinct "nonorganic process of evolution," which depended not on the inheritance of acquired characters but on the social transmission and accumulation of knowledge. If biologists did not admit this crucial distinction and persisted in fallaciously asserting that the social was organic, the "scientists of the social" would in the end, Kroeber prophesied, "revolt violently," and "attain their own separateness by force."[11]

As these sentiments indicate, Kroeber, like other social scientists of the day, felt keenly oppressed by biological determinism, both Galtonian and Lamarckian. Early in 1915 he published an anthropological confession of faith (as Lowie called it) proclaiming the autonomy of culture in eighteen professions. "In poignant sentences," as Lowie later reported, "Kroeber outlined the sole end of ethnology as the study of culture regardless of organic phenomena." Biology, he asserted, had nothing whatsoever to do with human history, which "involved the absolute conditioning of historical events by other cultural events." There was thus, according to Kroeber, a total separation between history and biology, and his eighteen professions were primarily directed to the elimination of any kind of continuity or interaction between biological and cultural processes. The physical environment, he stipulated, was not a factor shaping or explaining culture, nor was man's biological nature of any possible relevance.[12]

After the propounding of his eighteen professions, Kroeber spent 1915 on sabbatical leave in Europe, and returned to the United States early in 1916. In his absence he was charged by H. K. Haeberlin (in the *American Anthropologist*) with having committed, in his eighteen professions, the "cardinal sin of arbitrary elimination," but there were others who were attracted to his transilient ideas, and, as Lowie (who at this time was less decided than Kroeber) reported, eminent sociologists and ethnologists were tending to accept that sociological data were *sui generis*. Yet Kroeber himself was haunted, in 1916, by a major doubt. As in earlier years, it was an anxiety that the inheritance of acquired characters might, after all, turn out to be true. Everything hinged, Kroeber realized, on the rejection of Lamarckian doctrine by both biologists and anthropologists and the establishment of the nonorganic nature of cultural processes.[13]

At this time Kroeber began referring to the nonorganic, or social, as the "superorganic." The crux of the matter, he declared in April 1916, lay in the question of whether or not there was anything superorganic. Although the very possibility of the superorganic was widely denied, there were those, he intimated, who had already recognized its existence. That this recognition was not more general among anthropologists was, he declared, "a reproach and a cloud" on the so-called enlightenment of the day. For Kroeber, by 1916, anthropological enlightenment was only to be had by initiation into the "scope and nature of the superorganic." "If there is nothing beyond the organic," he adjured his colleagues, "let us quit our false and vain business and turn biologists ... but if there is a superorganic phase, it behooves us not merely to rest supine within our knowledge, but to press this great truth at every opening and every turn."[14]

In the article on which he was working in November 1914, Kroeber had strongly urged that biologists should bury the already dead doctrine of Lamarckian inheritance and admit the nonorganic nature of cultural processes. If this were done it would be possible, he said, for biology and anthropology to join hands in alliance across the gulf that separated them. Kroeber had fully grasped that the rejection of Lamarckian doctrine was an essential precondition for the scientific study of culture. However, there were still within biology many who remained undecided about the inheritance of acquired characters. For these individuals Lamarckian doctrine was by no means defunct and Kroeber's appeal for an alliance between anthropology and biology fell on stony ground. Indeed, even a decade later in 1925, the conclusion that Lamarckism was "a possible but unproved factor in evolution," represented, in the view of G. H. Parker, professor of zoology at Harvard, "the opinion of the majority of modern biologists."[15]

In 1914 and the immediately following years, biologists were too preoccupied with developments within their own discipline to give any attention to the problem that seemed so important to Kroeber. In 1914, in the addresses of Bateson and De Vries, the onslaught on Darwinism reached a peak, and the following year the Mendelians made what was immediately recognized to be an epoch-making discovery, namely the discovery that certain inherited characters were "transmitted from one generation to the next by being associated with small bodies called chromosomes contained in the germ cells." Later in 1915 Thomas H. Morgan and his colleagues published *The Mechanism of Mendelian Heredity,* in which their chromosome theory was fully explicated. Morgan felt justified in venturing the opinion that the problem of heredity had been solved. In 1916 the journal *Genetics* was founded, with Morgan and nine other eminent geneticists (including William Castle, Davenport, and Pearl) on its editorial board, all of them proponents, with varying degrees of enthusiasm, of the eugenics movement, in which there had been an accompanying upsurge of interest.[16]

With these developments, as E. G. Conklin noted in 1916, heredity became the central problem of biology, which was burgeoning as never before. Biologists, particularly in the United States, were buoyantly confident in their science and in no mood to respond to Kroeber's proposed delimitation of spheres of inquiry. There was to be no joining of hands in alliance. Instead, by about the end of 1916, the leaders of the anthropological profession in the United States were so overshadowed by the spectacular advances of their hereditarian opponents as to feel that their only viable course was to escape forever from the toils of biological determinism by proclaiming the complete independence of cultural anthropology.[17]

Kroeber and Lowie, who by this time had emerged as the intellectual leaders of the "irreverently skeptical" younger generation of cultural anthropologists, were very much in the mood to assert their independence. They believed they were pitted against alien and engulfing forces. Their battles, wrote Kroeber in 1917, were against an ever re-arising brood of dragons of superstition; while according to Lowie a monistic ogre was abroad, ever casting about for new victims. They were engaged, declared Lowie, in a life and death struggle for the sovereignty of cultural anthropology, and this longed-for sovereignty could only be gained by (as Kroeber later put it) a "proclamation of independence from the dominance of the biological explanation of sociocultural phenomena." The goal was no longer a coming to terms with biology, as it had been a year or so earlier, but the assuming of a theoretical position in which biology and cultural anthropology would be totally separated, once and for all.[18]

Kroeber's main pretext for the independence on which his heart was set was the concept of the superorganic, which he had developed from his eighteen professions of 1915. Using this uncompromising notion, he proceeded to dissociate cultural phenomena from every conceivable connection with biology. Individual capacity was wholly eliminated; heredity, he declared, maintained not one particle of civilization; between the organic and the superorganic, which were the outcomes of wholly disparate evolutions, there was an utter divergence—a difference that was absolute.[19]

This divergence had been created, Kroeber asserted, by a profound alteration in the course of human evolution: culture was "not a link in any chain, not a step in any path, but a leap to another plane." Kroeber had derived this notion from the theory of the Dutch botanist De Vries that species had originated by sudden leaps, or saltations. Kroeber's consuming objective was the complete separation of cultural anthropology from biology, and the notion that the superorganic had originated in a sudden leap, or saltation, springing fully formed from the organic as did Pallas Athena from the brow of Zeus, was immensely appealing. Undeterred by the lack of empirical evidence, Kroeber predicated his whole case on this convenient supposition. The superorganic, he announced, was without antecedents in the beginning of the organic, from which it was entirely separate and which it transcended utterly. Then, on the basis of this wholly unsubstantiated supposition, convinced that he was standing "at the threshold of glimpsing vague, grand forces of predestination," Kroeber instigated an intellectual schism, proclaiming that between cultural anthropology and biology there was an abyss, an "eternal chasm" that could not be bridged.[20]

Kroeber's revelation of this unbridgeable chasm was at once accepted by Lowie. In this book *Culture and Ethnology,* which appeared later in 1917, Lowie gave vigorous support to Kroeber's claims by declaring culture to be "a thing *sui generis"* and by propounding, in oracular fashion, the formula *omnis cultura ex cultura.* It was the contention of both Kroeber and Lowie, as *The New International Year Book* for 1917 reported, that the domain of culture constituted a distinct sphere of investigation, and from this contention the complete autonomy of cultural anthropology necessarily followed. By this drastic maneuver Kroeber and Lowie, as they had threatened in 1916, had attained "their own separateness by force." Their triumphant success in their "life and death struggle" with "the universalist monster" of deterministic biology was celebrated by Lowie in an article in *The New Republic* in November 1917. Ethnology, he recorded with great glee, had, with Gargantuan precocity and lusty kicks, won a victory over this cradle-snatching monster, and would soon gain its rightful place in the sun.[21]

As Lowie's metaphors indicate, the struggle in which he and Kroeber had been involved was essentially political and ideological. Their mission had been to throw off, at any cost, the oppressive intellectual dominance of the extreme hereditarian doctrines which, since the advent of eugenics in 1901, had been impinging ever more forcefully on the young science of anthropology. That these doctrines were indeed extreme, extending, as in the case of Davenport, to an absolute biological determinism, there can be no doubt. In this predicament Kroeber and Lowie were impelled, with momentous consequences for anthropology, to devise a doctrine quite as extreme as that of their hereditarian opponents. It was expressed in the formula *omnis cultura ex cultura,* which, in asserting that cultural phenomena can be understood only in terms of other cultural phenomena, was predicated on the existence of an unbridgeable chasm between biology and cultural anthropology, and so inexorably involved an absolute cultural determinism. The absolute nature of this specifically cultural determinism was promptly confirmed by Kroeber himself. While culture permeated the lives of the individual members of a society, it was, he declared, utterly uncontrollable by these individuals, and had a causality entirely of its own.[22]

In his insistence that the cultural was "in its very essence non-individual," Kroeber was arguing in the same way as had Durkheim in 1894 in his *Les règles de la méthode sociologique,* when propounding the doctrine that society is "a thing in itself" (which was, through its adoption by A. R. Radcliffe-Brown and others, to become the ruling assumption of British social anthropology). In adopting this extreme stance Kroeber went beyond the views of Boas and some of his other followers. Edward Sapir in July 1917, thought that Kroeber's desire to take a sharply defined position had led him into dogmatism, shaky metaphysics, and a point of view "amounting practically to abstractionist fetishism"; it required, said Sapir, a "social determinism amounting to a religion to deny to individuals all directive power, all culture-moulding influence." Nonetheless, despite these misgivings, Sapir (as he told Lowie at the time) sympathized on the whole with the spirit of Kroeber's "superorganic." Other Boasians responded similarly. Kroeber and Lowie, it was realized, had gone beyond the limits of the more muted cultural determinism that Boas, citing Waitz, had begun advocating in 1894: yet Kroeber's assertion of the existence of an absolute difference between the superorganic and the organic varied in but slight degree from Boas' pronouncement of November 1916 that "the social stimulus is infinitely more potent than the biological mechanism." And so, despite some differences of opinion, the Boasians, with the total exclusion of biology from the purview of cultural anthropology, had by about the end of 1917 fully established their independence. The breach with biology—at least in theory—was complete.[23]

Several historians of the development of anthropological ideas have applied the term "paradigm" to the general doctrine of cultural determinism as it crystallized in 1917. In Kroeber's own opinion, the conceptualizing of culture as "wholly non-organic" involved "almost as fundamental a shifting of mental and emotional point of view" as "when the Copernican doctrine challenged the prior conviction of the world." However exaggerated this opinion may have been, it is evident that a fundamental change was indeed involved, and if the term paradigm is understood in T. S. Kuhn's modified sense of "disciplinary matrix" its use is clearly warranted. It should be noted, however, that, in its insistence on the existence of an unbridgeable chasm between biology and cultural anthropology, this paradigm was also very much an ideology. It was, indeed, essentially a *system of belief,* which, in claiming to represent something like revealed truth, required the suppression of whatever did not conform with its central dogma. And it was to such suppression, as we shall see, that the principal conclusion of Mead's Samoan researches was directed.[24]

While it was primarily Kroeber and Lowie who precipitated the disjunction of cultural anthropology from biology and so made way for the unqualified acceptance of cultural determinism, this doctrine, it is important to note, had stemmed directly from Boas' preoccupations from the outset of his anthropological career. In his address of 1900 on "The Mind of Primitive Man," Boas explicitly argued for the recognition of culture as a construct to which the laws of biology did not apply, and from that time onward his presiding genius shaped the course that culminated in the momentous schism of 1917. In the struggle for the independence of cultural anthropology, in which Boas took the lead with his sweeping denunciation of the assumptions of Galtonian eugenics and his talk of a parting of the ways, Kroeber and Lowie were acting as the loyal, if somewhat over-zealous, lieutenants of their revered teacher. Ruth Bunzel, another of his students, has argued that the first two decades of the twentieth century should be known as the Age of Boas, so completely did this "giant" dominate the field, and Alexander

Lesser has described Boas as "the builder and architect of modern anthropology." I shall, then, refer to the explanation of human behavior in purely cultural terms as *the Boasian paradigm*. In the 1920s and 1930s this paradigm rapidly assumed a position of commanding importance in American anthropology. Since those years anthropology in the United States and elsewhere has become greatly diversified. However, while there have always been individuals whose views have radically diverged from those of Boas and his followers, the notion that human behavior can be explained in purely cultural terms has remained widely influential.[25]

With the emergence of this new paradigm the independence of cultural anthropology was swiftly attained, but at an enduringly crippling intellectual cost, for it was an independence that had been won not by any reasoned resolution of the age-old nature-nurture problem but instead by the stark stratagem of arbitrarily excluding "nature" from any kind of consideration whatsoever.

At this recherché maneuver the "universalist monster" of deterministic biology suffered no sudden weakening or loss of will. Indeed, early in 1918, a number of biologically oriented activists in the United States, many of whom had strongly supported the eugenics movement from the days of its inception, joined forces for "the promotion of study of racial anthropology, and of the origin, migration, physical and mental characters, crossing and evolution of human races, living and extinct." This organization, the founding of which had been initiated by Madison Grant and C. B. Davenport, was pointedly named the Galton Society, and Davenport became its chairman. Accepting evolution by natural selection and Galton's principle of "the like inheritance of mental and physical characters," the members of this new anthropological society were at rooted variance with the notion that human behavior could be explained in exclusively cultural terms.[26]

The contending schools of thought of which Boas and Davenport had been the principal spokesmen since 1911 had, during the years 1914 to 1918, become more implacably opposed than ever. The radical controversy over the relative importance of nature and nurture—Kroeber's "eternal chasm" notwithstanding—was to persist, with increasing intensity, into the third decade of the twentieth century, and to spur Boas into devising Margaret Mead's Samoan researches.

4

Boas Poses
an Intractable
Problem

By ABOUT 1920 the Boasian paradigm had taken definite shape, and a defiantly independent new school of American anthropologists, dominated, as Sapir observed, "by the sympathetic yet acidly critical spirit of Prof. F. Boas," had come into being. By this time Boas' students held positions in most of the major American universities, and (in Regna Darnell's words) "in spite of internal disagreements and personal enmities, these individuals considered themselves a group and cooperated to promote their version of anthropology—which in its broad outlines was shared by all."[1]

This version of anthropology had been specified in the notion of culture as *sui generis* and in the formula *omnis cultura ex cultura;* in his *Primitive Society,* which appeared in 1920, Lowie completed the break with the evolutionist tradition, which for the Boasians had become "a pseudo-science like medieval alchemy." In one of his three reviews of *Primitive Society,* Sapir, a close friend of Lowie's and himself a prominent Boasian, reported exuberantly that "the new school of American anthropologists" was convinced that a culture was "an historical datum, a thing of time, of place, of contiguity, of that divine accident that results from the intertwining of thousands of antecedent factors that are themselves of time, of place, of contiguity," and further that "the psychological necessities of man" were "capable of infinitely multiform solution." By the early 1920s, then, the Boasians had won their independence and were firmly in possession of a specific set of beliefs, yet the central element of their paradigm, the postulate that "the social stimulus is infinitely more potent than the biological mechanism," had been put to no empirical test, and the long-standing controversy between the Boasians and their hereditarian opponents was still wholly unresolved.[2]

The eugenics movement had continued to flourish. In 1919 H. L. Laughlin of the Eugenics Record Office announced that the newly organized science of eugenics had so advanced during the previous decade as to make its future secure. Preparations were being made for the 1921 International Congress of Eugenics in New York and the Galton centenary of 1922. In the United States in the early 1920s, eugenics was thus, as Lowie noted, very much in the air. The International Congress of 1921, which had been delayed since 1915 because of the war, would furnish, it was announced, an opportunity for the geneticists and eugenicists of the world to meet together at the American Museum of Natural History for "discussions of the results of their researches and their application to race improvement." Among the principal organizers of this congress were Davenport, Grant, and Osborn, who in 1918 had founded the Galton Society, and all of whom remained out-and-out hereditarians.[3]

Further, with the appearance of Madison Grant's *The Passing of the Great Race* (1916), and later of Lothrop Stoddard's *The Rising Tide of Color* (1920), there had taken place, particularly in the United States, a recrudescence of the theory that mental traits are determined by race, which Boas traced back to the Count de Gobineau. When Grant's book first appeared Boas thought it be so dangerous that he took it upon himself to expose the "fallacies" on which it was based in two separate reviews. Grant was in no way deterred. He continued to proclaim the marked superiority of the Nordic race and to ridicule those who bent the knee "in servile adulation to the great god, Demos." In this and similar statements Grant was jibing at, among others, the Boasians; he made unmistakable reference to Boas in his sardonic mention of the "anthropological expert" who in giving evidence to the Congressional Immigration Commission had "gravely declared" that he had observed alterations in the anatomy of immigrants to the United States "under the influence of a changed environment." For Grant any such belief in the influence of environment was "fatuous." H. F. Osborn took the same stance in his presidential address of September 1921 to the Second International Congress of Eugenics, declaring that he and his fellow eugenicists in the United States had woken to the consciousness that "education and environment do not fundamentally alter racial values." Davenport, in his address, persisted in his claims that mental states had a "hereditary basis."[4]

Following the victory of the Allies in 1918 there was intense enthusiasm for the belief that "the constructive spirit of Francis Galton" could "restore disordered and shattered society." George Adami, the vice-chancellor of the University of Liverpool, having told the 1921 Congress that "students of heredity are inevitably eugenists," went on to claim that the idea of aristocracy was both sound and natural, and to advocate the compilation of "an annual record of the A1 youths and maidens of the year—A, standing for the first class in physical fitness; 1, for the first class in intelligence." Such a record, said Adami, "would become the human stud book" and result in "the establishment of a veritable aristocracy ... personal and hereditary."[5]

The Boasians, in their newfound independence, responded to these developments with redoubled vigor. Boas himself in 1920 dismissed as "vicious propaganda" the views of both Grant and Stoddard, who, he said, were trying to "bolster up their unscientific theories by an amateurish appeal to misunderstood discoveries relating to heredity." That same year, dismayed at the prospect of the forthcoming International Congress of Eugenics, and arguing that the time had come to take a definite stand, Lowie declared that nothing in past, and especially recent, experience warranted the belief that "a council of learned men could be safely entrusted with the power of regulating once and for all the future of mankind"; rather, said Lowie, everything pointed to the need for those with liberal views to combat "not merely the half-knowledge of disinterested or at least subconscious bias but the deliberate malevolence of the reactionary cloaking his self-interest with high-flown scientific verbiage." Further dissension occurred with the appearance in 1921 of the fourth revised edition of *The Passing of the Great Race,* in which Grant once more extolled the superiority of the Nordic race and wrote derisively of "the dogma of the brotherhood of man" that had been derived from "the loose thinkers of the French Revolution and their American mimics." In a tirade of disapprobation Lowie castigated those who had become "monomaniacs" in their idolatry of the Nordic, and likened Grant to an *enfant terrible,* thrusting out his tongue at humanitarian idealism and slinging mud at the standard of liberalism.[6]

The Boasians and the hereditarians were now more sharply at odds than ever before. In *The Rising Tide of Color,* for which Grant had written the introduction, Stoddard had repeated the hereditarian doctrine that civilization was the result of "the creative urge of a superior germ plasm." This belief, like those of Galton, Davenport, and others in earlier years, remained totally antithetical to the views of the Boasian school of anthropology. Lowie made this clear in July 1920, in discussing Galton's ignoring of "the influence of the social environment," when he reiterated Boas' observation that "cultural differences supply no measure of racial differences" and emphatically declared that "momentous cultural differences may arise without any fundamental change of organic constitution."[7]

In 1911 Boas had been virtually alone in his opposition to the biological determinism of Galton and Davenport, but a decade later the situation had significantly changed. By 1921 a school of cultural anthropologists recognizing Boas as their intellectual leader had been formed, and within the allied discipline of psychology a major new movement called behaviorism had joined in the combating of hereditarian ideas. Behaviorism had emerged in the United States at about the same time as the Boasian paradigm. Its founding manifesto was the article "Psychology as the Behaviorist Views It" of 1913, by J. B. Watson. Watson's book *Behavior: An Introduction to Comparative Psychology,* published in 1914, which elaborated this manifesto, was (in the words of one reviewer) "virtually a declaration of independence," and it soon prompted the emergence of a new school of psychologists. The basic doctrine of behaviorism was the limiting of the purview of psychology to overt behavior. This led to rejection of theories of genetic determinism and gave rise, in about 1920, to the "anti-instinct movement," in which a number of behaviorally oriented social psychologists became actively involved.[8]

From about 1920 onward, following the publication in 1919 of Watson's *Psychology from the Standpoint of a Behaviorist,* behaviorism rapidly gained in popularity. Astutely fostered by Watson himself, this high popularity continued throughout the 1920s. Watson wrote numerous popular articles, from 1922 onward, extolling behaviorism, and in 1924 he gave lectures in which, in Robert Woodworth's words, he "came out almost savagely against the notion of human instincts." This was the culmination of the movement against instinct theory which had begun in about 1920. In that year, while grudgingly admitting the existence of some human instincts, J. R. Kantor had emphasized their "extreme modifiability." A few years later, however, after Z. Y. Kuo had reduced human behavior to "reaction systems," Kantor entirely abandoned the concept of instinct, roundly asserting in his *Principles of Psychology* of 1924 that "in no sense may we say that human behavior reactions are inherited." It was this same extreme position that Watson adopted in his lectures of 1924.[9]

In these stances, in which heredity was totally excluded, Watson and Kantor were reacting against what Kuo in 1924 called "the tyrannic domination of biology in psychology." Another outright rejection of this domination was made by L. L. Bernard, again in 1924, in his *Instinct: A Study in Social Psychology*. "A child who has reached a rational age," Bernard declared (directly contradicting Karl Pearson), "is reacting in nine-tenths or ninety-nine hundredths of his character directly to environment, and only in the slight residual fraction of his nature directly to instinct." Again, the environmentalists had, in 1922, been given the influential support of the philosopher John Dewey, who in his *Human Nature and Conduct* characterized human nature as a "formless void of impulses" and argued that "any impulse may become organized into almost any disposition according to the way in which it interacts with surroundings."[10]

With this rejection by behaviorists, social psychologists, sociologists, and philosophers, as well as by cultural anthropologists, of the Galtonian doctrine of the vastly preponderating effects of nature over nurture, the nature-nurture controversy became more intense than ever before. By 1924 there was in the United States no more controversial subject of intellectual inquiry than the relative importance of biological and cultural factors in human behavior. The pressing problem, as the zoologist H. M. Parshley posed it in 1924, was "How much does what a man is, depend on his inborn qualities, and how much upon the habits born of his education and environment." Over this crucial issue, which went back to Galton's paper of 1865, the hereditarians and environmentalists, after years of bitter disputation, were still, as Parshley noted, in irreconcilable conflict.[11]

In 1924 then, Boas, as the intellectual leader of American cultural anthropology, found himself faced yet again by an issue that had plagued him throughout his career: the "fundamental importance" (as he had put it in 1916) of knowing "what is hereditary and what is not." "The fundamental difficulty that besets us," he declared in October 1924, "is that of differentiating between what is inherent in bodily structure, and what is acquired by the cultural medium in which each individual is set, or, to express it in biological terms, what is determined by heredity and what by environmental causes, or what is endogene and what is exogene." There was, he continued, "a fundamental need for a scientific and detailed investigation of hereditary and environmental conditions." Within a few months he had planned just such an investigation, and had found in the twenty-three-year-old Margaret Mead the very person to carry it out.[12]

Margaret Mead, at this time, was one of Boas' graduate students, having formally commenced her Ph.D. course in anthropology at Columbia University a short time previously. She had first become interested in anthropology as an undergraduate at Barnard College, when, having entered her senior year committed to psychology, she elected to take Boas' introductory course in general anthropology. Boas at this time was, at the age of sixty-four, an internationally acclaimed scholar and the unchallenged patriarch of American anthropology. He enjoyed his teaching at Barnard, where, according to Kroeber, his young female students, sensing "the genius which underlay his unpalatable presentations," afforded him special rapport. To the twenty-one-year-old Margaret Mead, Boas was the greatest mind she had encountered, with an authority greater than she had ever met in a teacher. She soon decided to attend everything Boas taught. Combined with Boas' extraordinary influence was that of his talented teaching assistant, Ruth Benedict, who not long before had completed her own graduate studies with Boas. As Mead has recorded, it was the intensity of Benedict's interest combined with "the magnificent clarity of Boas' teaching" that, in the autumn of 1922, caused her to experience anthropology as "something of a revelation."[13]

Ruth Benedict had begun her study of anthropology at the New School for Social Research in New York in 1919, at a time when the doctrine *omnis cultura ex cultura,* which Kroeber and Lowie had advanced two years earlier, was being very actively promoted. Alexander Goldenweiser, one of her teachers at the New School, had taken his Ph.D. under Boas in 1910, and, despite some minor differences of opinion, was in "unequivocal agreement" with Kroeber's critique of biological determinism and with his conclusion that culture was "a closed system." Benedict had also taken a course with Lowie. Her Ph.D. dissertation, written under Boas' supervision, placed great emphasis on "social patterning"; so much so that Sapir, on reading it, inquired of her whether she had adopted the "extreme view" in which culture was "merely environment for the individual psyche."[14]

The strength of Benedict's commitment to cultural determinism at the outset of her career can be gauged from her writings of the early 1920s. Kroeber's *Anthropology* of 1923 she welcomed as the first book to make available the point of view of modern American anthropology. "The fundamental question," she wrote, "as Mr. Kroeber conceives it, to which the labors of anthropology are directed, is how far the forces at work in civilization are cultural, and how far organic or due to heredity; what is due to nurture, in the rhyming phrase, and what to nature." For Benedict, whose ideas had been shaped by the newly formed Boasian paradigm, the answer to Kroeber's "fundamental question" was plain. Man, she believed, was, above all else, a being whose responses had been "conditioned from birth by the character of the culture into which he was born." From this it followed that for the anthropologist it was "first of all necessary to be able to recognize those elements that are received from tradition, those which are ours because we have been brought up in a particular group." Human behavior, she was convinced, was to be understood through the study of "cultural patterns." It was the explication of these "causes of another order," she believed with Kroeber and the other Boasians, that would give anthropology its "place in the sun."[15]

During her first semester in anthropology, Mead reports, she became increasingly fascinated by Benedict. She was invited to attend a graduate seminar at which Benedict discussed John Dewey's newly published *Human Nature and Conduct,* and she was presented with the offprint of a paper containing the basic conceptions of Benedict's approach to anthropology, about which they had numerous impassioned discussions. It was this clear-cut approach, an extreme form of cultural determinism, into which Mead was inducted and that she soon came enthusiastically to share. Within a few months the eager young student and the shy teaching assistant with the consuming interest in cultural patterns had entered into an intimate friendship and a zealous intellectual collaboration that was to have momentous consequences for the development of cultural anthropology.[16]

It also happened that the approach to anthropology that Mead learned from Benedict and Boas was virtually identical with those imparted to her by another of her teachers at Barnard, William Fielding Ogburn, from whom in her senior year she took a course on psychological aspects of culture. Ogburn's book *Social Change with Respect to Culture and Original Nature,* which had appeared in 1922, was a major contribution to the nature-nurture debate. Ogburn had been profoundly influenced by the doctrines advanced by Kroeber and Lowie in 1917, and his *Social Change* was very largely a further development of these ideas. According to Ogburn, the social heritage and the hereditary nature of man were two distinct and separate things, the one organic and the other superorganic. From this conviction Ogburn derived a principle basic to his teaching: "good methodology," he stipulated, required the "consideration of the cultural factor" before any recourse was had to "biological causes." And so, from the inception of her anthropological studies, Mead, as she herself has noted, became convinced by Ogburn's procedural rule, as was her mentor Benedict, that "we should never look for psychological explanations of social phenomena until attempts at explanation in cultural terms had been exhausted." The procedure she was to follow in her as yet unplanned Samoan researches had already been set.[17]

Early in March 1923, Ruth Benedict began to talk with Margaret Mead about the possibility of Mead's becoming an anthropologist rather than a psychologist, as she at that time intended. Lonely and uncertain about her own future, Benedict (as she noted in her diary on 13 March 1923) felt the need for a "companion in harness," and had begun to hope that the gifted young student whose company she found so congenial would be moved to take up anthropology. Mead, by this time, needed little persuasion: listening to Boas' lectures she had been enthralled by the prospect of the comparative study of human culture leading to "a better knowledge of what man is"; all that was required was Benedict's assurance that in anthropology work that really mattered was waiting to be done. On 20 March

Mead told Boas of her wish to enroll for a Ph.D. in anthropology. At first he "poured cold water" on the idea. She held firm to her choice, however, and after taking a B.A. degree at Barnard, accepting an assistantship to Ogburn, and marrying Luther Cressman, a theology student to whom she had been engaged since she was seventeen, she turned in the autumn of 1923 to graduate work in anthropology. Boas at this time was still concentrating, in the training of his graduate students, on the comparative study of cultural traits. The topic allotted to Mead was the investigation, in the ethnographic literature, of canoe-building, house-building, and tattooing in the Polynesian culture area. By August 1924 her reading was sufficiently advanced for her to present a paper on "Rank in Polynesia" to the anthropology section of the meeting of the British Association for the Advancement of Science in Toronto. Her study of rank among the Samoans, the Hawaiians, and the Maori of New Zealand, she reported, had revealed "in each of these cultures . . . a different cultural emphasis." But the most instructive of her experiences at this international meeting of anthropologists was the discovery that everyone who was anybody had a "people" of his own to whom he referred his discussions. She returned to Columbia resolved to achieve this for herself as soon as possible after the completion of her dissertation. Before long she had formed the plan of following her library researches on cultural stability in Polynesia at large by a field study of cultural change in the remote and romantic Tuamotu Islands of Eastern Polynesia.[18]

At this juncture, after having emphasized in the *American Mercury* of October 1924 the fundamental need for "a scientific and detailed investigation of hereditary and environmental conditions," Boas, with Margaret Mead in mind, devised quite another research project. As Mead has noted, Boas was "always tailoring a particular piece of research to the exigencies of theoretical priorities." Over the years, as we have seen, Boas had taken the lead in combating, with whatever evidence he could muster, the hereditarian theory of the vastly preponderating effects of nature over nurture, and toward the end of 1924 he conceived the idea of challenging this theory through a study of adolescence in a culture markedly different from those of Western

Europe and the United States. Boas was well conversant with G. Stanley Hall's massive study of adolescence of 1904. In the early 1920s there was widespread concern with "reckless and rebellious youths," linked with what H. L. Mencken called "wholesale discussion of the sex question." The project, as Mead has described it, was to be a special inquiry into "the relative strength of biological puberty and cultural pattern." In 1924, ten years before the publication of Karl Popper's *Logik der Forschung,* the notion of subjecting one's own theories to rigorous testing was unknown. Rather, one sought to prove them to the very hilt, and Boas was intent upon obtaining evidence in support of his own deeply held convictions. He had long believed the social stimulus to be infinitely more potent than the biological mechanism. If this could be convincingly demonstrated it would bear on issues that were, Boas felt, of the utmost significance. In Margaret Mead there was at hand a spirited young cultural determinist ideally suited to the project he had in mind.[19]

Boas' initial plan was for the study he had devised to be undertaken in an American Indian tribe. This, however, Mead adamantly resisted. Her heart was set on field research in some "remote and 'untouched' place in the South Seas." She would be prepared, she intimated, to abandon culture change and study instead the relative strength of biological puberty and cultural pattern, as long as this was in the Tuamotu Islands, or some comparably remote part of Polynesia. But to this scheme Boas, in turn, was opposed. Fieldwork in the Tuamotu archipelago would, he considered, be too risky. Indeed, according to Mead, Boas disapproved of her working anywhere in the "unhealthful tropics" of Polynesia. Yet Boas, being "very definite about what he wanted done," was in a mood to compromise. The study, he agreed, could be in Polynesia if it were on an island "to which a ship came regularly—at least every three weeks." In this way, as Mead has recounted, Boas consented to her choice of Polynesia while she, in return, accepted Boas' special project for a comparative study of female adolescence. She would work, it was finally decided, in American Samoa, not because of any theoretical or personal preference, but because at that time Matson liners called at the deep water port of Pago Pago at about three-week intervals. To Mead herself, in later years, it seemed "crazy" that she should, in this way, have "got a culture" that, as she depicted it, so completely confirmed Boasian doctrine.[20]

At the end of April 1925, soon after Mead had completed the draft of her doctoral thesis on cultural stability in Polynesia, word came of the award of a fellowship from the National Research Council. The way was now clear. She would be going to Samoa, after two years of graduate study in anthropology, to do research among Samoan girls on Boas' special problem. She spent the next couple of months "frantically assembling . . . field equipment—spare glasses, cotton dresses, a camera, pencils and notebooks"; then in mid 1925 Mead set off for the South Seas.[21]

On the morning of 31 August 1925, "remembering Stevenson's rhapsodies," Mead was up early for her Matson liner's arrival in the romantically remote islands of Samoa. The "whole picture," alack, was badly skewed by the presence of numerous battleships of the American Pacific fleet, with airplanes screaming overhead, and a naval band playing ragtime. She was given a room in a ramshackle hotel by the edge of Pago Pago harbor, which Somerset Maugham had described a few years previously in his wry tale of the downfall of a prudish missionary. Margaret Mead's Samoan researches, which were to have such a profound influence on twentieth-century anthropology, were about to begin.[22]

II

MEAD'S SAMOAN RESEARCH

5

Mead Presents Boas with an Absolute Answer

THE TWENTY-THREE-YEAR-OLD Margaret Mead arrived in American Samoa in August of 1925. She did not, as she has recorded, "really know much about fieldwork," and in the rush before she left New York she had had no occasion for any study of the Samoan language. She was carrying with her a letter of introduction from the surgeon general of the U.S. Navy (who had known her father-in-law in medical school), and when this was presented to the chief medical officer of the naval station at Pago Pago, she was assigned within a few days of her arrival a young Samoan nurse, who had been in the United States and spoke excellent English, to work with her for an hour a day on Samoan. For the next six weeks or so, in the enervating heat of the port of Pago Pago and the "generally unco-operative atmosphere" of her hotel, Mead studied Samoan.[1]

Toward the end of September, as she cast about for a place in which she might study adolescence, she visited a girls' boarding school of the London Missionary Society at the western end of Tutuila, and by 11 October, when she reported to Boas on her first six weeks or so in Samoa, she had briefly inspected almost every village on the island of Tutuila that could be reached by road from the port of Pago Pago. The villages of Tutuila, she told Boas, were either very much influenced by American goods and American visitors or so very small and difficult to reach as to make them impossible places to work. In this predicament, she reported, she had decided to go to Ta'ū, one of the three small islands of the Manu'an archipelago, lying some seventy miles to the east of Tutuila, where there was a government outpost which was visited by a naval vessel at about three-week intervals.[2]

She was particularly anxious, she told Boas, to have his advice on whether when she got to Manu'a she should live with a Samoan family or in the household of the one white family on Ta'ū, that of Edward R. Holt, the chief pharmacist's mate of the naval medical dispensary. To the first of these alternatives Mead had, from her observations of Samoan life in Tutuila, developed a rooted antipathy. "If I lived in a Samoan house with a Samoan family," she told Boas,

> I might conceivably get into a little more intimate touch with that particular family. But I feel that such advantage as might be reaped would be more than offset by the loss in efficiency due to the food and the nervewracking conditions of living with half a dozen people in the same room in a house without walls, always sitting on the floor and sleeping in the constant expectation of having a pig or a chicken thrust itself upon one's notice. This is not an easy climate to work in; I find my efficiency diminished to about one-half as it is, and I believe it would be cut in two again if I had to live for weeks on end in a Samoan house.[3]

By 11 October when Mead wrote these words to Boas, she had already come to know Mrs. Holt, who was in Pago Pago

awaiting the birth of her second child, and her decision to live
with the Holts (as is apparent from another letter written two
days later) was in fact already made. The native food, she said
in this letter of 13 October 1925, was too starchy for her to live
on for six months, whereas with the Holts she would have a bed
to sleep on and the food would be much better, as Navy people
had canteen privileges.[4]

After seven weeks spent mostly in the vicinity of the naval
station at Pago Pago, Mead reported to Boas that her knowledge of Samoan was progressing more slowly than at first, and
she was intending to spend the next five or six weeks, before
Mrs. Holt and her baby would be ready to return to Ta'ū, partly
in the girls' boarding school she had visited earlier, where no
English was spoken, and partly with a half-caste family at
Leone, where she would be able to hear Samoan spoken most of
the time. Instead, with the help of the mother of some half-caste
children she had met in Honolulu, she spent ten days with the
family of Ufiti, county chief of Tualautu, of the village of Vaitogi, on the iron-bound coast to the west of Pago Pago. She had
been given a letter of introduction to Ufiti by the secretary of
native affairs in the naval government.

When Mead arrived in Samoa at the end of August 1925,
with her letter from the surgeon-general of the U.S. Navy, she
had been invited to dine on the flagship of the admiral of the
American Pacific Fleet, an honor that had, she reported, greatly
impressed the "very rank-conscious Samoans." Accordingly, on
her arrival in Vaitogi she was carefully chaperoned. Ufiti's el-
dest son was studying for the ministry, while his daughter,
Fa'amotu, was a *taupou,* or ceremonial virgin. Fa'amotu, who
spoke a little English, was given the responsibility of being
Mead's constant companion, even sleeping beside her under the
same mosquito net.[5] Because she did not know what "the consequences might be in the roles that would be assigned," Mead
concealed from her Samoan hosts that she already had a husband, and Ufiti, supposing her to be other than she was, conferred upon her the title of ceremonial virgin, this being, in Samoan eyes, a very high honor. During her stay in Vaitogi she
was also instructed for a few days in the rudiments of the re-

spect language and etiquette of Samoa, by two visiting talking chiefs.[6]

Although, according to Mead, she had never spent "a more peacefully happy and comfortable" ten days in all her life than in Ufiti's household at Vaitogi, she did not alter her determination to live with the Holts. When she reached Ta'ū, having made the crossing from Tutuila on 9 November 1925 in a U.S. Navy minesweeper, she elected to live in the comfort of the medical dispensary, with the local representatives of the naval government of American Samoa.[7]

At the time of Mead's arrival in Ta'ū, an island of about fourteen square miles, which rises like a huge cone to an elevation of nearly 3,000 feet, the Manu'ans had been converts to protestant Christianity for some eighty years, and governed by the United States for twenty-one years. When the islands of Tutuila and Aunu'u were ceded to the United States on 17 April 1900, following a treaty of the previous year among Great Britain, Germany, and the United States, the Tui Manu'a, as the sovereign chief of the highest-ranking polity in the whole of Samoa, initially resisted the heavy pressures being placed upon him; on 16 July 1904, however, Manu'a was finally erected into a territory or district of the United States, and those Manu'ans of rank who had signed the deed of cession each received from Theodore Roosevelt, the president of the United States, a proclamation diploma, together with "a silver medal (with case)" and "a silver watch and chain (with case)." From this time onward the people of Manu'a came ever increasingly under the influence of American institutions and values.[8]

On 30 June 1908 a government school was opened on Ta'ū, with "a most gratifying attendance." Just over seven years later, however, this school and most of the other buildings in Manu'a were destroyed in the devastating hurricane of 10 January 1915, after which about two-thirds of the population of 2100 were taken, in the U.S. naval vessels *Fortune* and *Princeton,* to live for a time on Tutuila and to acquaint themselves with the marvels of the port of Pago Pago. In April 1915 the building of the Manu'a Co-operative Society, which had been severely damaged in the hurricane, was taken over by the naval government to be converted into a medical dispensary and radio office. The government school was reopened in 1920 under Lieutenant A. J. Link, M.C., United States Navy, with the hospital corps man and the radio man as his assistants. By the time Mead began her researches, the government school had an enrollment of 202, with a staff consisting of a Samoan principal and three Samoan assistants. On Ta'ū at this time there were six copra sheds and a trading store of the South Seas Pacific Co. About every three weeks a naval vessel carried passengers and their freight to and fro between Pago Pago and Ta'ū, free of charge, while the radio office maintained regular schedules with the naval radio station in Tutuila, so that Mead could contact Boas, Benedict, and others in the United States by telecommunication, as the need arose. Tufele Fa'atoia, who was in 1925–1926 the district governor of Manu'a, spoke excellent English, having been educated in Hawaii at U.S. government expense, and, Mead herself (in a letter of 7 March 1926) remarked on the European character of the chiefs living at the western end of the island of Ta'ū, in the vicinity of her research headquarters. Albert F. Judd, president of the board of trustees of the Bernice P. Bishop Museum, who visited Manu'a early in 1926, during the course of Mead's fieldwork, judged the Manu'ans to be the leaders of American Samoa, in both "thought and progress."[9]

On her arrival on Ta'ū, Mead at once became a member of the Holt household. She was given a small room on the back veranda of the large, one-storied building which contained both the medical dispensary and the radio station, and this room in the main outpost in Manu'a of the naval government of American Samoa, a photograph of Boas having been placed on one of its walls, became her research headquarters. Before Mead left New York, Boas had specifically cautioned her against embarking on a general study of the ethnology of Samoa, and as soon as she had settled in, despite her limited knowledge of Samoan,[10] she began work on her special project. From the sixty-eight girls between the ages of eight and twenty in the three villages of

Lumā, Si'ufaga, and Faleasao at the western end of the island of
Ta'ū, Mead selected fifty for study, eleven of them being "children who showed no mammary signs of puberty," fourteen
"children who would probably mature within the next year or
year and a half," and twenty-five being "past puberty," or first
menstruation.[11] From these twenty-five girls, ranging in age
from fourteen to twenty years, all of whom were considered by
their communities to be not yet adults, Mead drew her principal
informants.[12]

In front of the medical dispensary, facing the sea, there was a
small Samoan-type house in which Mead was also able to work
with her adolescent subjects. After the school holidays began in
the second half of December, she was able to borrow the
schoolhouse to give intelligence and other tests, and to interview each girl privately. Being small and slight, Mead could
move comfortably among the fourteen-year-olds who were her
daily companions. Proceeding in this way, she gradually built
up a census of the village and worked out the background of
each of the girls she was studying. The Christmas and New
Year vacation of the U.S. government school on Ta'ū was for
eight weeks from the third Monday in December, and soon after
the school had resumed late in February 1926, the researches on
female adolescence into which Mead had plunged in mid-No-
vember 1925 were (as she noted in a letter on 7 March 1926)
"almost completed." They had been in progress for little more
than three months, and had been "terribly complicated" by a
severe hurricane on New Year's Day, 1926, after which for several weeks everyone was busy with repairing the widespread
damage and informants were "not to be had for love or
money."[13]

On 18 February 1926 an expedition from the Bernice P.
Bishop Museum arrived in Manu'a for a stay of some sixteen
days to collect shells and ethnological information. At the invitation of the district governor, its members together with Mead
made a short visit to Fitiuta at the eastern end of the island of
Ta'ū. With the resumption of the government school, it had become, as Mead noted after her return from this visit, "practi-

cally impossible" to get hold of her adolescent informants. On 8 March 1926 she went on a visit to the islands of Ofu and Olosega; from this point onward, most of her time was given to the general study of the ethnology of Manu'a.[14]

During her stay in Manu'a, Mead did not have "any political participation in village life," as there was in Manu'a in the 1920s a strict prohibition[15] against any woman participating in any of the chiefly assemblies in which decisions were made concerning economic, political, ceremonial, and religious life, and before which from time to time those who had seriously offended against Samoan custom were arraigned and punished. Again, during the final five months of her stay, when, in the aftermath of the hurricane of 1 January 1926, "adult energies were devoted almost exclusively to house building," she had "very little opportunity to witness social ceremonies of any kind."[16]

Faced by these severe disadvantages, Mead was compelled, in her study of many of the fundamental aspects of Samoan life, to "completely rely on informants." Working in this restricted way, from the environment of the medical dispensary, and coping as best she could with the terrible complications caused by the hurricane that had devastated Ta'ū only seven weeks after her arrival, Mead struggled to construct a picture of Samoa that would answer the problem that Boas had set her. When she returned to Pago Pago from Manu'a in May 1926, to embark on a six weeks' voyage to Europe, via Australia, she felt a "fierce longing" for contact with people who would understand her work, and who would give her some perspective on whether she had actually done what she had been "sent out to do."[17]

Throughout her nine months' stay in Samoa, Mead had been in constant correspondence with Benedict, who had become her anthropological alter ego. In the summer of 1925, when Mead set out for Samoa, the two women had traveled together as far as the Grand Canyon, from where Mead went on to San Francisco while Benedict returned to Zuni in New Mexico. From Zuni, Santa Fe, and Pena Blanca, in the month of August 1925, Benedict wrote to Mead seven times: she would be reckoning the time of their separation, she said, by the three-week inter-vals between the steamers carrying Mead's letters, rather as the Zuni counted off their year with prayerstick plantings.[18]

As we have seen, by as early as mid 1924, Benedict and Mead in their enthusiastic discussions together had become totally committed to the goal of achieving an understanding of human behavior through the study of cultural patterns. Mead had taken with her to Samoa all of the questions about deviance from pattern that Benedict had prepared for her, together with an anthology, which Benedict had compiled, containing Amy Lowell's poem "Patterns," with its final agonized line: "Christ! What are patterns for?"[19]

From Cochiti in September 1925 Benedict had written to Mead of her deep yearning to "find a really undiscovered coun-try." This she was to do, among the Pima, in the summer of 1927, some nine months after Mead's return to the United States. The process of discovery was expedited in September 1926, when Mead and Benedict, after their reunion in Rome at the International Congress of Americanists, began to discuss on their voyage home a "host of new problems," bearing on cul-tural patterning, which Mead had brought back with her from Samoa.[20]

Back in New York, Mead at once took up the position of as-sistant curator of ethnology at the American Museum of Natu-ral History, which had been offered to her by cable while she was still in Manu'a. With scarcely a pause she plunged into writing up her materials on Samoan adolescence, and by the spring of 1927 she had completed (except for chapter 2, which was added later) the first twelve chapters of what was to be-come *Coming of Age in Samoa*. During this same period she also acted as an assistant to Benedict in her anthropology course at Barnard College, and their discussions together (espe-cially of chapter 11 of Mead's manuscript on deviance from pat-tern among Samoan adolescents) continued unabated, until the summer of 1927, when Benedict went to work among the Pima and Mead traveled to Europe to make a study of Oceanic mate-rials in German museums.[21]

Earlier in 1927, Mead had sent the first draft of her account of adolescence in Samoa to Harper Brothers, only to have it rejected. At the instigation of the anthropologist and author George Dorsey she then went to see William Morrow, who was just setting up as a publisher. Morrow put it to her that she should round off her book with an account of the significance of her findings for contemporary Americans. To this Mead readily agreed, it being very much her view that "if one society could bring its children through adolescence painlessly," as did Samoa, "then there was a chance that other societies could do so also." She had in fact been lecturing to an assortment of audiences, in and about New York, on this very theme from soon after her return from Samoa.[22]

This then was the situation when, in the summer of 1927, from her research base in the Southwest, Benedict wrote to Boas describing the contrast between the Zuni and the Pima as "unbelievable." It presented, she wrote later, "probably the most abrupt cultural break" in America. Benedict had, with "a sense of revelation," recognized, according to Mead, the fundamental differences between "those American Indian cultures that emphasize ecstasy (for which she adopted Nietzsche's term Dionysian) and those that emphasize moderation and balance (for which she adopted Nietzsche's term Apollonian)." This brilliant insight, as Mead felt it to be, Benedict developed in a paper that was the precursor to her book of 1934, *Patterns of Culture*. Presented to the International Congress of Americanists in New York in 1928, it was entitled "Psychological Types in the Cultures of the Southwest." Nietzsche, in his studies of Greek tragedy, Benedict pointed out, had named and described two diametrically different ways of arriving at the values of existence, the Dionysian and the Apollonian. Comparable value systems, she claimed, were to be found in the region of the Southwest, so that among the Zuni, as among other Indian tribes of the Southwest, "a fundamental psychological set" had "created an intricate cultural pattern to express its own preferences."[23]

By the autumn of 1927 Benedict and Mead had become more convinced than ever that in all human cultures the traditional patterns of behavior set the mold into which human nature flowed. Mead was at work on her monograph on the social organization of Manu'a, and she eagerly grasped the opportunity of applying Benedict's newly conceived theory of culture as "personality writ large" to her Samoan materials. Together they "spent hours discussing how a given temperamental approach to living could come so to dominate a culture that all who were born in it would become the willing or unwilling heirs to that view of the world," taking as their example the Samoans about whom Mead was then writing. It thus transpired that the first written application of Benedict's new theory appeared in Mead's account, in *Social Organization of Manu'a,* of the "dominant cultural attitudes" of the Samoans, "every detail of the phrasing" of which was "thrashed out" by Benedict and Mead, as they "discussed at length the kind of personality that had been institutionalized in Samoan culture."[24]

There was among the Zuni, according to Benedict's new theory, an "Apollonian delight in formality," and in "the intricacies and elaborations of organization." While Mead excluded from her account of Samoa the actual terms Benedict had borrowed from Nietzsche, she nonetheless depicted the Samoans in unmistakably Apollonian terms. "All of a Samoan's interest," she wrote, was "centered upon his relationship with his fellows within an elaborate and cherished social pattern." Further, the particular implication of this social pattern was an "emphasis upon social blessedness within an elaborate, impersonal structure," the "formal social personality" of Samoa being that of "a devotee of a careful observance of all the decreed amenities." These descriptions could well have been applied by Benedict to the Zuni, and indeed Mead, on a later occasion, specifically noted that in both Zuni and Samoa it was "the individual endowed with a capacity to feel strongly" who was "maladjusted."[25]

There is thus the clearest evidence that with the emergence of Benedict's vision of culture as "personality writ large" in the summer of 1927, Mead construed her data from Samoa in this same way, and that Benedict's new theory powerfully influenced Mead in the writing of the three chapters she added to

Coming of Age in Samoa early in 1928. The first of these was chapter 2, Mead's idyllic vignette of "A Day in Samoa." Benedict's new configurational approach to culture had an even more important influence on the two final chapters of *Coming of Age,* which Mead wrote at William Morrow's suggestion. Benedict and Mead (to use a phrase from Benedict's letter to Mead of 5 March 1926) had both been brought up on "Papa Franz's milk," and after they had worked so intensively together on "the phenomenon of social pressure and its absolute determination in shaping the individuals within its bounds," Mead was ready to depict Samoa as possessing a culture congruent with the Apollonian characteristics she had described in her application of Benedict's "brilliant insight" to her Samoan materials, and to avow cultural determinism in absolute terms.[26]

Boas' devising of Mead's researches of 1925–1926, as we have seen, had stemmed directly from his recognition, in 1924, of the "fundamental need for a scientific and detailed investigation of hereditary and environmental conditions," and, as Mead herself acknowledged, his specific reason for sending her to Samoa was that he wanted "a study to see how much adolescent behavior is physiologically determined and how much culturally determined." This study he hoped would bear significantly on the nature-nurture problem, which had hitherto defied the best efforts of many of the leading intellects of the day, including that of Boas himself.

This was, however, an impossibly difficult problem to foist upon a graduate student as sparsely experienced as was the twenty-three-year-old Margaret Mead at the outset of her Samoan researches. For one thing, although she had for some three years been a student of anthropology as it was taught by Boas and his associates, Mead lacked any systematic training in biology, and was thus by no means scientifically equipped to investigate the subtle and complex interaction, in Samoan behavior, of biological and cultural variables. During her first two months in Samoa, when she was working in Tutuila, she found herself saying under her breath, "I can't do it. I can't do it." In the end, however, in Manu'a, despite numerous difficulties, she was able to collect information on some twenty-five adolescent girls. This, however, did not amount to anything like a "scientific and detailed investigation of hereditary and environmental conditions." Indeed, a critical reading of Mead's writings on Samoa reveals that she did not, at any time, either on Tutuila or in Manu'a, carry out any systematic comparison of hereditary and environmental conditions. Thus on her return to the United States in 1926 she was in no position to analyze the nature of the interaction between genetic and exogenetic variables in the behavior of Samoan adolescents. In this predicament she adopted the stratagem of using Samoa as what has come to be known in anthropology as a "negative instance."[27]

In his planning of Mead's Samoan researches, Boas had fully accepted that adolescence, in Europe and the United States, was a difficult period. For example, in a letter he wrote to Mead on the eve of her departure for Samoa, he noted that "we find very often among ourselves during the period of adolescence a strong rebellious spirit that may be expressed in sullenness or in sudden outbursts." That this was the case in the United States was also fully recognized by Mead, but, given the "determinism of culture" in which she had been taught to believe, it might be, she surmised, that in some remote part of the world, such as Samoa, things were wholly different. And from this she derived the supposition that "if a society could be found in which the growing boys and girls missed out on all this storm and stress, then the anthropologist would know ... that this storm and stress was not inevitable."[28]

This, then, became Mead's homespun approach to the immeasurably complex problem that Boas had required her to study. Having failed, in her perplexing predicament, to investigate scientifically the actual interaction of biological and cultural variables in Samoan behavior, she turned instead to the purported invalidation of a preexisting theoretical generalization by a "negative instance." That this was the method she adopted Mead confirmed in an interview in 1970 with T. George Harris and J. Diener, during which there occurred this exchange, referring specifically to her Samoan researches:

Harris: You had a beautiful technique going. There were all these theories around—piled up by centuries of philosophers and added to by psychologists—that claimed to apply to all mankind. You went after the single negative, one culture in which the theory broke down.

Diener: Sure, one negative is worth a thousand positives. It kills the theory.

Mead: That was the first stage of anthropology really. Up until 1939 we used primitive cultures—conveniently simpler than our own—to challenge assertions . . .[29]

Again, a few years later in another interview Mead remarked, "in anthropology you only have to show once that it is possible for a culture to make, say, a period of life easy, where it is hard everywhere else, to have made your point." Here also, Mead is alluding to her Samoan researches, and in particular to her conclusion that among the Samoans adolescence is the age of maximum ease, in a society "replete with easy solutions for all conflicts."[30]

This exemplary society in which, in conspicuous contrast to the United States, growing up was "so easy" became her negative instance, and, clutching it like a talisman, she swept on to an unequivocal answer to the general question she had posed in the introduction to *Coming of Age in Samoa:* "Are the disturbances which vex our adolescents due to the nature of adolescence itself or to the civilization?" Certain of the absolute truth of cultural determinism, and having attributed what she claimed to be the untroubled character of adolescence in Samoa to the ease of Samoan culture, Mead went on to pronounce her main theoretical conclusion:

If it is proved that adolescence is not necessarily a specially difficult period in a girl's life—and proved it is if we can find any society in which that is so—then what accounts for the presence of storm and stress in American adolescents? First, we may say quite simply that there must be something in the two civilizations to account for the difference. If the same process takes a different form in the two different environments, we cannot make any explanations in terms of the process, for that is the same in both cases.[31]

In other words, any explanation in biological terms of the presence of storm and stress in American adolescents was totally excluded. The conclusion to which Mead was led by her depiction of Samoa as a negative instance was thus of an extreme order. Instead of arriving at an estimate of the relative strength of biological puberty and cultural pattern, as Boas had anticipated, Mead dismissed biology, or nature, as being of no significance whatsoever in accounting for the presence of storm and stress in American adolescents, and claimed the determinism of culture, or nurture, to be absolute.

Boas had believed, according to Mead, that her researches in Samoa would indicate that culture was "very important." How then did he react to the revelation that Mead and Benedict, in their enthusiasm for cultural patterning, had prepared for him? Some time after *Coming of Age in Samoa* had been submitted to him for criticism, he said to Mead during a departmental meeting, "About that manuscript. Come to lunch with me next Tuesday"; and then, turning to Ruth Benedict, "You had better come too." Mead was "devastated" by his tone of voice, and on the "fatal Tuesday morning" she anxiously paced the floor of her office in the American Museum of Natural History saying to herself "I have betrayed him, like everybody else." She need not have worried. As she reports, the only criticism that Boas ever offered of what she had written in *Coming of Age in Samoa* was the quite trifling comment that she had not made clear "the difference between passionate and romantic love."[32]

By this time, at almost seventy years of age, Boas was the veteran of years of unrelenting opposition to the doctrines of extreme hereditarians like Davenport, Osborn, Grant, and Stoddard. To Jacob Epstein, who sculpted Boas during a visit to New York in 1927, he "seemed to be a man of great courage both mental and physical," and "as spirited as a fighting cock." After years of combating the battle-cry of "nature not nurture,"

Boas was still, in 1928, hopeful of turning the tables on the eugenicists and their supporters with a singular anthropological instance—an instance that would be a striking exemplification of his claim of 1916 that "the social stimulus is infinitely more potent than the biological mechanism." It was precisely with this kind of exemplification that, if credence were to be placed in her account, he had been presented by Mead, and so closely was it in accord with his own cherished beliefs that he voiced not a word of criticism of its conclusion that culture, or nurture, was the absolute determinant of the events of adolescence.[33]

This was the acceptance for which Mead had most hoped. In Sydney, Australia, in October 1928 she proudly told A. R. Radcliffe-Brown that it was Boas who had planned her work in Samoa, and in *Coming of Age in Samoa* she acknowledged that it was to Professor Franz Boas that she owed the inspiration and the direction of her problem, the training that had prepared her to undertake her investigations in Samoa, and the criticism of her results. Prodded by George Dorsey, who looked on Boas as, beyond all question, the world's greatest anthropologist, she asked Papa Franz if he would introduce her "psychological study of primitive youth" to the reading public. This he agreed to do, and when *Coming of Age in Samoa* (this title having been suggested by Dorsey) was published in New York at the end of August 1928, it contained a highly approving foreword by the intellectual leader of American anthropology.[34]

Anthropologists, explained Boas, had come to doubt that adolescence was an unavoidable period of adjustment through which everyone had to pass, and he was grateful that Miss Mead, by "having undertaken to identify herself so completely with Samoan youth," had in "the results of her painstaking investigation," confirmed "the suspicion long held by anthropologists, that much of what we ascribe to human nature is no more than a reaction to the restraints put upon us by our civilization." In his *Anthropology and Modern Life,* published very soon after *Coming of Age in Samoa,* Boas made this general conclusion more specific by declaring that "the studies of Dr. Margaret Mead on the adolescents of Samoa" had shown that "with the freedom of sexual life, the absence of a large number of conflicting ideals, and the emphasis upon forms that to us are irrelevant, the adolescent crisis disappears."[35]

When her book appeared at the end of August 1928, Mead had already embarked on her second field expedition to the South Seas. In Sydney, on the night of 26 October 1928, en route to the Admiralty Islands, she dreamed that *Coming of Age* had failed so completely that the publishers had withdrawn it from publication. This anxiety was misplaced, for her book, with a theme and conclusion wonderfully in accord with the pervasive intellectual mood of the late 1920s, was an immediate and spectacular success. By December 1928 there had been a second printing. *Coming of Age in Samoa* had become a best-seller, and a book said to be of exceptional scientific significance.[36]

While Mead had been writing *Coming of Age in Samoa,* behaviorism had continued to flourish. J. B. Watson, in a steady flow of articles (published in book form in 1928 under the title *The Ways of Behaviorism*), had continued to proclaim that nurture not nature was responsible for human behavior.[37] In 1927, V. F. Calverton, the editor of the *Modern Quarterly,* in discussing Watson's doctrines, claimed that environmentalism had become the great movement of the age. For Calverton, this movement was the expression of a glorious faith in environment and possibilities of change and progress, and he depicted the environmentalists of the late 1920s as standing in unqualified opposition to those "heredity fiends, the eugenists."[38]

The struggle against hereditarian doctrines in which Boas and his followers had been openly engaged since 1916 was, then, still very much alive in 1927 when Mead, with Benedict's active assistance, was formulating her general conclusion about her Samoan researches. Further, although with the vigorous campaigning of Watson and others the balance of opinion had shifted in favor of the environmentalists, the nature-nurture issue, as it applied to human behavior, remained unresolved. The mood of the day, as R. L. Finney noted in 1927, was one that craved "finality."[39]

It was this longed-for finality that Mead purported to provide, and it was precisely as a conclusive contribution to the protracted nature-nurture debate that *Coming of Age in Samoa* was greeted by the intellectuals of the day. One of the first reviews to appear, in the *New York Times* of 4 November 1928, noted that the question at issue was whether "the difficulties of the transition from childhood to adult life" were "due to adolescence itself, and, therefore, universal and unavoidable" or "the result of the impact between developing youth and a civilization which at once restrains and complicates." This question, which was, of course, Boas' special instance of the problem of determining "what is hereditary and what is not," had, the reviewer declared, been answered "in an extraordinary fashion" by an anthropologist.

This providing, by Margaret Mead, of a definitive answer to the problem that Benedict had identified as the fundamental question to which the labors of anthropology were directed, was, for the Boasians, the most heady of triumphs. Boas, in his foreword, had emphasized the painstaking nature of Mead's Samoan researches. Benedict, who had followed Mead's researches even more closely than had Boas, gave the same assurance. Adolescence, she wrote in the *Journal of Philosophy,* had been "an excellent choice as a test problem," both because conditions in American society had focused so much attention upon it and because it was "by definition tied up with a biological fact in human development." In studying this test problem Dr. Mead had, said Benedict, "learned to know intimately, in their own language, the girls of three villages," and had "made herself familiar with the minutiae of their civilization." And, through these meticulous inquiries, Dr. Mead had found that "it was precisely at adolescence that, for the Samoan girl, emotional stress is at a minimum." For Benedict, as for the rest of the Boasians, *Coming of Age in Samoa* was above all significant as an exemplification of "the enormously variable social determinants that fashion our flexible human nature," and a demonstration that the human animal was "unbelievably plastic." Cultural determinism had been proved to the very hilt.[40]

6

Mead's Depiction
of the Samoans

DURING THE LAST FEW MONTHS of her fieldwork in Manu'a,
Mead turned, as we have seen, to the general study of Samoan
society. With the information she collected during this period,
supplemented by her reading of the earlier literature on Samoa,
she produced *Social Organization of Manu'a,* which she dedicated to Ruth Benedict. Mead's general study of Samoan society and culture was also of quite crucial significance for the
argument she presented in *Coming of Age in Samoa.* As we
have already seen, rather than attempting a direct study of the
interrelation of cultural and biological variables, Mead followed
the course of presenting Samoan society as a negative instance,
that is, as a society with special characteristics that had resulted in the disappearance of the disturbance at adolescence
that tends to occur elsewhere in human populations. In defining

these special characteristics she had perforce, as she noted in
the introduction to *Coming of Age,* to "give a picture of the
whole social life of Samoa." It was Mead's view in 1925 that a
trained student could "master the fundamental structure of a
primitive society in a few months," and, supposing the Samoans
to have a "very simple society," she had no compunction, despite the cursoriness of her inquiries, in constructing her own
picture of Samoan culture and character.[1]

It is with the scientific adequacy of Mead's picture of Samoan society that I shall be concerned from now on, for to the
extent that this picture is defective, Samoa ceases to be a negative instance and Mead's central conclusion that culture, or
nurture, is all-important in the determination of adolescent and
other aspects of human behavior is revealed as ungrounded and
invalid.

In chapter 13 of *Coming of Age in Samoa,* having announced
her conclusion that in the case of adolescent behavior "we cannot make any explanations in terms of the process" and must
therefore look wholly to the "social environment" for an answer, Mead at once went on to outline the aspects of Samoan
life that "irremediably affect" the life of the Samoan girl. "The
Samoan background," she wrote,

> which makes growing up so easy, so simple a matter, is
> the general casualness of the whole society. For Samoa is
> a place where no one plays for very high stakes, no one
> pays very heavy prices, no one suffers for his convictions,
> or fights to the death for special ends. Disagreements be-
> tween parents and child are settled by the child's moving
> across the street, between a man and his village by the
> man's removal to the next village, between a husband and
> his wife's seducer by a few fine mats. Neither poverty nor
> great disasters threaten the people to make them hold
> their lives dearly and tremble for continued existence. No
> implacable gods, swift to anger and strong to punish, dis-
> turb the even tenor of their days. Wars and cannibalism
> are long since passed away, and now the greatest cause
> for tears, short of death itself, is a journey of a relative to

another island. No one is hurried along in life or punished harshly for slowness of development. Instead the gifted, the precocious, are held back, until the slowest among them have caught the pace. And in personal relations, caring is as slight. Love and hate, jealousy and revenge, sorrow and bereavement, are all matters of weeks. From the first months of life, when the child is handed carelessly from one woman's hands to another's, the lesson is learned of not caring for one person greatly, not setting high hopes on any one relationship.[2]

Elsewhere in her writings, Mead elaborates this picture of the background that, for Samoans, "makes growing up so easy," the leitmotif of her depiction being the notion of *ease*. Samoan life, she claims, is above all else "characterized by ease"; Samoan society is "replete with easy solutions for all conflicts." She remarks, for example, on "the ease with which personality differences can be adjusted by change of residence," on "the easy acceptance of innovation," and on a prevailing "ease in sex relations." Adolescence is "the age of maximum ease," and Samoans develop into "easy, balanced human beings" in a society that "emphasizes a graceful, easy, diffuse emotional life, a relaxed dependence upon reliable social forms."[3]

This picture of an easeful society was powerfully conveyed in the chapter immediately following the introduction to *Coming of Age*. Entitled "A Day in Samoa," it was originally written for inclusion in *Social Organization of Manu'a*, in the section on which Mead worked in close collaboration with Benedict. It was, however, judged to be "too literary" for this monograph, and in 1928 it became part of the text of *Coming of Age*. This piece of writing has been frequently republished, and Mead herself in 1965 gave it prominence in *Anthropologists and What They Do* as giving an idea of "the whole gentle rhythm of life" in Samoa. Her beguiling vignette begins at dawn as lovers slip home from trysts beneath slender palms at the edge of the gleaming sea, and ends long past midnight, with the mellow thunder of the reef and the whispering of lovers as the village rests before another golden dawn. The sole disturbing element is the death of a relative in another village; and there is no hint of the grim realities, as, for example, the violent quarrels, the punishments, the jealousies, the insults, and the disturbed emotional states that are as much a part of Samoan existence as the alluring features of which Mead's "A Day in Samoa" is so artfully compounded.[4]

The further depiction that Mead gives of Samoan character stems directly from her account of the pervasive ease of the Samoan way of life. Samoans, so Mead would have it, display a "lack of deep feeling" and "no strong passions." Children, before age six or so, have "learned never to act spontaneously, even in anger, but always after reviewing the social scene." After thus acquiring "a relaxed dependence on reliable social forms," the individuals reared in Samoan society, according to Mead, have "a peaceful harmonious development which holds few situations for conflict." The minds of adolescents being "perplexed by no conflicts," there is among Samoans an "absence of psychological maladjustment." Indeed, in discussing the adolescent girls of whom she made a detailed study, Mead claims that in almost all cases the benign social environment in which they had grown up had resulted in "a perfect adjustment." Samoan society, in Mead's judgment, "never exerts sufficient repression to call forth a significant rebellion from the individual." Among Samoans, there is "practically no suicide," and suicides of humiliation do "not exist."[5]

The Samoans, given the "pleasant, mild round of their way of life," are "well-adjusted" and "contented," the "adult personality" being "stable enough to resist extraordinary pressures from the outside world and keep its serenity and sureness." A culture such as that of Samoa, claimed Mead, probably assured "the greatest degree of mental health in its members." In 1963, in response to the question "Is there any one society that you have observed in which the people seem considerably happier than those in other societies?" she answered that "a happy society would be one like Samoa."[6]

In these statements from her general purview of Samoan society and character, the central argument on which Mead relied in *Coming of Age in Samoa* is clearly evident. If, as she claimed, the Samoans were so well-adjusted, with adolescence being the age of maximum ease, and if, as she assumed, the shaping of the character of individuals is absolutely determined by their culture, then the Samoan social environment had also to be free from any significant stress and conflict. It was in these terms then that Mead depicted Samoan culture, so creating her negative instance of a society singularly different from those, like twentieth-century America, in which there was, to use Boas' words, an "adolescent crisis." Mead's argument, reduced to its simplest form, was one in which she purported to demonstrate that the "perfect adjustment" which she claimed to exist in almost all of the adolescents she studied had been shaped by processes of harmonious development in a virtually perfect society. She was thus obliged, by the logic of her central argument, to depict the whole social life of Samoa as being free of happenings that might generate tension and conflict.

The ease that pervades Samoan life, and especially that in sex relations, is made possible, Mead claims, by "the whole system of child rearing." As depicted by Mead, the Samoan extended family, of some fifteen or twenty people, is undifferentiated internally, and characterized by casual relationships and generalized affection. In this situation, "the child is given no sense of belonging to a small intimate biological family," and "the relationship between child and parent is early diffused over many adults." Because they are treated with "easy, unparticularistic affection" by a large group of relatives, children "do not form strong affectional ties with their parents." And so it comes about that "children do not think of an own mother who always protects them," but rather of "a group of adults all of whom have their interests somewhat but not too importantly at heart." This amounts to a claim that in the Samoan family primary bonding between mother and infant does not occur; indeed, Mead leaves us in no doubt that this is her position by asserting that in Samoa "the child owes no emotional allegiance to its father and mother." This being the case, so Mead argues, "the setting for parent fixation vanishes," the relationship between Samoan parents and children being "too casual to foster such attitudes." This means that as children grow up "they are schooled not by an individual but by an army of relatives into a general conformity upon which the personality of their parents has a very slight effect." "In such a setting," Mead concludes, "there is no room for guilt."[7]

This depiction of a family system without bonding or guilt, Mead then uses to explain the remarkable ease that, so she claims, characterizes life in Samoa, especially during adolescence. If the Samoan girl, she wrote in 1929, ever learned "the meaning of a strong attachment to one person," this would be "a cause of conflict." But this she does not learn. Rather, Samoan children grow up with "easy, friendly warmth and no idea that one human being is unique or that one lover cannot be substituted for another." Thus, "adolescence is not a period when young people rediscover the violent feelings of early childhood, because early childhood provided them with no such feelings to discover."[8]

Closely linked with Mead's depiction of the "easy, friendly warmth" of the diffused relationships that surround a child within the Samoan family is her claim that a child who suffers the domination of a parent or anyone else is readily able to move to another more congenial household. Indeed, from the time they can run about, according to Mead, Samoan children are permitted to, and often do, "show their preference for relatives other than their parents by going to live with them." Under Samoan custom, then, as Mead would have it, Samoan children "choose their own homes," little truants being "welcomed by any relative." This freedom of choice, furthermore, "serves as a powerful deterrent of specific adult tyrannies," so that a child is "often content to remain in one household serene in the reflection that he can always run away if he wishes." This way of dealing with difficulties within the family persists, according to Mead, into adolescence. In *Coming of Age in Samoa,* in discussing girls who deviated in temperament or conduct, she states that "any strong resentment results in the angry one's leaving the household," and that "to escape from a disagreeable situation" an individual "simply slips out of it into the house next door."[9]

Samoan society, as depicted by Mead, is very far from being

harsh or punitive. Instead, it is a society of "diffuse but warm human relationships," in which "neither boys nor girls are hurried or pressed." Within Samoan culture, claims Mead, each child is "given the means to satisfy his desires completely." In the case of a girl, development from childhood to womanhood is "painless," while "the boy who would flee from too much pressure hardly exists in Samoa."[10]

Nowhere does Mead make mention of anything resembling severe or grievous punishment of the young. Samoan children, she reports, "are not carefully disciplined until they are five or six"; the avoidances they are required to observe are "enforced by occasional cuffings and a deal of exasperated shouting and ineffectual conversation." In later childhood "violent outbursts of wrath and summary chastisements do occur, but consistent and prolonged disciplinary measures are absent." Occasionally, adults will "vent their full irritation upon the heads of troublesome children" by soundly lashing them with palm leaves or dispersing them with a shower of small stones, but "even these outbursts of anger are nine-tenths gesture," and "no one who throws the stones actually means to hit a child." Such punishment as does exist, if Mead is to be believed, is thus infrequent and slight, with a negligible effect on character formation. In brief, Samoan society, as depicted by Mead, is in essence kindly, permitting in both children and adolescents "a gradual development of the emotional life free from any warping compulsory factor."[11]

Just as Samoan culture has eliminated strong emotion, so also it has eliminated any interest in competition. Samoan social organization, claims Mead, places "each individual, each household, each village, even (in Western Samoa) each district, in a hierarchy, wherein each is dignified only by its relationship to the whole," each performing tasks that "contribute to the honor and well-being of the whole," so that "competition is completely impossible." Samoa, according to Mead, is thus in its basic composition a cooperative society in which "competition is muted and controlled." Even in everyday life, a growing boy "must never excel his fellows by more than a little," as going faster than one's age mates is "unforgivable." Parents, says Mead, will blush and hang their heads in shame if one of their children exceeds someone else's child. In this situation those individuals who are less proficient than others in social skills do not experience during either childhood or adolescence any disabling stress. Instead, "the pace is always set by the slowest"; "this is the child to whom everyone points with pride."[12]

In a comparable vein, Mead makes light of the significance in Samoan society of rank, which is "so arranged that there are titles for all those capable of holding them." In Samoa, she states, the sanctity surrounding chiefs is "minimal for the Polynesian area." The *ali'i*, or titular chief, does not "make his own speeches in council." Instead, "his talking chief speaks for him" and "also makes most of his decisions for him."[13]

The traditions of Samoa, according to Mead, are "almost unprecedentedly fluid and variable"; the kava ritual, which is performed whenever chiefs meet in a fono, or formal assembly, is a "dexterous graceful play with social forms," and "so flexible is the social structure, so minutely adapted to manipulation, that it is possible to change the appearance of the *fono* in twenty years." Furthermore, "competition between holders of titles is covert and always expressed as the manipulation of the rank of a title, not as any overt alteration which affects the individual," who is important only in terms of the position he occupies, being of himself nothing.[14]

Not only is competition muted and covert within village communities, but also, Mead claims, "competitiveness between villages usually does not reach important heights of intervillage aggression." Thus, "warfare was stylized as part of the interrelationship between villages that were ceremonial rivals, and occasioned few casualties." Being but a "matter of village spite, or small revenge, in which only one or two individuals would be killed," warfare was "slight and spasmodic." In Manu'a there were "no war gods" and "no war priests." Wars were "fought for no gains other than prestige, nor were there any important rewards for individual warriors." In Manu'a, "bravery in warfare was never a very important matter," and the warrior did not hold any important place in Manu'an society.[15]

Samoan society as depicted by Mead is thus markedly unaggressive. The Samoans, she states, "decree that all young people must show the personality trait of unaggressiveness and punish with opprobrium the aggressive child." Again, given their casual attitude toward life, there is among Samoans an "avoidance of conflict," with hostility between individuals being "expressed covertly in the form of gossip and political machinations rather than in open clashes." This setting, Mead argues, does not produce "violent, strikingly marked personalities." The Samoans "never hate enough to want to kill anyone," and are "one of the most amiable, least contentious, and most peaceful peoples in the world." In such a society, if Mead is to be believed, there is obviously little or no possibility, during adolescence or at any other time, of serious stress from acts of aggression. As depicted by Mead, then, "the whole gentle rhythm of life" in Samoa is integral to the benign background that, for Samoan children and adolescents, "makes growing up so easy."[16]

By the time Mead began her researches in Samoa toward the end of 1925, the Manu'ans had all been Christians since the 1840s, and for several generations had taken pride in the rigor of their adherence to the strict ordinances of the protestant London Missionary Society. Yet Mead, in the main text of *Coming of Age in Samoa,* beyond evocative allusions to "the soft barbaric singing of Christian hymns" and "brief and graceful evening prayer," makes virtually no reference to the fundamental significance of the Christian church in the day-to-day lives of the Manu'ans. Instead, the place of the Christian religion in Samoa in the mid 1920s is relegated to a single paragraph in an appendix. It was also Mead's view that in aboriginal Samoa religion had "played a very slight role." The premium that was set by society on religion was very low, with all contacts with the supernatural being "accidental, trivial and uninstitutionalized." The gods "were conceived of as having resigned their sacredness to the chiefs"; as being "concerned about their own affairs" and "presiding graciously over the affairs of men" as long as men kept quiet and conformed to the rules.[17]

Further, the Samoans she studied in 1925–1926, despite having been Christian for almost a hundred years, had only, according to Mead, taken such parts of Western culture "as made their life more comfortable, their culture more flexible" and were "without the doctrine of original sin." Indeed, the missionary influence had failed to give Samoans any "conviction of sin," and, in particular, because of "the great number of native pastors with their peculiar interpretations of Christian teaching," it had been impossible to establish in Samoa "the rigour of Western Protestantism with its inseparable association of sex offences and an individual consciousness of sin." Again, although the Christian church required chastity for church membership, in actual practice, according to Mead, no one became a church member until after marriage, for the authorities made "too slight a bid for young unmarried members to force the adolescent to make any decision." There was thus a "passive acceptance by the religious authorities themselves of premarital irregularities," and in this way the adolescent was relieved from the stress of religious conflict. Any strong religious interest, according to Mead, might have disturbed the nice balance of Samoan society and so had been outlawed. The Manu'ans, then, while having accepted protestant Christianity, had "gently remoulded some of its sterner tenets" so that it had come to be taken "simply as a pleasant and satisfying social form" in the "elaborate and cherished" traditional pattern of Samoan society.[18]

The Samoans, according to Mead, as well as having no conviction of sin, regarded lovemaking as "the pastime *par excellence,*" made "a fine art of sex," and had, of all the people she had studied, "the sunniest and easiest attitudes towards sex." Samoan society, she reported, "works very smoothly as it is based on the general assumption that sex is play, permissible in all hetero- and homosexual expression, with any sort of variation as an artistic addition." "Love between the sexes is a light and pleasant dance," and "the expected personality is one to which sex will be a delightful experience expertly engaged in" while not being "sufficiently engrossing to threaten the social order." Thus, "the Samoans condone light love-affairs, but repudiate acts of passionate choice, and have no real place for anyone who would permanently continue, in spite of social experiences to the contrary, to prefer one woman or one man to a more socially acceptable mate." Romantic love, Mead claims, does not occur in Samoa, and "jealousy, as a widespread social phenomenon, is very rare." Samoan culture, so Mead argues, has eliminated many of the attitudes that have afflicted mankind, and "perhaps jealousy most importantly of all." "Marriages make no violent claims for fidelity" and adultery "is not regarded as very serious." Many adulteries occur "which hardly threaten the continuity of established relationships." A man who seduces his neighbor's wife simply has to settle with his neighbor, as "the society is not interested." The assumption that sex is play provides a cultural atmosphere in which "frigidity and psychic impotence do not occur and in which a satisfactory sex adjustment in marriage can always be established"; the Samoan adult sex adjustment is "one of the smoothest in the world."[19]

This exceptionally smooth sex adjustment of adult Samoans is preceded, Mead reports, by a period of free lovemaking and promiscuity before marriage by adolescents. During this time of premarital freedom, sex is regarded as play and as a skill in which one becomes adept; the whole emphasis is on "virtuosity in sex techniques rather than upon personality." This freedom of sexual experimentation, Mead states, is "expected," and the casual love life of a female adolescent begins two or three years after menarche. All of the interest of such a girl is "expended on clandestine sex adventures," and her favors are "distributed among so many youths, all adepts in amorous technique, that she seldom becomes deeply involved." A girl's promiscuity, Mead writes, "seems to ensure her against pregnancy." Illegitimate children are rare and when they do appear are enthusiastically welcomed. In Samoan society then, with its sanctioning of "an easy expression of sexuality" during adolescence, young females "defer marriage through as many years of casual lovemaking as possible," it being one of their "uniform and satisfying ambitions" to live as girls "with many lovers as long as possible" before marrying and settling down to have many children.[20]

In the case of male adolescents, a successful lover is defined as one who is able to make a female "sexually contented and who is also himself contented in doing so." Lovemaking is seen as something that must be approached gradually while "the girl's body is prepared to enjoy a lover." In Samoa, then, male sexuality is "never defined as aggressiveness that must be curbed, but simply as a pleasure that might be indulged in, at appropriate times, with appropriate partners." "The idea of forceful rape or of any sexual act to which both participants do not give themselves freely is," according to Mead, "completely foreign to the Samoan mind."[21]

This picture of "the whole social life of Samoa" was constructed by Mead, as we have already seen, with the express purpose of producing a negative instance, by showing that in the mild, gentle, graceful, easy, pleasant, and happy Samoan social environment "adolescence represented no period of crisis or stress." In making this substantive claim, Mead did admit that there were a few girls who deviated in temperament or in conduct, and so lacked the perfect adjustment of the great majority of Samoan girls, but she in no way allowed these deviations to interfere with her general conclusions, arguing that in many cases they "actually had no painful results," and further, that "the causes for absence of conflict in the even tenor of development of the average girl" were actually "corroborated by the turbulent histories of the few cases where these causes did not operate." In almost all of her statements after the publication of *Coming of Age in Samoa* no mention whatever was made of these deviants, and her readers were told, in absolute terms, as in her article "Adolescence in Primitive and Modern Society" of 1930, that "in Samoa there is no conflict because the adolescent girl is faced by neither revelation, restriction, nor choice, and because society expects her to grow up slowly and quietly like a well-behaved flower."[22]

Adolescence in Samoa, according to Mead, is thus "peculiarly free of all those characteristics which make it a period dreaded by adults and perilous for young people in more complex—and often also, in more primitive societies." What is the most difficult age in American society becomes in Samoa the age of maximum ease, "perhaps the pleasantest time the Samoan girl will ever know." With "no religious worries," "no conflicts with their parents," and "no confusion about sex" to vex the souls of Samoan girls, their development is "smooth, untroubled, unstressed," and they grow up "painlessly ... almost unselfconsciously." And this being so, Mead states, she was left with "just one possible conclusion": that "the woes and difficulties" of American youth could not be "due to adolescence" for, as her researches had shown, in Samoa adolescence brought "no woes." In other words, the crisis and stress of adolescence are determined not by nature but by nurture.[23]

On the basis of Mead's writings, Samoa came to be recognized in intellectual circles and in the social sciences as providing conclusive proof of the cultural determinism central to the Boasian paradigm. This paradigm, as we have seen, had been launched in 1917 in the theoretical formulations of Kroeber and Lowie; what was sorely needed, thereafter, was an empirical demonstration of the validity of these purely theoretical formulations. Just over a decade later, this demonstration, so it seemed to the Boasians, had been decisively given by the publication of the "painstaking investigation" conducted in Samoa by Margaret Mead. So enthusiastically was Mead's vision of Samoa accepted that her conclusions, as they were elaborated by herself and others, gave rise to what has become the most widely promulgated myth of twentieth-century anthropology.

7

The Myth
Takes Shape

"SHOULD A TRAVELLER, returning from a far country, bring us
an account of men wholly different from any with whom we
were ever acquainted; men who were entirely divested of avarice, ambition, or revenge; who knew no pleasure but friendship,
generosity and public spirit; we should immediately, from these
circumstances, detect the falsehood, and prove him a liar, with
the same certainty as if he had stuffed his narration with stories
of centaurs and dragons, miracles and prodigies."[1] So wrote
David Hume, in 1748, in *An Inquiry Concerning Human Understanding.* And yet when Mead depicted the Samoans as a
people without jealousy, for whom free lovemaking was the
pastime *par excellence,* and who, having developed their emotional lives free from any warping factors, were so amiable as to
never hate enough to want to kill anybody, no anthropological

or other critic, in the fervid intellectual climate of the late 1920s, seriously questioned these extravagant assertions.

It was a time when human nature was being "newly conceived as flexible and malleable and plastic" by both behaviorists and cultural anthropologists, and when, in the United States, prominent intellectuals like V. F. Calverton and Samuel D. Schmalhausen (both of whom eagerly accepted Mead's glowing account of the utopian character of Samoa) were proclaiming the advent of "a new enlightenment." Indeed, the years before and including 1928 were, in J. B. Watson's judgment, a period of "social Renaissance, a preparation for a change in mores," that was likely to become much more of an epoch in history than the scientific Renaissance which began with Bacon.[2]

To many, during this time of awakening and change, "the new Russia" was a source of hope that human nature could in fact be molded into other patterns than the Western world had hitherto known. Advertisements in *The Nation* exhorted American intellectuals to "Go to Soviet Russia," where the world's most gigantic social experiment was being conducted. And those who made the pilgrimage returned to write of having been "thrilled by the spirit of the children . . . trained under the Soviet regime," and of never having seen a more engaging picture of happy childhood. There were reports of human nature having been decisively changed, as, for example, in the form that jealousy took under the Soviet regime, and of "mental hygiene" being inherent in the social organization of the new Russia. In particular, Soviet Russia was thought to be "in advance of the rest of the world in its attitude towards sex." Socialism, it was widely claimed, would (as the Communist Manifesto had predicted) bring about the destruction of the bourgeois family and substitute "the free union of the sexes."[3]

The free union of the sexes was also being much talked about in the United States. It was the age, as Calverton proclaimed in 1928, of the flapper, with her "wild Corybantian antics" in "the contortions of the Charleston," and her insatiable cravings for "sexual excitement and ecstasies"; a time when in America, more than any country in the world, as the Hon. Mrs. Bertrand Russell observed, there was "an immense amount of excitement about the relations of men and women" both within marriage and outside of it. This excitement, according to Schmalhausen, had been generated by a sexual revolution in which "ancient degrading taboos" were being repudiated, and "passion's coming of age" was heralding "the dawn of a new orientation in the life of the sexes." This new gospel, Schmalhausen declared, was one in which, amid "a jazzing of sexual eagerness" and open-hearted invitations to sensual playful experience, infidelity was no longer deemed a violation of a sacred vow and virginity was sacrificed to felicity.[4]

Promiscuity, in Schmalhausen's view, was "in the nature of things the fundamental reality," and the only important problem for the civilized minds of the 1920s was the discovery of educational and social and artistic and recreational forms of behavior that would assist the erotic nature of human males and females to express itself "with ease and dignified naturalness from the cradle to the grave." Any primitive community that indulged, or was said to indulge, in "unrestricted sex behavior," Sapir noted in the *American Mercury*, was considered "an interesting community to hear from." By those who were part of this "awakening," with its fantasies of sexual freedom and sensual playful experience, Mead's portrayal of Samoan society was hailed as the most significant of revelations.[5]

In *The Nation*, under the heading "Sex in the South Seas," Freda Kirchwey began her review of Mead's "impressive study" by musing that "somewhere in each of us, hidden among our more obscure desires and our impulses of escape, is a palm-fringed South Sea island . . . a languorous atmosphere promising freedom and irresponsibility . . . Thither we run . . . to find love which is free, easy and satisfying." And thither, to the sexual paradise engagingly described in Mead's anthropological account of Samoa, the enlightened social critics of the day did indeed run. Schmalhausen, convinced by Mead's evidence of what he called "the innocent, strangely impersonal, naively mechanistic-behavioristic sexing of the light-hearted youths and maidens of far-off Samoa," felt there were but "two roads of heart's fulfillment: Samoa or Calvary: happy-go-lucky felicity or tragic intensity"; in his widely read book of 1929, *Our Changing*

Human Nature, his heartfelt cry was "Back to the South Sea Isles!" to "naturalness and simplicity and sexual joy."[6]

In a similar vein Bertrand Russell, who had become well known in New York as an advocate of sexual freedom, having read Mead's account, expatiated on how Samoans "when they have to go upon a journey, fully expect their wives to console themselves for their absence." And Havelock Ellis, the venerable seer of the sexually enlightened, was unreserved in his praise for Mead's "highly competent" and "judicious" study of sex life among the youth of a Pacific island on which, he declared, Americans could profitably meditate. Miss Mead, wrote Ellis, had revealed the existence of a society of wholesome simplicity, where freedom of relationships was practically unhampered before marriage, and which had, furthermore, developed a system of rearing children that had legislated "a whole field of neurotic possibility out of existence," so that Samoa had become a place where there was "no neurosis, no frigidity, no impotence."[7]

This unmitigated claim was made by Ellis in his contribution to a massive volume richly expressive of the ethos of the environmentalism of the late 1920s. Published in 1930 with the sanguine title *The New Generation,* and edited by Calverton and Schmalhausen, it had a soaring introduction by Bertrand Russell in which he dwelt on the changing attitudes of the day and on how it had become clear that "the scientific psychologist, if allowed a free run with children" could "manipulate human nature" as freely as Californians manipulated the desert. Calverton and Schmalhausen were passionately dedicated to the notion that human beings could attain "beauty and high utility" by "a courageous transformation of the social system," and in their preface they singled out for special mention, among their many distinguished contributors, J. B. Watson, and Margaret Mead, the gifted young anthropologist whose "enlightening study" of Samoa had furnished those who had a "faith in the environment" with evidence of a singularly significant kind.[8]

In 1924, when the nature-nurture controversy was at its height, J. B. Watson had baldly asserted that there was "no such thing as an inheritance of capacity, talent, temperament,

mental constitution and characteristics," and in subsequent
years he had repeatedly spoken of human nature as having
"limitless plasticity." However, as the hereditarians were quick
to point out, Watson's sweeping assertions were unsupported by
any experimental or other substantial evidence, and in this
highly insecure situation Mead's depiction of Samoa became of
fundamental significance, not only for the proponents of cultural determinism but equally for the wider environmentalist
movement that, originating in the nature-nurture controversy,
continued into the 1930s.[9]

In their preface to *The New Generation*, Calverton and
Schmalhausen referred with the keenest of appreciation to
Mead's "remarkable essay" in which, with Samoa as her negative instance, she reiterated her conclusion that "with a different social form" human nature could radically change. By 1930
this conclusion, in addition to having been vouched for by Boas
and Benedict, had also been given the unqualified approval of
other prominent anthropologists. Lowie, for example, found
Mead's "graphic picture of Polynesian free love" convincing
and, in his review in the *American Anthropologist*, he accepted
her major conclusion that the stress and strain characteristic of
American adolescents were "not rooted in original nature" but
in the "repressive agencies" of society. J. H. Driberg, in reviewing *Coming of Age in Samoa* in *Man*, described it as being both
in method and presentation as "competent a piece of research
as could be required"; while Bronislaw Malinowski let it be
known that in his eyes Miss Mead's book was "an outstanding
achievement," and "an absolutely first rate piece of descriptive
anthropology."[10]

As George Stocking has shown, "the working out of all the
anti-biological tendencies in behavioral science and the complete dissemination of Boasian thinking were not accomplished
until after 1930." In this working out, such as it was, Mead's assertion of the absolute sovereignty of culture, in answer to the
problem that Boas had sent her to Samoa to investigate, was of
quite pivotal importance. The acute dilemma as to what, in
human societies, was determined by heredity and what by environmental causes, which had loomed so large for the Boasians

in the early 1920s, had to all appearances been solved. With this outcome, Mead's Samoan researches came to occupy a uniquely significant position in the development of anthropology, as of other of the social sciences.[11]

"A myth," Erik Erikson has remarked, "blends historical fact and significant fiction in such a way that it 'rings true' to an area or an era, causing pious wonderment and burning ambition." When Mead's account of the pleasant innocuousness of human nature in Samoa was communicated in 1928 to an intellectual world still deeply absorbed in the nature-nurture controversy, it was indeed received with something akin to wonderment. George Dorsey, whose immensely successful *Why We Behave like Human Beings* had been a kind of harbinger to *Coming of Age in Samoa*, hailed it as an extraordinary and illuminating book, while the formidable H. L. Mencken was moved to declare that the Samoans lived in Miss Mead's "precise, scientific pages" more vividly than in popular romantic writings on the South Seas. Most momentous of all was the way Mead's account rang true for the cultural determinists and environmentalists of the day. For these advocates of nurture, as Ruth Benedict feelingly announced in *The New Republic*, *Coming of Age in Samoa* was the book for which they had all "been waiting"; the concrete evidence of its "excellent ethnological picture of an alien culture" was, as Benedict pointed out in a second review in the *Journal of Philosophy*, "more convincing than any *a priori* argument" as to the plasticity of human nature. To demonstrate this plasticity once and for all had long been the burning ambition of the Boasians. Mead's "painstaking investigation," so it seemed, had at last achieved this objective. As the Boasians continued their campaign against biological determinism, Mead's conclusions soon took on the status of absolute truths.[12]

If Samoa was to be an entirely effective negative instance, leaving no loopholes for captious biologists, it was in such wholly unequivocal terms that Mead's conclusions had to be stated, and, within a few years, so indeed they were. In 1934, for example, in her widely read *Patterns of Culture*, Benedict, ignoring completely the numerous instances of conflict which Mead herself had reported, blandly advanced the greatly exaggerated claim that in Samoa adolescence was "quite without turmoil" and a "particularly unstressed and peaceful period" during which no adolescent conflicts were manifested. *Patterns of Culture*, like *Coming of Age*, had an approving foreword by Boas, who in that same year propounded the major generalization that "the study of cultural forms"—an obvious reference to the work of Benedict and Mead—had shown that the "genetic elements" that may determine personality are "altogether irrelevant" as compared with the powerful influence of the cultural environment. From this time onward, the conclusion that in Samoa adolescence represented no period of crisis or stress was purveyed in absolute terms, and in subsequent years it was with this rhetoric that the complete sovereignty of culture over biology was attested by ardent cultural determinists.[13]

Throughout the 1930s, the campaign to achieve general recognition of the sovereignty of culture remained Mead's principal preoccupation. At the beginning of the decade, using language quite as extreme as that of Watson, she advanced the view, on the basis of her researches in Samoa and New Guinea, that human nature was "the rawest, most undifferentiated of raw material." "The whole of a man's life," she claimed in a paper of which Boas approved when he read it in manuscript in 1931, was determined by his culture, this being effected (as she argued elsewhere) by a process in which the "almost unbelievably malleable" raw material of human nature was "moulded into shape."[14] Her task from 1925 onward had been, as she described it in retrospect, to document over and over again the fact that "cultural rhythms are stronger and more compelling than the physiological rhythms which they over lay and distort." By 1939, so she claimed (by which time Boas, at eighty-one years, had retired), the battle that the Boasians had had to fight had been won. By this time, too, the example of Samoa had become duly incorporated into the literature of the social sciences—as, for example, in Otto Klineberg's *Social Psychology* of 1940, in which the conclusions Mead had launched in the late 1920s were accepted without question as established facts.[15]

Later in the 1940s Mead's central conclusion about Samoa was taken up by other intellectual disciplines, as, for example,

by philosophy, as in L. J. Russell's contribution of 1946 to a
symposium of the Aristotelian Society. Others of her findings
were relied upon by anthropologists. In 1949, for example, Leslie
White, in *The Science of Culture*, cited Mead's report that the
Samoans "cannot understand jealousy among lovers" as proof
that jealousy was not a natural emotion in humans.[16]

In 1950 *Male and Female* appeared. "A study of the sexes in
a changing world," which has become, after *Coming of Age in
Samoa*, the most influential of all Mead's books, it gave special
prominence to the "harmonious and unintense" Samoans, and
several of Mead's earlier conclusions were set down in considerably exaggerated form. In 1949 *Coming of Age* had been presented in the New American Library as an "incisive and original" scientific classic, and it soon became, as Mead herself has
noted, standard reading in courses in the human sciences
throughout the world.[17]

By this time Mead was already something of a celebrity. In
January 1950 the London *Observer* featured her in its Profile
series. By showing that adolescence in Samoa was "a peaceful
and gentle flowering towards maturity," Mead had proved, the
readers of the *Observer* were told, "that it was culture, not
physiology, which determined the calmness or explosiveness of
adolescence." Quite soon after this, in the winter of 1950, E. E.
Evans-Pritchard, in the fifth of his authoritative lectures on social anthropology given on the Third Programme of the B.B.C.,
singled out *Coming of Age in Samoa* as a good example of a
modern anthropological study that treated "only a part of the
social life for particular and limited problems of investigation."
The aim of Mead's book, Evans-Pritchard told his listeners, was
"to show that the difficulties of adolescence . . . do not occur in
Samoa, and may therefore be regarded as the product of a particular type of social environment." He went on to record that
Mead had shown that in Samoa there was no crisis or stress
during adolescence, and that it was one of the ambitions of adolescent Samoan girls to live with many lovers as long as possible. Also in 1950, Melville J. Herskovits, in his *Man and His
Works*, dwelt on the point that Mead's demonstration that the
adolescent crisis of Euro-American societies was absent in

Samoa had forced on anthropologists the conclusion that the emotional reactions of adolescence were "culturally, not biologically determined."[18]

This uncritical acceptance of Mead's conclusions in centers of higher learning in both Europe and America could occur because none of the anthropologists who had published the results of research undertaken in Samoa subsequent to Mead's expedition of 1925-1926 had in any way questioned her findings. In 1934, in the bibliography of his *Modern Samoa*, Felix M. Keesing had listed *Coming of Age in Samoa* as giving "an excellent picture of life in the isolated Manu'a islands"; while W. E. H. Stanner, who visited Western Samoa in 1946–1947, described, in his *The South Seas in Transition*, the "percipient analysis" of Mead's writings on Samoa as having revealed Samoan thought, behavior, and values in a "brilliant light." During the 1950s, then, Mead's conclusion about adolescence in Samoa came to be regarded as a proven fact which had demonstrated, beyond all question, the sovereignty of culture. Within anthropology, the Boasian paradigm had become quite generally accepted, and such was the intellectual climate that in 1955 Lionel Trilling remarked that an entrancement with the idea of culture had produced an inclination "to assign to culture an almost exclusive part in man's fate."[19]

At this same time, Lowell D. Holmes was working on a doctoral dissertation entitled "A Restudy of Manu'an Culture," which he was to submit in 1957 to the department of anthropology at Northwestern University. Holmes had gone to Samoa early in 1954, after preliminary training under Melville Herskovits, who was a follower of Boas, a friend of Mead, and a fervent cultural determinist. Because of the crucial role Mead's writings on Samoa had played in the establishment of the Boasian paradigm, there was, from a scientific point of view, every reason to subject her conclusions to detailed testing by further investigations in the field. These conclusions had, however, become so well established in the anthropological departments of Northwestern and other universities as to seem eternally true, and Holmes made their systematic testing no part of his concern. Instead he devoted his energies to an "acculturation study" in

which his objectives were the description of contemporary
Manu'an culture and the documentation of changes that had
"taken place in the course of the history of European contact."
To this end Holmes spent five months in Manu'a followed by
four months in Tutuila.[20]

Both in his thesis and in an account published in 1958 by the
Polynesian Society, Holmes reported numerous facts widely at
variance with the picture Mead had given of the same population of Samoans a generation previously. He reported, for example, that rank and prestige constituted "the focal point of
Samoan culture" to which all other aspects of life were secondary in importance: that the whole pattern of oratory was "based
upon a competition between talking chiefs in order to win prestige both for the orator himself, and for the village or family he
represented"; that "competitive behavior and efforts to gain
praise through excelling one's peers" were believed by the Samoans to be "one of the traditional aspects of their culture";
that the people of Manu'a were "almost fanatical in their practice and observance of Christianity"; that the punishment of
children could be severe; that "larger children often hit smaller
ones with no apparent provocation"; that a woman had committed suicide because she was prevented from marrying the
man she desired; that male informants said that frigidity often
produced family tensions; that the chief ground for divorce in
Manu'a was adultery, with a woman caught in this act being
usually subjected to violence of some type; and that a government report of 1953 had listed rape as the fifth most common
crime in American Samoa.[21]

This ethnographic report provides substantial grounds for
seriously questioning the validity of Mead's picture of Samoa as
a place where competition was muted, the excelling of rivals
unforgivable, the Christian religion merely a pleasant and satisfying social form, punishment slight and ineffectual, unaggressiveness the ruling personality trait, suicides of humiliation
nonexistent, frigidity entirely absent, adultery a peccadillo, and
"the idea of forceful rape . . . completely foreign to the Samoan
mind."

Logically, if Holmes's ethnography was factually correct (as indeed it is) this could only mean, given the general stability of Samoan culture during the first half of the twentieth century (which I shall describe in Chapter 8), that many of the elements on which Mead had based her depiction of Samoa as a negative instance were in serious error, and ipso facto, that the central conclusion she had reached in *Coming of Age in Samoa* about the sovereignty of nurture over nature was false. This, however, given the intellectual climate of the mid 1950s in the department in which he was studying, was a deduction from his own ethnography that Holmes did not make. Instead, in his doctoral dissertation, he gave it as his opinion that the reliability of Mead's account of Samoa was "remarkably high."[22]

Holmes's conclusion was discussed by Donald Campbell, a professor of psychology at Northwestern University, in 1961. Campbell observed that with several of the broader aspects of Mead's account of Samoa, such as the lack of competitive spirit and the lack of crisis in human relations, Holmes's findings were in "complete disagreement." These differences, in Campbell's judgment, could not be explained by cultural change between 1926 and 1954, but rather had to be interpreted as "disagreement in the description of aspects of 'the same' culture." This judgment might have been expected to generate a degree of skepticism about Mead's writings on Samoa. So towering, however, was Mead's reputation as against that of Holmes, who had in any event personally testified to the "remarkably high" reliability of her writings, that there was no lessening of enthusiasm for them. Indeed, with Holmes's apparent confirmation of its findings, *Coming of Age in Samoa* came to be regarded more widely than ever before as a classic of American cultural anthropology, and by the 1960s it had become the most widely read of all anthropological books.[23]

Mead herself had actively contributed to this widespread acceptance by making, in successive editions of *Coming of Age,* extensive claims for the validity of her Samoan researches. In 1949, for example, she averred that "to the extent that the anthropologist records the whole pattern of any way of life, that record cannot fade, because it is the way of life itself," and "once written down . . . can become a precious permanent possession." In 1952, when invited to choose one of her books for inclusion in the Modern Library, she chose *Coming of Age in Samoa,* remarking that it was the Samoans themselves and their culture and life as they were at the time of her researches that gave her book "its right to continue to be." It seemed, she wrote, "an extraordinary historical accident that some few children of some one South Sea island should be given by camera and printing press an enduring existence far beyond the world that their imaginations could have dreamed of." In 1961 she wrote of "the absoluteness of monographs of primitive societies," which "like well-painted portraits of the famous dead ... would stand forever for the edification and enjoyment of future generations, forever true because no truer picture could be made of that which is gone." *Coming of Age,* she indicated, was just such a monograph, and she dwelt on "the historical caprice which had selected a handful of young girls on a tiny island to stand forever like the lovers on Keats' Grecian urn."[24]

During the 1960s, as *Coming of Age in Samoa* edified yet another generation of readers, its reputation, like that of Mead herself, continued to effloresce. In 1963 John Honigmann, in his *Understanding Culture,* called *Coming of Age* a classic description of "institutionalized premarital sexuality," and Morris Carstairs, in his influential B.B.C. Reith Lectures of 1962, relying on Mead's ethnography, described for the edification of the people of Great Britain how "every young Samoan ... has had many sexual experiences before marriage." George Devereux, in his incisive *From Anxiety to Method in the Behavioral Sciences,* ranked Mead's study of Samoan adolescence as "a brilliantly effective exploitation of cultural differences between the subject's and the object's traditional attitudes to certain age groups," and as "markedly free from age linked countertransference distortion," while D. Price-Williams emphasized that in *Coming of Age* Mead had made use of "heavy and detailed documentation." In 1967 E. L. Schusky and T. P. Culbert recounted how Mead, by performing in Samoa an experiment that paralleled "the method of the chemist or physicist," had found that "biological adolescence did not cause problems there." And *Time* magazine told the world at large that Margaret Mead, who by 1969 was being referred to as "Mother to the World," had in Samoa in the distant 1920s provided "solid proof" for her conclusions.[25]

By the late 1960s, however, despite these high-flown claims, Mead's account of Samoa had already begun to be revealed by the work of other ethnographers of Samoa as markedly idiosyncratic. In 1969, confronted by a range of well-substantiated facts about the Samoan ethos recorded by Fa'afouina Pula and others, Mead was compelled, in "Reflections on Later Theoretical Work on the Samoans," which she appended to the second edition of *Social Organization of Manu'a,* to admit the "serious problem" of reconciling the contradiction between her own account of Samoa and other records of historical and contemporary Samoan behavior.[26] This contradiction was heightened by the fact that after her investigations in Manu'a in 1926 Mead, while extremely active elsewhere in the South West Pacific, visiting Manus six times between 1927 and 1975, had never returned to conduct further field research in either eastern or western Samoa, and so was unable to produce supplementary evidence in support of her inexplicably aberrant account of the Samoan ethos.[27] Nor had she, over the years, as evidence wholly inconsistent with her own account of Samoa was published,[28] revised in any way whatsoever the 1928 text of *Coming of Age in Samoa,* or any of her other writings about the Samoans.[29]

By the 1970s, however, Mead had come to be viewed, in Morton Fried's words, as "a symbol of all anthropology," and such was her prodigious reputation that, despite the contradictions she herself had admitted in 1969, *Coming of Age in Samoa* continued to be accepted by the vast majority of anthropologists as presenting an accurate picture of the Samoan ethos as it had been in the 1920s. Thus, in *Anthropology Today,* published in 1971 with thirty-four senior anthropologists from universities throughout the United States as contributing consultants, the reader is told that in Samoa Mead found that "the inner turmoil characteristic of adolescent girls simply was not present"; while in 1972 E. A. Hoebel, in his textbook *Anthropology: the Study of Man,* referred to "Margaret Mead's famous study of adolescence" as a classic example of the use of fieldwork as the equiva-

lent to the experimental laboratory, in which she had demonstrated that "Samoan adolescents do not go through the period
of psychological stress that characterizes American adolescence, because Samoan culture is free of certain stress-produc-
ing features."[30]

In the course of fifteen months of field research in American
Samoa in 1972–1973, Eleanor Gerber, a highly percipient anthropologist from the University of California, observed that
sexual relations in Samoa, far from having a carefree and adven-
turous tone as reported by Mead in 1928, were marked by "premarital chastity or the semblance of it," and her informants all
agreed that in their grandmothers' day (at the time when Mead
was in Samoa) Samoan custom had been even more severe,
with parents being "extremely strict, and all daughters virginal." Further, the educated Samoans known to Gerber who
had read *Coming of Age in Samoa* rejected out of hand what
they called "all that sex stuff," insisted that their parents and
grandparents had told them how hard it was in the old days,
and declared that "Mead's informants must have been telling
lies in order to tease her." Yet Gerber's assessment of this immensely significant information was that the sexual morality of
the Samoans must somehow have become more stringent since
the time of Mead's researches. She construed the unequivocal
statements of her Samoan informants as a "rewriting of history," so accepting Mead's fanciful account of Samoan sexual
behavior in preference to the unanimous and direct testimony
of the Samoans themselves about their own values and history.
Could any myth, one wonders, have acquired, within the confines of a scientific discipline and during the second half of the
twentieth century, a greater potency?[31]

According to Vera Rubin the publication of *Coming of Age
in Samoa* in 1928 marked in many ways "the coming of age of
contemporary anthropology." Since that time Mead's book has
come to be accepted as a scientific classic, and its conclusions
continue to be regarded by anthropologists and others as
though they were eternal verities. Robert LeVine, for example,
has recently referred to Mead's Samoan fieldwork as an example of research conducted in a single cultural setting that "com-

pelled revision of generalizations about adolescence" for "the species as a whole." In the chapters that follow evidence will be adduced to show that the main conclusions of *Coming of Age in Samoa* are, in reality, the figments of an anthropological myth which is deeply at variance with the facts of Samoan ethnography and history.[32]

III

A REFUTATION
OF MEAD'S
CONCLUSIONS

8

The Historical Setting of Mead's Research

IN THE PREFACES she wrote from 1949 onward for successive editions of *Coming of Age in Samoa*, Mead argued, as we have seen, that the account she had given of Samoa in 1928 was "a precious permanent possession" of mankind, "forever true because no truer picture could be made of that which was gone." And when in the early 1970s she encountered, from Samoan university students in the United States and elsewhere, radical criticism of her portrayal of Samoa, together with the demand that she should revise what she had written, she asserted that any such revision was impossible. She admonished these irate Samoan critics of *Coming of Age in Samoa* with the words: "It must remain, as all anthropological works must remain, exactly as it was written, true to what I saw in Samoa and what I was able to convey of what I saw, true to the state of our knowledge of human behavior as it was in the mid 1920s; true to our hopes and fears for the future of the world."[1]

This pretext that anthropological works cannot possibly be revised and have forever to remain exactly as they were written is manifestly without scientific justification. Even if Mead had been the first European to undertake the study of Samoan culture, which she certainly was not, there would still be the possibility of retrospective revision of her conclusions in the light of the findings of subsequent investigators. In fact, however, there is an immense corpus of detailed historical information on the Samoans dating from the year 1722; indeed, as Mead herself noted in 1958, "the literature on Samoa is one of the most complete and varied . . . available for any culture." This means that the propositions about the nature of Samoan culture contained in Mead's writings are fully open, as are the propositions of any other writer on Samoa, to an empirically based examination of their truth or falsity.[2]

Although the Navigators' Archipelago, as it was at first called, was discovered by Roggeveen as early as 1722, and then visited by de Bougainville (1768), La Pérouse (1787), Edwards (1791), Kotzebue (1824), and other voyagers, it was not until 1830, with the arrival of the pioneer missionaries John Williams and Charles Barff, that comprehensive and detailed information about the Samoans and their ways began to be recorded. During his second voyage to Samoa in 1832, Williams took aboard his schooner one Mr. Stevens, a surgeon, who had gone ashore from a whaler and spent some months living with pagan Samoans. From the reports of teachers from eastern Polynesia whom he had left in Savai'i in 1830, his own observations, and the recollections of Stevens, who accompanied him back to Rarotonga, Williams put together an account of the Samoans as they were during this period.[3]

This remarkable narrative was later supplemented by the observations of many other missionaries, whose letters, journals, and published works make up an enormously rich fund of information on Samoan culture and behavior. Particularly valuable are the writings of George Pratt, George Turner, and Thomas Powell, each of whom lived among the Samoans for several decades. Powell, after a visit to Ta'ū in 1853, took a special interest in the traditions and history of Manu'a. The observations of Williams, Barff, and the other missionaries of the early 1830s were notably augmented in 1839 by the wide-ranging investigations in Samoa of the United States Exploring Expedition under Charles Wilkes, one of whose associates was the pioneer ethnographer Horatio Hale, and later by Captain J. E. Erskine's account of his visit in 1849 in H.M.S. *Havannah* and by John Jackson's plain-spoken narrative of his forced sojourn in Manu'a in 1840. Then followed the writings of consular officials such as W. T. Pritchard, T. Trood, A. P. Maudslay, and W. B. Churchward; of the incomparable Robert Louis Stevenson, who lived in western Samoa from 1889 to 1894; and of erudite German scholars, notably O. Stuebel, E. Schultz, and Augustin Krämer, the first volume of whose monumental *Die Samoa-Inseln* appeared in 1902. And from 1900, when western Samoa became a protectorate of Germany and eastern Samoa a territory of the United States, there are official reports aplenty.[4]

The institutions and traditions of Samoa had thus been very extensively documented long before Mead first set foot on Ta'ū in 1925. Indeed, when George Brown's *Melanesians and Polynesians* (which contains a valuable account of Samoa based on Brown's observations from 1860 to 1870) was published in 1910, a reviewer in the *American Anthropologist* remarked that it added little that was really new, so often had Samoa been described by navigators, missionaries, and later investigators, such as Krämer. It is in this context of copious observation and research from 1830 onward that Mead's investigations of 1925–1926 have to be assessed, in particular her supposition of 1969 (voiced after sustained criticism of her findings), that Manu'a in 1925 "might have represented a special variation on the Samoan pattern, a temporary felicitous relaxation," of the quarrels and rivalries, and the sensitivity to slight and insults that other observers had reported as characteristic of Samoan society both before and after the time of her research.[5]

Although Mead's investigations in 1925–1926 were confined to the islands of eastern Samoa, she fully recognized that these islands were part of the Samoan archipelago, which prior to Eu-

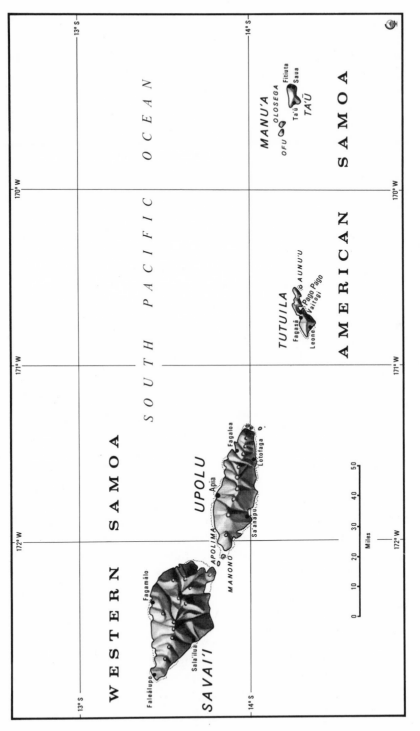

The Samoan Islands

ropean contact was a "closed universe," whose inhabitants conceived of "the Samoan people as all members of one organization." The Samoan archipelago (see map) contains nine inhabited islands. Of these, Savai'i, Upolu, Apolima, and Manono
make up Western Samoa, which after periods of German and
then of New Zealand rule became an independent nation in
1962. The other islands, consisting of Tutuila and Aunu'u and of
Manu'a, are in American Samoa, a territory of the United
States. Manu'a has three islands, Ofu, Olosega, and Ta'ū; the
main settlement of Ta'ū also goes by the name of Ta'ū. As
George Turner notes, the Samoans have but one dialect and
have long been in free communication from island to island; in
Bradd Shore's words, "culturally and linguistically, the entire
Samoan archipelago reveals a remarkably unified identity and
striking homogeneity."[6] Historically, then, all of the local polities of the Samoan archipelago have a common way of life, described by the people themselves as 'o le fa'aSamoa, a phrase
meaning in the manner of the inhabitants of the Samoan archipelago.[7]

In 1930 Su'a, a chief from Savai'i who after fifteen years' residence in Tutuila had become a naturalized citizen of American
Samoa, stated in evidence before the U.S. Congressional Investigation Commission on American Samoa (referring to Upolu
and Savai'i as British Samoa): "All the Samoan people are of
one race. Our customs, genealogies, legends and languages are
the same. The chiefs and village maids (taupou) of American
Samoa when they visit British Samoa are recognized as chiefs
and taupous of certain villages in accordance with their genealogies. Their visitors from British Samoa are likewise recognized in the chief councils of Tutuila and Manu'a."[8] In what
follows, therefore, as is warranted by their common cultural
history, I shall make use of pertinent evidence from any of the
Samoan islands—from Ta'ū in the east to Savai'i in the west.

Margaret Mead was in Samoa from 31 August 1925 to early
in June 1926, spending some three months in Tutuila and about
six months in Manu'a. What is the evidence for her later supposition that at the time of her inquiries there might have been a
temporary relaxation of quarrels and rivalries, and of sensitivity

to slight and insults? This question can be readily answered: as the historical documents show, in American Samoa the 1920s were in fact a particularly turbulent period, with deep and widespread disaffection among the Samoans of both Tutuila and Manu'a. As Governor H. F. Bryan recorded in 1926, in April 1920 "a period of unrest" began which had "a very disastrous effect on the material prosperity of the islands" of American Samoa. This unrest stemmed from a movement which came to be known as the Mau, a Samoan term signifying to stand fast in opposition, and took the form of a demand for civil government. Its counterpart in Upolu and Savai'i was directed against the governing of those islands by New Zealand under the mandate of the League of Nations. After serious trouble in 1928, during which sailors and marines from two New Zealand cruisers arrested some 400 Samoans, the Mau of Western Samoa culminated tragically in Apia in 1929, in the fatal shooting by police of eleven Samoans, including the high chief Tupua Tamasese Lealofi, who were participating in a procession of protest.[9]

On 14 April 1926, while Mead was still in Manu'a, an article appeared in *The Nation* that discussed "abuses and evils" in American Samoa and drew attention to a letter that 344 Samoan chiefs had addressed to the President of the United States in 1921. This letter, which had been published in *The Nation* of 15 March 1922, mentioned "grievous wrongs" against the Samoans committed by the naval government of American Samoa. In another letter of 1921, also published in *The Nation*, 971 Samoan signatories complained, among other things, that the chiefs and people of Tutuila and Manu'a were "forbidden to assemble to consider Samoan affairs and the welfare of the Samoan people." Also in 1921, seventeen chiefs and orators were imprisoned for "conspiring to kill the high chiefs who had signified their loyalty to the Governor."[10]

The involvement of Manu'ans in this unrest became acute in July 1924, when three of their high-ranking talking chiefs, Taua-nu'u, Tulifua, and Ti'a, in open defiance of the government of American Samoa, formally conferred the title of Tui Manu'a on Christopher Taliutafa Young. The high chief Sotoa, who held the position of acting district governor, participated in the kava ceremony that marked the installation of the new Tui Manu'a. These events precipitated a major crisis. Some fifteen years previously, on the death of Tui Manu'a Eliasara in 1909, the then governor of American Samoa, Captain J. F. Parker, had proclaimed that from the date of the hoisting of the American flag in Manu'a (in 1904), the title of Tui Manu'a had been changed to district governor. This step was taken because, as J. A. C. Gray notes, "the Tui Manu'a was royal in nature and therefore inadmissible under the Constitution of the United States." In 1924, when the Manu'ans restored their sovereign chieftainship in direct defiance of this ruling, Captain E. S. Kellog, who had been governor of American Samoa since 1923, at once dispatched the U.S.S. *Ontario* to Ta'ū to summon the newly installed Tui Manu'a, together with Taua-nu'u, Tulifua, and Ti'a, to the naval station in Pago Pago. On 7 August 1924 they were arraigned before him. Their actions, he said, "smacked of conspiracy." Sotoa, who was held to be primarily at fault, was suspended from office, and the newly installed Tui Manu'a was detained in Tutuila. Taua-nu'u, Tulifua, and Ti'a remained wholly defiant, telling Governor Kellog that they were "dissatisfied to the death" with his interference in the affairs of Manu'a. In Gray's judgment the deposed Tui Manu'a, Christopher Taliutafa Young, became the means by which the Mau of American Samoa "came of age and assumed something of the status of a political party."[11]

This then was the tense and troubled political situation at the time of Mead's brief sojourn in Manu'a and Tutuila. According to A. F. Judd, who as a member of a Bishop Museum expedition visited both Manu'a and Tutuila for six weeks early in 1926, when Mead was on Ta'ū, the Mau was widespread at this time, and there were few Samoans who did not sympathize with it.[12]

Throughout 1927 and 1928 Mau leaders continued to confront the naval governor with demands for civil government and American citizenship. In response to these demands, a congressional investigation commission was finally created in 1929 and visited American Samoa in September and October 1930. The hearings of this commission, published in a volume of 510 pages in 1931, provide a detailed chronicle of events in American Samoa during the 1920s, just as does the report of the Royal Commission Concerning the Administration of Western Samoa of 1927 of events in Upolu and Savai'i. The evidence presented to these two commissions refers specifically to events in the Samoan islands from the early 1920s onward, including the months of Mead's researches in Tutuila and Manu'a, and thus provides a conclusive empirical check on many of Mead's assertions, as for example her statement that in Samoa "no one suffers for his convictions." Indeed, in the light of the facts established by these two commissions, Mead's claim that her picture of Samoa had become forever true is at once revealed as nugatory.[13]

Felix Keesing, in his study of the history of cultural change in Samoa, concluded in 1934 that during the years from 1830 to 1879, when the Samoans were converted to Christianity and traders became established, a postcontact "equilibrium of culture" was reached, which persisted virtually unaltered into the 1930s. Gray, in his history of conditions in Tutuila and Manu'a between the end of World War I and the American entry into World War II, asserted that during this period, despite the disturbances of the Mau in the 1920s, "the *fa'aSamoa* hung on tenaciously." There is thus no reason to suppose that Samoan society and behavior changed in any fundamental way during the fourteen years between 1926, the year of the completion of Mead's inquiries, and 1940, when I began my own observations of Samoan behavior. In the refutation that follows, in addition to making use of the rich historical sources that date from 1830 onward, I shall draw on the evidence of my own research in the 1940s, the years 1965 to 1968, and 1981.[14]

By way of introduction to my refutation of Mead's conclusions, I now turn to a brief conspectus of Samoan society, giving particular attention to the traditional system of rank, which is fundamental to the organization of Samoan society. Samoan society is exceedingly intricate and varied in the details of its structure, and this conspectus must necessarily omit many of the finer distinctions of Samoan traditional lore. Readers who wish further to acquaint themselves with the social history of

Samoa should consult the first volume of Augustin Krämer's *Die Samoa-Inseln,* in which he gives detailed information on the constitution, genealogies, and traditions of all the islands of the Samoan archipelago, or chapters 1 and 2 of R. P. Gilson's *Samoa 1830 to 1900.*[15]

Traditionally, the population of Samoa is organized into discrete local polities, known as *nu'u,* each with its own clearly demarcated territory, and each with its own *fono,* or governing council of chiefs. These settlements, which varied in size in the nineteenth and early twentieth centuries from several score to several hundred inhabitants, are dispersed along the palm-fringed coasts of all the islands of the archipelago, with each nu'u comprising a series of family homesteads grouped around a common *malae,* or ceremonial ground. Inland of each settlement are the swiddens in which taro and other crops are cultivated, and beyond these the rain forest, in which there were once stone-walled forts for use in time of war. The communities of these settlements are composed of a number of inter-related *'āiga,* or localized extended families. The members of each 'āiga reside in a cluster of houses, using the same earth oven in the preparation of their food. The descent system is optative with an emphasis on agnation. Each of these families (which averaged in 1943, in the village of Sa'anapu on the south coast of Upolu, some nineteen members) lives and works under the direct authority of the individual (almost always male) whose succession to its chiefly title has been both approved by its members and ratified by the village fono, in the hierarchy of which he takes his appointed place as the titled representative of his 'āiga.[16]

Each village polity has its own *fa'avae,* of constitution, in which the relative rank of the chiefly titles of its constituent families are laid down in strict hierarchical order. Sanctioning this hierarchy are the all-important genealogies, through which chiefly families trace their descent from illustrious forebears, whose primal rank had almost always been vindicated by victories in war. As Samuel Ella has recorded, in ancient Samoa the genealogy of chiefs, especially of high chiefs, was preserved with great care, those who had been charged with its custody being very jealous of their responsibility. Indeed, so crucial is genealogy to the traditional hierarchies of Samoan communities and districts that the unauthorized recitation of genealogies is strictly forbidden, out of a fear that the airing of issues of relative rank will lead to altercation and bloodshed.[17]

Instead, the genealogically sanctioned hierarchy of each local community and district and, indeed, the whole of Samoa, is expressed in a set of traditional phrases, or *fa'alupega*. These fa'alupega, which Dr. Peter Buck, when in American Samoa in 1927, likened to Burke's Peerage, extend over the whole of the rank hierarchy and operate at all levels of segmentation within this structure, are ceremonially intoned at all fono and other important gatherings in formal recognition of the relative rank of those participating.[18] Now as in the past, when a chief enters a fono all activity is suspended until he takes up his appointed place, at which all of the other chiefs present intone his fa'alupega. The newcomer then recites, in order of precedence, the fa'alupega of all those present. This elaborate procedure follows the arrival of each chief until the whole fono is assembled, and is gone through again immediately prior to its dispersal. Further, all speeches made at a fono begin and end, and are often punctuated with, the conventional declamation of fa'alupega.

A fa'alupega, whether it refers to a local polity or district or the whole of Samoa, is thus an institution of quite fundamental importance, for, with the formal reiteration of the relative rank of titles on every significant social occasion, a chiefly hierarchy becomes so firmly established as to make it exceedingly difficult to effect any fundamental change in its order of precedence, except, as happened in ancient Samoa, by force of arms.

Furthermore, as Robert Louis Stevenson has described, in Samoa "terms of ceremony fly thick as oaths on board a ship," so that even commoners "my lord each other when they meet— and the urchins as they play marbles." This elaborate courtliness, as Stevenson calls it, has made the Samoans, in George Pratt's words, "the greatest observers of etiquette in Polynesia, if not in the world." Because of the rigors of their rank system, the Samoans place a particular emphasis on the precise practice of the verbal niceties that go with precedence, and over the centuries they have evolved a distinctive respect language with specific vocabularies for addressing and referring to those of chiefly rank. In pagan Samoa, as John Fraser notes, the rules of precedence and the ceremonious deference to authority among chiefs were identical with those observed by and in relation to the gods. Thus, in the myths of the Samoans, the gods are called chiefs, and "when they speak, they themselves use, and are addressed in, chiefs' language."[19]

This polite language, as G. B. Milner has suggested, "probably grew out of the elaborate system of social intercourse adopted against the 'sin' and in fact the hazard of insulting or lowering the 'dignity' of a chief or guest in any way," and in practice the respect language acts as "a kind of verbal lubricant" and is "a most effective device for the purpose of avoiding clashes, forestalling quarrels, and soothing the vexation of wounded pride and imagined or genuine grievances."[20]

However, while this system of punctilious social intercourse operates effectively most of the time, it does on occasion fail to prevent the tensions generated by the Samoan rank system from breaking out into violent conflict. Thus, in the words of George Brown, while the Samoans are arguably "the most polite people in the world" in their formal language and manners, they are equally "a people quick to resent an insult or injury and quite ready to fight with their neighbors" for what non-Samoans would consider to be the most trivial of causes.[21]

With rank goes the right to exercise power (*pule*), to assert priority of access to scarce resources,[22] and to make and enforce decisions. Samoa is thus a highly authoritarian society, based principally on socially inherited rank, with those in subordinate positions being required to listen to and obey the instructions of those who have pule over them.

Chiefly titles, which vary considerably in rank, belong to one or the other of two quite distinct categories: *ali'i,* or titular chiefs, and *tulafale,* or talking chiefs (or orators, as they are also called in the anthropological literature). The general term for any chief, whether titular or talking, is *matai.*

The ali'i, in contradistinction to the tulafale, is, in J. W. Da-

vidson's words, "the ultimate repository of political power."
The ali'i, furthermore, having in Samoan tradition a personal
sanctity, is accorded special deference and respect; those of the
highest rank were known in former times as sacred chiefs. In the
presence of these sacred chiefs, as Pratt observed in 1842, "no
inferior dare eat," and on ceremonial occasions they were carried from place to place on a litter preceded by a talking chief
blowing on a conch shell. John Williams, in July 1830, witnessed
the chief Fauea (himself of considerable rank) salute his sacred
chief, Malietoa Vai-inu-po, to whom he was related, with "the
greatest possible respect, bowing sufficiently low to kiss his feet
and making his child even kiss the soles of his feet."[23]

The expressions used to describe a chief of high rank dilate
upon size, height, and brilliance. Such a chief is likened, for example, to a lofty mountain or a star, or is compared to a huge
banyan tree towering over the rest of the forest. The power of
sacred chiefs, as Pratt records, was believed to be of divine origin, and the most august of them, as the sacrosanct sovereigns
of their ancient realms, were given the transcendent title of
Tui.[24]

The sanctity that attached to these sacred chiefs is also possessed in some degree by titular chiefs of lesser rank. For example, a titular chief has the right to be addressed in honorific language; the right to a ceremonially named house site, the height
of the base of which is a measure of his rank; and the right to a
kava cup title, which is used whenever the place of his chiefly
title in the hierarchy of his polity is given formal recognition in
a kava ceremony. He may also possess the right to confer the
taupou title of his family on one of his nubile and virginal
daughters and its coveted *manaia* title on one of his sons, who
then becomes his heir apparent. Further, an ali'i of paramount
rank in his local polity enjoys, together with his taupou and
manaia, the right to wear on ceremonial occasions a *tuiga,* an
elegantly ornamented headdress of human hair bleached to a
golden hue and symbolic of the sun. This right is a mark of distinction which, as Judge Marsack notes, is very jealously
guarded, with any unsanctioned attempt to assume it being met

with "speedy and violent objection." Finally, a high-ranking ali'i is entitled to have performed on his death a prolonged and elaborate series of funeral rites.[25]

In contradistinction to the ali'i is the tulafale, or talking chief, who in Davidson's words performs for the chief a variety of duties, which it is "contrary to propriety for the chief to perform for himself." A talking chief is thus subservient to the titular chief to whom he is attached, deriving such rank as his own tulafale name possesses from the fact of his association with his ali'i. Judge Schultz, who was for many years president of the Land and Titles Commission under the German regime in Western Samoa, was of the view that in the course of history tulafale had sprung from the servants or dependents of the ali'i they served. The families of the titular chiefs, in Schultz's view, had in former times, through the warlike character of their members, obtained supremacy, and so formed a titled aristocracy, the members of which also laid claim to supernatural descent. In this process others in the population "became their subjects, and the word *tulafale* took the meaning of an inherited office."[26]

The relationship in which tulafale stand to ali'i is a social linkage in which the ali'i, although superordinate, very much depends on the support of the tulafale. This interdependence is well expressed in the use of the word *tula* as the term of respect for a talking chief attached to a high-ranking titular chief. A tula, as Schultz notes, is a stick bent at a slight angle, on which in ancient Samoa a tamed and prized pigeon was carried, and is thus a telling metaphor for the way in which a talking chief acts as the prop or support of his illustrious ali'i. It is the responsibility of talking chiefs to safeguard and enhance the dignity of their ali'i by carrying out a wide range of duties. In particular, talking chiefs are responsible for the sharing out of food and property, and, as the agents of their ali'i, for the making of speeches in both political and ceremonial settings. The marks of authority of the tulafale are a staff and a switch of sennit, and he is expected to attend to the policing of regulations and the like drawn up by ali'i. In some polities, moreover, through the vicissitudes of history talking chiefs have come to occupy positions of exceptional power. For example, Sala'ilua, in Savai'i, as Shore reports, is "striking in the pre-eminent position enjoyed by certain of its orators, a position eclipsing that normally enjoyed by ali'i in a village."[27]

In addition to being regularly reiterated in its fa'alupega, the rank hierarchy of a village is also expressed in the seating plan of its fono (see figure 1) and in its accompanying kava ceremony. During a fono, the traditional venue for which is an elegant round house, the participants sit cross-legged at the wall posts that mark its perimeter, in a rigidly prescribed seating order that clearly demarcates the titular from the talking chiefs and also designates the rank order within each of these categories. The wall posts of the two lateral sections of a round house, known as *tala,* are reserved for titular chiefs, while those of the *itu,* the front and back of the house, are kept for talking chiefs. Within each of these sections the central post is of principal importance, and the posts on either side of this central position decrease in importance in proportion to their distance from it. Again, within each of the tala that are the prerogative of titular chiefs, the wall posts extending to the front of the house take precedence over the equivalent posts in the rear section. When the paramount chief of a village takes up his position at the central post of one of the tala, the post in the opposite tala is left vacant in recognition of his being without peer within the local rank order.[28] Within the itu, the front is all important, the back section being used for the preparation of kava, the division of food, and other tasks that fall to low-ranking talking chiefs.

A third conventional summation of the rank structure of a Samoan polity is the kava ceremony, in which a drink prepared from the pulverized root of *Piper methysticum* is ritually partaken of during a fono. A formal kava ceremony is a sacrosanct occasion. As it has primarily to do with rank, which is the most grave and delicate of issues, the demeanor of the participants is serious. At kava ceremonies today, libations are poured to Jehovah. In pagan times they were offered to Tagaloa, and there are numerous myths associating kava with the gods of pagan Samoa, for whom it was a hallowed fluid. For example, it is said

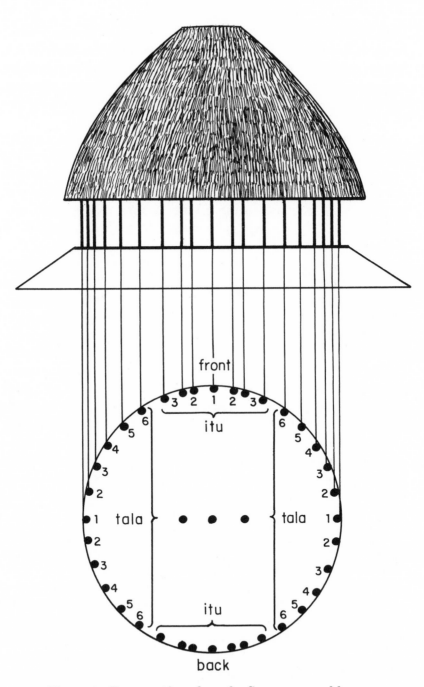

front

3 2 1 2 3

itu

6 6
5 5
4 4
3 3
2 2
1 tala • • • tala 1
2 2
3 3
4 4
5 5
6 6

itu

back

Figure 1. Fono seating plan of a Samoan round house.

that when the young son of a man named Pava fell into a kava bowl, desecrating it, Tagaloa became so enraged that he cut the boy in two with the stem of a palm frond. (After having thus struck fear into Pava's heart over his failure to restrain his son during a kava ceremony, Tagaloa mercifully restored the child to life.)[29]

A kava ceremony provides a great variety of ways in which formal recognition is given to rank. The principal of these is the order of distribution. The first cup to be announced is of prime distinction and next to this the last cup. The remaining cups progressively decrease in importance from the second to the penultimate. The order of precedence in a kava ceremony is thus another ritualized expression, like the fa'alupega, of the rank hierarchy of a local community or district.[30] A sharp distinction is also made in every kava ceremony between titular and talking chiefs. A titular chief possesses in his own right a kava cup title which is used whenever his kava is announced. For example, the kava cup title of 'Anapu, the paramount chief of Sa'anapu, is made up of these vaunting words: "The honor conferred by Malie and Vaito'elau [two centers of high importance in the rank order of western Samoa], fetch the war club that quickly springs to life." Again, a titular chief's kava cup is always prefaced by the honorific phrase *Lau ipu,* meaning, "Your cup." In contrast, a talking chief has no kava cup title, and his name is prefaced by the commonplace words *Lau 'ava,* meaning "Your kava." Further major distinctions are expressed in the modes of presenting kava to chiefs. In the case of a titular chief the kava cup (of highly polished coconut shell) is presented with a graceful sweep of the arm that culminates with the inner surface of the forearm and hand facing toward the recipient; in the case of a talking chief kava is offered with no sign of display and with the back of the hand thrust foward.

The fono, then, in its structure and conventions, is a prime expression of the ethos of Samoan society as well as of the particular characteristics of a village or district, and in its fa'alupega, seating order, and kava ceremony it provides a demonstration that rank, as Lowell Holmes has remarked, constitutes "the focal point of Samoan culture," in comparison with which all other aspects of Samoan life, including even religion, are of secondary importance.[31]

With the conversion of the Samoans to Christianity the sanctity that once surrounded sacred chiefs as the earthly descendants of Polynesian gods was gradually transferred to chiefs in general as the elect of Jehovah. For example, during the constitutional convention of Western Samoa in 1955, Afamasaga, a high-ranking titular chief of A'ana, declared that chieftainship was "a birthright from God," and it has long been averred by Christian chiefs that the institution of chieftainship was founded by God. This doctrine, furthermore, is given a scriptural sanction. In Proverbs 8:16, Jehovah is reported as proclaiming: "By me princes rule and nobles govern the earth." On the basis of this and other texts in the Bible, it is widely maintained that the Samoan chief is "a god of this world."

The Samoans, in addition to being preoccupied with rank, are deeply steeped in the Christian religion. However, the Christian pastor or priest of a village community is held to be in a special relationship with the village as a local polity, and is excluded from participation in the deliberations of its fono. This means that a local polity is held to be under the direct authority of God, or the Atua—*atua* being the term that was once applied to the high god of pagan Samoa, Tagaloa. Samoan chiefs, as Christians, think of their society as a hierarchy with Jehovah, instead of Tagaloa, at its apex. Today, in fonos throughout Samoa, libations of kava are poured to Jehovah, the all-powerful God who, as the source of the Samoan system of chiefly government, is said to be unrelenting in the punishment of those who disobey the dictates of its divinely constituted authority.

In every local polity the rank order of its fono is repeated in a series of interrelated social groups involving all of the adult members of the village (with the exception of the family of the pastor). All of these groups are under the direct authority of the fono, which they are obligated to support and serve. Traditionally these groups comprise the *'aumaga,* consisting of untitled men, the *aualuma,* consisting of women who are resident members, by birth or adoption, of local families, and groups consisting of the wives of titular and talking chiefs and the wives of untitled men. Each of these groups when it meets follows the basic structure of the fa'alupega, the seating plan, and the kava ceremony of the fono of chiefs to which it is subservient. The principle of rank thus applies to the members of all these groups, as also to all of the children of the community. Any individual's rank is that of the position of the title of the family to which he or she belongs in the community's constitution.

It is also said by chiefs that the relationship between themselves and untitled individuals is set apart, and that a chief (whether titular or talking) is entitled to the respectful obedience of all those over whom he has authority. A child is first taught to obey all those within his family, with one of the main instruments of instruction being physical punishment. He is expected to remain obedient to those in authority over him whatever his age. Central to Samoan society, then, are the closely related principles of the right of those of superordinate rank to exercise authority over those who are below them in the social order, and of the obligation of those in positions of subordination to obey the dictates they receive from above. The Samoans are thus a proud, punctilious, and complex, God-fearing people, whose orators delight in extolling the beauty of mornings that dawn with the sanctity and dignity of their ancient polities serenely intact. Yet, as we shall see, such are the rigors of the Samoan rank system and so intense is the emotional ambivalence generated by omnipresent authority that this goal is all too frequently not attained; instead, the morning dawns in fearful trembling and shaking, for as anyone who has grown up within a Samoan polity well knows, "the Samoan way is difficult indeed."[32]

9

Rank

BECAUSE MARGARET MEAD had no participation in the political
life of Ta'ū, being denied entry to all chiefly fonos, she had no
direct experience of the rank system as it operates among chiefs
in formal conclave. In this insurmountably difficult situation
Mead formed numerous misconceptions about fono behavior
and the rank system of Samoa. For example, presumably from
her experience as a participant in the *malaga*, or traveling
party, from Ta'ū to Fitiuta that she entertainingly described in
a letter dated 7 March 1926, Mead reported that a titular chief
is of "too high rank to make his own speeches in council," and
further, that in a fono the titular chief is "a noble figure head"
and the talking chief "makes most of his decisions for him."[1]

In the ceremonies associated with the reception of a malaga

it is indeed customary, as Mead observed, for only talking chiefs to speak (as the agents of their ali'i). This, however, is by no means the practice in a formal political fono, particularly in the case of a *fono manu,* a council especially summoned to consider an issue of major concern. On such an occasion, titular chiefs voice their opinions in the most forthright terms, with that of the highest-ranking chief being of decisive importance. This active participation in the deliberations of fonos of any substantial political significance has long been the established practice. In his journal of 1832, Williams specifically notes that in fonos of moment "the chiefs themselves speak," while leaving a speaker to represent them at meetings where subjects of minor importance are discussed, it being considered "below the dignity" of a titular chief to make speeches on these routine occasions.[2]

In a local polity, while the titular chiefs commonly consult with one another when a judgment on any major issue is being formed, the actual making of this judgment and its announcement to the fono is the prerogative of the ali'i of highest rank, who is known as the *sa'o* of his village. The term *sa'o* has the meaning of right or true, and when applied to the paramount ali'i of a local polity carries these same connotations. The judgment, in fono, of a paramount chief is also called a *tonu,* meaning an exact decision. The pronouncing of a tonu by a high-ranking ali'i is usually accomplished with few words and with what Robert Louis Stevenson called "that quiescence of manner which is thought becoming of the great." This aristocratic demeanor may, however, be accompanied by an imposing flourish. For example, at a fono at Malua in May 1966, Mata'afa Fiame Faumuina Mulinu'u II, one of the four highest-ranking chiefs of Western Samoa, issued a tonu with the words "Let it be thus . . . " at the same time striking the palm of his left hand with his right index finger. Furthermore, when a tonu has been laid down by an ali'i, it is, as the leading talking chief of Sa'anapu averred at a fono in March 1967, something that the talking chiefs present are bound to treat with the utmost respect. These same principles (as my inquiries in 1967 showed) are observed in the fonos of Manu'a, about which Mead wrote. For example, in Si'ufaga (one of the three villages from which

Mead's adolescent informants came) I was told that in the event
of an altercation in a fono, the paramount ali'i would, with
chiefly words, swiftly bring it to an end.[3]

In her ignorance of the traditional political life of Samoa,
Mead thus gives a quite false impression of the relationship,
within a fono, of titular chiefs and talking chiefs. She is equally
mistaken in asserting that "the sanctity surrounding chiefs in
Samoa was minimal for the Polynesian area." As Powell noted
in 1886, the Samoans, although they had been converted to
Christianity, remained "very tenacious of their traditional
myths." These myths Powell was able to record in the early
1870s, from Taua-nu'u, the main keeper among the *sacri vates*
of Manu'a (as Fraser called them), "whose duty it was to preserve in their memories and to recite the old legends and
myths."[4]

Fraser, who in the late nineteenth century edited various of
the traditions collected by Powell, has likened Ta'ū, the principal island of Manu'a, to Delos, the island birthplace of Apollo in
the ancient Aegean. This is an apposite comparison. In the
"Solo 'o le Va," which recounts the creation of Samoa, Manu'a
is described as the first of lands and the high peak of the island
of Ta'ū as the abode of Tagaloa. Further, the first of all Samoan
titular chiefs is said to have been the son of Tagaloa. According
to their most sacred traditions then, the ali'i of pagan Samoa
were descended from the gods, with the title of Tui Manu'a, as
we have seen, being the highest in rank and sanctity of all the
chiefly titles of Samoa, as also of all the other islands of the
southwest Pacific known to the Samoans.[5]

The ritual prohibitions surrounding the Tui Manu'a were (as
Mead herself noted in 1930) of a most elaborate kind. Similar
prohibitions and extreme marks of respect to high-ranking ali'i
were also observed throughout the Samoan archipelago. As
Thomas Nightingale noted in 1834, no one dared pass in front of
the chiefly residence of the paramount chief of western Samoa
"under penalty of the severest punishment"; or, as Hood observed in 1862, during the meeting of a fono attended by the Tui
Atua, any canoe passing by was, as a mark of respect to the Tui
Atua, vacated and pushed across the lagoon, its occupants wad-

ing up to their shoulders in the water. The sanctity surrounding Samoan chiefs of high rank was most certainly not "minimal for the Polynesian area."[6]

Mead also states that in Samoa "rank is so arranged that there are titles for all those capable of holding them"—the implication being that all competition for titles is thus eliminated. This is by no means the case. There is in fact intense competition for titles at all levels of the rank structure, particularly for titles of special distinction. Indeed, the principal tradition of Manu'a concerns the struggle between two paternal half-brothers for its paramount title: the legendary account of how the village of Ta'ū, by force of arms, wrested this title from Fitiuta, the original center of power in Manu'a. According to this tradition, Le Lologa Tele threw down the title of Tui Manu'a between Ali'a Matua and Ali'a Tama, his sons by different wives, telling them to settle its possession between themselves. It was at once claimed by Ali'a Matua on the ground of his seniority. However, Ali'a Tama, being of higher rank on his mother's side, became determined to seize from Ali'a Matua the headdress of white bark cloth that was the distinctive mark of a Tui Manu'a. This he finally contrived to do, and Ali'a Matua, in seeking to regain his dignity, was killed in the ensuing battle. Since that time "there have been many wars between Ta'ū and Fitiuta."[7]

Similar struggles over titles have occurred throughout the archipelago in the course of Samoan history, disputed succession to chieftainship being, as W. T. Pritchard noted in 1866, one of the "most prolific sources of war." In Tutuila in the 1880s, for example, fighting over the succession to the high-ranking Mauga title, by the factions of the son and the sister's son of the previous incumbent, resulted in the destruction of the settlements of Fagatoga and Pago Pago, and led to violence that had to be quelled by a British warship, H.M.S. *Miranda*.[8]

In the western islands even fiercer rivalry occurred over possession of the four sacrosanct titles that are known collectively as the *tafa'ifa*, the holder of which was regarded as the paramount chief of western Samoa. From the time of its institution, there were, as Krämer relates, violent conflicts between rival contenders for the four titles of the tafa'ifa. For example, after

Galumalemana named as his successor to the tafa'ifa the un-born child of his fifth wife instead of one of his other sons, "se-vere conflict took place between the brothers until the chosen child, I'amafana, attained the supremacy." This rivalry resulted in the division of western Samoa into two large factions, the conquerors and the defeated, and caused fiercely fought wars in which, over the years, thousands were killed.[9]

With the cessation of warfare at the end of the nineteenth century, disputes over succession to titles began to be taken to the Land and Titles Court (or Commission as it was at first called) that was set up in 1903 by the German authorities. Since that time, although the proportion of chiefs to untitled men is high (in the census of Western Samoa of 25 September 1945, the proportion was 1 to 3.7), hundreds of disputes over titles have reached the Land and Titles Court each year. For high-ranking titles, there are often numerous claimants. For example, in the case of the disputed succession to the paramount title of Sa'anapu, which was heard by the Land and Titles Court in 1964, there were no fewer than eight claimants, with the most intense rivalry between the two main contenders.

The Samoan rank system thus tends to generate bitter ri-valries. These rivalries, moreover, may erupt in any social con-text in which precedence becomes a crucial issue, as, for exam-ple, in a kava ceremony. As part of her depiction of what she called the "innocuousness" of Samoan culture, Mead described the kava ceremony as "a dexterous, graceful play with social forms," and went on to claim that the social structure of Samoa is "so flexible, so minutely adapted to manipulation, that it is possible to change the appearance of a *fono* in twenty years." These are major misconceptions. In all fonos of any importance precedence is, in Pritchard's words, "strictly regulated by rank," and, as Churchward noted in 1887, "many a quarrel in Samoa has had its origin in the kava distribution, merely from one chief receiving the cup before another believing himself to be of higher rank and as such entitled to higher service."[10]

When it impinges directly on the historically sanctioned constitution of a polity, such a quarrel may become violent. This happened (as I was able to document in detail) during a fono manu on the island of Upolu in the 1960s. This revealing case (the names used in the account that follows are pseudonyms) concerns a titular chief, Taeao, who for some time had on genealogical grounds been trying to gain acceptance of the enhancement of his title in his local polity. Having arrived somewhat late at a fono manu, Taeao, using the elaborate respect language of Samoa, requested the officiating talking chief, Taula, to hold a second kava ceremony. His intention was to use the occasion to press the issue of the change in rank he had long been seeking. Taula replied, with the same formal politeness, that the holding of a second kava ceremony would be quite contrary to custom. Vave, Taeao's talking chief, then intervened telling Taula not to bandy words with an ali'i, only to be told by Fusu, a talking chief of a family grouping of rival titular chiefs, to shut his mouth. At this Vave shouted, "Is it trouble you want?" "Indeed I do!" retorted Fusu, springing to his feet, and soon the two talking chiefs were fighting furiously just outside the fono house, close to where Taeao was sitting. When Taeao rose to his feet as if to go to the assistance of his talking chief, he was at once struck by Tumau, the senior titular chief of a rival faction. He fell to the floor of the fono house and was immediately set upon by several others of the Tumau faction, including several untitled men who had been sitting nearby. Taeao was violently beaten until he was unable either to stand up or to lift a hand to protect himself. His talking chief, Vave, was also heavily attacked and suffered a fractured skull. The affray was finally stopped by several neutral chiefs and the village pastor. Some time later the fono manu resumed without any kind of alteration of its rank order.

The intense rivalries of the Samoan rank system may also lead to violence between the branches of the same family, particularly when the same title has two or more holders and there is lack of agreement as to which of them is senior in rank. In 1968, for example, again on Upolu, I witnessed violence of this kind when the representative of one branch of an 'āiga of titular chiefs asserted, in a fono, his right as its senior rank holder to take precedence both in receiving kava and in speaking. Having made this challenge he was then and there heavily battered about the head by three members of the rival branch of the same family that had for some years exercised this right. Once again, there was no change in the status quo.

The prerogatives of rank are just as fiercely defended beyond the confines of the fono, as, for example, at a general conference of the Methodist Church in Samoa which was held at a village on the south coast of Upolu in 1965. As there would be many visitors from all over Samoa at this conference, it was decided to hold a *ta'alolo,* a ceremony in which a large body of people, often as many as a hundred or more, slowly approach a group of visitors, singing and dancing, while bearing gifts of food and other valuables, with the main body being preceded by one or more individuals of rank wearing traditional headdresses. In the village concerned, the wearing of such a headdress is the prerogative of two, and only two, chiefly families. However, when the ta'alolo was held, before hundreds of onlookers, it was headed by a low-ranking titular chief named Fiapoto (once again I am using pseudonyms), bedecked in a headdress and accompanied by a talking chief bearing an orator's staff. This spectacle was too much for the members of one of the chiefly families entitled by rank to wear a headdress, and as Fiapoto approached the vicinity of this family's residence, Isa, the 33-year-old daughter of its principal chief, ran out on to the malae, lifted her clothes to expose her bare buttocks, and bent over to point them directly at Fiapoto. This action is, among Samoans, insulting in the highest degree. In Isa's gesture, Fiapoto's wearing of a headdress, ostensibly the highest of honors, was identified with the lowest part of the human body. Isa and eight of her kindred, including three adolescents, then threw stones at Fiapoto and his talking chief. The assailants were subsequently arraigned before the District Court and fined. All of them, however, appeared well satisfied at having chastised those who had violated a cherished prerogative of their rank.

Such incidents are fairly rare in Samoa, for the elaborate conventions of the rank system are usually sufficient to contain its tensions. However, the fact that violent conflicts do erupt from time to time in highly formalized settings is a clear indication that the Samoan rank system, far from being "hospitable to innovation" and characterized by "extreme mobility" as Mead claimed, is, in fact, an essentially conservative system, which, beneath the punctilio of chiefly etiquette, is fraught with intense and long-standing rivalries.

So keen are these rivalries that major issues of rank often turn on the finest of distinctions, as is well exemplified in a celebrated case that occurred soon after the establishment of American government in eastern Samoa in 1900. One of the earliest actions of Commander B. F. Tilley, the first commandant of the naval station at Tutuila, was to appoint three high chiefs to district governorships. One of these was Mauga of Tutuila, and another, the Tui Manu'a, whose rank at that time was the highest in all Samoa. Among the many rules concerning the Tui Manu'a was that in kava ceremonies the term *ipu,* or cup—which elsewhere in Samoa was used to refer to the kava cup of any titular chief of whatever rank—was reserved within Manu'a for the Tui Manu'a alone. In August 1901, the high chief Mauga visited the Manu'an island of Ofu. At a ceremony held in his honor, he was given pride of place, and his personal kava cup title was announced, in accordance with custom. At this, Mauga demurred, insisting that as one of the newly appointed district governors, he be offered an ipu as was the Tui Manu'a. At first the talking chiefs of Ofu were reluctant, but in the end, after Mauga had quoted the Bible (Romans 13:7) to them ("Render therefore to all their dues: tribute to whom tribute is due; custom to whom custom; fear to whom fear; honour to whom honour") they complied with his demand. When word of this innovation reached the Tui Manu'a he was furious. The talking chiefs who had officiated at the ceremony were apprehended and had imposed upon them the most severe penalties: their property was to be confiscated, their families banished, and they themselves set adrift on the high seas in a canoe.[11] At this stage the American authorities intervened, and the case went to trial before a European judge. The judge ruled that it was not wrong to employ the term *ipu* when kava was being served to high officers of the American government of eastern Samoa—a judgment that initiated the gradual decline of the Tui Manu'a as a chief of unsurpassed rank and sanctity.[12]

In this historic case we have an example of one of the apparently trivial causes for which Samoans, who are ever ready to "find quarrel in a straw, when honour's at the stake," are prepared to fight. In truth this case was, within the values of the Samoan system of rank, very far from being trivial, for the exclusive right to the word *ipu* was a principal mark of the Tui Manu'a's preeminent rank, as was made evident in the testimony of one of the witnesses at the trial of September 1901. "Could a Tongan have an *ipu?*" a Manu'an chief was asked. "No," he replied. "Could a Fijian have an *ipu?*" "No." "If the King of England came here, could he have an *ipu?*" "No . . . the Tui Manu'a is higher than all other kings."[13]

This same punctilio also exists at lower levels in the rank structure, as, for example, at the installation ceremony for a newly elected talking chief in a village on Upolu in the mid 1960s. Such installations are attended by all of the titular and talking chiefs of the polity concerned, as well as by chiefly visitors from further afield, who, in contemporary Samoa, are presented at the beginning of the proceedings with a light repast of bread, biscuits, and tea. Convention requires that talking chiefs have their tea served in enamel mugs, while each titular chief is provided with a china cup and saucer and a teapot. Further, all those present must be served in strict order of precedence. On the occasion in question the officiating talking chiefs served a young ali'i, Afoa, before Vaiola, an older ali'i, despite the fact that Vaiola was sitting at a house post of higher rank and took precedence over Afoa in the fa'alupega of their polity. Vaiola vociferously condemned the talking chiefs responsible before the assembled guests. What had happened, he said, was wholly improper and he shouted at the erring talking chiefs, "Don't do new things within this polity! Keep to its constitution!" He added that if not for his respect for the visitors who were present he would have flung from the house the teapot that had been served to him in wrong order of precedence. On another occasion, the attempt to serve a teapot to a low-ranking titular chief, whose title was not mentioned in the fa'alupega of his polity, resulted in a brief melee in which corms of taro were violently thrown by the members of rivalrous branches of the same extended family.

As these examples show, the manifold conventions that surround the Samoan rank order, far from being "adapted to manipulation" as Mead claimed, are designed to ensure that any attempt to alter precedence will be at once detected. These conventions, moreover, are both aggressively safeguarded and meticulously observed. Fortunately, we have for virtually all of the local polities of Samoa the detailed fa'alupega that Augustin Krämer collected during the years 1897 to 1899. These fa'alupega, as already noted, are a direct reflection of the constitutions of the fonos to which they refer. In every case that I have investigated during the years 1941 to 1981, the fa'alupega in use in modern Samoa remain essentially the same as those recorded by Krämer at the end of the nineteenth century. There is thus no substantive historical evidence for Mead's assertions of 1928 that "it is possible to change the appearance of a *fono* in twenty years," and that in Samoa, where "the social innovator runs against . . . no jealously guarded body of tradition," the social landscape can, with ease, be "completely altered." Rather, the ethos of Samoa, when it comes to rank, is that expressed by the chief Tuato, at the Constitutional Convention of Western Samoa on 20 December 1954: "No one will ever dare to take away or add anything to the dignity of Samoa."[14]

10

Cooperation
and Competition

IN THE EARLY 1930s, largely in response to the writings of Benedict and Mead, the Social Science Research Council in the United States became "actively interested in developing as one of its areas of concentration, the field of personality and culture." A major expression of this interest was the publication, under the editorship of Mead, of a survey of the competitive and cooperative habits of the members of thirteen different "primitive societies." As well as appending a lengthy interpretative statement to this survey, Mead contributed chapters on the Arapesh and Manus and a specially written study of the Samoans.[1]

In 1928 Mead had asserted that in Samoa a youth must "never excel his fellows by more than a little," and in 1931 she advanced the sweeping generalization that Samoan culture had taken the road of "eliminating ... interest in competition." In

1937, in *Cooperation and Competition among Primitive Peoples*, where cooperation is defined as "the act of working together," and competition as "the act of seeking or endeavouring to gain what another is endeavouring to gain at the same time," Samoa was classified as a markedly cooperative society. Although in Samoan social organization a tendency for individuals to rebel against subordination and to foment trouble and rivalry is always present, this, Mead argued, is not so strong as the opposite tendency, which is to "place each individual, each household, each village, even (in Western Samoa) each district, in a hierarchy, wherein each is dignified only by its relationship to the whole ... and competition is completely impossible." Thus, "competitiveness between villages usually does not reach important heights of intervillage aggressiveness," and when "rivalry situations occur between young men in the free lovemaking which precedes marriage ... it is notable that these have the same unrealistic character as the rivalries which occur between villages." The Samoans then, as depicted by Mead, are markedly cooperative, having a society (as she stated in 1950, when expatiating on the ease of Samoan life) in which "competition is muted and controlled."[2]

As I noted in Chapter 8, the individuals, families, and local polities of Samoa are indeed, as Mead states, arranged in hierarchies according to rank; it is, however, a cardinal error to suppose that within these hierarchies, with their ceremonious formalities, competition has been eliminated. While it is true that within all Samoan polities there are established orders of precedence, it is crucially important to realize that these orders of precedence are the institutionalized expression of an intense and pervasive competitiveness, and that while they are generally effective in its regulation, this competitiveness nonetheless remains inherent in the entire system. Indeed, among a people as obsessed with rank as the Samoans, there is a marked accentuation of competition for the numerous benefits that rank confers. Situations are generated at all levels of the social structure in which, as we have seen, the omnipresent competitiveness is liable to break through the constraints of convention into open contention and conflict.

This is certainly how Samoans see their own society. For example, during a political fono held on the south coast of Upolu in February 1967, one of the participating titular chiefs remarked of Samoa: "This country is indeed competitive," and went on to warn his fellow chiefs that intense competitiveness almost always ended in trouble and often in outright fighting. At this, another ali'i agreed that competitiveness was truly the principal feature of Samoan life, being intrinsic to the age-old rank system of Samoa, and therefore a much more potent force than the ethics of the Christianity of which Samoans had been adherents for only a relatively short time. Again, the 44-year-old daughter of a titular chief remarked to me, quite spontaneously, in September 1966: "The Samoan way is truly difficult, with constant competition for land and titles, nothing being gained but discord."

Similar conclusions have been reached by numerous European observers of Samoan behavior. In his 1832 journal Williams noted the "extreme jealousy" of respect for rank that existed among the Samoans, and made mention of the "very favourite" Samoan amusement of fighting with clubs made from the butt-ends of coconut palm fronds, saying it was no uncommon thing for one of the contestants to be severely injured and fall senseless to the ground from a blow on the head. Arms were also frequently broken.[3]

In 1834 Thomas Nightingale witnessed one of these ritualized club-fighting contests that were so common in pagan Samoa. Held on the island of Manono, in western Samoa, it was attended by "three thousand persons habited in their war costumes," a great number of whom had "arrived from adjacent islands, each desirous of outvieing his neighbor in dexterity and warlike prowess." As Nightingale reports:

> The scene commenced by each warrior menacing the other, partly in words, but still more forcibly by expressive gestures, thus mutually signifying a wish that the opposing party should begin hostilities—then, retiring to their respective stations, they successively engaged in single combat, in a most scientific, and sometimes too ef-

fective manner, each warrior inflicting blows of such overwhelming force on the head of his opponent, as to render it a matter of surprise, to the bystanders, how any human skull could escape unfractured. No quarter was granted, until one of the contending parties was rendered insensible, or his club broken. Should any unfair advantage be assumed during the encounter, on either side, immediate death was the offender's portion. At the conclusion the successful combatant seats himself before his chief, whose approbation he receives, then retires amongst his own party, who further celebrate the victory by loud yells and acclamations.[4]

Nightingale goes on to remark that these contests, although commenced as a mere trial of skill, are so "stimulated by rivalry and competition" as to often become means of exciting serious jealousy and revenge. Such a breakdown of ritualization was witnessed by the missionary Charles Hardie during a club-fighting contest between two local polities on Savai'i in July 1837. On this occasion one contestant was disabled and his club shattered, whereupon the party of his opponent raised a shout, which, because the defeated combatant had not fallen, gave offense to his supporters. Immediately, there were "manifest signs of war in earnest" as the offended party rushed upon their rivals with stones. Hardie commented that "civil and mild as the Samoans generally appear to us, they are as bears and tigers when excited by anger."[5]

Ritualized club fighting, which, as these accounts show, was fiercely competitive, took place at all levels of the rank structure between the members of different extended families of the same village, between villages, and between such great districts of the island of Upolu as Atua and A'ana, which were virtually separate realms, each with its own high chief. Stair has given an account of club fighting between Atua and A'ana and of the highly sarcastic songs that were sung in the excitement of competition, when the champion of one district triumphed over that of another. Thus when a contestant from A'ana fell and was unable to rise, those of Atua, after emitting shouts of triumph and derision, would sing a song that ended with the wounding words, "A'ana, whose pastime is fighting, you are eating earth and rolling in the grass!"[6]

Club fighting among young warriors was paralleled in pagan Samoa by the highly competitive chiefly sport of netting pigeons, which was conducted at especially cleared and constructed mounds in the forest. At these sites, chiefly contestants from all over Samoa would assemble, each with his favorite decoy pigeons. These birds had been trained to fly, as directed by their owners, at the end of long strings. When a wild pigeon approached, the contestants would try to entangle it in a net fastened to the end of a long pole. The chief who netted the greatest number of wild pigeons was, in Turner's words, "the hero of the day," and received from the less successful competitors the food and other property they had all wagered. Pigeon netting, as Krämer records, was first and foremost the sport of high chiefs, whose ardor for it was such that "at times nothing could move them to call a halt to their passion" and they would "spend many weeks without interruption in the forest." The competition for the renown that came to an especially skilled netter of pigeons sometimes had tragic consequences. Schultz records a case, famous in Samoan history, that took place at Olo, a pigeon-netting site in Savai'i. Uluma, a celebrated exponent of the art, was struck down by Tapusoa, "who was jealous of his reputation as a hunter," and then subjected to the grievous insult of being "cut up like a pig." For this flagrant act Tapusoa himself was treated in like manner by one of Uluma's kinsmen. The incident is remembered in the proverbial expression 'O ula i Olo, which is applied to any extreme form of retaliation.[7]

Turner, Stair, and others have described diverse other competitive activities of the pagan Samoans, such as spear-throwing, dart-throwing, "boxing," and wrestling, as well as numerous other contests like that reported by Turner in which a man engaged to "unhusk with his teeth and eat five large native chestnuts" before another could "run a certain distance and return," this being for a wager of a basket of coconuts.[8]

In the second half of the nineteenth century these traditional forms of ritualized competition were gradually supplanted by new forms of sport, particularly by cricket, which was introduced by the crew of a British naval vessel and was taken up throughout the islands with immense enthusiasm. Having been adapted to Samoan conditions with a bat shaped like a war club, cricket matches were soon being arranged, as a mission report of 1888 records, with "two hundred a side," and with play continuing "during the whole day for a month at a time, to the utter neglect of home, plantations and worship." This total absorption in a new form of contest led to attempts by both church and government to outlaw cricket; it has, however, become a game that is played with lively competitiveness by males and females of all ages in virtually every Samoan village. All manner of other contests have also been introduced, as, for example, racing in long-boats, volleyball and baseball, and, in Western Samoa, rugby football.[9]

In villages it is still the custom for any number of individuals to make up a side in cricket, and such is the competitiveness of children that it is common to see one fielder hitting another of the same side who has beaten him to the ball. Cricket matches are taken most seriously, and I have often seen fights on a cricket pitch over disputed decisions. Usually there are elders or talking chiefs at hand, armed with staffs, who swiftly intervene to restore the peace. On occasion, however, the fighting can be serious, as for example during a cricket match in a village on the north coast of Upolu on 27 July 1966. A 22-year-old man, Solomua, was so put out when his side was beaten that he hurled the ball at one of the opposing team, Motu, who at once retorted, "Don't play with such bad spirit, you excrement eater!" A fight ensued in which Motu was stabbed in the thigh by Solomua, who was later convicted and sentenced to nine months' imprisonment. As this example indicates, as do the many others that I might instance, the rank-conscious Samoans become so deeply involved in contests that there is an ever present likelihood that participants in ritualized competition will resort to outright violence against their opponents.[10]

The evidence I have presented reveals the Samoans to have long been an intensely competitive people in contests of all kinds. This same competitiveness is to be found in virtually all other areas of their society. This is not to say that Samoans are not capable of cooperation. They are, in fact, conspicuously proficient at working together in diverse ways. This cooperation, furthermore, is most effective when one unit in their society, say a local polity, is openly competing with another unit of the same kind, whether it be in playing cricket, staging a major ceremony, or making a collective offering to the church. This cooperation, moreover, exists side by side with intense competition at other levels; thus, within the local polity its component sections are in competition, and within these sections their component families.

Tales of highly competitive encounters abound in the traditions of Samoa. I have already dealt in Chapter 9 with the most celebrated of all these encounters, that of the lethal rivalry of Ali'a Matua and Ali'a Tama in ancient Manu'a. Dr. Peter Buck was told in Manu'a in 1927 that when in ancient times Malietoa arrived from Savai'i, and one of his talking chiefs was outwitted by Le Polo of Ta'ū, he killed this unfortunate retainer "for not being able to compete." In Savai'i there is the well-remembered tale of Fatu and Sala who belonged to different sections of the village of Safune. Having become involved in an argument, these two women set out for their taro gardens to establish which of them did the most work, a contest that ended when Sala died of exhaustion. In Upolu, probably the most historic rivalry is that of the two talking chiefs Ape and Tutuila, of the closely related polities of Fasito'outa and Fasito'otai, who, in the late sixteenth century, went to Safata on the south coast of Upolu to carry off the high-ranking infant son of Vaetamasoa, who became the founder, as Krämer notes, of the Tui A'ana line. When these two talking chiefs returned to their own district, so fierce a quarrel took place over the possession of the royal infant that it has become enshrined in ritual. An account of this ritual, as it was performed at a kava ceremony attended by the Tui A'ana in 1901, has been given by S. Osborn. When, during this sacrosanct kava ceremony, the current holders of the titles of Ape and Tutuila began to quarrel ritually, so convincing was their performance that Governor Solf intervened to try to stop them. In the full version of this ritual, as Osborn describes it, Ape and Tutuila contend so violently for the possession of a live piglet that they tear it in two, each of them making off with his own portion—a primevally competitive ritual if ever there was one. Again, Shore has given a detailed account of the long-standing competitiveness of two talking chiefs of Sala'ilua in Savai'i which led to the murder of one by the other after a violent quarrel instigated by an accusation of cheating at cards.[11]

Competition in the making of orations is especially marked among talking chiefs, the whole pattern of oratory, as Holmes has noted, being based upon "competition ... in order to win prestige both for the orator himself and for the village or family he represents." Engaging in this activity is termed *fa'atau,* which literally means to provoke contention, and such competition is the standard practice among talking chiefs at a fono or any other important social occasion at which orations are made. The main form of competition is for the right to speak first. Any talking chief present has the right formally to contend with any other for this highly coveted privilege. The competition is often settled by the rank of one or another of the contending talking chiefs, but the depth of an individual's traditional knowledge (especially of fa'alupega and genealogies), his eloquence, and his age are also major factors. Each talking chief argues his own case, and, as Brother Herman notes, the number of contestants gradually decreases as the participating individuals concede defeat, until only one is left. This form of competition is of great antiquity; as J. B. Stair, who arrived in Samoa in 1838, has noted, much stress was always laid upon the privilege of addressing a public assembly, and when the time came for a particular settlement to address the meeting "the whole of the speakers stood up and contended amongst themselves for the honour of speaking on that day." This custom is still followed, and on important occasions the competition may last for well over an hour. It also tends to be intensely emotional, with, for example, angry responses when one speaker interrupts another. Any opportunity to shame a rival into submission is eagerly grasped. For example, on 5 May 1966 Ape of Fasito'outa rebuked another talking chief, Tupa'i of Nu'usuatia, who had challenged his knowledge of genealogy, with the words: "You talk like a Fijian! Don't speak to me of that which lies beyond your understanding!" The humiliated Tupa'i at once withdrew from further contention. On another occasion, when an inexperienced but ambitious young talking chief made an egregious mistake in referring to the Tui Atua, his rival remarked crushingly, for all present to hear: "Laddie, just shut your mouth! Your mouth is fuddled, go back to school!"[12]

Sometimes the competitiveness of talking chiefs becomes so intense that they resort to physical violence. When making a standing oration a tulafale customarily grasps a long staff in one hand and a switch in the other; in Sa'anapu in 1967 I witnessed two visiting talking chiefs, competing for the right to speak, begin openly fighting for possession of the staff that they were both intent on using.

Because of the unsurpassed rank of the Tui Manu'a and his attendant talking chiefs, no tulafale from elsewhere in Samoa is able to win a fa'atau contest on the ceremonial ground of Ta'ū. I have seen talking chiefs of high rank from Western Samoa reduced to tears when faced with this overwhelming situation. Equally strong emotion is sometimes displayed by those who triumph in a fa'atau contest. On occasion even a seasoned talking chief will be so overcome as to weep in the elation of victory.

There is also, as will have become apparent from my discussion of rank, great competitiveness among titular chiefs. In Savai'i in 1835, George Platt observed that every chief was "jealous of his neighbor, wishing to be as great as he in every respect." As already noted, competition for succession to the position of paramount rank in western Samoa, the tafa'ifa, was almost always marked by violent conflict between rival contenders and their supporting districts. If one of these districts, as Robert Louis Stevenson remarked in 1892, bestowed its high title "on competitor A" it would be the signal and sufficient reason for the rival district to bestow its high title "on competitor B or C." This competitiveness, moreover, persisted long after the actual conferment of titles. Thus, as T. H. Hood noted in 1863, there was great jealousy among the principal chiefs, so much so that they never went to sleep "without guards on the watch lest they should be murdered by the often unbidden retainers of some rival chief." Although large-scale fighting over the succession to high titles ceased at the end of the nineteenth century with the establishment of the governments of German and of American Samoa, there is still in modern Samoa intense competition over titles, with frequent recourse, as in Western Samoa, to the Land and Titles Court. This competitiveness, furthermore, pervades the entire rank structure, so that throughout contemporary Samoa, as Franklin Young (who conducted research in both western and eastern Samoa in 1970 and 1971) has noted, "vying for *matai* . . . titles and social position" is of paramount importance. Again, Margaret Mackenzie (who did field research in Savai'i in 1976) has observed that in Samoa "competitiveness and manipulation pervade political contexts."[13]

Vying for titles now most commonly occurs within the confines of an extended family. I have on several occasions been privileged to join the assembled members of a family in their private deliberations on the succession to a chiefly title. Each occasion was marked by intense rivalry. Further, this rivalry is freely recognized by those involved. It is usual, indeed, for the dignified proceedings to begin with a solemn warning by the senior members of the family as to the perils of excessive competitiveness within an extended family. Despite these warnings there are often disputed successions and occasionally outbursts of rivalrous aggression. For example, in one case when the daughter of the sister of a talking chief, acting in accordance with his dying will, secured succession for his adopted son, a more senior holder of the title at issue assaulted her with a bamboo headrest.

Intense rivalry also frequently occurs among the different families making up a local polity. For example, in 1961 a note was found in front of the chiefly residence of Taimalie, one of the high-ranking titular chiefs of the village of Nofoali'i. It bore the words, "Taimalie, you have no power in this village, nor have you any rank in Nofoali'i." Fetu, a 19-year-old female member of the Taimalie family, who found this note, at once suspected Leuila, a 15-year-old female of a rival family. Fetu thereupon assaulted Leuila's 14-year-old sister. In the ensuing affray fourteen individuals varying in age from 14 to 62 and of both sexes, joined in the fighting. They were all convicted of provoking a breach of the peace, and Leuila, who admitted to writing the note, was fined £2.[14]

Addressing the U.S. Congressional Investigation Commission in 1930, Chief Su'a described the Samoans as a people steeped in family pride who "consider feasts and ceremonies that are not elaborate as a disgrace to the family." This pride in family is paralleled by a comparable pride in one's local polity and paramount chief. Mead was thus mistaken in claiming, as she did in 1937, that "Samoa relied to a very slight degree upon group rivalry as a cohesive force within the group." Rather, as John Soloi, the pastor of Fitiuta, remarked when I was discussing this point with him in 1967, "group rivalry is basic to Samoan politics." He instanced the intense rivalry between the two sections of Fitiuta, between the entire village of Fitiuta and the village of Ta'ū, and between the whole of Manu'a and Tutuila. Segmentary rivalries of these kinds, as I have already noted, abound in Samoan history, and they were certainly active in both western and eastern Samoa in the 1920s. Frances Hubbard Flaherty, who was in Savai'i in 1924, has recounted that when she and her husband brought a ceremonial virgin to Safune from the neighboring and rival village of Sasina, to appear in a film they were making, the women of Safune vowed this taupou would die before morning, such was "the intense rivalry that exists between Samoan villages." Mead herself, in a letter, mentions that the 'aumaga of the village of Ta'ū was thinking of burning down what was left of the village on the island of Ofu (an ancient rival of Ta'ū) for having stoned their pastor. It was the fiercely rivalrous spirit evident in contentions such as these to which George Drummond was referring, when in 1842 he described the "natural character" of the Samoans as being one "of ungovernable pride."[15]

This pride is also conspicuously displayed in elaborate and extravagant prestations. For example, when a chapel, measuring 120 feet by 40 feet, was opened in Leone, Tutuila, in 1839,

2300 pigs were slaughtered for the occasion, with other articles of food in proportion. A. W. Murray, in reporting this display by a local polity, attributed it principally to "a spirit of rivalry." Again, W. B. Churchward has noted that, when in competition with others, everything a village can afford is "ungrudgingly sacrificed" to add to the glorification of its highest ranking ceremonial virgin, as the principal ornament of its rank. On such occasions the rivalry between villages knows no bounds and may easily lead to altercation. For example, at the end of the great kava ceremony held at Fasito'otai in September 1901, to which I have already referred in discussing the ritualized rivalry of Ape and Tutuila, two quite separate ceremonial processions, one from the village of Fasito'outa and the other from Faleasiu, each bearing fine mats and other valuables and each headed by several taupou, happened to enter the ceremonial ground from different directions at the same time. As Osborn, who witnessed this event records, neither would give precedence. An altercation resulted, with more serious fighting being narrowly averted by the strenuous efforts of the local leaders and police.[16]

The main valuables disbursed on major ceremonial occasions are the exquisitely made fine mats, which for the Samoans are among the most important measures of traditional wealth and rank. These mats frequently become the objects of rivalrous contention, as revealed in an excerpt from the minutes of the Fono of Faipule (the appointed leaders of the people of Western Samoa) dating from 1909. In these minutes, fine mats, although described as being the wealth of Samoa, as bringing dignity to titular chiefs, and as being a help in time of trouble, were also called a principal source of misunderstandings and squabbles between chiefs and orators and between families and of poverty because of the propensity of Samoans to try to "equal the number of mats given by others" or to try to "outdo others." In 1916 this competitiveness over fine mats led the Faipule and the High Chiefs of Western Samoa to condemn what they considered to be the resultant underhand-scheming, quarreling, falsehood, selfish ambition, arrogance, avarice, and self-glorification. These, I would emphasize, are the judgments of the Samoans themselves about the competitiveness over fine mats that pervades their society.[17]

The lively consciousness of rank and the intense competitiveness that pervade the secular life of Samoans have also penetrated their religious institutions. When John Williams made his second voyage to Samoa in 1832 he found that the paramount chief of western Samoa wanted all of Williams' eastern Polynesian teachers of the Christian gospel to be brought to him first, and soon after this a serious quarrel broke out between the factions of the chief's sons about where the first Christian chapel in Samoa should be built, "each party wanting it on their own ground." Directly comparable difficulties arose with the arrival of the first resident missionaries. For example, when the new missionary, Alexander Chisholm took up residence at Sala'ilua on the south coast of Savai'i in June 1843, the people of Fogatuli, a village further to the west, were "so much under a discontented feeling," having wanted an English missionary for themselves, that they refused to let their teachers go to Chisholm for instruction, this reaction being rooted in "the jealousy which one land manifests against the other."[18]

In later years this rivalry was exploited by missionaries to raise funds for the London Missionary Society both in Samoa and other parts of the Pacific. The whole of Samoa was divided into religious districts, which were enjoined to compete with each other in the raising of funds, with the results being publicly announced each year. This was a new version of the competitive disbursement of food and property that had been a major social institution in pagan times, and the Samoans took to it with alacrity. The pioneer missionary George Pratt records that when in 1868 he visited a district extending from Safata to Aleipata (on the south coast of Upolu) they issued a challenge to all the other districts in Samoa to beat them in the making of contributions to the church. Pratt reminded them that his district (on the north coast of Savai'i) had once beaten them in a traditional game of chance. Taking up the challenge from Upolu, the people of Pratt's district surmounted every difficulty to raise "hard on £700 for the L.M.S." and to win the contest.[19]

This competitive raising of funds for the church soon became a major preoccupation of the Samoans. The initial competitiveness is among the families within a village, then among the villages of a district, and, finally, among all the districts of the Samoan archipelago. Considerable shame accompanies defeat by a rival family, village, or district, and those who come out on top are immensely proud of their competitive success. For example, when I visited the village of Fitiuta in Manu'a in 1967, one of the first pronouncements haughtily made to our traveling party was that Fitiuta had achieved the highest total in all Samoa during the previous year, with donations exceeding $3,000, and that 13,000 kegs of beef had been disbursed at the ceremonial opening of their new church.

The keenest competition is between the ancient village polities of Samoa. To avoid the shame of being outclassed, entire communities are ready to put themselves into debt. For example, on 17 December 1942, the people of Sa'anapu village arrived at the district meeting with the sum of £110 as the annual gift for their pastor, only to find that their closest rival village, Sataoa, had raised £130. After a hurried consultation, the Sa'anapu delegation anounced its total as £130; the resulting debt of £20 was gradually paid off during the following months. At the next such district meeting I attended, on 15 December 1966, Sa'anapu's gift to its pastor was £501 7s 4d., easily excelling the Sataoa total of £320 15s. At this there was general elation, and the next Sunday the senior deacon praised the Sa'anapu congregation with the words "Thanks for raising up our village." On another such occasion the comment made was, "Being below some other village is not what is wanted, but rather, the victory of Sa'anapu."

This same system of competitive giving was, as the records of the London Missionary Society show, fully established throughout Samoa at the time of Mead's research. This is confirmed by the report of Aletta Lewis, who was in American Samoa in 1929, that a pastor was able, "by stimulating the naturally strong competitive spirit" of the Samoans, to divert to himself perhaps half of the money that was earned by the people of a village in copra cutting, or by services to the naval population of Pago Pago.[20]

As further evidence of the lack of competitiveness among Samoans, Mead asserted in 1931 that "the Samoans deprecate all precocity." Each individual, she stated, was expected "not to exceed by any more than is possible the typical achievement of the slowest and stupidest member of the group." In 1937 this statement was embellished by the improbable generalizations that those who exceeded the slowest in a group brought "blushes to their parents' cheeks," and that when children who had achieved success in their formal education came home from school to report they had been put ahead of former companions "their parents hung their heads in shame."[21]

While it is true that in Samoa individuals who impudently question the views of those senior to them in age or rank are roundly condemned, there is commonly much competitiveness between peers, of whatever age. Mead's account is once again directly contradicted by the observations of other investigators. F. M. Keesing, who carried out field research in both American and Western Samoa within just a few years of Mead's sojourn in Manu'a, paid particular attention to education. Having noted "the urge to emulate and excel in forms of activity valued by the group" as being basic to the traditional pattern of Samoan life, Keesing went on to describe the "competitive spirit" that had emerged in the education systems set up by the New Zealand and American authorities. The competitive spirit among students and the overweening pride of parents in the outstanding educational achievements of their children were also phenomena that I regularly observed from 1940 onward as a member of the Education Department of Western Samoa. G. B. Milner, in his excellent *Samoan Dictionary*, illustrates the use of *felosia'i*, meaning "to compete against others," with the sentence "The children are competing for the first place in the class." This they indeed do in both the modern government schools and in the much older church schools, presided over by the village pastor, which were instituted soon after the arrival of the pioneer resident missionaries in 1836.[22]

When the Samoans encountered writing for the first time in the early 1830s, they flocked to the houses of the teachers John Williams had brought from eastern Polynesia "to learn this mysterious art, many of them coming eight to ten times each day, to be taught their letters." By 1842 there were in the Samoan islands, in addition to 11 missionaries, some 224 native teachers, most of them Samoan, and such was the eagerness for instruction that paper for writing had become a principal medium of exchange. From about this time onward prizes were given, and later certificates were issued, for superior educational achievement. Today such certificates can be seen prominently displayed in homes throughout the Samoan islands, including Manu'a.[23]

Further, as Holmes reported on the basis of his observations in American Samoa in 1954, "ability in formal education is always acclaimed." Indeed, I have often seen parents with tears in their eyes in intense pride at the public recognition (as at a school prize-giving ceremony) of the competitive success of one of their children. This pride in exceptional achievement also extends to entire communities. Thus, when on 18 December 1966 the pastor of Sa'anapu told the assembled people that for the first time in the history of the village a youth had succeeded in passing his university entrance examination, he began to weep and his voice trembled and broke with emotion. He had, he said later, been overcome with pride that one of his former students had brought such renown to Sa'anapu.[24]

The Samoans, then, within their social conventions based upon dominance and rank, are a highly competitive people, among whom the "extreme jealousy" and "ungovernable pride" on which the early missionaries remarked are conspicuously present to this day. These characteristics indeed are even present in the migrant Samoan communities in New Zealand, some of which I visited in 1968 and again in 1979. David Pitt and Cluny Macpherson report the observation of a European supervisor in a New Zealand factory (in which a number of migrant Samoans worked) that "if they see another Samoan rising above them they get jealous and try to pull him down."[25]

11

Aggressive Behavior and Warfare

IN HER DEPICTION of the ease and casualness of their society, Mead, as we have seen, gave special emphasis to the "unaggressiveness" of the Samoans, describing them as "one of the most amiable, least contentious, and most peaceful peoples in the world." They were, she reiterated in 1950, a "peaceful and constructive people" among whom warfare had been "stylized as part of the interrelationship between villages that were ceremonial rivals and occasioned few casualties." These assertions, on which Mead so relied in her general theorizing about Samoa, are markedly at variance with the facts of Samoan history.[1]

The reputation of the Samoans as an unusually bellicose people began, for Europeans, in 1787, with the fierce affray in which twelve members of the ill-fated La Pérouse Expedition and some thirty Tutuilans lost their lives. La Pérouse observed of the Samoans, "the least dispute between them is followed by blows from clubs, sticks or paddles; and often, no doubt, costs the combatants their lives. Almost all of them are covered with scars, which must have been the consequences of these private quarrels." In 1824 Otto von Kotzebue, who had had to force the Tutuilans from the sides of his ship with long poles when they tried to storm it, considered them to be "perhaps the most ferocious people to be met with in the South Seas." It was not, however, until the early 1830s that the bellicosity of the Samoans became firmly established through the observations and inquiries of the pioneer missionary and explorer John Williams.[2]

When Williams reached Savai'i from Tonga in 1830, a "devastating war" occasioned by the assassination of the chief Tamafaiga was raging in the district of A'ana at the western end of the island of Upolu. Williams could clearly see the villages of A'ana enveloped in flames and smoke. When the paramount chief, Malietoa Vai-inu-po, returned from the fighting to greet Williams and his fellow missionary Charles Barff, he gave them to understand that war was "his great delight" and said that the thing he most wanted, as he would be the laughing stock of his brother chiefs if he were not given it, was a musket. This war between the inhabitants of A'ana and the more numerous forces of Manono and its allies lasted for eight months, with frequent set battles involving hundreds of warriors. Williams recounts that during the course of this war, in which well over a thousand people lost their lives, canoes would arrive in Savai'i with the remains of those who had fallen, and that "the dismal howlings and lamentations of the relatives, their frantic behavior, the frightful lacerations they inflicted upon themselves with shells and shark's teeth, together with the horrid appearance of the victims," kept everyone in "a state of intense excitement and distress." When A'ana finally surrendered, more than four hundred of its inhabitants, including many women and children, who had been sheltering in forts, were "thrown indiscriminately into large fires," while others, according to Williams, were cut open and had their hearts torn out. At the end of this war those who had been defeated were, in accordance with Samoan custom, driven from their lands, and their houses and plantations were laid waste, so that when Thomas Heath toured A'ana some five years later he could "scarcely see a hut in a distance of ten miles, where formerly had dwelt perhaps 5,000 or 6,000 people."[3]

Whether any of the numerous wars of the earlier history of Samoa, many of which also involved entire districts, were as devastating as the A'ana war of 1830–1831, we cannot be sure; there is, however, substantial evidence that wars in pagan Samoa were "exceedingly frequent." Williams records that although ignorant of the art of writing the chiefs of Manono kept, in a sacred house on the nearby island of Apolima (which they used as a fortress), a basket in which each war in which they had fought had been marked by the depositing of a stone, the size of each stone indicating the magnitude of the war it commemorated. When these stones were counted in 1832, they numbered 197, and when Stair later took possession of this basket he found that some of the stones were much larger than others.[4]

Williams' landfall on 17 October 1832, on his second voyage to Samoa, was Ta'ū in Manu'a. He found that about four months earlier the settlement of Ta'ū, when attempting to invade and conquer the nearby island of Olosega with a fleet of about one hundred canoes (in retaliation for a previous killing in a long-standing feud), had suffered a severe defeat. Thirty-five of their number had been slain, a loss that more than decimated the able-bodied adult male population of the settlement of Ta'ū. Comparable death rates occurred, as I shall presently substantiate, in a war that took place between Ta'ū and Olosega some fifty years later.[5]

Such intervillage conflict, albeit in a less severe form, continued into the twentieth century. Thus, some four years after Mead's research in Manu'a there was, in direct continuation of their ancient feud, a major affray between Ta'ū and Olosega. Again, as Holmes noted, following his research in Manu'a and Tutuila in 1954, "serious conflicts between villages" often occurred and it was "not unusual for the government anthropologist in Tutuila to be summoned in the middle of the night to try to settle differences between two outlying villages before violence occurs." In Western Samoa in 1964, when its inhabitants numbered approximately 123,000, there were forty-nine affrays sufficiently serious to require intervention by the police, yielding the high rate of forty affrays per annum per 100,000 of population.[6]

Such affrays, which may involve from ten to fifty or more individuals of both sexes and all ages from rival local polities or from families of the same village, are in effect small-scale undeclared wars, in which fists, sticks, and stones tend to be used rather than more dangerous weapons. Affrays have long been characteristic of Samoan society; there are numerous reports of them in mission and other records. In 1836, for example, on Savai'i, Platt and Wilson observed a "regular fight" in which the members of two neighboring polities were "belaboring one another's heads with sticks and stones," a conflict occasioned by the people of one polity having "killed and baked a hog belonging to another."[7]

Affrays also commonly occur between rivalrous extended families of the same village, and may continue intermittently over several days until those involved are either apprehended and fined by the local fono or restrained by the police. In 1961, for example, such an affray occurred between two families, the Sa Oloaga and the Sa Manu'o, in Lufilufi on the north coast of Upolu. It began when Lusia and Peone, the 10- and 11-year old daughters of Suapusi, the chief of the Sa Oloaga, encountered Pota'e and Fa'ani, two adolescent female members of their long-standing rivals, the Sa Manu'o. Seeing Pota'e and Fa'ani, Peone remarked, for all to hear, "How superior are those excrement eaters' mouths!" This at once led to a fight in which Lusia and Peone, who were conveniently armed with sticks, managed to drive off their older rivals. The next day Maria, an older sister of Peone and Lusia, as she was going to church, came upon Pota'e and Fa'ani in the roadway. As she passed them, Pota'e coughed loudly. "Who are you coughing at?" said Maria. "At no one other than you!" retorted Pota'e. In the ensuing fight, which involved three girls from each family, Pota'e was hammered on the head with a stone so that she had to be taken to the hospital. At this Fetuana'i, the chief of the Manu'o family, sought out the wife of his rival chief, Suapusi. After further wounding insults, there was another serious affray between five members of each family, during which females on both sides bared their buttocks at one another. That night Opapo, of the Sa Manu'o, who had been drinking, was heard shouting (in English) outside the house of Oloaga Suapusi: "Oloaga! Come and have a war!" This "war" took place the following day with a fierce stone-throwing affray in which several individuals were badly injured. It was finally stopped by a number of staff-wielding talking chiefs. Nine members of the Sa Oloaga and ten members of the Sa Manu'o were later convicted of assault and provoking a breach of the peace. Lusia, the 10-year-old who had started it all, was fined £10.[8]

This case well illustrates various facets of the rivalrous aggression that is so characteristic of Samoan society: for example, the concern of rivals about their relative rank, the way in which fights are willfully provoked by verbal insults or other displays, the quickness with which a rival takes offense, the readiness of others of the same group to be drawn into the fighting; the vigor with which talking chiefs act to quell an affray; and finally, the fact that adolescent girls are prone to rivalrous aggression, just as are adolescent boys. In 1963, for example, also in Lufilufi, an 18-year-old girl, Fa'atupu, having become incensed with Pese, a 32-year-old woman of another 'āiga, for having remarked that Fa'atupu had "sucked up" to the village pastor, rushed with her brothers into the house of Pese and her mother and struck each of them repeatedly on the head with a stone while her brothers held their arms. During the attack on the mother, moreover, Fa'atupu's father, who was also present, shouted, "Bash her until her brains burst forth!" Both Pese and her mother were admitted to the hospital with suspected concussion. Fa'atupu and her two brothers were convicted of having caused "actual bodily harm" and were heavily fined.[9]

Affrays involving males tend to result in much more serious injuries. In Safotu on the north coast of Savai'i in October 1961, a 25-year-old Safotu man fought with and knocked unconscious a male rival from the nearby village of Avao. He was pursued by ten young men of Avao, hit twice on the head with a Samoan cricket bat, and then stoned to death. Five of his assailants were adolescents. All ten assailants were convicted of manslaughter and given sentences ranging from three to seven years.[10]

Affrays also occur in American Samoa. On 30 October 1967, for example, in the village of Fagasa on the north coast of the island of Tutuila, after a rock throwing fight between two families who had long been locked in a feud over a plot of land, five people were taken to the hospital, and the fono of Fagasa threatened to exile from the polity one of the families concerned.[11]

With affrays such as these having an annual incidence (in Western Samoa) of 40 per 100,000 of population, and with the annual incidence of assault with bodily injury (see p. 164) being 105.1 per 100,000 of population, no credence can be given to Mead's assertion of 1950 that in Samoa "hostility between individuals" is expressed "covertly in the form of gossip and political machinations rather than in open clashes," nor is there any empirical ground for accepting her assertion that Samoans "never hate enough to want to kill anybody."[12]

The Samoan term for the cherishing of anger is *ita fa'amoe-moe,* literally "anger that has been slept upon," and such anger readily turns into hatred. And when hatred has taken root, murderous attacks do sometimes occur. In 1963, for example, Sio, a 20-year-old youth of Lotofaga on the south coast of Upolu, became so suffused with hatred for Aupito, a 39-year-old chief of a collateral branch of Sio's family, "because of his ungrateful and wrongful doings" over the possession of a title that after midnight he crept into Aupito's house and slashed at his head with a long-bladed bush knife. Had not Aupito managed to avoid this blow he would certainly have been killed, for it cut deeply into the pillow and mattress on which he had been lying. Sio was convicted of attempted murder and sentenced to ten years" imprisonment.[13]

In another case of the many I might instance, Salu, a 23-year-old man of Vailoa village in Aleipata at the eastern end of Upolu, became incensed following the hearing of a dispute over his family's title at the Land and Titles Court on 15 December

1964, at which Saumalu Tui, a 65-year-old ali'i had given evidence that Salu judged to be in error. Salu came bitterly to hate this older member of his 'āiga, who was a first cousin of his deceased father. On New Year's Eve, 1964, in the Methodist Church at Vailoa, a service was held in which Saumalu Tui preached the sermon, while his nephew Salu played the organ. Toward the end of his sermon, Saumalu Tui exhorted the assembled villagers to "give up both lying and contending against chiefly authority in the hope that in the New Year they could achieve a new village." When Salu heard these words, and, in particular, Saumalu Tui's adjuration to give up lying, he was so overcome with hatred (as he later confessed to the police) that he at once left the church. Some time later, when Saumalu Tui was sitting outside his home scraping taro, Salu shot him in the head. When Saumalu Tui recovered consciousness in the hospital and was told who had been his assailant, he was "astonished," for, as he told the police, he had always looked upon his organ-playing nephew as "very good and quiet." Salu was convicted of having caused grievous bodily harm and sentenced to three years in prison.[14]

That their society is conducive to aggressive behavior is well recognized by the Samoans themselves. In the words of Anesone, the pastor of Mulinu'u, at a public reconciliation on 9 November 1966 between two litigating villages from the south coast of Upolu: "Conflict comes easily in this country of Samoa; a village that lives in peace is rarely found."[15]

Again, Sir Angus Sharp, a former New Zealand Commissioner of Police, on retiring in mid 1978 after seventeen months as Commissioner of Police in Western Samoa, while praising the Samoans as a people with "a well deserved reputation for courtesy, hospitality and generosity," went on to observe that despite these virtues, the amount of violence among Samoans was "frightening." In 1977, he noted, 10 murders had been committed in Western Samoa, with a population of only 150,000. This is a rate of 6.66 per 100,000 of population. In American Samoa, in 1977, when the population was about 31,000, there were 8 criminal homicides, which equals a rate of about 25 per 100,000.[16]

In *Studies in Homicide,* M. E. Wolfgang presents a table of homicide rates of sixty-one countries that reported to the United Nations, ranging, in 1960, from Colombia, with 34.0 per 100,000, to Ireland with 0.2; the rate for the United States was 4.5. Western Samoa's homicide rate in 1977 was more than three times higher than that of Singapore, the median country in Wolfgang's list, while the rate in American Samoa was more than thirteen times higher.[17]

In cases of serious assault, that is of assault resulting in some kind of bodily injury, the comparisons are even more significant, for it is violence of this kind that has long been especially characteristic of Samoan society. There are, I am aware, numerous pitfalls in the path of those who would compare the crime rates of different countries. In Samoa, for example, a very high percentage of delicts, including assault, are dealt with directly by the chiefs of a local polity in an especially summoned fono, and so are not communicated to the police. This means that the percentage of cases of assault actually reported to the police in Samoa is likely to be considerably smaller than in some other countries. Again, there may be differences from one country to another in the definition of serious assault. All I am interested in, however, is a general and approximate indication of the comparative level of violence in Samoan society. If then we concentrate on cases of assault "causing bodily injury" that were reported to the police in Western Samoa during the three years 1964–1966, the rate per 100,000 of population was 105.1 per annum. This compares with rates of 11.1 for New Zealand (for the male population aged 16 and over during the years 1957–1964), of 17.7 for Australia (1964–1966) and of 62.9 for the United States (cases of aggravated assault in 1965). On these figures the Western Samoan rate of cases of serious assault was, in the mid 1960s, about 67 percent higher than the U.S. rate, 494 percent higher than the Australian rate, and 847 percent higher than the New Zealand rate.[18]

If we next turn to cases of common assault known to the police in Western Samoa during the years 1964–1966, the rate per 100,000 of population was 773.35 per annum. The comparable U.S. rate (arrests during 1965) was 154.8, which means that the

Western Samoan rate for common assault in the mid 1960s was about five times higher than that of the United States.

These Samoan rates of homicide and assault, even if the above comparisons be only very approximate, when taken together with the cases I have presented, do demonstrate clearly that the people of Samoa are greatly given to interpersonal aggression, and are thus very far from being, as Mead claimed, one of the "least contentious and most peaceful peoples in the world."

In constructing her picture of the "general casualness" of Samoan culture, Mead also made light of the significance of warfare in Samoan history. For example, in her monograph of 1930 on the social organization of Manu'a, she stated that war, in the Manu'an islands, was "slight and spasmodic." Indeed, she attributed what she supposed to be the rudimentary development of religion in Manu'a to "the small population and lack of war." It was "plausible," she wrote, to suggest that "the numerous tales of conflict in myths" might "all have been inspired by the same few intervillage clashes." War in Samoa then, as depicted by Mead (in 1928), was merely "a matter of village spite, or small revenge, in which only one or two individuals would be killed," or (as she stated in 1937) "a part of the ceremonial rivalry between villages" being "fought for no gains other than prestige," in which case, once again, "casualties were low." In Manu'a, according to Mead, there were "no war gods," "bravery in warfare was never a very important matter," and the warrior did not hold "any important place in the society."[19]

Mead's depiction of Samoan warfare is deeply at variance with the judgments of both the Samoans and the Europeans who witnessed Samoan warfare, in both the eastern and western islands of the archipelago, during the nineteenth century. Moa, an ali'i of Olosega, one of the islands of Manu'a, began his statement to the American Samoan Commission in 1930 with the observation that the Samoan people had been "very fond of war," and Tuitele, of Tutuila, told the Commission that in former centuries "district warred with district" and "island warred with island." Again, the ali'i Tuatagaloa, of the Falealili District of the island of Upolu, in a speech to the Western Samoan

Royal Commission in 1927, said that Samoans had long been "accustomed to wars and bloodshed."[20]

In the words of Murray, whose experience of Samoa, including Manu'a, extended over several decades from 1836 onward, "domestic and other feuds often disturbed the peace of the community, and wars, on greater or smaller scale, were of frequent occurrence and sometimes were attended with deeds of revolting cruelty." Stair, who was in western Samoa from 1838 to 1845, reports that wars amongst the Samoans were "frequent and bloody," and that the islands were seldom free from "actual warfare or local quarrels." When Wilkes arrived in Manu'a in October 1839, where, as Williams records, there had been a major conflict in 1832, he found the people again on the verge of war. Of the Samoan archipelago at large Wilkes notes that "scarcely a month passed without quarrels being avenged ... with blows." He also records that in the war of 1830–1831 the inhabitants of A'ana in Upolu, had been "almost exterminated." King, in September 1864, following the outbreak of hostilities between Falealupo and a number of other villages at the western end of Savai'i, observed that war was "the one absorbing thought of all"; and Whitmee, who was (like King) in Samoa from 1863 to 1872, described the Samoans as being "in war ... furious," and as exhibiting, when the war spirit was upon them, characteristics "totally different from anything one would think them capable of when seen in time of peace," being ready to "butcher and mutilate one another in the most barbarous manner." These statements are confirmed by Krämer, who has described the "violent passions" of the otherwise amiable Samoans, which in time of war were "set recklessly free."[21]

Krämer records that in Samoan warfare it was usual for male captives to be killed, after which everything that had fallen into the hands of the victors was carried away, while the settlements of the defeated were plundered and their plantations destroyed in the general devastation. That such devastation occurred is fully substantiated by Powell's eyewitness account of the war that broke out in Tutuila in 1859, following the murder of a young man of the family of Mauga, the high chief of Pago Pago. Because Le'iato, a rival ali'i, gave refuge to the kindred of those responsible for this murder, "war mania" was soon rampant among the forces led by Mauga, and when Le'iato and his allies abandoned their villages and fled for safety to an off-shore island, all of their houses were burnt, their plantations destroyed, their coconut and breadfruit trees cut down, and the graves of their dead desecrated. Such desecration commonly involved the taking of skulls, and, as Hardie recorded in 1844, it was a widespread practice in ancient Samoa, when invasion was apprehended for the skulls of departed relatives to be disinterred "to secure them from the insults of the invaders."[22]

The slain on the battlefield were also, in Frazer's words, "treated with great indignity," their heads being hacked off and carried in triumph to be paraded before the high chiefs of the victors. Pritchard, who witnessed Samoan warfare during the decade 1848–1858, has given an account of the excitement and pride of the successful warrior as he capered before his approving chiefs with the head he had acquired, shouting in triumph "I've taken a man!" "To a young Samoan," writes Pritchard, "this is the realization of his highest ambition, to be thus publicly thanked by the chiefs for slaying an enemy in mortal combat" and then to become known, far and wide, as a *toa,* or "brave."[23]

Such ferocious warfare produced, as Krämer notes, a longing for vengeance and retribution and frequently led to atrocities and other forms of revengeful behavior. In 1886 Josia, a Samoan pastor, recorded that in a war at Lepā, on the south coast of Upolu, numbers of children were killed, some being hung in trees to have spears thrown at them, while others were cut in half. Again, Williams records that following the war of 1832 between Ta'ū and Olosega, a young woman obtained the head of the man who had killed her father. This head she burnt gradually upon a fire and, having beaten it to a powder, "cooked food on it which she ate with great delight." In some instances, as Hunkin reported from Manu'a in 1845, cannibalism was practiced "in the case of prisoners taken in war." Extremes of retaliatory aggression were also practiced following the assassination of the tyrannical Tamafaiga in 1830 by the people of A'ana, and, in particular, for the mutilation of his body. As Williams records, after Tamafaiga's head had been severed from his body, his legs were hacked off for his "gadding about to other people's settlements," his hands for his "seizing of other people's property," his "parts of generation" for his having had "connection with other men's wives," and his tongue for his "intolerable insolence." Because of these extreme indignities the war of 1830–1831 was fought, as Williams reports, with "frightful severity." Thus, as already noted, some hundreds of women and children were cast into huge fires, and according to Heath several human victims, mostly boys were "baked and eaten like hogs."[24]

The casualties in the Samoan wars for which we have historical information, as I have already indicated, were very far from being trivial. When the people of A'ana reoccupied their devastated lands in 1836, some 3000 returned to a district where, according to Heath, perhaps 5000 or 6000 people had formerly lived. From this and other evidence it would seem likely that from 1000 to 1500 people, or up to a quarter of the population of A'ana, lost their lives in the war of 1830–1831, and the dead of Manono and her allies probably ran into some hundreds. While this is certainly the most devastating war of which we have reliable knowledge, there is also evidence of substantial loss of life in other conflicts. For example, when hostilities broke out anew between Manono and A'ana and their allies in June 1848, there was further large-scale destruction of the houses and plantations of A'ana; as Hardie reported in August 1848, 130 were killed in the first two months of fighting.[25]

There is well-substantiated evidence that warfare in Manu'a, where the total population in the mid nineteenth century was little more than 1400, was comparably destructive. Indeed, during the nineteenth century the people of Manu'a had the reputation of being exceptionally bellicose. For example, Murray, from his own observations as well as those of Matthew Hunkin, who was stationed in Manu'a for six years from 1842 onward, has noted that it was "the universal testimony of all the islands," as of the Manu'ans themselves, that they greatly exceeded the Samoans of the western islands in "barbarity and ferocity." Similarly, Young has noted that historically the

Manu'ans have had the reputation of "being the fiercest of warriors." As already recounted, the war of 1832 in Manu'a resulted, if Williams' testimony be accepted, in the deaths of approximately 16 percent of the adult male population of the settlement of Ta'ū, a very severe rate of loss. Heavy losses also occurred with the resumption of warfare between Ta'ū and Olosega during the years 1866–1871, a period for which Powell's reports provide detailed and reliable information. Of either this war or that of 1832, Mead makes no mention whatsoever.[26]

The war of 1866–1871 was precipitated when Lalolagi, a young chief of Olosega, usurped the age-old prerogative of the Tui Manu'a of having a conch-shell trumpet blown by a talking chief when he went on a ceremonial journey. In retaliation for this insult to their paramount chief, the polity of Ta'ū in 1866 launched an attack on the island of Olosega, in which seven warriors of Olosega and three of Ta'ū were killed. After another affray in August 1867, in which six from Ta'ū lost their lives, the forces of Ta'ū, in September 1867, with a loss of nine of their own number, killed fifteen of their enemies, after which the entire population of Olosega fled to Tutuila, leaving their lands to be devastated by Ta'ū. Two years later, in 1869, after their return to their island, a newly elected Tui Olosega and the members of his party were attacked and killed during a ceremonial visit to Ta'ū, and the polity of Fitiuta, the ancient rival of Ta'ū, gave refuge to the followers of this murdered chief. Ta'ū attacked Fitiuta in January 1871, and eight men from Ta'ū lost their lives, two of them having their heads taken. By the time Powell finally succeeded in bringing a halt to these protracted hostilities in May 1871, he had recorded 55 male deaths over a period of six years. In 1862, a few years before this war began, the total population of Manu'a consisted of 688 females and 780 males. From data recorded by Powell, it is known that approximately 40 percent of these 780 males were boys, leaving a total of about 470 men. On these figures, the 55 men killed in warfare between 1866 and 1871 represents a loss of 11.7 percent of the adult male population of Manu'a, which is, once again, a severe rate of loss. Indeed, from the available data on Samoan warfare during the nineteenth century there is good reason to accept

Brown's view that "the wars of the Samoans tended for a long time to check the natural increase of population." These same data, furthermore, make it plainly evident that warfare in Samoa, far from being characterized, as Mead asserted, by low casualties, was, in fact, decidedly destructive of human life.[27]

Moreover, instead of having been, as Mead supposed, a form of stylized "ceremonial rivalry," warfare in Samoa was in reality a violent and ruthless struggle for political dominance. As Ella has noted, each of the political spheres of Samoa was "divided into two parties" the *mālō*, or "conquerors," and the *to'ilalo*, or "conquered and enslaved." This divisiveness gave rise to an unending struggle for supremacy, with first one alliance of local polities and then another gaining dominance. A war, Erskine noted in 1853, was not considered at an end until the conquered party made "with many degrading ceremonies and promises, full submission to the victors," and this outcome could only be achieved when one side had inflicted a crippling defeat on the other. Samoan warfare was thus a violent struggle between rival polities for outright dominance, and it is this fact which accounts for the ferocity and tenacity with which wars were fought, as also for the numerous casualties and not infrequent atrocities. In September 1853, for example, more than five years after the struggle between Manono and A'ana and their allies had again erupted into open conflict in June 1848, Turner reported that Manono and Savai'i were "as determined as ever on having the upper hand" while A'ana and her ally Atua, rather than submit to their traditional rivals, were ready to "die first," with each side being "bent on the other's ruin." Similarly, in Manu'a, as Williams observed in 1832, there was a mālō that held supremacy in consequence of being the strongest. In Manu'a this supremacy rested with the paramount chief of the local polity of Ta'ū, the Tui Manu'a, and, as already recounted, when the people of Olosega challenged this supremacy in 1866 by the usurping of one of the Tui Manu'a's traditional prerogatives, they were defeated and forced to surrender their lands, for a time, to the mālō of Ta'ū. In Samoa then, as the history of their warfare demonstrates, the rank system was derived from, and continuously depended upon, the attainment of political dominance by force of arms. Further, the high levels of aggression noted earlier in this chapter, which still obtain in Samoa, stem predominantly, today as in the past, from the numerous situations of contentious rivalry generated by dominance and rank.[28]

In Samoan society, in which those who conquered were of the highest rank, the prowess of the warrior (contrary to Mead's assertion) was valued above all else, with bravery in warfare being esteemed as the most important of all manly attributes. In Samoan values, as the novelist Albert Wendt has noted, the coward was execrated beyond all others. Krämer, following Pratt, lists no fewer than twelve terms in the Samoan language, all of them derogatory, referring to cowards. It is to Mead's assertions about the Samoans' lack of appreciation of bravery in warfare, and her related claims as to the "scant premium ... upon fortitude and endurance," that Samoan men take the keenest exception. For example, in Si'ufaga in 1967, when I repeated Mead's statement that the warrior did not hold any important place in Manu'an society, the immediate and irate response of one of the orators of the high chief Lefiti was, "How could a warrior who has demonstrated his prowess on behalf of his polity possibly lack importance!"[29]

As Williams noted in 1832, warriors were in fact "held in great estimation by the chiefs," who supplied them with their every need and forbade them to engage in ordinary work. Throughout Samoa, furthermore, the holders of the highest chiefly titles were all descendants of illustrious warriors. In the eastern islands, as noted in Chapter 9, Ali'a Tama was the warrior from whom the paramount rank of Ta'ū and the Tui Manu'a stemmed, while in the western islands the august title of Malietoa (which is at present held by Malietoa Tanumafili II, the Head of State of Western Samoa) was acquired in the thirteenth century when the brothers Tuna and Fata, as they drove the last of the Tongan invaders from Samoan shores, were hailed by the departing Tui Tonga Talakaifaike with the words, "Brave warriors! Well fought! I will not again venture to Samoa in a war canoe!" The memory of this occasion still excites the pride of Samoans, as does Marathon that of the Greeks.[30]

R. S. Moore and J. R. Farrington, who accompanied the congressional commission to American Samoa in 1931, were shown a 150-year-old war club with which, they say, a "hero had slain many enemies and won a place in village history similar to that of George Washington in American history." When such a warrior fell in battle his obsequies were marked, as Pratt notes, by a fire that was kept burning for seven days, and his war club, as Pritchard mentions, was often laid on his grave as a "mute record of his valor and prowess." Further, in most Samoan polities there were traditionally vanguards, the warriors of which, as Turner notes, boasted of their right to lead any attack and, like Spartans, of the "glory of dying in battle."[31]

In Samoan society, then, in the nineteenth and earlier centuries, the warrior held a place of high importance. Even today, decades after the suppression of open warfare by European governments, young Samoan men can be heard, especially when intoxicated, giving voice to the high-pitched challenge of former times and volubly claiming the vaunted status of a warrior of some local polity.

Among such a warlike people there were, not surprisingly, numerous war gods. Turner in his classic account of the religion of pagan Samoa discusses about seventy superior gods (as he calls them), more than half of whom were war gods, with Le Fanoga, who was incarnate in the owl, being one of the most important of them in both the eastern and western islands.[32] Here, once again, Mead's account is both mistaken and confused. For example, having asserted in *Social Organization of Manu'a* that there were "no war gods" in Manu'a, she goes on to record that the owl, whose cry "meant war," was "a war spirit" on Ofu, one of the islands of Manu'a. Further, Le Fanoga, the "war god" of whom she makes mention, had, as Powell (whom she cites) makes clear, originated in Manu'a. He was a son of Tagaloa, and incarnate in the owl, which was, as Mead herself records, the incarnation of a god "formerly worshipped" in Ta'ū.[33] Hardie, writing in the late 1830s, identified the war god Le Fanoga as an attendant upon the Tui Manu'a, and recorded the following prayer offered to Le Fanoga "in time of war":

O Fanoga, compassionate us, receive our offerings and be propitious to us and make us prosperous; save us from injury and death. When our enemies pursue us make our backs invisible to them, and let it be bright and clear before us. May no yam holes or other pits or snares be in our way, and make us strong and quick of foot that we may escape unhurt. When we pursue our enemies, let their backs be visible to us but we invisible to them; let yam holes, and other pits and snares and obstacles be in the way that we may overtake and kill them and obtain the victory and ruling power![34]

That the Manu'ans did indeed have war gods, upon whom they called for strength and assistance, is made clear not only by Powell and Hardie but also by Williams, who in Ta'ū in October 1832 recorded, in Samoan, a prayer that he translates: "O Tagaloa! Make your people valiant! Conquer and drive away those who make war on us!" In Manu'a, as in the rest of Samoa during the nineteenth and earlier centuries, far from being "slight and spasmodic" as Mead would have it, warfare was a common occurrence and often highly destructive of human life and property.[35]

12

Religion: Pagan and Christian

MEAD'S GRADUATE STUDIES, which she completed under Boas' supervision shortly before leaving for Samoa in 1925, involved the comparative study of canoes, houses, and tattooing as described in the then available literature on Hawaiians, Tahitians, the Maori of New Zealand, Marquesans, and Samoans. In 1928 she approached the pagan religion of Samoa in a similar way, asserting that Hawaii, Tahiti, New Zealand, and the Marquesas all out-distanced Samoa "in richness and variety of religious forms and beliefs and in the relative importance of religion in the lives of the people." As compared with other parts of Polynesia, the pagan Samoans (especially in Manu'a) gave, she claimed, but "the slightest attention to religion," and had "no temples," and "no religious festivals." "A libation poured to the family god" at the evening kava ceremony completed an individual's religious duties; "all contacts with the supernatural were accidental, trivial, uninstitutionalized," and both "institutionalized religion and personal psychic experience" were "exceedingly underdeveloped." Mead offered an apparently plausible explanation to accompany these assertions: "A strong religious interest," she surmised, was among the things that would have disturbed "the nice balance of Samoan society," and so it had been "outlawed" from a "social structure" that simply had "no room for the gods."[1]

These views, at which Mead arrived at a time when the pagan religions of western Polynesia were still little understood by anthropologists (Raymond Firth's *The Work of the Gods in Tikopia* was not published until 1940) almost wholly misconstrue the nature and significance of religion in both ancient and twentieth-century Samoa. Fortunately, the writings of John Williams and others provide a detailed and accurate account of the highly developed religious life of the pagan Samoans of the early 1830s as well as of Samoan Christianity from that time onward.[2]

Having had extensive experience of Raiatea and other parts of eastern Polynesia from 1817 onward, Williams, when he encountered the Samoans in the early 1830s, was immediately impressed by the "very peculiar" nature of their system of religion, which differed greatly from that "of every other group" then known "in the South Seas." What initially struck Williams was that, in marked contrast to eastern Polynesia, there were in Samoa no idols, "no altars stained with human blood, no *maraes* strewed with the skulls and bones of its numerous victims," and no elaborate temples devoted to special rites. Because of the conspicuous absence of these basic elements of eastern Polynesian religion it was common for Rarotongans and others to refer to the Samoans as "godless," yet, as Williams emphasized, the pagan Samoans in fact had many gods to whom they constantly offered "mouth worship" and with whom they were wont "on all occasions" to converse. "Each chief and almost every man," as Aaron Buzacott noted in 1836, "had his god, or *aitu*, the representations of which he would consider sacred, and treat ... with the utmost respect." These aitu, which were commonly incarnate in some bird, fish, reptile, or insect, were looked upon, however, as inferior deities, far above which was Tagaloa-a-Lagi, the "supreme god and creator of everything."[3]

These accounts by Williams and Buzacott are confirmed by Horatio Hale, the ethnographer who accompanied the Wilkes Expedition on its visit to Samoa in 1839. According to Hale, when a Samoan woman was in pains of child birth, numerous gods were invoked in succession, and the deity whose name was being invoked at the moment of birth became the "tutelary deity" of the infant. Connected with each tutelary deity was "some particular prohibition" (generally against eating the creature in which this deity was supposed to be incarnate), which the person under this god's protection was required scrupulously to observe. Again, when an individual swore by his god nothing would "induce him to make a false asseveration." George Turner, whose study of Samoan religion extended over some forty years from 1841 onward, mentions a total of 120 of these tutelary deities. In addition to this personal or tutelary god, according to Turner, everyone revered at least four other gods: a family god, a village god, a district god, and a war god. In his classic *Samoa a Hundred Years Ago and Long Before*, published in 1884, Turner lists the names of some four score of these deities. He also records that "a flaming fire" was the "regular evening offering to the gods," at which time the members of a family bowed their heads while their chief "prayed for prosperity from the gods great and small." Again, W.T. Pritchard records that at every kava ceremony the first cup was offered to some god, most comonly to Tagaloa, by being "held up and waved with a circular motion towards the heavens," and then "solemnly poured on the ground."[4]

These beliefs and practices were all peculiarly Samoan, yet what made their system of religion so very peculiar in Williams' eyes was the fact that pagan Samoans had direct oracular communication with their gods. As Williams graphically describes in his journal of 1832, the first sign of an individual's coming under the influence of a god was a violent muscular agitation with which he was suddenly seized. This generally commenced in "one of his breasts," which became greatly agitated while the rest of his body remained quiet. At length, however, the other parts of his body yielded to the agitating influence of the indwelling god until the medium shook "most dreadfully" and became "frantic." The god then spoke through the lips of his chosen vessel. If there was, says Williams, any subject that happened to be under consideration, it would be decided by the god's utterances. Again, if a polity or family was suffering under any calamity, the god would "upbraid the chief with his crimes," saying that "he, the god," had been "privy to all his actions." At last the inspired medium, worn out with fatigue, would become quiescent, and, having slept, would awake as if unconscious of anything having happened to him.[5]

Williams is here describing the institution of spirit mediumship on which the remarkable pagan religion of Samoa was centrally based. A spirit medium was said to be a *taula aitu*, or anchor of the spirits, or alternatively a *va'a aitu*, or vessel of the spirits, and was believed to be especially prone to possession by gods and spirits. As George Brown also noted, the gods and other spirits, including on occasion ancestral ghosts, were supposed to enter into and take temporary possession of spirit mediums. Then, the presence of a god having been evidenced by the medium's profoundly altered (and in fact dissociated) psychological state, the transformed voice with which the medium spoke was taken to be the actual voice of the entity possessing him. A sacred seance followed between the immanently present god and his human audience, who, "in the most polite language," held converse with him, seeking his counsel and hanging on his every word.[6]

It was usual, as J.B. Stair notes, for each family to have its own taula aitu, and this office could be held by the chief of a family, by his sister, or by some other member with the requisite oracular powers. Through this medium the members of a family were able to maintain contact both with their family god and with the ghosts of their ancestors. Various maladies were believed to be caused by the anger of some ghost in which case a special seance was held to ascertain what might be done to assuage this anger and so heal the hurt it had caused. According to

Pritchard, there was also in each local polity a particular taula aitu whose office was hereditary, with "a nephew, perhaps more frequently than a son, assuming the holy and coveted functions." It was the privilege of this medium to appoint feast days in honor of the god of his community, and on occasion to be possessed by him. Again, in time of impending conflict, the war god of a village would be consulted by spirit mediums.[7]

At other times, when kava and food were offered in their honor, the gods of a major family would possess for a time one of its acknowledged mediums. Such a medium, as in Tikopia, could be of high rank, and was often one of the titular chiefs with whom the gods of a family were especially identified. Thomas Powell was informed in Ta'ū in 1870 that the thirty-fourth Tui Manu'a, who had been killed in about 1820 in a war with Fitiuta, had been a medium of the gods. In Manu'a in 1832, Williams was told that the people "went into the bush . . . to hold conversations" with their "great spirit" Tagaloa; it was on such occasions that the Tui Manu'a would have been possessed by Tagaloa, the supreme god from whom the Tui Manu'a was believed to be descended.[8]

In pagan Samoa, then, a medium could emerge from anywhere in the rank structure as long as he or she had the capacity to evince, when in a dissociated state, oracular powers. Thus, while in most instances, as Ella notes, the office of medium belonged to chiefs, and, if suitable individuals were available, was hereditary, it was also "often taken up, or given, on account of some malformation, or from a striking peculiarity in temper or disposition." Further, because of the central importance that was given in ancient Samoa to direct communication with gods, ghosts, and spirits, spirit mediums were, as Brown records, very important personages who often came to exercise great influence. The most celebrated instance of this in Samoan history was Tamafaiga, who, having become the taula aitu of Manono, the ruling power in the western islands in the early nineteenth century, went on to become the tupu, or "king" of western Samoa, and, because of his seeming occult powers, to be worshipped as a god, before being assassinated for his tyrannical excesses by the people of A'ana in 1830.[9]

The islands of Ofu and Olosega viewed from Lumā on the island of Ta'ū, the site of Mead's fieldwork in 1925–1926. These three islands collectively are known as Manu'a.

The island of Ta'ū at about the time of Mead's stay there in 1925–1926. The U.S.S. *Ontario* is at anchor beyond the reef of the village of Lumā. Faleasao bay and village are at the far left.

The naval medical dispensary on Ta'ū, where Mead made her headquarters. This photograph was taken in 1967 when the building was no longer in use.

A Samoan round house, photographed in 1967.

A *taupou* (ceremonial virgin) wearing the traditional *tuiga,* photographed in 1967.

Franz Boas in 1906.

Ruth Benedict in about 1925.

Margaret Mead in the late 1920s.

Mead was thus plainly in error in asserting in 1928 that in ancient Samoa "the individual whose religious interest and unstable temperament gave him a reputation for oracular powers was given no accepted place in a pattern where religion claimed so little attention," and that "all contacts with the supernatural were accidental, trivial and uninstitutionalized" and personal psychic experience "exceedingly underdeveloped."[10]

Similarly, Mead's statements that there were no temples and no religious festivals in pagan Samoa are directly contradicted by the historical evidence. The house in which sacred seances were regularly held was termed a *malumalu*, and, as the setting in which the gods communicated directly with humans, was very much a temple. Indeed, the term *malumalu* is now used to refer to the Christian churches, one or more of which is to be found in every Samoan village. Again, as both Pratt and Turner record, almost every month in the Samoan year was the occasion for some kind of festival for a god. The first month of the year, for example, was called Tagaloa Fua (*fua* meaning fruit), and was preeminently the season for great offerings to Tagaloa. This festival of pagan times still persists, moreover, in modified form, in many parts of Samoa, with the principal offerings of food now going to the village pastor as the earthly representative of Jehovah, who supplanted Tagaloa in the mid-nineteenth century.[11]

The ancient Samoans, then, quite contrary to Mead's assertions, were a highly religious people with a system of religion which was, it is now known, essentially similar to that of pagan Tikopia. Firth, in his illuminating *Rank and Religion in Tikopia*, lists nine major elements of Tikopia paganism, all of which are also characteristic of the pagan religion of the Samoans. These elements, in abbreviated and slightly modified form, are, in the case of Samoa: (1) belief in a pantheon of spirits and gods, culminating in the supreme creator god, Tagaloa; (2) an ancestor cult directly linked with the family system; (3) the worship of gods and ancestors, involving prayers and offerings: (4) the use of material media, including temples and other sacra; (5) a concept of a soul which at death goes to an afterworld; (6) elaborate myths of creation and of the deeds of the gods; (7) numerous spirit mediums, aligned with the system of rank, with the titular chiefs in ultimate control; (8) a series of periodic celebrations at specific seasons of the year, involving social expression in dancing and elaborate ceremonies; and, finally (9) a sense of integral relationship between religious practices and the general welfare of the community. Firth comments that this form of pagan religion was "a highly integrated system with a moral jurisdiction over the Tikopia community." This was also true for pagan Samoa, and particularly so because of the development there, much more than in Tikopia, of a supreme god, Tagaloa, who overlooked the affairs of those he had created. This development, moreover, was one that Mead conspicuously neglected, as a result of having been "very doubtful," in her ignorance of the historical sources I am about to cite, that Tagaloa was "especially the god of the Manuans."[12]

When Williams arrived off the island of Ta'ū in 1832, his schooner was boarded, to his astonishment, by Paraifara, a Christian convert from Raivavae in Eastern Polynesia who with a number of others had reached Ta'ū after becoming lost at sea during a voyage from Tabuai. By 1832 these castaways had been on Ta'ū for about three years, had built a small chapel, and, having acquainted themselves with the religious beliefs of the Manu'ans, had persuaded some of them to become Christians. Williams was thus able to obtain from Paraifara a valuable account of the pagan religion of the Manu'ans. The Manu'ans, Paraifara reported, worshiped a "great spirit" called Tagaloa, who "resided in the skies." As well as going to special places in the bush to hold conversations with this great spirit, all of the people, including the chiefs, prayed and made offerings to Tagaloa. For example, "at their great feasts, prior to the distribution of food, an orator arose, and, after enumerating each article, exclaimed, 'Thank you great Tagaloa, for this!' " Again, in 1837, in reviewing his experiences in both eastern and western Polynesia, Williams noted that "the Samoans, in particular, had a vague idea of a Supreme Being" known to them as Tagaloa, whom they looked upon as "the creator of all things and author of their mercies"; and in 1839 Anamia, a Rarotongan teacher stationed on Ta'ū, wrote that some Manu'ans, in rejecting Jehovah, had claimed that "Tagaloa, of the skies" was the "true God."[13]

These accounts by Paraifara, Williams, and Anamia were later amplified by Powell on the basis of his discussions, from the 1860s onward, with the keepers of the sacred traditions of Manu'a. By this time Powell had lived in both the western and eastern islands of the Samoan archipelago for more than twenty years, and was able to collect, with scholarly exactitude, a series of traditional texts of the utmost importance for the understanding of the pagan religion of Samoa. These texts reveal a concept of a supreme being, which far from being vague, as Williams had supposed, is to a remarkable degree for a preliterate people theologically sophisticated and mature. Indeed, so impressed was Powell with the "monotheism" of the Samoan myth of creation that he was led to conjecture that "those who had handed it down, from father to son, from time immemorial, as an inviolable trust," must have been "closely allied to the original possessors of the Mosaic record." Fraser, similarly impressed, compared Tagaloa to Brahma of the Hindu pantheon, in that Tagaloa, like Brahma, is, in the words of Dowson, a "supreme spirit manifested as the active creator of the universe." Thus, the Samoan myth of creation begins, "Tagaloa is the god who dwells in the illimitable void. He made all things. He alone, at first, existed."[14]

The myth goes on to describe how Tagaloa created both mankind and the other gods. The most important of these deities are his agents and bear, in many cases, modifications of his own name. Tagaloa created the first two human beings, Fatu and 'Ele'ele, male and female, from the primordial matter that took shape beneath his feet, and endowed them with souls (*agaga*), affections (*loto*), wills (*finagalo*) and the power of thought (*masalo*; literally doubt), which, when mingled together, gave them intelligence (*atamai*). This recognition of *finagalo*, the capacity for alternative action, and of *masalo*, the capacity to assess experience critically, as vital components of human intelligence, is an indication of the great sophistication of theological speculation in pagan Samoa. These tasks accomplished, the primeval creator retired to the tenth "heaven" above the heavens of all the other gods he had brought into being, where, in Fraser's words, he reigned supreme as Tagaloa of the Skies (Tagaloa-a-Lagi) manifesting himself only as necessary "in accordance with the work" he wished to do. Further, it was the son of Tagaloa-a-Lagi, Ta'e 'o Tagaloa, who descended to the world below and became (as Taua-nu'u confided to Powell in 1871) the first Tui Manu'a. It is thus from their supreme god that the paramount chief of the Manu'ans was held to derive his unique sanctity.[15]

The gods of the skies were believed to assemble in the tenth "heaven," on the Ground of Tranquility, there to hold their sacred fonos in the *Fale 'Ula*, or Crimson House, of Tagaloa-a-Lagi. At these fonos perfect peace and order prevailed, and when kava was ceremonially served it was Tagaloa-a-Lagi who received the first cup. As myth has it, when a second Fale 'Ula was established by Tagaloa in Manu'a as the sacrosanct fono house of the Tui Manu'a, its practices duplicated those which had originated in the skies. Tagaloa, then, was conceived of by the Samoans not only as the creator of all things but also as the originator of the chieftainship basic to their society. There was thus in ancient Samoa a profound fusion of the theological and the social, and the Samoans were, and still remain, quite contrary to Mead's assertions, a profoundly religious people.[16]

Pagan Samoans, Turner records, firmly believed that if in their daily lives "there was no prayer to Tagaloa there could be no blessing." Prayers, with appropriate offerings, were made on all occasions of any importance, such as "before going to fish, before planting some fresh section of bush land," and also in times of sickness and war. Fraser notes that Tagaloa was believed to be especially partial to bonito; if those who went angling beyond the reef wished to secure his favor in their ventures, they had to show him respect by the prestation of a bonito as soon as they returned to shore. Thunder was thought to be a sign that a prayer had been heard, and disaster was the lot of those who had neglected their obligations.[17]

As these facts indicate, Tagaloa was believed to take a vital interest in the doings of the Samoan people. In one myth he is "keen-eyed Tagaloa," whose "all-seeing eyes" follow a guilty man wherever he goes. So, as Turner notes, when Pava fled to the earth below after desecrating the kava of the gods he still saw the "terrible eye" of the indignant Tagaloa looking down on him. When angered by those who had behaved improperly Tagaloa swiftly became a dreaded punishing force. When his son Le Fanoga negligently spoilt an oven of food, Tagaloa pelted him with burning yams, marking his body with reddish spots, like that of the owl in which Le Fanoga later became incarnate as a war god. When carpenters constructed a house for the Tui Manu'a without first consulting Tagaloa, "The rafter-breaking god came down / With wrath inflamed and angry frown," to scatter all before him. When Sina had the temerity to go off with Tagamilagi, a suitor from Tonga, Tagaloa, with lightning and darkness, turned these wayward lovers into stones. And when Sa and Manu pointedly disobeyed Tagaloa by pilfering fish he had given them to tend, he transformed them into sea urchins, to spend the rest of their lives face downward. Tagaloa, then, was an all-seeing, all-powerful creator god, remote yet ever present, peaceloving yet ever ready to punish the disobedient and wayward, who bore a distinct resemblance to the supreme and demanding god of the ancient Hebrews and of the strait-laced Protestant missionaries by whom the pagan Samoans were so rapidly converted during the fourth and fifth decades of the nineteenth century.[18]

When Williams reached Ta'ū in 1832 he was met by Manu'ans who, having been converted by Paraifara, pleaded, as sons of the word of Jehovah, to be sent a missionary. By as early at 1840, soon after teachers from Rarotonga and Rurutu had been stationed in Ta'ū, the Tui Manu'a himself became a Christian. The following year the missionary Matthew Hunkin arrived, and by the beginning of 1846 the entire population of Manu'a had been converted to Christianity, having found in Jehovah a god apparently superior to Tagaloa. The pagan religion of the Samoans had been thick with prohibitions, and as Wilkes observed in 1839, wherever Christianity had taken root in Samoa the ten commandments rapidly became law, with any infringement of them being punished by immediate withdrawal of the privilege of attending worship. The observance of Sunday also became very strict; it became "impossible to get a native to do anything whatsoever on that day, but perform his religious duties." These duties, which included morning and evening prayers on every day of the year, were attended to "with a devotion rarely to be seen among civilized men."[19]

At the time of Mead's brief sojourn in Samoa this strict adherence to Christian principles had long been integral to the lives of Manu'ans, who, as Holmes has noted, have a history of being "almost fanatical in their practice and observance of Christianity." Governor H. F. Bryan, in his report of October 1926, which covers the period from September 1925 to June 1926, during which Mead was in Tutuila and Manu'a, describes the Samoans as "innately and intensely religious," with "family prayers in the morning and evening in every Samoan home" and with Sunday "very religiously observed as a day of rest." A. F. Judd, who visited American Samoa early in 1926, when Mead was still in Manu'a, emphasized in his notes on the ethnology of Samoa the extraordinary preoccupation of the Samoans with the Christian religion, remarking on the well-attended congregational services at Ta'ū, which were held twice each Sunday in a church standing partly in Lumā and partly in Si'ufaga. Bruce Cartwright, after a tour of Tutuila in September 1927, described the Samoans as being very religious, with services "participated in every evening in every family by every individual"; Dr. Peter Buck, on the basis of his observations in Manu'a, Tutuila, Upolu, and Savai'i from September 1927 to February 1928, wrote of the Samoans as being "strongly religious," and of their pastors as occupying high positions of great influence; while Tufele Iosefa averred of the Samoans in 1929 (to the Congressional Commission on American Samoa) that "probably no people on the face of the earth" had "accepted the teachings of Christianity with such wholesome enthusaism and sincere purpose."[20]

At the time of Mead's Samoan research, then, the Manu'ans were devout adherents of the strict ordinances of protestant Christianity. Yet instead of analyzing the consequences of this situation for the adolescents she was studying, Mead, as part of her depiction of a society essentially "characterized by ease," misdescribed Samoan Christianity as being just "a pleasant and satisfying social form in which choirs sing and married women wear hats and pastors pray and preach in the most beautiful language." Indeed, the sterner tenets of protestant Christianity had been so "remoulded," according to Mead, that there was "passive acceptance" by religious authorities of the premarital promiscuity which was, so she claimed, customary among female adolescents, with the result that, as she asserted in 1929, "no one" became a church member "until after marriage."[21]

To this misrepresentation of a crucially important aspect of their social and religious lives, Samoans take the keenest exception. For example, when I discussed this statement of Mead's with To'oa Salamasina Malietoa in 1967, she called it "a most mistaken story" and added that throughout Samoa girls were prepared for church membership from as young as 10 years, with many adolescent girls becoming full members of the church, or Ekalesia, from 15 or 16 years of age onward. This was borne out by my detailed study in Sa'anapu in 1967 of all of the girls of this community aged between 12 and 22. In this sample of sixty-seven girls and young women the youngest full member of the church was 13 years of age, and of the twenty-two fully pubescent unmarried girls aged 16 to 18, no fewer than eighteen, or 82 percent, were members of the Ekalesia. All of these eighteen girls, moreover, being church members, were regarded by others of their community as virgins, as fornication is strictly forbidden to all church members and any suspicion of indulgence in this "sin" results in expulsion from the church. Indeed, it is largely as a safeguard to their socially valued virginity (as is further discussed in Chapter 16) that Samoan girls when they reach puberty are strongly enjoined by their parents, their chief, and their village pastor to become church members. In January 1943, for example, after the pastor of Sa'anapu had made an appeal for new members of the church, Lauvi Vainu'u, a senior talking chief, cried out from the front of the church were he was sitting "Fly a banner for our family!" At this his adopted daughter, Taotasi, aged 13, walked forward, under considerable emotion, to join the Ekalesia.

In Ta'ū in 1967 I was assured, by both male and female informants who had been adults at the time of Mead's reseaches and well remembered the years 1925-1926, that an identical system—with the recruiting of unmarried pubescent girls to church membership and the strict prohibition of fornication to all members of the Ekalesia—had also existed in Manu'a at that time. That this was the case is also evident from the information that Mead herself gives, despite her lack of attention to the religious behavior of the adolescents she was studying. Thus, table 1 in *Coming of Age in Samoa* reveals that no fewer than nine of the twenty-five adolescents listed were resident members of a pastor's household, which means they would have been either actual or prospective members of the Ekalesia. Again, in chapter 11 Mead makes specific mention of a girl who had become a "church member" in compliance with the expressed wish of her pious father, and of another who, while a church member, had "transgressed her vows." Mead, then, was plainly in error in generalizing that in Manu'a in 1925-1926 "no one" became "a church member until after marriage"; nor is there any substantive evidence for her assertion that premarital promiscuity on the part of female adolescents was passively accepted by the "religious authorities" in Manu'a. Rather, in the 1920s the female adolescents of Manu'a lived in a moralistic society that specifically interdicted premarital sexual intercourse. Mead's failure to give due attention to this socioreligious regime (which is accorded great prominence in the accounts of other contemporary observers, such as Judd and Buck) can only be construed as an active—albeit unconscious—denial of the realities of Samoan life.[22]

With the rapid conversion of Manu'a and other parts of Samoa from their pagan religion to Christianity, many pagan practices survived in but slightly modified form. Just as Tagaloa had "all-searching eyes," so was Jehovah, the Samoans were told by their missionaries, able to "see ... in the dark"; and just as Tagaloa, as Fraser notes, was believed to be "swift to know, and to requite the evil ... done among men," so, the Samoans were instructed in their catechisms, did Jehovah become greatly angered at the sinful actions of mankind, which he never failed to punish.[23] As in pagan times, chiefs and their families prayed directly to Jehovah, while the pastor of a local polity came to be viewed, like the pagan taula aitu, as its major intermediary with the deity, being often referred to as "the representative of God." Whereas in pagan times a person under suspicion of stealing would, as Turner records, touch a sacred stone and say, "In the presence of our chiefs now assembled, I lay my hand upon the stone. If I stole . . . may I speedily die," this same imprecation came to be sworn on a Bible, in the belief that death would result if such an oath were falsely sworn. Again various of the prohibitions of the pagan religion were transferred to Christianity. For example, each evening when the heads of families pray to Jehovah there is a curfew during which no one is supposed to be abroad and unseemly behavior is forbidden on pain of divine retribution. In March 1966, for example, when the 13-year-old daughter of one of the titular chiefs of Sa'anapu, climbing in a *pua* tree instead of attending evening prayers, fell and broke her arm, it was said that God had punished her. Again, the thunder and lightning that were once the awesome attributes of Tagaloa have been transferred to Jehovah, to whom, in one of their hymns, Samoans sing:

> Your voice, Jehovah,
> That I hear
> In the thunder clap
> Fills me with fear;
> The lightning is also yours
> And conveys your tidings.[24]

Jehovah is conceived of as being, in the words of a Samoan pastor, "full of anger against those who sin." Thus, when in October 1966 a 2-year-old of Sa'anapu who had been playing untended in the lagoon was found drowned, his mother exclaimed, again and again, in her distress, "Alas! O God! I fear Thee, God!" At the burial service the officiating pastor, as is common in such cases, openly attributed the child's death to the potency of human sinfulness, adding that he had died as a substitute for some other sinful person.

The Samoan Jehovah, then, like Tagaloa before him, is an austere, all-seeing God who is believed to punish relentlessly those who willfully disobey his commandments. There is thus no truth in Mead's assertion, in *Coming of Age in Samoa*, that the even tenor of the life of Samoan adolescents is disturbed by "no implacable gods, swift to anger and strong to punish." Equally at error are Mead's parallel assertions that the Samoans she studied in Tutuila and Manu'a had "no conviction of sin" and that, having taken only such parts of Western ways as made their own culture "more flexible," they were "without the doctrine of original sin." These, once again, are unhistorical statements, to which Samoans take immediate exception, pointing out that sinfulness, or *agasala* (literally, behavior in contravention of some divine or chiefly ruling and so deserving of punishment), is a basic Samoan concept antedating the arrival of Christianity, and, further, that the doctrine of original sin contained in the scriptures is something with which, as converts to Christianity, they have long been familiar.[25]

The early missionaries, as Pratt notes, readily adapted the Samoan concept of agasala to the Hebrew notion of sin, as is shown in the first Samoan catechism of 1842, the fourth chapter of which tells how the original sin of Adam and Eve in disobeying Jehovah was visited on all minkind. This doctrine, from the mid-nineteenth century onward, has been conscientiously imparted to all Samoan children, and the sinfulness of humans, because of their frequent disobedience to God, is said, as in the words of a nineteenth-century Samoan hymn, to be exceeding great.[26] It is thus commonplace in Samoa to hear speakers in fonos and the like expatiating on sinfulness. For example, in Sa'anapu in February 1967 I listened as the titular chief Lea'ana Satini declared to his fellow chiefs that "no one in this life is straight, all are sinful." Such homilies, moreover, are apt to end with a repetition of St. Paul's warning that the wages of those who sin is death. So, in one of their well known hymns the Samoans have for a century and more been admonished:

> Put down sin,
> Cast it away,
> Lest disaster flourish
> And you come to an evil end.[27]

It was in the spirit of this nineteenth-century hymn that after a devastating hurricane in 1966 the prime minister of Western Samoa, in a national broadcast, attributed this disaster to the fact that many Samoans had been following bad paths and admonished the nation to "lift its eyes to Jehovah and to fear him."[28]

Yet another seriously erroneous statement about Samoan religious behavior is Mead's assertion that "transgression and non-transgression are matters of expediency," there being "no room for guilt." This is by no means the case. Rather, growing up in an intensely religious society in which there is constant talk of sinfulness, Samoans are keenly aware of guilt, which in the ordinary course of their lives they are frequently called upon to confess to those in authority. For example, toward the end of a judicial fono in 1966, Sene, an untitled man who had committed the enormity of striking a chief, publicly acknowledged the error of his ways, whereupon the officiating tulafale at once remarked, "You are then conscious of your guilt, for that we are thankful." Further, as Brown notes, the Samoans have long "attached great value to the confession of wrong-doing in times of danger," as when a canoe on the high seas is in danger of being swamped. In 1940, for example, when our long boat was overtaken at night by a squall and seemed likely to founder in the Apolima strait, I witnessed confessions of guilt and fervent appeals to Jehovah by several of the Samoans with whom I was traveling. [29]

This practice of confessing guilt is even more significantly displayed in a major Samoan ceremony, the *ifoga*, in which those who have done others wrong ritually humiliate themselves before them. This they used to do by taking stones and firewood from which an oven is made and, sitting with bowed heads covered with fine mats, so offering these fine mats in reparation and themselves (as Brown notes) as pigs to be cooked and eaten. Such a gesture, which to Samoans is deeply moving, almost always leads to reconciliation. In contemporary Samoa it is usually made with fine mats alone. An ifoga, in my experience, is always accompanied by the public confession of guilt. Thus, when in 1966 the chiefs of Sa'anapu made an ifoga to the chiefs of the neighboring polity of Sataoa, the senior titular chief of Sa'anapu, in offering the fine mat he had brought with him, began with the words, "I have come because of my guilt." Guilt, then, is a quite major element in the religious and social life of the Samoans, particularly associated with the demand for obedience to divine and chiefly authority and with the punishment that is meted out to those, of all ages, who transgress this basic social requirement.[30]

13

Punishment

ALTHOUGH IN *SOCIAL ORGANIZATION OF MANU'A* Mead does mention that in ancient Samoa "violent breaches of the pattern" were "vindictively punished" (giving the example of someone who stole being made to sit in the sun and toss a poisonous fish in his hands), she declares that this punishment was only "vaguely glimpsed as a deterrent," and elsewhere records that by the 1920s extreme measures of this kind had been outlawed. Samoan society as depicted by Mead was neither severe nor punitive. Rather, so she asserted, the Samoans inhabit a social order that "is kind to all and does not make sufficient demands upon any." These assertions are inaccurate and misleading. In recounting the myth of Tagaloa's punishing of the disobedient Sa and Manu by turning them into sea urchins, to which I have referred in Chapter 12, Fraser commented that if any special truth was burnt into the minds of pagan Samoans by such tales of Tagaloa's powers it was that "any transgressions of the commands of their gods or their chiefs" were "sure to be visited with punishment." As this indicates, the Samoans give particular emphasis, through the imposition of various kinds of punishment, to the active maintenance of obedience to those in chiefly authority.[1]

The Samoan term for obedience, *usiusita'i*, refers specifically to the action of listening to an instruction and then unquestioningly carrying it out. In Samoa such obedience, to chiefly instructions in particular, is greatly lauded, especially in untitled men, members of the *'aumaga*, whose principal obligation is to serve the chiefs of their local polity. Thus, when the men of an 'aumaga are summoned before their chiefs it is common for a senior talking chief to remind them of "the supreme importance of obedience," as also of the fact that their obedience should be marked by a proper submissiveness. In April 1966, for example, in my hearing a senior talking chief of Sa'anapu told the assembled members of the 'aumaga that "in an untitled man, a lowly heart is praiseworthy," and in March 1967 another high-ranking talking chief admonished the Sa'anapu 'aumaga: "You must obey in everything! Obey completely! Even though your chief be in error."

In other words, in Samoan society untitled men are called upon to be the submissive and wholly obedient agents of their chiefs. This customary requirement of absolute obedience is sometimes advanced as a defense in Samoan courts. For example, in the Supreme Court of Western Samoa in April 1941, Miss O. F. Nelson pleaded on behalf of seven untitled men who had assaulted a man of their village that they were merely, as Samoan custom required, "blindly obeying" the edicts of their chiefs. In this case, some twenty chiefs of a village on the north coast of Upolu had taken it upon themselves to impose upon a fellow chief who had defied a ruling of their fono the most demeaning of all Samoan punishments, that of *saisai*, which involves tying up an offender as though he were a pig about to be baked in an earth oven, and then inflicting upon him various other indignities.[2]

A comparable case also occurred in April 1941 in another village on the north coast of Upolu. The chiefs had become incensed because a man of their village (I shall call him Tala) had given evidence against them during a hearing in the Land and Titles Court in September 1940. In October 1940 these chiefs convened a fono to decide what punishment they would mete out to Tala. Their decision, so the court was told, was to tie him up "like a pig, and bring human excrement and put it in his mouth, and make an oven to symbolize the cooking of man." The forced ingestion of excrement, which is eaten by pigs, and the treating of a man as though he were, like a pig, fit only to be eaten, are ultimate forms of subjugation. This extreme form of punishment, as Stuebel recorded in a text collected in the late nineteenth century, was once meted out to anyone who cast aspersions on the genealogy of a chief. As Stuebel's informants remarked of such an offender: "Even his children and sisters could be slain, or they might be publicly shamed by being led to the oven or by having human excrement thrust into their mouths, while the malefactor himself would certainly be killed."[3]

Tala fled and was not apprehended until 19 April 1941. He was struck on the head with a heavy husking stick, then suspended naked, trussed like a pig, from a thick rough pole about ten feet long, and in his abject state displayed for all to see. As the court was told by the Crown Prosecutor, "this is the greatest insult, according to Samoan custom, that can be inflicted on anyone." All those directly responsible were given prison sentences varying from two to three months.[4]

This punishment of saisai, as the reports of Turner, Brown, and others show, is very much a part of the traditional culture of Samoa, and, although Mead makes no mention of saisai in her discussion of "the offenders and the offended" in *Social Organization of Manu'a*, it was certainly being practiced during the 1920s when she was in Samoa. For example, F. H. Flaherty has reported that in Savai'i in 1924 culprits were brought before a chief "swinging between bamboo poles, trussed like pigs"; she adds that in Samoa "no more terrible disgrace" can befall a man. Further, this dire punishment is still occasionally inflicted;

a prosecution for saisai was heard in the Supreme Court of Western Samoa as recently as January 1981.[5]

As recorded in an official report of 1950 in Western Samoa, the trial and punishment of those guilty of offences against custom has "always been among the major functions" of the titular and talking chiefs of a local polity. And as mentioned in *Institutions and Customs of the Samoans* (a compilation by the Education Department of Western Samoa), those guilty of "repeated impudence or disobedience" toward the fono of their community are the most heavily punished. Thus in 1862 Ta'unga, a Rarotongan pastor stationed in Manu'a, wrote that the chiefs of Ta'ū would not "countenance any wrong-doing" and when one of their laws was broken would seek very carefully to find a punishment that was "appropriate" to the offense.[6]

When a sufficiently serious offense does occur, a juridical assembly, or *fono manu*, is immediately summoned, a special kava ceremony held, and, after detailed consideration, a specific punishment decided upon by the assembled titular and talking chiefs. A distinction is made, as Stair notes, between punishments imposed on an entire family and those inflicted on an individual. An especially severe form of traditional punishment by a village fono was the banishment of an entire family, which was for a time legalized under the laws proclaimed by Malietoa Laupepa in 1892, before being prohibited in Western Samoa by Governor Solf in 1901. When a fono decided on the banishment of a family it was usual, as Stair has described, for its chiefs to walk to the house of the offending family, there to seat themselves on the ground while the highest-ranking talking chief formally announced their decision. This done, others of the judicial party would appropriate the family's pigs and other property, cut down or ring-bark their breadfruit trees, and, after their enforced departure, set fire to their houses. The 1927 Report of the Royal Commission on Western Samoa lists a number of such banishments in the late nineteenth century, including one in which an entire village was permanently "ordered away." On other occasions an individual who had offended the fono was banished, and from time to time in twentieth-century

Samoa a chief is formally expelled from a fono. In 1946, for example, a titular chief was expelled for acting in defiance of the ruling of the fono of Sa'anapu that village land should not be leased to outsiders for the purpose of erecting a trading store, and in 1966 another ali'i was similarly expelled for disobeying the instruction to accompany his fono in an ifoga to the village of Sataoa after untitled males of his family had killed and eaten one of the cattle of Sataoa.[7]

In former times there were many other forms of severe personal punishment, particularly for acts of disobedience or disrespect to chiefs. Krämer mentions the beating of an offender until his head bled and his bones cracked. Wilkes and Turner record the cutting off of ears and noses, and Stair describes a punishment that involved compelling an offender "to inflict severe wounds and bruises upon himself, by beating his head and chest with a large stone, until the blood flowed freely," this being enforced, if necessary, by "the prompt and unsparing use of a war club." Yet another painful punishment described by Stair, Turner, Brown, and others was the enforced biting, five times, of the noxious *teve* plant, which besides inflicting intense agony on an offender would cause his gums to become so inflamed, according to Krämer, "that death often resulted." Stair also lists the punishments of being forced to handle poisonous spined fish, of being exposed in the broiling sun, and of being suspended head downward for many hours from a tall coconut palm. Again, in *Institutions and Customs of the Samoans*, mention is made of a punishment of olden times in which an offender, having been tied hand and foot, was "thrown into the pigsty, to eat and sleep with the pigs until he died."[8]

These personal punishments, with the exception of severe ad hoc beatings and expulsion from village groups such as the fono and 'aumaga, are now no longer practiced, their place having been taken by an extension of the ancient Samoan custom of imposing fines. As Turner notes, it was common in nineteenth-century Samoa for a fono to impose "fines of large quantities of food, which provide a feast for the entire village." Brown mentions fines of "as much as a thousand head of taro, and a thousand fish, all cooked," or of "from one to twenty or thirty pigs."

Under Samoan custom it is usual when an offender is an untitled individual for a fine to be imposed on his chief, who then draws on the general resources of the family of which he is head. In January 1943, for example, when a 23-year-old man surreptitiously raped an 18-year-old girl of another family, his chief was fined two pigs and ten six-pound tins of meat by a specially summoned juridical fono; this food was then shared among all the other families of Sa'anapu.[9]

It is also customary for fines to be imposed on any chief who fails to obey a ruling of the fono to which he belongs. It is usual, for example, for a fono to require all its members to plant a certain amount of taro, or to make standard contributions to village enterprises, such as the building of a school. Those chiefs who do not meet these obligations are almost always penalized, the most common fine in the 1940s and 1960s being a six-pound tin of meat. Both the imposition and the collection of these and other fines are strict, the principle being, as a senior talking chief of Sa'anapu remarked to his fellow chiefs in 1967, that "no one may make light of something that has been decided upon by the fono."

This principle is also followed in all the other social groupings of a village community, such as the 'aumaga. For example, in 1942 the Sa'anapu 'aumaga ruled that all of its members were to join in a malaga to a village on the north coast of Upolu. When one of them, Filipina, aged about 40, disobeyed this injunction he was fined £2, and when he refused to pay this fine he was expelled from the 'aumaga and formally ostracized, all other members being forbidden, on pain of a heavy fine, to communicate with him. After a few months of this punishment Filipina formally admitted his wrongful behavior and, on the prestation of a large pig and other food to the 'aumaga in lieu of the fine he had refused to pay, was readmitted to its membership.

In other village groups, such as church choirs, there are often elaborate sets of rules, each with its own fine for disobedience. In 1943 the church choir of Sa'anapu had a total of some thirty finable offenses, ranging from a fine of sixpence for sitting down too quickly after the singing of a hymn, to £1 for the divulging of a choral arrangement to a rival village. As this example indicates, the imposition of punishment is very much a part of the religious life of Samoa. Thus, it is commonplace to hear Samoan pastors admonishing their congregations that eternal torment in hellfire is the punishment of those who disobey the commandments of God. This notion is no great novelty to Samoans, for their traditional afterworld, as Stair records, contained, in addition to an Elysium called Pulotu, a dread place of punishment known as Sa le Fe'e. Again, very strict discipline, with the infliction of physical punishment as necessary, is maintained during church services. For example, Moore and Farrington, when they attended a protestant service in Tutuila in 1930, noted that an elder armed with a fly switch patrolled the church swatting unruly boys and shaking them "by winding his fingers in their hair." Often the punishment inflicted for misbehavior at services or when under religious instruction is more severe, and I have recorded several instances of both male and female adolescents having had a bone fractured by a punishing blow inflicted by an irate pastor.[10]

Fines may also be imposed directly upon an individual when marked disrespect has been shown to a chief. In 1946, for example, when Pomate threatened a talking chief with a bush knife during an argument over a plot of land, the fono summarily sentenced him to banishment from Sa'anapu. When Pomate pleaded for his case to be reconsidered, he was made to crawl on hands and knees with head bowed into the house where the chiefs of Sa'anapu were meeting in fono, and to remain in this abject posture while his behavior was condemned in the roundest terms. Pomate, who was married to a Roman Catholic woman from the nearby village of Mulivai, was in the habit of attending Mass with her there on Sundays. From the nineteenth century onward Sa'anapu had been exclusively protestant, with one of the main rules of its fono being that any villager who became a Roman Catholic must leave the community. Pomate was heavily fined and told that he could remain in Sa'anapu only if he gave up attending Roman Catholic services, an imposition which, in fact, drove him from his natal village.

In 1966 I witnessed another case of severe punitive action by chiefs, which involved the disputed boundary of the plantation of Samala, an untitled man of Sa'anapu. Several chiefs, acting on behalf of the fono, marked the boundary by planting a line of breadfruit saplings, depriving Samala of a few yards of land to which he claimed he was entitled. Samala uprooted these cuttings and threatened to shoot the chiefs who had planted them. At a specially summoned fono Samala was fined one bullock and one very large pig, animals he had been rearing for some years with the intention of selling them. When Samala saw his animals being killed he threw himself on the ground, groaning and weeping in a paroxysm of frustrated rage, and tore the shirt from his body in a violent display of redirected aggression.

The imposition of heavy punishment frequently provokes rage, yet the penalized individual well knows that any action he might take against the chiefs of his community would be certain to lead to even heavier punishment. This situation sometimes has tragic consequences, as in the case of Tulei, an untitled man of the village of Safa'atoa. Early only morning in June 1966, the boundaries of a plot of newly cleared agricultural land of the family to which Tulei belonged were formally inspected, as is usual in Samoan villages, by the chiefs. During this inspection Tulei was overheard to say of these chiefs, "What's the point of their frequent measuring of the land, the earth is befouled by their tread." After the inspection the chiefs at once met in fono and imposed on Tulei's family the fine of ten sows, ten cases of tinned fish, five large tins of biscuits, and 5000 corms of taro, stipulating that this food was to be provided if not that very day then without fail on the morrow, under the threat of further penalties. Their fono was still in progress when the news reached them that Tulei, having heard of the severity of this punishment, had killed himself with a shotgun.

Samoa then, far from possessing a social order that "is kind to all and does not make sufficient demands upon any," as Mead would have it, has a culture in which it is traditional to have recourse to punishment, and frequently very severe punishment, in the interests of obedience and respect for authority. Furthermore, those who have erred are expected to accept their punishment without demur. This is especially so when a chief is

being found fault with by his fellow matai. I was present in October 1966 when a 53-year-old titular chief, who had disobeyed
a ruling of the Sa'anapu fono, tried to justify his actions. He was
peremptorily told that his only course was to admit the error of
his ways and to sit patiently without a word while the indignation of his polity was vented upon him. This, as we shall see, is
what is also required of children who are being reproved or
punished by their parents, or, for that matter, by anyone else
set in authority over them.

14

Childrearing

THE "EASE IN SEX RELATIONS" that Mead claims is so much a
feature of Samoan life, especially during adolescence, is "made
possible," she argues, "by the whole system of child rearing."
Samoan children, she asserts, never learn "the meaning of a
strong attachment to one person," and because early childhood
does not provide them with "violent feelings" there are no such
feelings to be rediscovered during adolescence. The Samoan
family, she claims, is "just a long series of people of different
ages, all somehow related to one another." This means that Samoan children are "given no sense of belonging to a small intimate biological family," and so "do not form strong affectional
ties with their parents." Instead, "filial affection is diffused
among a large group of relatives," with the result that "in
Samoa the child owes no emotional allegiance to its father and

mother," and children "do not think of an own mother who always protects them," but rather of "a group of adults all of
whom have their interests somewhat but not too importantly at
heart." This view of the relationship between a child and its
parents, which is basic to Mead's whole account of adolescence
in Samoa, is markedly at variance with the facts of Samoan existence.[1]

In the 1920s, as Mead has recorded, behaviorism was
"treated hospitably" by American cultural anthropology, and it
is notable that her assertions about infancy in Samoa closely
reflect the views of J. B. Watson that were fashionable in the
United States when Mead was writing about Samoa in the late
1920s and early 1930s. In his *Psychological Care of Infant and
Child*, for example, Watson argued that when a mother picked
up and caressed her child she was "slowly building up a human
being totally unable to cope with the world it must later live in."
Instead, he favored as ideal a system in which a mother would
not know "the identity of her own child," and which, so he predicted, would make of adolescence "just a stretch of fertile
years." Samoa, as depicted by Mead, had a culture in which
these Watsonian conceptions had apparently been fully realized, and, as I have described in Chapter 7, her account was received with something akin to rapture by the behavioristically
oriented generation of the late 1920s.[2]

This was all some years before the publication of Konrad
Lorenz's pioneer inquiries on imprinting in birds, which were
soon followed by comparable research on mammals, including
non-human primates, and then by the work of John Bowlby and
others on attachment behavior in the human species. In
Bowlby's researches, attachment behavior became intelligible
in evolutionary terms as a phenomenon that occurs when certain behavioral systems (such as sucking, crying, smiling, clinging, and following) are activated in an infant within its environment of adaptedness. Thus the attachment of a human infant to
its mother is, in Bowlby's words, "a class of social behaviour of
an importance equivalent to that of mating behaviour and parental behaviour" with "a biological function specific to itself."
During the years 1966 and 1967, assisted by my wife, I made a

detailed study of attachment behavior in Samoan infants, including a repetition of the reseaches by René Spitz and others on the onset of smiling behavior.[3]

As I have reported elsewhere, my inquiries showed that attachment behavior in Samoan infants has all of the characteristics described by Bowlby. In Samoa, as in other human populations, an infant during its first year of life becomes behaviorally attached to its caretaker, whoever she or he may be. For example, when Aperila, who was born on 19 April 1955, was left by her mother, Lei, at five months of age, she was cared for by Uiese (the elder sister of Lei's mother), who was then 59 years old. By 1966 Lei had returned to the village, but it was Uiese to whom Aperila was bonded, sleeping and eating with her and going to her for all her needs. Her genetic mother, Lei, she ignored. Those of the family concerned were well aware of what had happened: "Aperila knows that Lei is her mother, but has no love for her; the heart of Aperila adheres to Uiese."[4]

Instances of this kind, in which an infant becomes attached to some caretaker other than its genetic mother, do occur in Samoa, as elsewhere. However, the incidence of such adoptive attachments is low. On 31 December 1967, when there were 483 individuals 18 years of age and under in Sa'anapu village, there were twenty-eight cases of intrafamily and twelve cases of interfamily adoption, making a total of forty adoptions in all. This means that approximately 92 percent of individuals 18 years of age and under were living with their genetic parent, or parents. As Mead failed to observe, biological families of parents and their offspring do in fact exist as distinct units within the extended families into which Samoan society is organized; it is customary for a cohabiting couple to have their own living quarters within the cluster of houses belonging to an extended family.

As Mead also describes, there is in Samoa a well-developed system of child-minding in which infants are handed over for extended periods to the care of an older girl, usually a sister or a cousin. This relationship results in the formation of a secondary bond of major significance. This *tei* relationship does not, however, supplant the attachment of a child to its genetic or adoptive mother. As was clearly evidenced in our study of Samoan infants during their first two years of life, the behavioral attachment of an infant to its mother antedates the formation of a secondary bond to its tei or to any other relative.[5]

It is a common practice in Samoa to separate an infant from its mother to facilitate weaning. When a male infant we were studying was taken at thirteen months of age to his maternal grandmother in another village, he became so severely depressed and debilitated during a month's separation from his mother that to ensure his survival he had to be reunited with her. After about seven days he began gradually to recover, although after this traumatic separation he would cry whenever his mother made to leave him. Indeed, so attached does a Samoan infant become to his mother that during his early years there is almost always marked emotional agitation at the prospect of her leaving.

We conducted the simple experiment of testing Mead's assertion that in Samoa "filial affection is diffused among a large group of relatives," by having the women of an extended family walk away from an infant one at a time. The agitated reaction of the infant to being separated from its own mother (and her alone) demonstrated that attachment in Samoa, as elsewhere, is with but rare exceptions monotropic. Again, when one particular mother moved away from all of the younger children of an extended family, it was only her own children who evinced distress. The primary bond between mother and child is very much a part of the biology of Samoans, as it is of all humans.

The behavior of Samoan children when a death occurs also dramatically demonstrates how intense is the bond between a child and its parents. For example, when a 56-year-old talking chief of Sa'anapu died on 24 July 1966, only his own offspring among the numerous children of his extended family evinced acute distress, in particular his 12-year-old daughter, who reproached her dead father again and again for having abandoned her. Mead's statement that "in Samoa the child owes no emotional allegiance to its father and mother" is one to which Samoans take particular exception. For example, when I mentioned this assertion to the people of Si'ufaga in Manu'a in 1967 a talking chief immediately responded, "In Samoa the feelings of a child for his parents are most intense."

Mead also makes the related assertion that in Samoa "residence in the same household with one's parents is not obligatory." According to Mead, Samoan children, from the time they can run about, are able to "chose their own homes," with the result that few of them "live continuously in one household." In Samoa, she says, a child is "serene in the reflection that he can always run away if he wishes," and she instances this "freedom of choice" as "a powerful deterrent of specific adult tyrannies."[6]

These statements, which I discussed in Manu'a with informants who well remembered the 1920s, were strongly denied. I was told that under Samoan custom a child is not permitted to change its place of residence without parental approval, and that such approval is seldom granted before a child is 12 or more years of age, and then only in special circumstances. These statements I tested in 1967 by studying all the children of between 3 and 18 years of age from eight neighboring extended families in the village of Sa'anapu. This yielded a total of 108 children, for all of whom reliable observational data were available. Of this total, ten had been adopted. An analysis of the residential behavior of all 108 children showed that 105 of them, or 97 percent, were permanently resident with either their genetic or their adoptive parents. Further, one of the three not in this category was a boy of 7 who had, because of his poor health, been sent to live on the coast with his mother's sister. There were thus only two instances of children having moved out of their parents' household. One was a 14-year-old girl who, after a heavy beating by the adult daughter of her adoptive father, had gone off with the tacit approval of all concerned to live with an aunt in another village. The second was a 15-year-old boy who, after a beating for an attempted surreptitious rape, had gone off to live in another family and had been allowed to remain there. There were also during the years 1966–1967 two children, a boy of 12 and a girl of 8, who attempted to move to a new place of residence. In each of these cases, however, the runaway child was recovered and subjected to severe parental punishment. The boy's hands were tied behind his back and he was made to walk back to his parents' home, a distance of some three miles, with his irate father hitting him from time to time with an iron fishing spear as he walked behind him.

Eleanor Gerber, who worked in Tutuila in 1972-1973, also reports that parents may "display considerable anger" should a child run away, and that the shaving of a runaway child's head is a common punishment for this offense. One of Gerber's informants suggested that parents would even have a runaway put in jail, while another told her that "if he ran away and stayed in a friend's house for a few nights, he would be afraid that his father would sneak in and attack him with a knife as he slept." Mead's claim that in Samoa a child's freedom to choose its own place of residence is "a powerful deterrent of specific adult tyrannies" is thus at variance with the realities of Samoan existence.[7]

Mead's account of the ethos of the Samoan family is also inadequate. As Mead would have it, within a Samoan extended family an infant is succored by "women of all ages . . . none of whom have disciplined it." "Samoan children," she states, "are not carefully disciplined until they are five or six." Further, although from this time onward "violent outbursts of wrath and summary chastisements do occur . . . consistent and prolonged disciplinary measures are absent." Samoan culture is thus, according to Mead, "based on diffuse but warm relationships," in a family setting in which "neither boys or girls are hurried or pressed," and this family environment, through the "avoidance of conflict," brings its children "through adolescence painlessly."[8]

While it is true, as Wilkes noted during his visit to Tutuila in 1839, that Samoan parents are "extremely fond of their offspring," it is also true that from infancy onward Samoan children are subjected to quite stringent discipline. Thus Samoan children, as Stair observed during this same period, are alternately "indulged in every wish" and "severely beaten for the most trivial offence." That such punishment is customary in Samoan families has been confirmed by other observers. Holmes, on the basis of his observations in Manu'a in the 1950s, writes of the early training of children being "often accompanied by severe punishment." Hirsh, who worked in a village near Apia in 1957, reports that while beatings within the family were not frequent, they were "apt to be severe." Cooper, who did field research in Manu'a in the early 1960s, reports children being "severely punished in private," and felt Samoan parents to be "extremely harsh," and Gerber, writing of family life as she observed it in Tutuila in the early 1970s, states that "by the time a child is three, he is being hit frequently" for such offenses as making noise and balking at an adult's request. These beatings, Gerber reports, last well into adolescence, and may frequently be severe, there being occasional stories of "children being injured severely enough to require attention in hospital." The youngest child she observed being hit was an infant less than three months old.[9]

As Gerber correctly reports, Samoans believe in "the unique efficacy of pain as a means of instruction" and that "beatings are necessary to ensure that children will be 'good,' or at least stay out of trouble." These beliefs, which were integral to the pagan culture of Samoa, have been powerfully reinforced since the mid nineteenth century by the admonitions of the biblical king Solomon. It was Solomon's belief that "a father who spares the rod hates his son" and that if a parent will only "train up a child in the way he should go," then "even in old age he will not depart from it." These admonitions the Samoans have long taken to heart, and when asked why they punish children they answer that this is the best way to teach them what they must not do. The Samoans, then, scold and punish their disobedient children not only in anger but in the pious belief that they are doing right. The consequences of this method of rearing children are, as I shall show, severe.[10]

The peculiarly Samoan way of administering punishment to children is illustrated in the following account from my field notes of 15 November 1942:

Punishment is almost always physical and severe. Despite the severity of the punishment the child is not permitted to show emotion. Thus, if a child persists in crying aloud the parent continues to punish him, shouting *Uma!*

Uma! ("Have done! Have done!"). Not until the child sits
stock still with his legs crossed and head bowed, and sup-
presses his emotions by not overtly crying, does his punishment cease. This treatment is meted out to young children of both sexes from as young as three or four years of
age.

In other words, Samoan children are early taught, through
this particular mode of punishment, to accept without question
the dictates of those in authority. This specifically Samoan system of discipline, which I had observed in the early 1940s, was
still being practiced a generation later in the mid 1960s, as also
in the 1980s, with those who had been thus treated during their
childhood imposing the same form of punishment on their own
young children. This method of dealing with the misbehaving
young is used by all those in authority, however marginal; for
example, in 1966 I witnessed a 10-year-old boy disciplining his
8-year-old brother in precisely this way.

When young children are first subjected to this punitive regime it is usual for them to respond with temper tantrums. As
Gerber has described, the temper tantrums of young Samoan
children (a phenomenon Mead ignores) begin in earnest after a
child has been "hit for crying." The child will then "throw himself down and wail loudly and rhythmically" in a display that
can last for fifteen or twenty minutes. Of young children in
these fits of passion the Samoans say that the seat of their affection is distressed and angered. The anger is almost always
directed against someone in authority, such as a mother or
older sibling, who has dominated and then punished the child.
Often a tantrum becomes violent, with the distraught child
flinging his limbs in all directions in repeated paroxysms of passion as he voices his indignation, until at last he collapses from
nervous exhaustion.[11]

Although temper tantrums are indulged for a time, young
children sooner or later have imposed on them the traditional
Samoan mode of discipline in which they are required, while
being punished, to sit cross-legged and to suppress both their
anger and their distress. The youngest child I have observed

being subjected to this kind of discipline was eighteen months old: a female infant named Sasa, born on 2 October 1965, was punished by her mother on 18 April 1967 for going out in the sun after having been told not to do so. After hitting her daughter heavily and repeatedly about the head and body with her open hand, the mother shouted angrily: "Have done! Have done! Shut your mouth!" When the child continued to cry, the mother clamped her hand over the child's mouth to stifle all expression of emotion.

At the outset of this encounter, when she was first smacked, Sasa had shouted angrily at her mother the most common of all Samoan expletives, "Eat shit!" From this and other cases it is plainly evident that when they are forced to suppress their indignation and inhibit their crying Samoan children are subjected to considerable psychological stress. Further, being forced so frequently to assume an outward demeanor fundamentally at variance with their emotions produces in Samoan children an isolation of affect which is of quite fundamental significance in the formation of Samoan character.

As the case of Sasa shows, Samoan children are in fact very seriously disciplined well before the ages of five or six, mentioned by Mead. Of thirty-eight children 10 years of age and under, whose punishment my wife and I observed in Western Samoa in 1966 and 1967, nineteen were under 5 years of age, with eight of these nineteen being under 3 years of age. In Manu'a in 1967 I observed a number of similarly young children being physically punished.

Punishment may also be meted out to a child by any older family member. It is customary for an older to punish a younger sibling. In one of the families in which we lived in 1966-67, a girl of 7 was regularly punished by her brother, aged 9, for all manner of supposed offenses. Further, this punishment of a younger sibling by an older one often closely follows the punishment of the elder by some more senior member of the family. For example, in January 1967, 9-year-old Tunu was very severely beaten with a leather belt by his 42-year-old uncle, receiving numerous bleeding welts on his back. Soon afterward, Tunu launched an unprovoked attack on his 7-year-old cousin, forcing his head down onto some stones and causing the side of his face to bleed. This redirection of anger and retaliatory aggression following punishment account, in my view, for the fact that, as Holmes and others have observed, "larger children often hit smaller ones with no apparent provocation."[12]

The punishment of younger siblings by older ones continues well into adult life. For example, in March 1967, when Papa, 33 years old and a married woman with three children, did not prepare an evening meal as she had been told to do, her 53-year-old sister hit her heavily, several times, over the head. Similarly, some parents continue to punish their daughters long after they have become adults. An extreme case of this occurred on a Sunday in March 1967, when a 53-year-old talking chief began beating his 30-year-old daughter because she had not obeyed his instruction to have food ready at the close of the afternoon church sevice. So severe was this beating that others of the family intervened to lead the father away, while his daughter, who was in an advanced stage of pregnancy (she gave birth to her seventh child some twelve days later) wailed aloud in distress. The response of her 54-year-old mother was to shout at her daughter, just as though she were still a child: "Have done! Have done! Don't open your mouth so!"

Occasionally those in authority punish a child so severely that a lasting injury is inflicted. In one case that I investigated, a pastor's wife, whom I had known in 1943 as a devoutly religious woman, struck her 14-year-old second cousin over the back with a heavy carrying stick with such force as to cause a crippling and permanent injury to her spine. In other cases, as I learned from my researches in the police records of Western Samoa, the punishment of a child may be fatal. For example, in Savai'i in April 1958 a 12-year-old girl, after being heavily punished by her 19-year-old brother, died from a cerebral hemorrhage. And in Upolu in August 1963, a 53-year-old man, angered by the disobedience of his 13-year-old son during a ceremony, jabbed the boy in the back of his head with the end of an umbrella, causing brain damage from which the boy died two days later.[13]

Samoan social organization, then, is markedly authoritarian and depends directly on a system of severe discipline that is visited on children from an early age. By the time this discipline begins to be imposed, the great majority of children are already bonded to their mothers. The mother is thus experienced as alternately caring and punishing. This means that she comes to be feared and hated as well as loved and longed for, a combination of emotions that, in addition to producing ambivalence, significantly intensifies the feelings of an infant for the individual to whom it is bonded. The initial reaction of an infant to the onset of maternal punishment is usually one of anger, and I have observed young children actually attack the mothers who are chastising them. This response is soon beaten out of a child, however, as it is coerced into submitting to discipline out of fear of even heavier punishment.

The physical infliction of punishment is also commonly accompanied by scolding and verbal threats. For example, in May 1966 I heard a 40-year-old mother shout at her 2-year-old son, who was crying after being punished, "Stop it! or I'll break your neck!" Such threats continue well into adolescence, as when a mother threatened her disobedient 15-year-old daughter that she would return as a ghost and devour her.

The fact that children submit to discipline does not mean that they cease to feel intense resentment toward those who punish them. The reaction of the eighteen-month-old Sasa to being smacked by her mother was to shout "Eat shit!" This same imprecation is often angrily muttered by older children after being punished. Children who have especially punishing mothers may come to harbor death wishes against them. For example, in April 1967, when the corpse of a chief's wife was brought into Sa'anapu village prior to burial, an 8-year-old girl who had been subjected to much heavy punishment was heard to remark how good it would be if her adoptive mother were likewise dead.

When my wife and I talked to children of how they felt about the stringent discipline to which they were subjected, it became clearly evident that they experienced severe punishment as a terrifying attack. Further, they would sometimes confess to feelings of intense anger and hatred toward their punishing mothers. Thus, while outwardly expressing nothing but love, respect, and obedience to those in authority, children of 6 or 7 would, when we gave them paper and crayons, depict their mothers as threatening monsters.[14]

Samoan folklore is inhabited by towering and ferocious ogresses, with staring eyes and lolling tongues, who tear their victims apart as they devour them, as also by female spirits who suddenly change in appearance. One of these is Sauma'iafe, who may take on either the appearance of a beautiful maiden with long tresses of black hair and an enchanting smile or that of an ugly old woman much given to hitting people. This fickle phantom, who is known throughout Samoa, is an obvious projection of the Samoan mother. It is also a manifestation of the deep-seated ambivalence generated in Samoans by the form of the punitive discipline to which they are subjected in infancy and childhood, an ambivalence that is basic to the structure of Samoan character.[15]

15

Samoan Character

CENTRAL TO MEAD'S DEPICTION of Samoan character is her claim that among Samoans there are "no strong passions." Samoa, she asserts, has taken the road of "eliminating strong emotions." "Love, hate, jealousy and revenge, sorrow and bereavement," we are told, are all matters of weeks; "the social patterning of personal relationships has to contend with no deeply channeled emotions"; a "lack of deep feeling" has been "conventionalized" by Samoans "until it is the very framework of all their attitudes to life."[1]

This assertion that Samoans have no strong passions, while consistent with her depiction of them as "easy, balanced human beings," is plainly contradicted by Mead's own accounts of Samoan behavior. In *Social Organization of Manu'a*, for example, she writes of the "loudly proclaimed rage" of those who have been "injured" by offenses such as insult and adultery, and of the "very genuine horror" of Samoans at the accidental uncovering of unidentified bones. In *Coming of Age in Samoa* there is an account of a 22-year-old woman, devoted "to the point of frenzy" to an older man whose mistress she had been, whose "fury" when she discovered he had seduced her younger sister "knew no bounds," and who displayed "the most uncontrolled grief and despair" when he "announced his intention of marrying a girl from another island."[2]

As these accounts and the reports of numerous other observers demonstrate, Samoan behavior, in a wide range of situations, is very much marked by strong passions. William Harbutt, for example, who witnessed hysterical possession during a religious service in 1841 on Upolu, wrote of Samoan character as being "*excess* of feeling whether grief or joy has possession of their minds." This phenomenon of becoming possessed during a Christian service, which was a direct continuation of the pagan religion of Samoa, greatly astonished the early missionaries, who had never witnessed such outpourings of emotion at revival meetings elsewhere as they did among Samoans. George Lundie, who attended a service led by the Reverend A. W. Murray in Tutuila in 1840, saw dozens of men and women who became so convulsed "as to drive five or six men about like trees in wind," or who dropped down "as dead," after "struggling with their bursting emotions until nature could bear no more." In his journal, Murray himself recounts a service attended by over a thousand Samoans at Leone in June 1840, at which "the tide of feeling rose higher and higher, and became more and more deep and powerful till bursting through all restraint it vented itself in loud weeping and violent bodily convulsions, or laid its subjects on the floor in helpless prostration," in one of the "most affecting scenes" he had ever witnessed.[3]

Mead's assertion that in Samoa "no one feels very strongly," is also feelingly dismissed by the Samoans themselves. To'oa Salamasina Malietoa, for example, in a conversation with me in December 1967, rejected this assertion of Mead's, referred to the Samoans as "an intensely emotional people," and mentioned as an instance that a chief of Fasito'otai, in making a ceremonial apology to Papauta School in 1967 on behalf of an ill-mannered youth of his village, had wept in public. Such reactions, under the sway of intense emotion, are very common in Samoa. For example, when Powell and his family returned to Tutuila in 1869 after a sojourn in England, men, overjoyed at their return, sat "weeping and unable to utter a single word." Comparable emotion is displayed at times of parting. Elation at the attainment of some significant victory is also commonly accompanied by tears, even on the part of senior chiefs. For example, in 1966 when a 64-year-old talking chief of Sa'anapu, with the support of his close kindred, foiled an attempt to confer on a disliked rival the same title he himself held, he wept profusely in the presence of his kindred. One of them commented that he wept "from joy at his victory, being unable to contain the pride with which his heart was filled." Similarly, as reported in the official gazette of Western Samoa in 1967, when after two hours of heated debate, Mata'afa Fiame Faumuina Mulinu'u II was reelected as prime minister, he was in tears as he thanked the members of the parliament for their confidence in him.[4]

Weeping is also associated with states of shame and anger. Throughout Samoa children are required each year on White Sunday (a local religious festival) to recite before their assembled community an excerpt from the scriptures which they have sedulously memorized over the previous months. When on White Sunday, 1942, the 7-year-old daughter of the pastor of Sa'anapu, of all people, completely forgot the verses she had learned, her mother collapsed in tears, at which many of the other women present wept in sympathy. Again, in July 1967, during the private conclave of an extended family over the keenly contested succession to its chiefly title, there was also much sympathetically induced weeping, most markedly when a 59-year-old contender for the title, known for his hardness of heart, broke down and sobbed aloud when insistently challenged by his sister's son, a man fully fifteen years younger than himself.

The Samoan language, as Pratt records, contains a term for horripilation and one for trembling with terror, and states of fear, including abject fear, are by no means uncommon in

Samoa. Further, Samoans, like other humans, are apt to panic in highly frightening situations. Williams, for example, had recorded that during a severe earthquake in the early 1830s the people of a settlement in Savai'i "rushed from their houses, threw themselves upon the ground, gnawed the grass, tore up the earth, and vociferated in the most frantic manner" as they called on Mafui'e, the spirit believed to cause earthquakes, to desist. Many Samoans display comparable extremes of emotion at the death of someone to whom they are behaviorally attached. Turner, having observed Samoan behavior during the years 1841–1861, wrote of the "indescribable lamentation and wailing," with doleful cries audible from two hundred yards away, that marked a death. These vocalizations were accompanied by other most frantic expressions of grief such as "rending of garments, tearing the hair, thumping the face and eyes, burning the body with small piercing fire-brands," and (as Pritchard also reports), "beating the head with stones" until "blood freely flowed." Although in twentieth-century Samoa the more extreme of these displays no longer occur, a death is still marked by heartrending expressions of grief. For example, when in April 1967, a 72-year-old woman lost consciousness and was thought to have died, the harrowing screams of her 37-year-old daughter could be heard from at least two hundred yards away. Summoned by these screams, I found the daughter in a distraught and agitated state, clutching frantically at her disheveled hair and tossing her head and body from side to side, as, with tears streaming down her face, she wailed aloud.[5]

There can be no doubt that Mead was mistaken in claiming that among Samoans there are no strong passions. She was equally in error in asserting that in Samoa emotions such as hatred and revenge are but matters of weeks. As Brown notes, one of the most widely quoted of Samoan proverbs avers that while stones decay, words do not. So, as Turner recounts, reports of an ignominious event involving any member of a Samoan community are "brought up to the shame of the members of his family, for generations afterwards." Such reproaches, which are commonly expressed in a succinct phrase, are, as I discovered when I returned to Samoa in 1981, remembered over many years. For example, in 1929 a 20-year-old youth of Sa'anapu, whom I shall call Manu, assaulted and raped an 18-year-old girl from another family. Manu was subjected to the dire punishment of saisai (see Chapter 13) and as an added indignity had a rope (*maea*) tied about his neck, as though he were an animal. This ignominy led to the phrase 'o le 'au maea, meaning "they of the rope," being applied to the family to which Manu belonged. In 1981, this reproach and the hatred of which it was an expression were, after more than fifty years, still well remembered. Again, at a family conclave that I attended in June 1967, a major issue was a serious intrafamily quarrel that had taken place in 1943, with the resentments that had been generated on that occasion being, after twenty-four years, both deep and active.[6]

As well as depicting the Samoans as lacking either deep or lasting feelings, Mead also claimed in *Coming of Age in Samoa* that among Samoans there was an "absence of psychological maladjustment," and a "lack of neuroses." These claims, as we shall see, are without foundation. As I have already described, those who grow up and live within the highly authoritarian Samoan society are frequently subjected to emotional and mental stress, and this experience sometimes results in psychopathological states, suicides, and other violent acts.[7]

Samoan character, as I have suggested in Chapter 14, is very much the product of the way in which discipline is imposed upon young children. As Robert Louis Stevenson has noted, if a child is sufficiently frightened "he takes refuge in duplicity"; it is into this response that Samoans are commonly forced by the anxiety-provoking demands of their often stern and punitive society. The child learns early to comply overtly with parental and chiefly dictates while concealing its true feelings and intentions. As a result, Samoans, whatever may be their real feelings about a social situation, soon become adept at assuming an outward demeanor pleasing to those in authority. By the time they are adults, males in particular have acquired the ability to hide their true feelings behind, as Wendt puts it, "an impregnable mask of controlled aloofness."[8]

In both men and women this aloofness is commonly joined,

as is socially appropriate, with an elaborate politeness and engaging affability. For example, when in a fono a chief is being
criticized by others, however severely, it is usual for him to respond, even when deeply angered, by intoning at regular inter-
vals the words *Malie! Malie!* ("How agreeable! How agreeable!), so maintaining his social mask. Indeed, the maintenance
of this mask becomes a source of special pride; for example, at a
fono in Sa'anapu in 1966, a high-ranking talking chief (who later
confessed to me that he had at the time been furious), suavely
assured his detractors that not a hair of his body was ruffled. As
these examples indicate, it is usual, especially in demanding social situations, for Samoans to display an affable demeanor
which is, in reality, a defensive cover for their true feelings—to
be, as they themselves put it, "smooth on top but whirling beneath."

The Samoans, then, as Wilkes noted as long ago as 1841, are
"adepts" in "giving a false impression relative to their feelings
and designs," and "particularly when they think their personal
interest may be promoted by their dissimulation." Thus,
Cartwright reports that although the high chief Tufele
"thoroughly hated" Captain H. F. Bryan, who was governor of
American Samoa from March 1925 to September 1927, he said
in a speech on 9 September 1927, that the twelve apostles at the
Last Supper were "happy men" compared with himself and
other Samoans as they bade Bryan a final farewell. Such dissimulation is also common in purely Samoan contexts, as in a revealing incident I observed in 1966 during a communion service
in a village church: During this service, Masima, a talking chief
and lay preacher, having taken his piece of bread from the cir-
culating communion plate, at once, in conformity with local
custom, swallowed it, only to hear the visiting pastor solemnly
announce that all members of the congregation were to perform
the act of communion together. Giving no outward sign of his
embarrassment, the worthy Masima elaborately simulated the
eating of a second piece of communal bread, lifting an empty
hand to his mouth and moving his jaws in unison with the rest
of the congregation.[9]

However (as in the case of a child who had been forced to

suppress his emotions to escape further punishment), there are often, and particularly among adolescents and young adults, feelings of deep resentment and anger against those in authority. When these feelings pervade the mood of an individual he or she is said to be *musu*, a term which Williams recorded as early as 1832, and which, as Pratt notes, has no exact equivalent in English. According to Stevenson, the word *musu* means "literally cross, but always in the sense of stubbornness and resistance"; it is used by Samoans to refer to any unwillingness to comply with the wishes or dictates of others, and especially of those in authority. It is, moreover, common for a mood of stubborn unwillingness so to dominate an individual's behavior that, in Judge Marsack's words, "he becomes completely intractable; will do little or no work, will deliberately misunderstand instructions, will go about with a look of sulky tragedy on his face and will reply to no questions."[10]

An individual who has become seriously musu (as do virtually all Samoans from time to time, and especially during childhood and adolescence), is thus in a disaffected and emotionally disturbed state, and this psychological condition is of key significance for the understanding of Samoan character. What did Mead make of this state of being musu, the widespread incidence of which among Samoans is manifestly at odds with her depiction of Samoan life as being essentially "characterized by ease"? The word *musu*, Mead tells us, "expresses unwillingness and intractability," but she offers no explanation at all of why it is that this disaffected state is so widely prevalent among Samoans. If Mead's analysis had penetrated to the heart of what being musu means, she could never have sustained her claims about the untroubled character of Samoan adolescence. All she tells us is that the state of being musu is "a mysterious and widespread psychological phenomenon" which the Samoans themselves out of "an odd incuriousness about motives" find "inexplicable." These assertions are unwarranted, for there are many Samoans who are by no means incurious about motives, and who well understand why it is that someone becomes musu.[11]

As we have seen, individuals growing up in Samoan society

are regularly subjected to the dictates of those in authority over them, with punishment being meted out to the disobedient and refractory. On occasion the demands of this stringent system generate such internal resentment and stress that an individual can take no more and becomes intractable, or musu, sullenly refusing all commands and admonitions. A person in this state is very near the breaking point, and if harried further may become violent or even commit suicide; therefore when an individual does become seriously musu he is usually left to his own devices until his dangerous mood has subsided. Becoming seriously musu is thus, as my investigation of numerous cases has revealed, a direct result of the stress caused by the excessive demands of punitive authority. This, furthermore, is the interpretation of the Samoans themselves. For example, in discussing a case of musu behavior in February 1966, the 44-year-old daughter of a titular chief attributed being musu to "resentment at being dominated by another." She added that a person in a musu state, while "angered in his heart" at the dominance of those in authority, was unable because of his fear of them to vent this anger.

This accords closely with Otto Fenichal's definition of stubbornness as "a passive type of aggressiveness, developed where activity is impossible," and the widespread incidence of musu states (which Mead herself reports) is evidence of the latent aggression that has been remarked upon by many observers of the Samoans. Ronald Rose, who did field research on Manono in the late 1950s, found that "a very large percentage of the population had compulsive mannerisms of various sorts." One of the most common of these mannerisms is the agitated moving of the fingers of the hand in states of frustration: for example, drumming them rapidly on a mat, a behavior known to the Samoans as *fitifiti*. This behavior, in ethological terms, is a form of redirected aggression, and its prevalence among Samoans is evidence of the tension generated within individuals by the mode of discipline imposed upon them from childhood onward.[12]

This tension also occasionally finds expression in outbursts of uncontrollable anger. Turner, for example, writing in the mid nineteenth century, has described how a man or woman in a passion of anger not only would pull off an upper garment and tear it to shreds, but then, rushing up and down like a demon, would smash coconut water bottles and the like, before sitting down to weep over "the folly, wreck, and ruin of the whole affair." Again, when the 29-year-old Samala was heavily disciplined by the chiefs of Sa'anapu (see Chapter 13), he flung himself to the ground and tore to shreds the shirt he was wearing.[13]

Such fits of destructive rage closely resemble the temper tantrums of infants who are subjected to severe parental discipline, and Samoans prone to uncontrollable rage have told me of being overwhelmed as if by a kind of madness. This anger may also be released in redirected assaults upon others, as in the case of Tunu (see Chapter 14), who after being painfully punished by his uncle launched an unprovoked attack on one of his cousins. Thus, the high rates of aggression in Samoan society are certainly due, in part, to the tense and easily provoked characters of those who have been subjected to its severe regime of discipline and punishment.

In yet other instances, the aggressive impulses that individuals who have been heavily disciplined feel toward those in authority are redirected onto themselves in acts of suicide. In her paper of 1928, "The Role of the Individual in Samoan Culture," Mead asserts that the "emotional tone" of Samoan society "never exerts sufficient repression to call forth a significant rebellion from the individual," and that "the suicides of humiliation so common in parts of Polynesia do not exist in Samoa." These statements are seriously in error.[14]

During my researches in Western Samoa in 1966-1967, I collected from various sources detailed information on twenty-two cases of suicide (sixteen males and six females) that had occurred from 1925 onward[15]

Fourteen of these twenty-two persons (64 percent) had committed suicide in a state of anger at having been scolded or punished by a parent or some other elder. This accords with the opinion of Pratt, who lived in Samoa from 1839 to 1879, that among Samoans suicide is "mostly caused by anger with family"[16] Most of these fourteen individuals, had, moreover, also been musu toward a parent during the emotional crisis that immediately preceded their suicides, as the following cases illustrate.

Tupe, a 16-year-old girl of Solosolo, left her parents' house on 29 September 1964 and spent the next two days staying and working at the house of the village catechist. On her return she was scolded and beaten by her father, who suspected her of having gone off with a boy. After this punishment Tupe became musu, flatly refusing her father's instruction to weed the family's cocoa plantation. After further scolding and punishment from her father, she went off and hanged herself, with a piece of bark, from the branch of a tree.

On 26 October 1958 Sio, a 16-year-old boy of Leulumoega, wanted to go to the town of Apia for the day. His adoptive father forbade him to go, on the ground that it was Sunday. Intensely angered at this domination, Sio became musu and, as he had threatened when arguing with his father, went off and hanged himself from a breadfruit tree.

In 1942, Malu, the beautiful 17-year-old daughter of a titular chief of a village on the north coast of Upolu, who had been installed as a ceremonial virgin, was seduced and became pregnant by a handsome 25-year-old bus driver of part-European descent. Malu's father, on discovering this, subjected his daughter to severe scolding and punishment. When Malu pleaded to be allowed to marry her lover, her father took down a shotgun and told her that if she tried to elope he would kill her. At this Malu became angered and musu. One Sunday, having refused to go to church, she hanged herself with a clothesline from a rafter in her father's house.[17]

Six of the twenty-two individuals who committed suicide did so out of shame at illicit sexual liaisons (the remaining two killed themselves after being jilted). The six who acted out of shame all either had been scolded by others or feared that they would be. One of them, for example, a youth of 19, wrote (in English) of not being able to carry his "big load of blame," and a man of 28, who had been severely scolded, left a note (in Samoan) saying that he was taking his life because he was "so weighed down with shame."

A further point of significance is that nine of the twenty-two persons who committed suicide were adolescents, eight of these (36 percent of the total) being between the ages of 15 and 19. This proportion of adolescent suicides is high in comparative terms. In 1975, for example, only 4.6 percent of the 1,528 suicides in Australia were committed by individuals aged between 15 and 19. For New Zealand the percentage (for the years 1940-1964) is even lower: approximately 3 percent. Thus, the information I have been able to collect from police records and other sources indicates that the incidence of adolescent suicide relative to that of older age groups is, in fact, considerably higher in Samoa than in some other countries. This is scarcely a confirmation of Mead's claim that in Samoa adolescence is "the age of maximum ease" (a point to which I shall return in Chapter 17). Further, it is plainly evident from my analysis of twenty-two cases that Mead's assertion that "suicides of humiliation . . . do not exist in Samoa," is in error. Indeed, these cases show that the majority of the suicides that occur in Samoa directly involve the humiliation of an individual by those in authority. Examples are the case of Tulei (see Chapter 13) who shot himself after being punitively fined by the chiefs of his village; and that of Amoga (aged 25), who was humiliated in front of his brothers by his father for having broken the handle of an axe, and who then stormed off to take his own life by swallowing the powdered root of a poisonous plant.[18]

As we have seen, the tensions that sometimes develop within Samoan families in response to excessive scolding and punishment not infrequently result in states of psychopathological stubbornness, or musu behavior, and even, from time to time, terminate in suicide. Yet another expression of these tensions is a form of hysterical dissociation known to the Samoans as *ma'i aitu*, or ghost sickness. Although Mead was aware of the presence of this psychological malady—she specifically refers to a sickness in which an individual becomes "possessed" by "an angry ghostly relative" and "speaks with a strange voice"—she did not relate this sickness to the structure of Samoan character.[19]

As described in Chapter 12, the principal institution of the pagan religion of Samoa was spirit mediumship, in which a medium was believed to become possessed by a spirit or god who then spoke through his lips. This state of possession in which "normal individuality is temporarily replaced by another" with intense motor and emotional excitement is, as T. K. Oesterreich documents, a widespread phenomenon in human populations. As William Sargant's researches have shown, it is associated with the "hypnoid, paradoxical and ultraparadoxical states of brain activity" first studied by Pavlov, which can result in a splitting of the stream of consciousness and so a state of hysterical dissociation. As I have already described, because of the mode of punishment in which children are forced to assume an outward demeanor totally at variance with their actual feelings, the psychology of Samoans is especially characterized by states of marked ambivalence, particularly toward those in authority. Thus, I have often had a Samoan tell me that while one part of his character is under the power of God, another part of it is under the power of Satan. Shore reports a pastor's characterizing Samoan existence as being "an ongoing war between Satan and God within each person," and it is common to hear a Samoan account for having violently attacked someone, or for some other antisocial act, by saying "Satan overcame me." This kind of character structure, in which the emotionally impulsive is split off from the socially acceptable, makes Samoans particularly prone to dissociated reactions, such as were once displayed by their spirit mediums, and which, as noted earlier in this chapter, are also sometimes evinced in Christian settings.[20]

A further major expression of this susceptibility to dissociated reactions is a form of possession in which the sickness of an individual is attributed to his or her having been entered by the angry ghost of an ancestor. This condition, which existed in pagan times (it was witnessed by 1836 by Buzacott), has been reported from all parts of Samoa. Holmes, for example, in confirming the occurrence of ma'i aitu in Manu'a, describes it as involving, among other things, the symptoms of delirium and "sudden aimless running about"; while Goodman, writing of

Western Samoa, describes a case in which a boy shouted "bad words" at the woman who was treating him and then tried to bite her.[21]

These disturbed behaviors are attributed by Samoans to the anger of the ghost that is possessing the individual. Their way of treating the condition is to hold a seance to discover the cause of this ghost's resentment, and then to placate and thus exorcize it. A person skilled in this task (who may be either male or female) is called a *taulasea*. The usual way of proceeding is to have the possessed individual drink an herbal potion, drops of which are also often placed in all the orifices of the body. This done, the taulasea addresses the ghost directly, asking why it has come. In a successful seance the ghost replies through the lips of the psychologically dissociated individual, voicing angry complaints at recent happenings within the family, until finally, after promises of rectification and reparation have been made, the placated ghost leaves and the sickness subsides. My own inquiries in both the 1940s and the 1960s indicated that this form of psychological sickness is always associated, as Buzacott noted in 1836, with "some quarrel or ill-natured words" within an extended family, and, further, that it tends to occur especially in adolescents who have been subjected to excessive emotional stress. For example, the two cases of ma'i aitu that I investigated in 1943 were of 18- and 19-year-old girls, and the case I studied in detail in 1966 was of an 11-year-old boy, Mu, whose hysterical illness well illustrates the psychodynamics of the ma'i aitu syndrome.[22]

Some eight months after his birth in 1944, Mu was given in adoption to Moana, the sister of his father, Sami. It was to Moana and her husband, then, that Mu became behaviorally attached. He lived contentedly with them until 1954, when after a searing quarrel between Moana and Sami, he was forcibly taken to his father's household. When he tried to return to his adopted mother, he was repeatedly and heavily punished. In this highly stressful situation Mu finally became hysterical, complaining of pains in his head and body, talking incoherently, and making to bite those who approached him. When a Samoan medical practitioner could find nothing physically wrong with

him, he was declared to be stricken with a ma'i aitu. In the seance that followed he was revealed to be possessed by the ghost
of his grandmother (whose voice he had often heard as a young
child), who, speaking through Mu's lips, so berated Sami for
taking his son away from Moana, that Sami broke down and
wept, promising then and there to let Mu return to Moana's
household, so temporarily resolving the crisis that had led to
Mu's illness.[23]

As this case indicates, the sickness that the Samoans call
ma'i aitu is one in which an individual, having been subjected to
excessive stress within the family, develops an hysterical illness.
A ma'i aitu is thus revealed as a psychopathological consquence
of the stringent authority system in which the young grow up.
Although the Samoans have developed their own techniques for
coping with hysterical illness, in seances which allow the source
of the trouble to be identified and then rectified without undue
threat to the authority system, such illness is nonetheless, for
the individuals afflicted by it, a severe psychophysiological disturbance.[24]

The fact that such hysterical illnesses are endemic to Samoan society, occurring in adolescents as well as in adults, is a
further indication that Mead's depiction of Samoa as a place in
which there is "no psychological maladjustment" is in error. Instead, as I have shown in this and earlier chapters, Samoans, as
children, adolescents, and adults, live within an authority system the stresses of which regularly result in psychological disturbances ranging from compulsive behaviors and musu states
to hysterical illnesses and suicide.

16

Sexual Mores
and Behavior

THAT COMING OF AGE IN SAMOA so rapidly attracted popular
attention was due more than anything else to Mead's alluring
portrayal of Samoa as a paradise of adolescent free love. In September 1928, in the *American Mercury*, Miss Mead was said to
have found in Samoa an entire absence of the sex problems of
western civilization, while in Frederick O'Brien's estimation
Coming of Age in Samoa was an extraordinary accomplishment
in "the domain of erotics." These judgments are understandable, for it was Mead's claim that in Samoa, in the romantic
South Seas, there was a people with one of the smoothest sex
adjustments in the world, among whom, before marriage, love-
making—which was their "pastime *par excellence*"—was free,
and girls deferred marriage "through as many years of casual
love-making as possible." Indeed, so widely was this view dis-

seminated that many came to believe that Samoan culture included, in John Honigmann's words, "institutionalized permarital sexuality." An early adherent of this view was Boas' student Robert Lowie, who said in reviewing *Coming of Age in Samoa*, "Miss Mead's graphic picture of Polynesian free love is convincing. It falls into line with the reports of early travellers."[1]

This judgment may possibly have been true for Tahiti, the Nouvelle Cythère of Bougainville, to which Lowie had made a "purely recreational" visit in 1925. It does not hold, however, for Samoa, which in numerous respects, as Burrows has documented, significantly differs from Eastern Polynesia. In no area is this difference in culture more marked than in that of sexual mores. Thus, as Charles Wilkes, a well-informed early traveler to the Samoan islands, noted in 1839, among the Samoans "there was no indiscriminate intercourse," the women of Samoa "exhibiting a strange contrast to those of Tahiti." Again, the Rarotongan teacher Ta'unga, in a report written in Ta'ū in 1862, recorded that in Manu'a fornication was "not habitual" as in Rarotonga. This difference in culture stems from the fact that in pagan Samoa *taupou*s, or ceremonial virgins, occupied positions of great social importance and virginity at marriage was very highly prized. So, as Pritchard noted in 1866, among the Samoans "the chastity of the daughters of the chiefs was the pride and boast of their tribes," with old duennas guarding "their virtue and their honor from an early age." Pritchard is here referring specifically to the taupou system, in discussing the values of which Krämer observed in 1902: "The esteem felt for maidenhood in the old heathen times reminds us of the Vestal Virgins, of the Huarimaguadas of the Guansches, and of the Inca Maidens of the Sun, this esteem placing the Samoan people on an ethical height that accords with the spirit of their traditions." Again, the Samoans themselves give a special preeminence to their ceremonial virgins. At the constitutional convention of Western Samoa, for example, one of the chiefly delegates proudly declared that compared with Samoa there is "no country under the sun" where the "question of virgins" is "so upheld."[2]

How did Mead depict the taupou system in which this high

valuation of virginity is conspicuously expressed? The taupou, she tells us, who has the tokens of her virginity ceremonially taken at marriage by the talking chief of her bridegroom, is "excepted" from the "free and easy experimentation" of other young females. Further, although this virginity-testing ceremony was "theoretically observed at weddings of people of all ranks," it was possible, according to Mead, for a taupou who was not a virgin, to tell this to the officiating talking chief, and so "not be ashamed before all the people." The taupou system was thus depicted by Mead in 1928 as a curious appendage to the general practice of "promiscuity before marriage" in which the "onus of virginity" was taken from "the whole young female population" and placed on the taupou, the "legal requirement" of her virginity being something that could easily be circumvented with the connivance of the talking chief of her intended husband. This, as we shall see, is a confused travesty of the traditional taupou system of Samoa.[3]

As noted in Chapter 8, in pagan Samoa a titular chief had the right to confer on one of the sexually mature virginal girls of his family the rank of taupou, the girl chosen being usually one of his own daughters. In the Samoan family, female agnates possess a special rank vis-à-vis their brothers, and so a taupou was the apotheosis of the honorific standing of a chiefly family, with her hand in marriage being much sought after by other titular chiefs of rank, or by their heirs apparent. A taupou, like a titular chief, was given a ceremonial installation, in which all the members of a local polity participated, after which, as the Samoans phrase it, "they protectively encircle the luster of that lady." Such taupou were to be found in every local polity in which there were titular chiefs, and their traditional titles were known and revered throughout Samoa. Thus, Stevenson calls the taupou the sacred maid of her village, a phrase that conveys something of the special aura of her position. A taupou was, for example, entitled to sit on ceremonial occasions in that part of a house reserved by custom for high-ranking chiefs, and on such occasions was addressed in honorific language. As Ella notes, from the time of her first menstruation a Samoan girl was "strictly watched and guarded." A taupou in particular was placed in the care of the *aualuma*, a group consisting primarily of the sexually mature unmarried female agnates of a village. Once within the aualuma, she was assiduously chaperoned by its old women, who, like Spanish duennas, "never for a moment" lost sight of her.[4]

A taupou then was a sexually mature *virgo intacta* of rank. Her virginity was distinctively different from the virginity valued within Christendom. The Christian ideal, which stemmed from the musings of Gregory of Nyssa and others on the prelapsarian virginity of Adam and Eve, aspired to an asexual mode of existence and the overcoming of all concupiscence in the interests of a total identification with the risen Christ. The Samoan taupou, in contrast, was an engaging young lady of rank, enchantingly erotic in her very virginity, which in the eyes of Samoans gave her unique value, it being an ineluctable fact that a maiden's virginity can be given up but once. And so, young chieftains would vie for the special prestige associated with the deflowering of a taupou.[5]

In John Williams' journal of 1832 there are several descriptions of taupous. Decorated with necklets and bracelets, their skins gleaming with scented oil, their breasts tinged with an orange-colored power made from tumeric, and shaggy white mats or skirts of red and green cordyline leaves about their loins girded up to leave the left thigh completely bare, they were highly sexual objects; indeed, according to Brown, even the pubic hair of the village virgin was oiled and combed. Their virginal state, furthermore, was made plain for all to see by the tresses of curled, and sometimes artificially colored, hair at the sides of their partially shaven heads, a style affected by all virgins of rank.[6]

When a titular chief or his heir apparent (*manaia*) took a fancy to some taupou, a formal courting party was sent to her family to sound out the possiblity of a union. This delicate task was entrusted to talking chiefs so that the ali'i or manaia, who did not accompany them, would not be too painfully shamed should they be turned down. As Turner notes, when it came to deciding whom she should marry, a daughter was "at the absolute disposal of her father, or elder brother," with, in the case of a taupou, the whole of her village becoming involved. So as Aiono Ma'ia'i, a modern Samoan scholar, has written, "it is not the wishes of the *taupou* but those of her village that count."[7]

When an agreement had been reached, the taupou was accompanied to the village of her intended husband by a large traveling party consisting of members of her extended family, her aualuma, and various of the titular and talking chiefs of her settlement, bearing with them a dowry of fine mats and other valuables. The ceremonies lasted for about three days, and were marked by large-scale exchanges of property, with the amount given being a measure of the rank of the donors. Often the amount of property exchanged was very substantial. Turner mentions fifty or a hundred fine mats and two or three hundred pieces of bark cloth being heaped before a bridegroom, and Williams records seeing a woman to whose family three hundred hogs had been given. These massive exchanges were then a major facet of the taupou system, in which, as Williamson remarks, virginity was "a social asset rather than a moral virtue."[8]

The culminating point in the marriage of a taupou was her ceremonial defloration in public. The account that follows is based on sixteen cases taken from the literature and my own field notes. The earliest of these deflorations is that described in John Williams' journal of 1832. The exchange of property having taken place, the bridegroom seated himself on the ceremonial ground of his village. The young woman was then taken by the hand by her elder brother or some other relative, and led toward her bridegroom, dressed in a fine mat edged with red feathers, her body gleaming with scented oil. On arriving immediately in front of him she threw off this mat and stood naked while he ruptured her hymen with "two fingers of his right hand." If a hemorrhage ensued the bridegroom drew his fingers over the bride's upper lip, before holding up his hand for all present to witness the proof of her virginity. At this the female supporters of the bride rushed forward to obtain a portion to smear upon themselves before dancing naked and hitting their heads with stones until their blood ran down in streams, in sympathy with, and in honor of, the virgin bride. The husband, meanwhile, wiped his hands on a piece of white barkcloth which

he wore around his waist for the rest of the day as a token of respect for his wife. With the bride's ceremonial defloration accomplished, the marriage was usually consummated forthwith,
with the utmost decorum, in a screened-off part of a house.[9]

In the event of there being no hemorrhage, the bridegroom
Williams reports, repeated the operation. If no proof of the
bride's virginity was obtained, she was sorely abused by her
friends, called a prostitute, and hastened away, while her intended husband, refusing to take her to wife, at once reclaimed
his property. Sometimes, according to Pritchard, when a taupou
was thus exposed as a nonvirgin, "her brother, or even her father himself, rushed upon her with their clubs, and dispatched
her on the scene of her fatal exposure."[10]

In the case of a high-ranking taupou, the defloration ceremony was even more elaborate, being performed, when the
bridegroom was a titular chief of high rank, by one of his talking
chiefs. We are fortunate in having an eyewitness account of
such a ceremony involving the highest-ranking of all Samoan
chiefs, the Tui Manu'a. It took place in 1840 and was witnessed
by John Jackson, a young Englishman who had been kidnapped
by the Manu'ans from a South Seas whaler out of anthropological curiosity.[11]

The union witnessed by Jackson was that of the Tui Manu'a
and a taupou of Fitiuta, the high-ranking primordial settlement
of Manu'a. The bride, Jackson reports, was led onto a mat on
which the Tui Manu'a was standing. About her loins was a large
fine mat, edged with red feathers, on her forehead a pearly
white decoration made from nautilus shells, and part of her hair
had been dyed a reddish hue. A large bowl of kava had been
prepared, and as the cup-bearer, with traditional aplomb,
walked forward with the cup of the Tui Manu'a, he was accompanied by another of the Tui Manu'a's retinue (almost certainly
one of his talking chiefs) holding in his hand a piece of white
bark cloth. At the moment the Tui Manu'a lifted his kava to his
lips, so expressing the supremacy of his rank, the taupou at his
side was ceremonially deflowered by his talking chief.[12]

As described in Chapter 8, in a Samoan kava ceremony the
titular chief of highest rank receives his kava before all others,

and is later presented with the choicest and most succulent foods, having to these goods a socially recognized priority of access. In pagan Samoa this same principle applied to the sexual possession of women, and it thus became a matter of the greatest moment to any man of rank that he should make quite certain of his absolute priority of access to the woman who was to become his wife. So, within the traditional Samoan system of rank, the proof of a bride's virginity was regarded, as Krämer remarks, as "indispensable." The public testing of her virginity was the established method of avoiding any possibility of the bridegroom's being shamed by some other male who might secretly have had sexual connection with her. It was thus the specific duty of the officiating talking chief to make absolutely certain that a taupou was indeed a virgin. Indeed, so seriously did the pagan Samoans take the issue of rank and sexual liaisons that, as Harbutt records, if a female had lived as a wife with a high chief, she was thereafter prohibited from contracting a new marriage, with any breach of this rule being, according to Pritchard, a sufficient cause for war.[13]

Female virginity, then, was very much the leitmotif of the sexual mores of the pagan Samoans. Indeed, for an uninformed outsider it is difficult to appreciate the peculiarly exalted significance, stemming from the notion of peerlessness, that the Samoans, with deeply felt emotion, once gave to their female virgins of high rank. Some inkling of it may be had from the marriage songs that were ecstatically intoned when it was proved, by her ceremonial defloration, that a manaia had succeeded in securing for himself and his local polity a virgin of rank. A stanza of one such marriage song, making direct reference to the public defloration of a taupou, runs as follows:

The way into the vagina, the way into the vagina,
The sacred fluid gushes forth, the sacred fluid gushes forth,
All others have failed to achieve entry, all others have failed to
    achieve entry;
Lilomaiava is the manaia,
Samalaulu, the titled taupou;

He is first by being foremost, being first he is foremost;
O to be foremost!
The dart has reached its goal,
O, what a goal![14]

The Samoan term for the hymen is *'afu'afu,* derived from
the proto-Polynesian *kahu,* meaning a covering. In Samoan the
term *'afu* refers, among other things, to the fine mats presented
by the family of a bride to the family of a bridegroom. These
mats are by custom fringed with the beautiful red feathers of a
parakeet, which in Manu'a as elsewhere in Samoa are recognized a symbolic of hymenal blood. Among Samoans there is
still a pronounced mystique surrounding fine mats. When displayed they are praised in adoring tones, in traditional phrases
such as *Saō! Fa'alalelei!* (meaning "Thank you! How beautiful!"—*lalelei* being a term that specifically refers to beauty in
women). Fine mats are thus a cultural symbol of the traditional
taupou, who in a defloration ceremony has been proved to be a
virgin and so, within the values of the fa'aSamoa, a true
tama'ita'i, or lady of excellence.[15]

As Williams notes, a female found not to be a virgin at a defloration ceremony was called a prostitute. Prostitute, however,
is only a very approximate translation of the term *pa'umutu,* by
which such a female who had failed to preserve her virginity
was publicly shamed. Intimately related with the cult of virginity, this word is derived from *pa'u,* meaning skin or hymenal
membrane, and *mutu,* cut off or defective. It is a very heavy
slur, and a common cause of strife among women when improperly used. Indeed, so crucial an issue is this that a young woman
who has been unjustly subjected to the insult of being called a
pa'umutu will sometimes obtain and make public a medical cer-
tificate as to her virginity. In November 1963, for example, Tala,
a 20-year-old married woman of Aleipata, Upolu, accused Loto,
a 19-year-old girl, of being a pa'umutu. Loto traveled all the way
to the General Hospital in Apia (about 40 miles away) to have
herself gynecologically examined by the medical superinten-
dent. His report confirmed that her hymen was intact. With

Loto's virginity thus established, the police charged Tala with using insulting words. Tala was convicted and fined £5. She confessed to the police that she had acted out of jealousy after her husband had boasted, falsely as she now knew, of having deflowered Loto, and having had sexual intercourse with her. The same values were in force in the 1920s, as evidenced by Dr. Peter Buck's report that in December 1927 a young man was convicted for having falsely claimed that he had deflowered and had coitus with a local girl.[16]

The cult of virginity, which is central to the sexual mores of the Samoans, is also found (as Mead seems to have been unaware when she went to Samoa in 1925) in Tonga, the Lau Islands, Fiji, the Gilbert Islands, Tuvalu, and Tikopia, and is one of the principal characteristics of the cultures of Western as against Eastern Polynesia. For example, Gifford reports of Tonga that a virgin of chiefly rank was called a *taupoou*, and that "a crucial part of the marriage ritual there was the testing of the bride by the bridegroom (with his finger) to determine if she were a virgin"; and Laura Thompson records that girls in the Lau Islands, who do not marry until at least 18 years old, desist from accepting lovers before marriage from fear of being ridiculed and reviled at their weddings when their virginity is publicly tested. Firth describes how in Tikopia males exalt and swagger in the possession of "the treasure that no other man has touched," and relates an instance in which a young man of rank, having found a young woman to whom he was attracted to be not a virgin, commanded her to swim out to sea, which in her shame she did, and was never seen again. A somewhat comparable case is known to me in which a highly religious Samoan girl of 22 cut her own throat in shame after it became public knowledge that she had, through surreptitious rape, lost her virginity. Again, in Samoa, as in Tikopia, young men are greatly given to boasting about having deflowered a virgin, this being an aspect of the traditional rivalry throughout Samoa on the part of manaia and titular chiefs for the possession of virgins of rank. Indeed, a titular chief acquired great fame if he was successful in ceremonially deflowering a succession of taupou. For example, 'Anapu Tui'i, a high chief of Sa'anapu who died in 1918, is still remembered as having consummated formally arranged unions with a succession of six taupous from various parts of Samoa, by each of whom he had a child.[17]

The individual most celebrated for his zeal and prowess in deflowering virgins is the legendary Vaovasa, of Savai'i. Vaovasa, so the story runs, had accumulated a total of no fewer than ninety-nine maidenheads. Each conquest he had commemorated with a large stone, in the overweening ambition of constructing a wall one hundred stones in length. Having reached ninety-nine, he set out for Falealili on the south coast of Upolu, from whence he would return with, as he vainly thought, his hundredth virgin. As he was paddling back to Savai'i he was accosted by Logona, the manaia of Sa'anapu, standing on a headland with a plaited package in his upraised hand. With unerring aim, Logona hurled this package at Vaovasa's loins. It contained a fluid made up in part of the hymenal blood of Vaovasa's hundredth virgin, whom Logona, with the kind of daring Samoans most admire, had contrived to deflower shortly before Vaovasa's arrival. No shaming of one chief by another could be more complete than this, and so humiliated was Vaovasa that no hundredth stone was ever added to his wall.

These legendary events, which are deeply expressive of Samoan sexual mores, are celebrated in a song of praise to Logona that is known throughout Samoa:

To the westward by the headlands of Utumalama and Utu-
    sauva'a
Stood Logona;
In his hand the palm-frond container
Which he hurled at the canoe of Vaovasa.
Loud were the lamentations of the crew of Salemuliaga,
Great the surprise of Vaovasa
As he gazed at his loins.
Alas! a calamity is upon them.
O wanton woman, like an empty shell exposed by the ebbing
    tide!
Pity these travelers as in sorrow they return to Savai'i
Vaovasa's wall will never be completed.

These heroic happenings are still vividly remembered in Samoa. Some years ago when a traveling party from Satunu-mafono, the family grouping to which Sa'anapu belongs, ventured to sing this traditional song of praise to Logona at Gatai-vai, a village in Vaovasa's district, it was more than the local people could bear, and there was an affray.

As this indicates, the sexual mores of pagan Samoa are still, in many ways, extant. Youths of no particular rank still vie with one another, and given half a chance will boast of their exploits in deflowering virgins. A Samoan youth, it is said, keeps count of his conquests, and I have often sat in an 'aumaga and heard bragging of such feats. Again, there are numerous terms, such as *le o'o* ("to fall short"), which are widely used to refer to, and shame, a man whose attempt to secure a virgin for himself has failed.

Samoa, then, is a society predicated on rank, in which female virgins are both highly valued and eagerly sought after. Moreover, although these values are especially characteristic of the higher levels of the rank structure, they also permeate to its lower levels, so that virtually every family cherishes the virginity of its daughters. For example, as Turner noted in 1861, and as Stuebel confirms, although the marriage ceremonies of common people were marked by less display than those of people of high rank, they still involved the testing of the bride's virginity. In other words, while the virginity of the nubile daughters of families of high rank was a matter of quite crucial importance to all concerned, the values of the taupou system also traditionally applied to the whole of Samoan society, albeit less stringently to those of lower rank.[18]

It is thus customary in Samoa, as Mead quite failed to report, for the virginity of an adolescent daughter, whatever her rank, to be safeguarded by her brothers, who exercise an active surveillance over her comings and goings, especially at night. Brothers will upbraid, and sometimes beat, a sister should she be found in the company of a boy suspected of having designs on her virginity, while the boy involved is liable to be assaulted with great ferocity. Gerber, from her work in Tutuila in the early 1970s, records that many girls reported that "they were afraid of their brothers beating both them and their boyfriends if they were found together"; while Young (who worked in both western and eastern Samoa in the 1970s), writes that a brother will fly into a "killing rage" at an attempt to seduce his sister. To cite a case from my own researches, on a Sunday in June 1959, Tautalafua, aged 17, found his 18-year-old classificatory sister sitting under a breadfruit tree at about 9:00 in the evening with Vave, a 20-year-old youth from another family. He struck Vave with such violence as to fracture his jaw in two places. For this attack he was later sentenced to six weeks' imprisonment. Again, in February 1964, when a girl of 15 was found at 10:30 P.M. with Tali, a youth of 19 from another village, two of her brothers at once attacked Tali, wounding him severely on the forehead with a thrown stone. Both were later sentenced to two months' imprisonment. On such occasions the girl involved is also liable to be scolded and punished by an adult male of her family. In December 1967 a 19-year-old girl of Sa'anapu, sitting on the malae, continued talking to some visiting youths after the sounding of the village curfew at 10:00 P.M. Her 30-year-old uncle knocked her to the ground and chastised her, complaining that after having been educated at great expense she was putting her maidenhood in jeopardy.[19]

With the interdicting of public defloration by Christian missions, the taupou system of pagan Samoa underwent major changes. Ceremonial deflorations, when they were arranged, took place within a house, behind a screen. Again, from the nineteenth century onward the house of the pastor supplanted the aualuma as a place for the virgin daughters of a village, and the family of any youth who attempted to seduce one of these institutionally secluded virgins was heavily fined, and even banished, by the fono of his village. This, as Holmes confirms, was the situation in Manu'a at the time of Mead's researches, as indeed it was thoughout Samoa in the 1920s. Thus, of the twenty-five adolescent girls aged, according to Mead, from 14 or 15 to 19 or 20, on whose behavior she based her conclusions, nine are listed in table 1 in *Coming of Age in Samoa* as being resident in a pastor's household. Further, of these same twenty-five girls, no fewer than thirteen are listed as having had no "heterosexual experience." In other words, more than half of those in this sample were virgins on Mead's own evidence, with one of them being a girl of 19 who in addition to being resident of the household of the pastor of Si'ufaga was a communicant member of the church. This situation, which Mead herself records, is obviously incongruent with her generalizations about Samoan female adolescents: more than half of the adolescent girls about whom she wrote in *Coming of Age in Samoa* were in fact virgins, and most of them, furthermore, institutionally secluded virgins.[20]

The traditional Samoan ideal of chastity for females before marriage tended, as Shore has noted, to be "quite rigidly upheld for the holder of a *taupou* title"; in Mead's words, it was virtually "a legal requirement." To what extent, then, in Samoa in the 1920s did the ideal of chastity for females before marriage also apply to adolescent girls who were not of taupou rank? According to the elders of Ta'ū who, when I interviewed them, well recollected the state of their culture in the mid 1920s, the requirement that sexually mature adolescent girls should remain chaste, was, at that time, very much the ideal of their strict protestant society. Thus, in the 1920s sexually mature adolescent girls were enjoined to become members of the Ekalesia, or communicant body of the church, it being one of the rules of the Ekalesia that sexual intercourse outside of marrige was strictly forbidden to its members (see Chapter 12). That in the prudish Christian society of Samoa in the 1920s, sexual intercourse between unmarried persons was held to be both a sin and a crime is confirmed by cases in the archives of the high court of American Samoa. For example, on 6 May 1929 in the district court at Fagatoga, Lafitaga, an unmarried man, having admitted that he knew it was wrong for a man and woman to have "intercourse with each other unless they were married," was accused of committing 'the crime of fornication" by "lewdly and lasciviously cohabiting" with a woman while not being legally married to her.[21]

Comparable values obtained in Western Samoa during this same period and also, as I was able to obseve at first hand, during the 1940s. In 1967 I was able to complete a detailed survey of the incidence of virginity in adolescent girls by making, with the assistance of my wife, a census of all the young females of a village on the south coast of Upolu born within the period 1945-1955. This gave a sample of sixty-seven individuals, varying in age from 12 to 22. We collected information on whether these girls and young women were virgins and whether they were members of the Ekalesia. If, to enable a comparison with Mead's data, we take from this sample the forty-one girls aged between 14 and 19, then thirty of them, or 73 percent, were virgins. The incidence of virginity in each of the years within this age range was as follows:[22]

Age	Number of girls	Number of virgins	% virgins
14	4	4	100
15	10	8	80
16	7	5	71
17	8	5	62
18	7	6	85
19	5	2	40
Total	41	30	73

In another detailed study, also in Upolu, of twenty-five women born between 1924 and 1947 whose ages were exactly known and for whom accurate data were available on the dates of birth of their children, we were able to calculate approximate age at first conception. In this sample only 12 percent had conceived when under seventeen and a half years of age—the youngest at sixteen years and three months. The mean age at first conception was nineteen and three-quarters years.

As this and the other evidence I have cited indicates, after the mid nineteenth century, when a puritanical Christian sexual morality was added to an existing traditional cult of virginity, Samoa became a society in which chastity was, in Shore's words, "the ideal for all women before marriage," and in which this religiously and culturally sanctioned ideal strongly influenced the actual behavior of adolescent girls. Although despite these severe moral values and the protective attention of their brothers, some girls (about 20 percent on the basis of the sample I have just discussed) became sexually active at about 15, the majority of pubescent females remained virgins until they were 17 or 18 years of age before going on an elopement. Further, the furtive sexual liaisons in which a minor proportion of adolescent females became, either willingly or unwillingly, involved were recognized by all concerned as shameful departures from the well-defined ideal of chastity.[23]

It is understandable, then, why Samoans are perturbed by Mead's depiction of them as a people for whom free lovemaking is "expected" among adolescent girls, so that the Samoans have come to be classed in the literature of anthropology as "one of the best known cases of institutionalized premarital sexuality." This conclusion is indeed so preposterously at variance with the realities of Samoan life that a special explanation is called for; as I shall discuss further in Chapter 19, all the indications are that the young Margaret Mead was, as a kind of joke, deliberately misled by her adolescent informants.[24]

While in all the Samoan communities I have studied a few girls remained virgins until they married in a religious ceremony, most of them lost the status of virgin by eloping from their families with the man who succeeded in deflowering them. Such an elopement, which is termed an *avaga*, is taken as establishing that the woman involved had previously been a virgin, and by eloping she avoids the shame of being subsequently revealed as some other man's pa'umutu. As Pritchard notes, a girl need spend no more than one night in the house of the man with whom she elopes for their union to be recognized and for any child born to them to be viewed as legitimate.[25] In many cases the defloration that precedes an avaga is the culmination of a seduction that the girl herself has actively encouraged. In other instances, the defloration occurs entirely without the girl's consent, through the use of either surreptitious or direct force; yet in these instances too, unless she follows the relatively rare course of going to the police, the girl will elope with her assailant to save her reputation and publicly demonstrate the fact of her erstwhile virginity.

A girl who elopes after a forced defloration will usually return to her natal household after an absence of one or more nights. Having lost the status of virgin, she is now more likely to accept the advances of a man; however, as N.A. Rowe, who was in Samoa at the same time as Mead, observed in the 1920s, "a Samoan girl's moral code opposes her going with a man unless, by living with him, she may be recognized as his wife." In cases where an avaga has been sought by a girl, it may lead to a lasting union, with the elopement being followed in some cases by a religious ceremony.[26]

Although, in Wendt's words, "marriage in church to a religious, conscientious, obedient virgin" is, in Samoa, "the dream of every aristocratic properly brought up son," this dream is not very commonly realized in the population at large. Of the marriages of the thirty-nine untitled males resident in Sa'anapu in January 1943, thirty-eight had originated in an avaga, followed in eleven instances (usually after some years) by a religious ceremony, and only one had begun with a religious ceremony. Under Samoan custom, however, an avaga is fully accepted as a form of marriage, with any sexual approach by another to either partner being viewed as attempted adultery.[27]

It was very much part of Mead's depiction of Samoan sexual mores that, in addition to free lovemaking being expected among adolescents, "adultery was not regarded as very serious." Many adulteries occurred, according to Mead, which hardly threatened the continuity of established relationships, and a man who seduced his neighbor's wife had simply to settle with his neighbor, as the society was not interested. To these assertions she added the claim that the Samoans had eliminated "many of the attitudes which have afflicted mankind, and perhaps jealousy most importantly of all" and that "jealousy, as a widespread social phenomenon" was "very rare in Samoa."[28]

All of these statements are seriously in error. As Pritchard records, and as Wilkes, Turner, Stuebel, and Brown confirm, Samoan custom in former times sanctioned "the summary punishment of adultery by death," with, as Turner also notes, the injured party being "at liberty to seek revenge on the brother, son or any member of the family to which the guilty party belonged." Again, an adulteress was liable, as Stuebel records and Turner and Brown confirm, to be punished by having her head fractured and bones broken or by having her nose or an ear cut off and cast away.[29]

Although these extreme punishments had been interdicted by the time of Mead's researches in Manu'a, adultery nonetheless remained a serious delict. It was listed, in recognition of Samoan attitudes, in the Regulations and Orders for the Government of American Samoa that were in force in the 1920s, as an offense for which those guilty "shall be fined not more than one hundred dollars, or imprisoned not more than twelve months, or both," and in the court archives of American Samoa for the 1920s there are cases of both men and women being fined for adultery. Again, the Royal Commission that met in Western Samoa in 1927 was told by Toelupe, the chairman of the Fono of Faipule, that adultery was "a very serious charge in Samoa" for which an offender together with his family might be banished from his village. This was also the custom, going well beyond the law of the day, in Manu'a in the 1920s, where, as I was informed by the talking chiefs of Si'ufaga in 1967, "the judgment of a local polity is exceedingly severe in the case of adultery, with the land of an offender being taken from him."[30]

It was thus by no means true, as Mead asserts, that Samoan society is "not interested" in the offense of adultery. Rather, as soon as an adultery, either actual or attempted, becomes known a special juridicial fono is promptly summoned. Thus, in Sa'anapu in February 1967 when Seu, an untitled 28-year-old married man with two children, was discovered to have made a sexual advance to a 17-year-old virgin of another titular family to whom he was distantly related, a fono manu was at once summoned. At this fono the chiefs of these two families, as well as Seu, were berated in the most extreme terms. Seu's action, said the officiating talking chief, was "a happening frightening to both ghosts and men." Then, turning in the direction of Seu and his father, who were held to be principally responsible, he shouted with great emotional force: "Ugly! Ugly! I am ashamed even to mention your act! It is forbidden! It is forbidden! Shame on you! Shame on you! Shame on you!" Seu's family was fined two large pigs, two large tins of biscuits, and one hundred corms of taro, while the family of the girl he had been with was fined half this amount.

Such a judicial fono is summoned promptly to forestall the possibility of revenge being taken by those who have been offended by an attempted or actual adultery. The taking of private revenge is by no means uncommon. In 1924, for example, as F. H. Flaherty recounts, when a young man from another village made advances to the wife of the son of the pastor of Safune, he was later accosted by two men of Safune, accused of having done "a very wrong thing *fa'aSamoa*," and so severely wounded by a stab in the neck that he subsequently died. On other occasions, adultery may lead to much more widespread trouble. Fay Calkins records a case in which a chief named Ofu, having eloped with the wife of another chief of the village of Salani, in Upolu, was subjected to the punishment of saisai (see Chapter 13) being "tied to a pole and presented to the offended chief for roasting," and then banished from Salani forever. This incident split the village in two, various of its chiefs finishing up in hospital and in jail, and twenty years elapsed before they met again as a single fono.[31]

Adultery in Samoa is then very far from being, as Mead asserted, merely a personal peccadillo; nor is it true that the Samoans have eliminated jealousy, as Leslie A. White was prepared to believe, arguing on the basis of Mead's reports that jealousy is not a natural emotion. In fact, in the words of C. C. Marsack, who was for many years the Chief Justice of Western Samoa, "Samoans are extremely prone to fits of jealousy ... A considerable proportion of cases of assault coming before the Courts—and such cases were very numerous—arose from jealousy." Many other observers of Samoan behavior have come to the same conclusion. Brenchley, for example, who visited Samoa in 1865, wrote of Samoan men being extremely jealous, and keeping "a sharp lookout on their wives."[32]

Sexual jealousy, furthermore, is most commonly displayed in cases of actual or suspected adultery. In 1956, for example, after Mata, the wife of Tavita, had accused his older brother, Tule, of making sexual approaches to her during her husband's absence,

Tavita attacked his brother, stabbing him five times in the back and neck. Again, when in 1964 Salau saw a schoolteacher making advances to his wife, he slashed him six times with a long-bladed bush knife, inflicting grievous wounds on his arms and shoulders. In court, where Salau was sentenced to six months' imprisonment, his wife attributed this attack to his intense sexual jealousy.[33]

Women are also prone to fits of jealousy. As Gerber records, one of her informants in Tutuila, in explaining the Samoan word for sexual jealousy, *fuā*, said: "That's if a woman gets angry if her husband goes to another woman. Then she says, 'Go to her, don't come back!' Then she starts a fight with the other woman." In one case, Gerber reports, a wife went looking for her husband's lover with a rope to strangle her. As this suggests, some women when jealous can be as violent as any man. In 1964, for example, Mele, aged 29, was left for another woman by her husband, Teo, soon after the birth of their second child. She sought out Teo and the woman and attacked them with a bush knife as they were sleeping together. She was later convicted of inflicting grievous bodily harm and sentenced to fifteen months' imprisonment. Jealousy, then, is by no means absent from the behavior of Samoans, and they most definitely do not—as Murdock, echoing Mead, asserted in 1934—"laugh incredulously at tales of passionate jealousy."[34]

Yet another aspect of Mead's depiction of Samoa as a place where "love between the sexes is a light and pleasant dance" is her claim that among Samoans "male sexuality" is "never defined as aggressiveness that must be curbed." Thus in 1928 she categorically stated that "the idea of forceful rape or of any sexual act to which both participants do not give themselves freely is completely foreign to the Samoan mind."[35] These assertions are, once again, wholly misleading, for in fact the incidence of rape in Samoa, both surreptitious and forceful, is among the highest to be found anywhere in the world.

Surreptitious rape, or *moetotolo* (literally "sleep crawling") is a peculiarly Samoan custom in which a man, having crept into a house under cover of darkness, sexually assaults a sleeping woman. As Mead herself notes, there was in pagan Samoa

on the part of the manaias and their male followers a preoccupation with the abduction and deflowering of the taupou of
some rival local polity, such a flamboyant feat being celebrated
far and wide by its perpetrators as a victory over their rivals. It
was, however, a dangerous pursuit, for an abduction party discovered lurking on the outskirts of a rival village would be
fiercely attacked, and, as Mead correctly reports, the abduction
and forced defloration of a taupou was sometimes the occasion
of warfare between villages. There is throughout Samoa a comparable preoccupation on the part of young men in general with
the deflowering, by whatever means, of any sexually mature
virgin, a success in this activity being deemed a personal triumph and a demonstration of masculinity. Given this preoccupation, rape, both surreptitious and forcible, is a common occurrence in Samoa. While in Samoa Mead had virtually no
contact with male groups, and thus she failed to understand this
situation. Although she refers to moetotolo behavior as "surreptitious rape" and as "definitely abnormal," she goes on to in-
terpret this custom, quite mistakenly, as the stealthy appro-
priation of "the favors that are meant for another," the sleep
crawler relying, so she claims, on a girl's "expecting a lover" or
on "the chance that she will indiscriminately accept any
comer." Thus, as viewed by Mead, the custom of moetotolo involves no force, only deceit.[36]

This is a major misinterpretation. As anyone who has studied the phenomenology of rape will know, successful persona-
tion by a rapist is an extremely rare event, and, in none of the
cases of surreptitious rape which I have investigated has perso-
nation been the method used by the assailant. The intention of
the sleep crawler is, in fact, to creep into a house in which a female virgin is sleeping, and before she has awoken to rape her
manually by inserting one or two of his fingers in her vagina, an
action patterned on the ceremonial defloration of a taupou.
This achieved, the sleep crawler at once or, as is more common,
on a convenient subsequent occasion, claims the female he has
forcibly deflowered as his wife, telling her in private that she has
no choice but to elope with him, and that if she does not elope
he will bring shame on her and her family by letting it be known

that she is not a virgin. These mores of the moetotolo are well depicted by the Samoan author Fa'afouina Pula in *The Samoan Dance of Life*, where he describes a Samoan youth waiting for a girl to go to sleep so he might "touch" her genitals ("touch" here being a euphemism for manual defloration), this being, as Fa'afouina Pula observes, a "trick" known to all Samoan youths. If the moetotolo is successful in his clandestine assault on her virginity, Fa'afouina Pula explains, the girl knows that the youth responsible "can go away and boast in front of her whole village ... and so she will come outside and let him do anything he pleases." Thus, as Matauaina, a taupou of Leasina, Tutuila, stated on 27 September 1922 in the district court of Fagatogo, "when the man came to me as I was sleeping he held me down and put his fingers in my private parts ... then I sat up and wept, and as it was no use for me to remain in my own family, we went to his family."[37]

The custom of moetotolo, patterned on the ceremonial defloration of a taupou, is then intrinsic to Samoan culture, having been reported from pagan times, as by Platt in 1836. Further, far from adding "zest to the surreptitious love-making that is conducted at home," as Mead asserts, surreptitious rape is greatly feared by Samoan girls, and is viewed with deadly seriousness by the family of any girl actually assaulted. A surreptitious rapist, if captured, is fiercely beaten by the brothers of his victim and then heavily punished at a specially summoned juridical fono. For example, in 1944 a 19-year-old youth of Sa'anapu was disturbed while attempting a moetotolo on a titular chief's daughter, and lost his loin cloth as he strove to escape. He was banished from the village, and his family was fined two large pigs, two large tins of bisucits, and two hundred corms of taro. Further, the youth himself was ridiculed by being given the demeaning nickname of Moetotolo Telefua, or The Naked Sleep-Crawler. Should a case of moetotolo be reported to the police in Western Samoa it is classed as indecent assault and a criminal offense, with a prison sentence being commonly imposed by the court. For example, when a 34-year-old man who had manually raped a sleeping 17-year-old virgin of Apia village in September 1967 was apprehended by two of her brothers, he was heavily beaten, then handed over to the police, charged with indecent assault, and later sentenced to three years' imprisonment for his "vicious attack."[38]

A detailed analysis of fifteen cases of surreptitious rape, drawn mainly from police records, shows that in all cases the victim was sleeping in a house at the time of the assault. Some 75 percent of assaults took place late at night, the remainder early in the morning. All assaults were wholly unexpected, and in no sense sought, by the female victims. In all of the twelve cases for which data are available, finger insertion was attempted; it was achieved in about 60 percent of instances, about half of the victims being virgins. Further, while sleep crawlers usually try to achieve their end by guile, my inquiries showed that there is recourse to violence in about 25 percent of cases.

Sleep crawling, properly described as a form of surreptitious rape, is clearly distinguished by Samoans from forcible rape, in which a man resorts to physical violence to overpower a fully conscious woman and then sexually assault her. In Samoa, however, forcible rape has the peculiar feature that the rapist, immediately after overpowering his victim, attempts to insert one or two of his fingers in her vagina. An analysis of thirty-two cases of forcible rape showed that finger insertion was attempted by all these rapists and successfully achieved by 88 percent. It will be seen, then, that surreptitious and forcible rape have much in common culturally, both involving force and both being characterized by the insertion of the male assailant's fingers in the vagina of his victim, in imitation of the defloration of a taupou.

Many Samoans aver that the principal aim of a male who engages in either surreptitious or forcible rape is to obtain for himself a virgin wife. This view is supported by the accounts, in court records, of the behavior of rapists after deflowering a female. For example, in December 1960, immediately after an 18-year-old youth had overpowered a 15-year-old virgin by striking her on the solar plexus with his clenched fist and had then manually deflowered her, he held up his bloodstained fingers to his male companion and shouted elatedly, "This girl has fallen to me!" He then added, "Now we shall live together as man and wife!" In another case, a youth of 20 who had manually raped a girl of 15 shouted at her mother, when she tried to rescue her daughter, to go away as the girl was now his wife.[39]

An analysis of thirty-two cases of forcible rape and attempted rape, again mainly drawn from police records, showed that 60 percent of the victims were virgins. In the typical case of forcible rape a girl of from 15 to 19 is alone and away from the settled parts of her village when accosted by a male of from 19 to 23 years of age. Often he is known to the girl, and he believes her to be a virgin. When she tries to escape, her assailant commonly resorts to the culturally standardized stratagem of knocking her unconscious with a heavy punch to her solar plexus. After inserting one or two of his fingers into his victim's vagina, the rapist usually also attempts penile intromission, which is achieved in approximately 44 percent of cases.

Many of the forcible rapes that occur in Samoa are dealt with at the village level by a special judicial fono, with even heavier fines being imposed than in cases of surreptitious rape. A proportion of cases, however, are reported to the police, and it thus becomes possible, by reference to the police records of Western Samoa, to form an approximate estimate of the comparative incidence of forcible rape in Samoa.

In the United States in 1968 there were 30 reported rapes or attempted rapes per 100,000 females. In his *Rape: Offenders and Their Victims*, J. M. Macdonald presents rape rates from several other countries. Norway has less than one rape per 100,-000 females per annum; England, three rapes; Poland, seven; Japan, twelve; and Turkey, fourteen rapes or attempted rapes per 100,000 females per annum. So, as Macdonald notes, the available statistics suggest that the United States has an unusually high rape rate. How then does the Samoan rate compare with that of the United States? In 1966, when the total population of Western Samoa was about 131,000, the number of forcible and attempted rapes reported to the police in Western Samoa was thirty-eight, which is equal to a rate of about sixty rapes per 100,000 females per annum, a rate twice as high as that of the United States and twenty times as high as that of

England. Further, if cases of surreptitious rape, or indecent assault, reported to the police be included, then the Western Samoan rate becomes approximately 160 rapes per 100,000 females per annum.[40] These figures, while only very approximate (for in Western Samoa a very considerable proportion of forcible and surreptitious rapes are, in fact, not reported to the police), do indicate that rape is unusually common in Samoa; the Samoan rape rate is certainly one of the highest to be found anywhere in the world.[41]

There is every indication that this high incidence of rape has long been characteristic of Samoan society. Cases are reported by the early missionaries, as by Pratt in 1845. The court records of American Samoa, which begin in 1900, note numerous cases of rape having been committed by Samoans during the first three decades of this century, and the jail statistics included in the exhibits attached to the hearings of the congressional commission on American Samoa of 1930 show that at the end of the 1920s rape was the third most common offense after assault and larceny, any male convicted of rape being liable to imprisonment for a term not exceeding ten years and not less than two. Again, in Western Samoa during the years to which Mead's findings refer, cases of rape by Samoans were regularly reported in the *Samoa Times*.[42]

Both surreptitious and forcible rape, it is important to emphasize, involve culturally transmitted male practices. In surreptitious rape the rapist's practice, or "trick," to use Fa'afouina Pula's term, is suddenly to insert his tautly extended index and middle fingers into his victim's vagina while she is asleep. In forcible rape it is the technique of knocking the victim unconscious by a heavy punch immediately over her solar plexus. Both of these practices are part of Samoan culture, and I have witnessed them being communicated by one individual to another within groups of Samoan males. Mead then was markedly at error in asserting as she did in 1938 that "the idea of forcible rape or of any sexual act to which both participants do not give themselves freely is completely foreign to the Samoan mind." Rather, as there is an abundance of evidence to demonstrate, both surreptitious and forcible rape have long been intrinsic to the sexual mores of Samoan men and are major elements in their sexual behavior.[43]

It should now be apparent that Samoa, where the cult of female virginity is probably carried to a greater extreme than in any other culture known to anthropology, was scarcely the place to situate a paradise of adolescent free love. How did Mead deal with the resounding enigma of a society which demanded that a girl should, in her own words, "be both receptive to the advances of many lovers and yet capable of showing the token of virginity at marriage"? The solution, according to Mead, was to place "the onus of virginity not on the whole young female population but on the *taupou*." Yet the enigma very much remains, for in functional terms what is this elaborate concern with ceremonial virginity doing in a culture in which "freedom of sexual experimentation by female adolescents" is, according to Mead, "expected"? The "onus of virginity" placed on a ceremonial virgin was, we know, extremely heavy, for as Mead's Samoan informants told her, should a taupou "prove not to be a virgin, her female relatives fell upon her and beat her with stones, disfiguring and sometimes fatally injuring the girl who had shamed their house."[44]

This punishment of the taupou who turned out to be not a virgin, which had been accurately reported to Mead by her informants in Manu'a, and which is confirmed by Williams, D'Urville, Turner, Pritchard, Brenchley, Riemann, Brown, and other writers on early Samoa, was, despite this weight of evidence, considered by Mead to be "too severe for the Samoan ethos," and in 1930 she published an entirely new ethnographic account of the ceremonial defloration of a Samoan taupou. A taupou, who was required to submit to ceremonial defloration on the occasion of her marriage, but who had lost her virginity, was only punished, Mead stated, if she concealed this fact. "If she confessed to having lost her virginity," Mead continued, "the old woman cannily substituted a bowl of chicken's blood and the ceremony proceeded without anyone knowing of the family's shame," while "with true Samoan courtesy in compromise, the talking chief of the husband connived also at the deception."[45]

This account, which Mead published in 1930 in *Social Organization of Manu'a,* betrays a complete ignorance of the function of ceremonial defloration in Samoa. As I have already indicated, ceremonial defloration is a social mechanism for making absolutely certain that a bridegroom of rank is taking to wife a female with whom no rival male could possibly have had sexual intercourse. The whole procedure is designed by an intensely rank-conscious society to avoid all possibility of a bridegroom of rank being shamed by a male rival who, if a bride's virginity were not publicly tested, might subsequently claim to have had prior sexual connection with her. It is thus entirely contrary to all expectation that a talking chief, being his chief's active supporter, would connive at having his chief's intended wife deceptively declared a virgin. When in 1967 I put this proposition to the chiefs of Manu'a, they indignantly rejected Mead's account, saying that if the supporters of a seeming taupou resorted to the unprincipled and highly insulting subterfuge of bringing chicken's blood to a ceremonial defloration they would at once be heavily attacked. They also denied that Mead could have been told of such a practice in Manu'a.

In this they were correct, for the account of ceremonial defloration that Mead incorporated in her monograph in 1930 had been obtained not from any inhabitant of Manu'a but from a Mrs. Pheobe Parkinson, whom she had met in New Britain in 1929, and who had, according to Mead, the "answer" for which she was seeking. A detailed account of what Mead was told by Phoebe Parkinson, whom she describes as possessing "singular gifts as a raconteur," is contained in Mead's article of 1960 "Weaver of the Border." As Mead reports her, Phoebe Parkinson declared, "If a girl is not a virgin she will tell her old women, and they will secretly bring the blood of a fowl or a pig and smear it on the *i'e sina*" (a kind of mat). This, as it stands, is a quite incredible tale, for in Samoa to associate anyone of rank with a pig is the heaviest of insults, and the use of pig's blood in substitution for that of a high-ranking taupou at her ceremonial defloration, being both insulting and sacrilegious, would at all costs be avoided.[46]

Who was Phoebe Parkinson, who indulged in such ill-in-

formed gossip? At the time of Mead's meeting with her in New
Britain in 1929, she was a 66-year-old widow. Her father, Jonas
Coe, was born in New York in 1822 and settled in western
Samoa in 1845. His daughter Phoebe was born in 1863 in Apia
on the island of Upolu, where her father had built himself a
large house, "all cut out and planned in San Francisco." Her
mother was a Samoan whom Coe had abandoned. Soon after
Phoebe's birth, however, he claimed her to bring her up strictly
as a European, sending her to the Convent School in Apia
where she was educated by French nuns and developed the wish
to become a nun herself. Instead, at 16 years of age Phoebe Coe
was married to Richard Parkinson, a German surveyor, and two
years later she sailed with her husband and child from Samoa to
New Britain, never to return. From her statements to Mead it is
evident that Phoebe Parkinson's knowledge of the traditional
culture of Samoa was essentially anecdotal, being mainly based
I would suppose on the gossip of European settlers to whom she
had listened when growing up in Apia. "Once," so she told
Mead, she had "a real glimpse of Samoan life" when as a young
girl she spent two weeks living in a Samoan village. Phoebe
Parkinson was then in no sense a reliable informant on Samoan
culture, and in particular not on ceremonial defloration in
Manu'a, where she had never set foot.[47]

It was, however, on no firmer foundation than the fible-
fables of Phoebe Parkinson that Mead based her apparently authoritative version of the deceptive form that ceremonial defloration took in Manu'a—the highest-ranking polity in all
Samoa. And she did this, in a technical monograph on Manu'an
social organization, without divulging that her information had
come not from the people of Manu'a, whom she ought to have
consulted on this crucially important issue, but from an old lady
living in New Britain who possessed singular gifts as a raconteur. In subsequent years, moreover, Mead embroidered her
version of 1930, going far beyond the outlandish tale she had
been told by Mrs. Parkinson in 1929. In 1935 she described how
in Samoa the defloration of a ceremonial virgin could be "grace-
fully faked," and in 1950 she published in her influential book
Male and Female the quite baseless statement that in a Sa-

moan defloration ceremony "the blood of virginity could always be counterfeited," adding without a jot of substantive evidence that a taupou who had lost her virginity in premarital intercourse was in danger of being "beaten to death" not "for her frailty, but for her failure to make an adequate provision of chicken blood"—so completely misrepresenting the attitude of the dignified and punctilious Samoans toward one of their most sacrosanct traditional institutions. It is difficult to imagine a greater travesty than this of the fa'aSamoa.[48]

17

Adolescence

WE HAVE SEEN that the "picture of the whole social life of Samoa" that Mead presented as an ethnographic background to her main conclusion in *Coming of Age in Samoa* is, in numerous respects, fundamentally in error. What then of her assertions about adolescence in Samoa? Both Mead and Benedict fully recognized adolescence as a biological process. Benedict, for example, wrote of adolescence as being "by definition tied up with a universal biological fact in human development," while for Mead the adolescent period was "the most striking instance" of "an innate pattern of growth." In Samoa, however, according to Mead the "disruptive concomitants" inherent in adolescence had, because of the mild and easy social environment, been "successfully muted." Adolescence among the Samoans, she claimed, being "peculiarly free of all those characteristics which make it a period dreaded by adults and perilous for young people in more complex—and often also, in more primitive—societies," was "the age of maximum ease." Thus human nature, within the "different social form" of Samoa, lacked "the conflicts which are so often characteristic of adolescence." On the basis of this claim, as I have recounted in Chapter 5, Mead unequivocally asserted the sovereignty of culture over biology.[1]

Is it in fact true, as Mead claimed, that the behavior of Samoan adolescents is untroubled and unstressed and lacks the conflicts that are so often characteristic of this period of development? As Herant Katchadourian notes, "research on ordinary adolescents has generally failed to substantiate claims of the inevitability and universality of adolescent stress." Nonetheless, the findings of W. A. Lunden, M. R. Haskell and L. Yablonsky, and others have clearly shown that the years of adolescence are hazardous for many, with delinquency in the United States and elsewhere reaching a peak at about age 16. To what extent, then, is adolescent delinquency present in Samoa? In particular, what can be concluded about delinquency among Samoan female adolescents from the information Mead herself has provided?[2]

Mead discusses delinquency in *Coming of Age in Samoa* in the general context of deviance. For Benedict and Mead deviance was a concept derived directly from their theory of cultural determinism, the basic notion of which was of the "undifferentiated" raw material of human nature being "moulded into shape by its society." One of the corollaries of this notion was that this molding process was sometimes ineffective, with the individual who "failed to receive the cultural imprint" becoming a "cultural misfit," or deviant.[3] These deviants from the cultural pattern of their society Benedict and Mead then relegated to a special category, as in the chapter of *Coming of Age in Samoa* entitled "The Girl in Conflict." In this chapter, which is crucially important for her whole argument, Mead distinguishes between what she calls "deviants upwards" from the pattern of Samoan culture, and deviants "in a downward direction." Upward deviants, she writes, are those who demand "a different or improved environment," and reject "the traditional choices." In this category she puts three girls, all of whom she lists as having had "no heterosexual experience." Lita, two months past menarche, who "wished to go to Tutuila and become a nurse or teacher"; Sona, three years past menarche, who was "overbearing in manner, arbitrary and tyrannous towards younger people, impudently deferential towards her elders," and who blatantly proclaimed "her pursuit of ends different from those approved by her fellows"; and Ana, aged 19, an intensely religious girl who was "convinced that she was too frail to bear children." All three of these girls, according to Mead, might, at any time, have come into real conflict with their society, but at the time of her inquiries they had not, and so remained deviants upwards, rather than deviants in a downward direction, or delinquents.[4]

A delinquent, Mead defined as an individual who is "maladjusted to the demands of her civilization, and who comes definitely into conflict with her group, not because she adheres to a different standard, but because she violates the group standards which are also her own." Of her sample of twenty-five adolescent girls, says Mead, two girls, Lola and Mala, had been delinquents for several years. Lola, aged 17, of Si'ufaga, was a quarrelsome, insubordinate, vituperative, and spiteful girl who had "continuously violated" the standards of her group. She "contested every point, objected to every request, shirked her work, fought her sisters, mocked her mother," had been expelled from residence in the pastor's house after a fight with another delinquent, and in a jealous rage had publicly accused a female rival of being a thief, so "setting the whole village by the ears." Mala, aged about 16, also of Si'ufaga, was insinuating and treacherous, as well as being a liar and a thief.[5]

In addition to these two girls of Si'ufaga, Mead also mentions under her "conception of delinquency" a girl of Faleasao, called Sala. Sala, three years past menarche, was a "stupid, underhand, deceitful" girl who had been expelled from residence in the pastor's house for "sex offences." This expulsion, which is a serious matter in Samoan eyes, shows that Sala had also violated group standards, and that she too, in terms of Mead's definition, was a delinquent. Another girl of Faleasao whom Mead discusses was Moana, 16 and a half, who, having begun her "amours" at 15, allowed her uncle, who had been asked by her parents "to adopt her and attempt to curb her waywardness," to avail himself "of her complacency." This sexual liaison, as Mead notes, was "in direct violation of the brother and sister taboo," Moana's uncle being young enough for her to call him brother. It was thus an instance of incest, a heinous offense, the perpetrators of which, according to Samoans, are liable to supernatural punishment. Thus Schultz recounts that when Mata'utia had sexual intercourse with his cousin Levalasi, he was attacked by a loathsome disease, while Levalasi gave birth to a clot of blood. Moana's incestuous liaison with her uncle resulted, Mead states, in a family feud. Moana's violation of one of the strictest prohibitions of Samoan society was thus unquestionably a delinquent act in terms of Mead's definition, although Mead inexplicably did not even class her as a deviant.[6]

It is evident, then, from Mead's own account that four of her twenty-five adolescent girls were delinquents. Further, from her descriptions of the actions of these four girls, it is apparent that instances of delinquent behavior by Lola and Moana occurred during Mead's brief sojourn in Manu'a from November 1925 to May 1926. If we assume, conservatively, on the basis of Mead's reports, that among the twenty-five adolescents she studied there was *one* delinquent act per annum, this is equivalent to a rate of forty such acts per thousand.

How does this rate compare with delinquency rates in other societies? Mead, as we have seen, defines a delinquent as one who violates the standards of her group. The examples she gives of delinquent behavior plainly caused considerable social disruption, setting a whole village by the ears in the case of Lola and resulting in a family feud in the case of Moana. They were, in other words, of a kind that would warrant their being considered by a juridical fono. It thus is possible, though Mead did not attempt this, to compare the incidence of delinquent behavior in Samoa with that of Western countries, where delinquency, as Sandhu notes, is defined as "any act . . . which might be brought before court and adjudicated." Mead's twenty-five female adolescents, as she notes, ranged in age from 14 or 15 to 19 or 20. If we assume an age range of 14 to 19, it becomes possible to make a comparison, on the basis of the rates given by D. J. West in *The Young Offender,* for indictable offenses by females per thousand of population of the same age, in England and Wales in 1965. In the age-group 14–19 the average rate per thousand was 4.00. In other words, the delinquency rate which seems likely to have been characteristic of Mead's Samoan female delinquents in 1925, was about ten times higher than that which existed among female adolescents in England and Wales in 1965.[7]

This comparison is obviously only approximate. It does, however, indicate that among the girls studied by Mead in 1925–1926 delinquency was in fact at quite a high level. Further, Mead's relegating of delinquents to a separate population of deviants, or "cultural misfits," to which her generalizations about Samoan adolescence supposedly do not apply, is revealed as a decidedly unscientific maneuver, for her four delinquents and three "upwards deviants," who, together, make up 28 percent of her sample of twenty-five female adolescents, are obviously every bit as much the product of the Samoan social environment as are the eighteen other adolescent girls who were, Mead tells us, untroubled and unstressed.

The conclusions about adolescence in Samoa to which Mead came in 1929 were based, as we have seen, on a few months' study of twenty-five girls. She had no compunction, however, in extending these conclusions, in later years, to male adolescents. Thus, in 1937 her statement that adolescence in Samoa was "the age of maximum ease" was applied to both males and females, and in 1950 she asserted that "the boy who would flee from too much pressure on his young manhood hardly exists in Samoa." These statements were made without specific investigation by Mead of Samoan male adolescents. As we have seen, the delinquency rate among Samoan female adolescents is, in comparative terms, high. It has long been known that delinquency in male adolescents is commonly four to five times higher than in females. In this respect Samoa is no different from other countries; the ratio of males to females among 932 adolescent first offenders in Western Samoa was five to one.

Mead's statements about Samoan male adolescents are, then, entirely unwarranted. As I shall presently show, Samoan delinquency rates for male adolescents are closely comparable to those of other countries.[8]

First, however, let me note that I have yet to meet a Samoan who agrees with Mead's assertion that adolescence in Samoan society is smooth, untroubled, and unstressed. Vaiao Ala'ilima, a graduate in the social sciences, who was born in Western Samoa and lived in American Samoa from the age of 12 onward, completely disagrees, as his wife Fay Calkins has recorded, that Samoan adolescence is not "a period of 'Sturm and Drang.'" Aiono Fanaafi Le Tagaloa, a graduate of the University of London, when in Australia in 1971 as Director of Education in Western Samoa, observed that although it had been claimed that the Samoan adolescent does not suffer the same stress and strains as an American girl, she knew that a Samoan girl, who showed her stress in different ways, did not go through "a less stormy adolescent period." And To'oa Salamasina Malietoa, who as principle of Papauta School in Western Samoa has extensive knowledge of Samoan adolescent girls, remarked to me in December 1967 that the lives of many of these girls are far from being untroubled and unstressed.[9]

These judgments from highly educated Samoans who possess direct personal knowledge of what it means to be an adolescent in Samoa are fully borne out by statements confided to my wife and me by adolescents, both male and female, whom we came to know particularly well. These adolescents would tell us of the tensions between themselves and their parents, and of their emotional distress during altercations with their families or when they were heavily dominated by someone in authority. One 17-year-old girl, for example, who wrote down for us in her own words the story of her life, described her feelings of intense resentment at being beaten by her mother, and her distress at what was often said to her, adding that her life and that of others like her was merely one of servitude.

These subjective statements are fully consistent with our observational data on adolescent behavior in Samoa. As I have noted, Samoan children continue to be physically punished well into adolescence. In the course of my fieldwork I observed fifty-six individuals aged 19 and under being physically punished by a parent, older sibling, or other senior member of a family. Of these, seventeen, or 30 percent, were between the ages of 11 and 19. Again, in eight cases, drawn from police records, of prosecutions for excessive punishment, half of the victims were aged between 12 and 15.

From this and other evidence I have presented it is clearly evident that not a few Samoans, during adolescence, are subjected to psychological stress. This stress, as I have documented in Chapter 15, is evinced in musu states, and in severe cases in hysterical illnesses and suicides—the Samoan suicide rate for adolescents being, the evidence suggests, significantly higher than in some other countries.

As Katchadourin notes, the attainment of puberty is marked by steady and rapid improvement in physical strength, skill and endurance, and this development is also marked by the involvement of adolescents in aggressive encounters of various kinds. A sample of first offenders drawn at random from the police records of Western Samoa yielded 528 cases of acts of violence by males and 218 by females in the age range of 12 to 22 years. As shown in figure 2, there is a rapid rise in the incidence of acts of violence from about age 14 onward, with this incidence reaching a peak at age 16. Again, as is apparent from the cases discussed in Chapters 10 and 11, from early adolescence onward both males and females tend to join in affrays.[10]

There is also a peak at age 16 in offenses against authority, particularly by males. From early adolescence onward Samoan youths may be observed grimacing and making threatening gestures at their elders, including chiefs, behind their backs, especially after having been punished or reprimanded; with the attainment of puberty, youths will occasionally lose control and openly attack those in authority over them. For example, in April 1965 a 31-year-old chief, patroling a village in Savai'i to enforce the ten P.M. curfew, came upon a group of five male adolescents who were breaking this curfew by playing a guitar and singing, and he at once set about chastising them with a board. Instead of scattering, as would children, at this show of chiefly

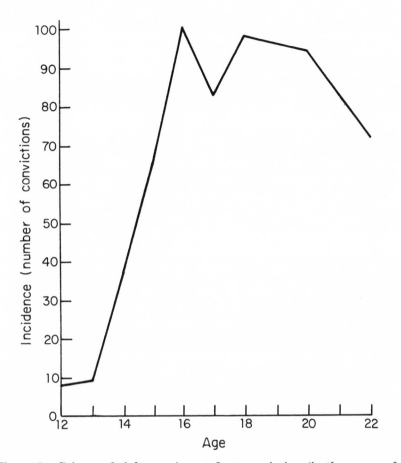

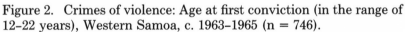

Figure 2. Crimes of violence: Age at first conviction (in the range of 12–22 years), Western Samoa, c. 1963–1965 (n = 746).

authority, one of these youths hurled a stone at the chief with such force as to expose the bone of his forehead and put him in hospital for a fortnight with concussion.[11]

Another measure of the involvement of adolescents in aggressive activity is obtained from a sample of forty cases, drawn at random from police records, of convictions for using insulting or indecent words. In this sample sixteen, or 40 percent, of those convicted were aged between 14 and 19, with thirteen of these sixteen adolescents being girls. As these figures indicate, verbal aggression is very common among adolescent girls in Samoa, and gives rise to much fighting between them.

Samoan adolescents from about 14 years of age onward begin to become involved in stressful situations that are sexual in origin. In a sample of 2,180 male first offenders there were no convictions for sexual offenses by individuals younger than 14. There was, however, one case of indecent assault by a 14-year-old youth, and of the total of forty-five convictions for indecent assault, rape, and attempted rape, nineteen, or 42 percent, of the offenders were males aged between 14 and 19, an incidence comparable to that existing in the United States. Menachem Amir, for example, records that in the United States 40.3 percent of forcible rape offenders are aged between 15 and 19. In the case of victims of rape, however, there is an appreciable difference between the United States and Samoa. Whereas according to Amir only 24.9 percent of rape victims in the United States are in the age-group 15–19, in a sample of thirty-two cases of rape and attempted rape from Western Samoa, 62 percent of the victims were in this age-group. A statistic available from Australia suggests that the incidence of virgins among rape victims is appreciably higher in Samoa than in other cultures: while according to J. P. Bush 30.5 percent of rape victims in Victoria, Australia were virgins before they were assaulted, the incidence of virgins in my Samoan sample of rape victims was 60 percent.[12]

As these incidences indicate, the traditional sexual mores of their society subject Samoan girls, from puberty onward, to formidable stresses. Within their families, and as members of the Ekalesia (as the great majority of them are), they are subjected

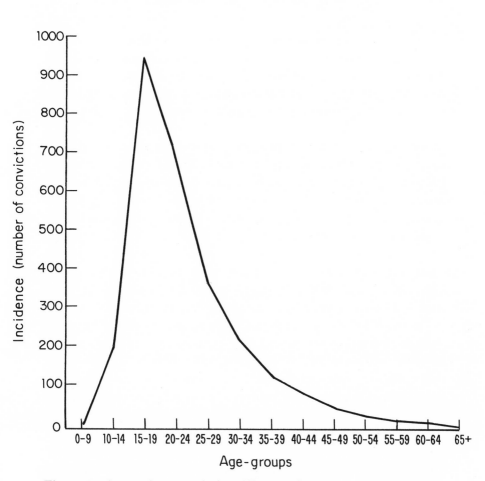

Figure 3. Age at first conviction, Western Samoa, c. 1963–1965 (n = 2717).

to a searching discipline aimed at safeguarding their virginity until a respectable marriage can be arranged—while during this same time they are exposed to the risk of both surreptitious and forcible rape. Thus, it is commonplace in Samoan villages for pubescent girls to be warned that they must sleep in the company of other girls of their family, so lessening the likelihood of becoming the victim of a moetotolo, and in particular that they must not walk alone beyond the precincts of a village for fear of being raped. Again, when a girl does finally elope from her family, as most do, from about 19 years of age onward, this occasion is commonly fraught with uncertainty and tension. These ordeals that the sexual mores of Samoa present to girls at puberty can generate very appreciable stresses, culminating from time to time in acts of suicide, as in the cases of Tupe and Malu (see Chapter 15) and of the 22-year-old girl (see Chapter 16) who took her own life after having lost her virginity to a moetotolo.

Now to return to the general discussion of delinquency among Samoan adolescents: as we have already seen, an analysis of the information that Mead herself provides on the behavior of Samoan girls aged 14–19 in Manu'a in the mid 1920s reveals what appears to have been a comparatively high rate of adolescent delinquency. In order to test further Mead's assertion that the adolescent period in Samoa in both males and females is untroubled and lacks the conflicts that tend to exist elsewhere, I decided, in 1967, to make a more detailed inquiry into the incidence of delinquency among adolescents in Western Samoa. At that time the only statistics available in Western Samoa on the incidence of criminal offenses were contained in the annual reports of the Police and Prisons Department, and these did not include information on the ages of offenders. A method that was open to me, however, was to compile, from police records, a *random* sample of convicted offenders, noting in each case the age and sex of the offender, the nature of the offense, and the date of conviction. The sample I compiled in this way totaled 2,717 convicted offenders. The offenses covered in this random sample included assault and various other crimes of violence; the "provoking of a breach of the peace"; theft and other offenses against property; trespass; rape and indecent as-

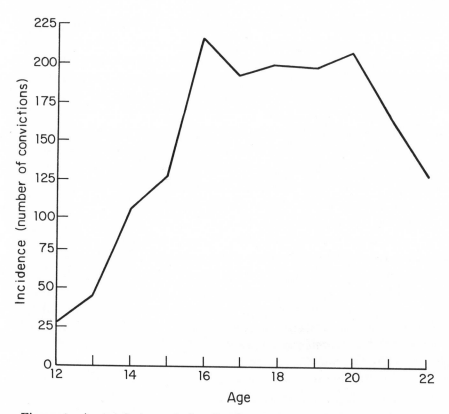

Figure 4. Age at first conviction (in the range of 12–22 years), Western Samoa, c. 1963–1965 (n = 1607).

sault; abduction; obstructing the police; uttering threatening, insulting, or indecent words; drunkenness; and perjury. In the great majority of cases they were offenses committed during the early 1960s, predominantly by inhabitants of the island of Upolu.

When this sample was tabulated in terms of age at first conviction the total range was from 9 to 80 years of age, and of the 2,717 offenders, 2,180 were males and 537 females, yielding a ratio of approximately four males to one female. However, of the 932 individuals whose age at first conviction was between 15 and 19, 777 were males and 155 females, a ratio of approximately five to one.

Figure 3 shows the relative incidence of age at first conviction for all 2,717 individuals of my random sample. It will be observed from this diagram that there is a marked increase, from age 14 onward, in the incidence of individuals committing offenses for the first time, with this incidence reaching a peak at the ages of from 15 to 19. A more detailed analysis (figure 4) of all the individuals in my sample who committed offenses for the first time between the ages of 12 and 22 also shows a sharp rise during early adolescence, a clear peak at age 16, and a high plateau through the remaining years of adolescence.

These incidences of age at first conviction among Samoan juveniles, while they are radically at odds with Mead's depiction of adolescence in Samoa, are closely in accord with findings from other countries. For example, Healy and Bronner's study of the Chicago Juvenile Court during the years 1909–1911 showed that the highest incidence among first offenders, both male and female, was of individuals 16 years of age. Adler, Cahn, and Stuart, in their study of juvenile delinquents in Berkeley, California, during the years 1928–1932, found that "the greatest percentage of the total number was found in the sixteen year age group." Bloch and Flynn, in 1956, gave 15 and a half years as the median age of delinquents in the United States. Haskell and Yablonsky, in discussing the crime statistics of the United States for 1972, record that "sixteen and seventeen year olds are arrested more frequently than persons of any other category." Challinger, in 1977, in discussing young offend-

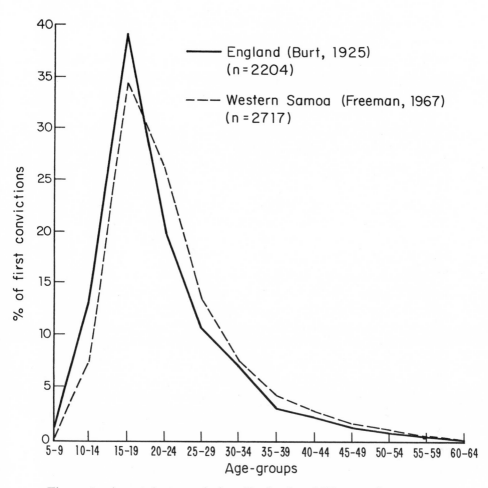

Figure 5.   Age at first conviction: England and Western Samoa compared.

ers in Australia, notes that "sixteen year olds always comprise the largest single group of those appearing in court."[13]

Again, if a direct comparison is made, as in figure 5, between my data, compiled in 1967, on age at first conviction in Western Samoa, with data on age at first conviction of offenders in England, from Cyril Burt's *The Young Delinquent,* it is evident that delinquency during adolescence has a generally similar incidence in Samoa and England. A comparable similarity exists between Samoa and the United States. Lunden, in his study of persons arrested in the United States in 1963, reports that 38.4 percent were under 20 years of age at the time of their first arrest, while in my sample of 1967 from Western Samoa those under 20 years of age at the time of their first conviction made up 41.6 percent of the total.[14]

From these data it is clearly evident that the adolescent period in Samoa, far from being "untroubled" and "unstressed" and "the age of maximum ease" as Mead asserted, is in fact a period during which, as in the United States, England, and Australia, delinquency occurs more frequently than at any other stage of life. Again, as I have shown earlier in this chapter, there is substantial evidence from Mead's own reports to demonstrate that this was also the situation in Samoa in the mid 1920s. Mead, then, was at error in her depiction of the nature of adolescence in Samoa, just as she was, as has been demonstrated in Chapters 9 to 18, in her portrayal of other crucial aspects of Samoan life. This being so, her assertion in *Coming of Age in Samoa* of the absolute sovereignty of culture over biology, on the basis of these erroneous depictions, is clearly invalid, and her much bruited "negative instance" is seen to have been no negative instance at all. In other words, Mead's presentation of Samoa as proving the insignificance of biology in the etiology of adolescent behavior is revealed as a false case.

18

The Samoan
Ethos

AS WE HAVE SEEN, the punishment traditionally meted out to an
erring taupou was deemed by Mead to be "too severe for the
Samoan ethos," which in all her writings she portrays as "mild,"
"relaxed" and "gentle." Thus, according to Mead, "The Samoan
system is a very pleasant way of reducing the rough unseemly
aspects of human nature to a pleasant innocuousness," and it
"lacks intensity in every respect." "Strong allegiances" are
"disallowed," and such is the "general casualness of the whole
society," Mead asserts in *Coming of Age in Samoa,* that "no
one suffers for his convictions, or fights to the death for special
ends."[1]

It is to this last depiction that Samoans, and especially male
Samoans, take particular exception, for, as they well know, it is
a major misrepresentation of their ethos and history. When in

1967 I discussed these generalizations from *Coming of Age in Samoa* with John Soloi, who was at that time the pastor of Fitiuta in Manu'a, he remarked testily that in these statements Mead was depriving the Samoans of deeply human characteristics and depicting them, wholly without justification, as a society of "spineless nonentities." Of the lack of justification for Mead's depictions there can be no possible doubt, for as their history amply proves, the Samoans are a people of exceptional punctilio and grit, with "the main virtue required of any male, children included," being, as Albert Wendt has described, "personal courage, especially in physical combat of any sort."[2]

As I have documented in Chapter 8, during the very period to which Mead's remarks specifically refer, the inhabitants of both American and Western Samoa were conspicuously suffering for their convictions. Thus, as we have seen, not long before Mead's visit to Manu'a a number of the chiefs of Ta'ū had defied the naval government by reinstating the title of Tui Manu'a; they told the governor, when he forcibly quashed what they had done, that they were "dissatisfied to the death" with his interference in their affairs.[3]

The announcement of Taua-nu'u and his fellow talking chiefs that they were dissatisfied to the death is an expression of one of the principal cultural values of the Samoans. In the course of a serious dispute with another village, for example, talking chiefs, on behalf of their titular chief, will extol the indomitable courage of those ready to die for their local polity and high chief. Such courage is believed to bring to those who display it honor, which the Samoans prize above all else. This attitude was pointedly expressed at a political fono in Satunumafono in February 1967, when a senior talking chief adjured the others of his district to stand fast forever and to die if need be, as this was true honor. Again, in 1966, in an incident I have described in detail elsewhere, an untitled man who had been provoked into fighting with a talking chief in the course of a territorial dispute came to fear that he might be attacked by this talking chief's retainers, but he remained defiant. What he had done, he said, he had done with good cause, and he was prepared for whatever the consequences might be. "If I have to die," he told me, "then I'll die." A Samoan then, whose blood is up, is all too ready, in a culture which extols violence, to go on and on fighting. There is, in the words of N. A. Rowe, "a peculiar tenacity about the Samoans which stamps them as being different."[4]

This tenacity is closely linked with the notion basic to Samoan warfare that one or other of the contending sides must achieve total dominance—the conquerers being called the *mālō* and the conquered the *to'ilalo*. It is thus commonplace to hear a Samoan averring "I will submit to nothing!" This spirit they have persistently displayed throughout their history. The high chief Mata'afa Iosefa, for example, who after rebelling against the political status quo was deported to Jaluit in the Marshall Islands, told the Commissioners of Great Britain, Germany, and the United States in 1899, as Tripp records, that he and his people would prefer "to become slaves, if they must, by compulsion, and not by cowardly submission." In 1902, various of the chiefs of Ta'ū defied the naval commandant of American Samoa over the curtailment of the traditional privileges of the Tui Manu'a to the point of being fined and exiled. In 1921 Levaleva, a chief of Tutuila who was opposed to the naval administration, informed that he was to be deprived of his title, exclaimed defiantly that "nobody in this world" would take it from him. For this gesture of independence he was charged with contempt of court and sentenced to three years' imprisonment. Similar acts of defiance, at no small personal sacrifice, were very frequent during the political opposition to the New Zealand administration of Western Samoa in the 1920s. In July 1927, for example, when Tuisila, a titular chief of Mutiatele, Aleipata, as ordered to desist from political activity in Apia and return to his local polity, he adamantly refused so to do and was sentenced to three months' imprisonment.[5]

The courage and tenacity of the Samoan people are palpably demonstrated in the actions and demeanor of the high chief Tupua Tamasese Lealofi III at the very time that Mead, in New York, was writing of how among Samoans "no one suffers for his convictions, or fights to the death for special ends." Lealofi, who as Tupua Tamasese was one of the tama'āiga, or highest-ranking titular chiefs of Western Samoa, first came into contention with the New Zealand administration as a young man when in 1924 he was ordered by the Secretary of Native Affairs to remove a hibiscus hedge from land that he believed to be his own. Certain of his right to the land in question, Tamasese staunchly refused to comply with the order, even when it was issued to him in person by His Excellency, Major-General Richardson, the supreme head of the New Zealand administration. Richardson, with a crass insensitivity to the eminence of the tama'āiga in the eyes of Samoans, ordered that Tamasese should refrain from using his title, and be banished to the island of Savai'i for an indefinite period. Later, when as J. W. Davidson records, Tamasese "left his enforced place of residence to ascertain the duration of his disabilities," he was sentenced to imprisonment, deprived of his title, and banished yet again. This oppressive treatment of a "royal son" of Samoa was one of the main causes of the Mau, the organized opposition to the New Zealand administration, of which Tupua Tamasese Lealofi III eventually became the active leader.[6]

Early in this movement some of its members had declared that the Samoans, in the words of one of their old proverbs, were moved by love, but never driven by intimidation. The oppression continued, and within a few years the Mau had the support of the vast majority of the Samoan people. So widespread was the disaffection that it amounted to an unarmed rebellion. In 1928, for refusing, with numerous others, to pay polltax to the New Zealand administration, Tamasese was summarily arrested at Vaimoso village, to which he had returned, by a posse of thirty-five military police armed with rifles and fixed bayonets. When the first of these military police broke in to Tamasese's house in the early hours of the morning he cried aloud, as one of them later reported, "I won't come, shoot me, kill me"—so evincing the implacable spirit of a true Samoan. For thus resisting arrest he was sentenced to a term of imprisonment in Mt. Eden Jail in Auckland, New Zealand. In Apia on 28 December 1929, some months after Tamasese had returned to Samoa to resume his leadership of the Mau, the authorities interrupted a procession by attempting to arrest Mata'utia

Karauna, the secretary of the Mau. In the ensuing melee Tamasese, who was appealing for the restoration of order, was fatally
shot by New Zealand military police. He was still in his twen-
ties. That evening, as he lay dying, Tupua Tamasese Lealofi III
issued to all Samoans these parting words: "My blood has been
spilt for Samoa. I am proud to give it. Do not dream of avenging
it, as it was spilt in maintaining peace. If I die, peace must be
maintained at any price."[7]

These magnanimous words are a notable expression of what
the Samoans call *'o le fa'atamāli'i,* the aristocratically restrained and far-seeing conduct characteristic of a chief of high
rank. Their spirit, moreover, epitomizes all that is best in the
Samoan ethos, for with their tenacity in altercation and combat, the Samoans also have a special genius for restoring order
and regaining amity in the face of outrageous fortune. Tupua
Tamasese Lealofi III stands in the history of Samoa as a great
patriot who, in rejecting the paternalist control of the New Zealand administration which had been imposed upon his people,
movingly demonstrated his willingness to suffer and to die for
his country while maintaining its highest ideals. In Auckland in
1929 a chaplain at Mt. Eden Jail remarked that in imprisoning
the Christian rebel chief Tamasese, the New Zealand government was defeating its own ends. This was even more evident in
the tragic shootings of 28 December 1929, in which ten other
Samoans were also killed. Tupua Tamasese Lealofi III had become the hero of his people, and each year the members of the
Mau would meet at his grave in commemoration of his sacrifice,
the final vindication of which was the establishment in 1962 of
Western Samoa as an independent Polynesian state.[8]

The preamble to the constitution of Western Samoa begins:
"In the Holy Name of God, the Almighty, the Ever Loving,"
and goes on to declare that the independent state of Western
Samoa is based "on Christian principles and Samoan custom
and tradition." As this declaration indicates, the Samoan ethos
derives from an admixture of institutions that emphasize rank
and the aggressive defense of ancient privilege, with Christianity and its ethic of mutual love and forgiveness. In the course of
history these divergent elements have become contained within

a uniquely Samoan ideology which equates the governance of Jehovah with the rank system itself. Thus, as described in Chapter 8 it is now one of the basic dogmas of Samoan society that the rank system is sanctioned by Jehovah. The stern values of this rank system, though fundamentally unchanged since pagan times, have thus been tempered by a belief in an all-seeing and all-powerful God, who, while he relentlessly punishes those who disobey his commandments, is also a God of love.

Behind the Christianity of the Samoans there still looms, however, the primeval rank system with its oppositions and tensions. In matters of precedence the Samoans, like the ancient Greeks as Thucydides describes them, "are as ashamed of being the second as they are proud of being the first." In this domain, where the dangers of rivalrous conflict are ever present, "terms of ceremony fly thick as oaths on board a ship," and the Samoan ethos remains one of obedience and submissiveness to those in positions of chiefly privilege and authority, as to the God who, it is said, stands at the apex of the rank hierarchy. Indeed, Samoan chiefs are much given to extolling obedience as the essential basis of virtue and concord, and to condemning freedom of action as the source of sin and social disorder. So, in Wendt's powerful novel *Pouliuli* (1977), which presents a searingly honest portrayal of the realities of Samoan existence, when a 67-year-old chief attempts, in the grip of an "almost unbearable feeling of revulsion," to renounce the fa'aSamoa, he is gravely warned by one of his oldest friends that "the individual freedom you have discovered and now want to maintain is contrary to the very basis of our way of life."[9]

The Samoan ethos, then, is scarcely pervaded by casualness as Mead claimed. Rather, for most Samoans there is no escape from the insistent demands of their society, one of its fundamental principles being (as described in Chapter 13) that anyone who disobeys the instructions of those in authority should be duly punished. This custom of inflicting punishment to maintain social order is therefore one of the basic characteristics of the Samoan ethos. Thus, while Samoans frequently talk of the boundless love of Jehovah, they also view him as a God who may become "full of anger for sinful people," and who will strike down, in infirmity or death, those who have broken his commandments. Jehovah, in other words, is believed by Samoans to be a punishing God, and the punishment he metes out, while it is greatly feared, is also looked on as being God's chosen and just way of dealing with the willfully disobedient. Thus, the punitive regime that, so the evidence suggests, has long been endemic among Samoans has, since their conversion to Christianity, been justified in terms of the principles by which Jehovah Himself is believed to rule Samoa. Punishment has become culturally established as the sovereign way of dealing with all those, including young children, who will not heed the dictates of authority.

In 1967, in scathingly dismissing Mead's depiction of Manu'an society as being "characterized by ease," John Soloi, the pastor of Fitiuta, remarked that on the contrary, Samoan society was characterized by "iron rule." He was referring, he said, to the way in which the chiefly fonos of local polities enforce their edicts with heavy fines and other forms of punishment. Within Samoan society there is very frequent resort to punishment, and I would argue that it is in particular a pervasive dependence on the physical punishment of children that makes Samoans so disturbingly prone to interpersonal aggression. The studies of M. M. Lefkowitz, L. O. Walden and L. D. Eron, and others have clearly shown that punishment enhances rather than inhibits the expression of aggression. And this conclusion has been corroborated by D. D. Woodman's finding that physical punishment is allied to aggression outside the home. Woodman's researches also suggest a biochemical component in interpersonal aggression, with an increase in noradrenaline being linked with increasing aggression in personality. It seems likely that it is the regime of physical punishment, and especially of children, that generates the "air of violence on a tight rein" reported by Mackenzie, and that results in Samoans flying "from feathers to iron" at the slightest provocation, to engage in the physical violence that they have come to accept as customary.[10]

Furthermore, while the punishment of children in Samoa

has the pious aim of correcting the young in the error of their ways, it is imposed, as described in Chapter 14, with such dominance as to produce in most Samoans a profound ambivalence toward those in authority, with respect and love alternating with resentment and fear. Because of this system of child rearing and the stringent demands that those in authority make upon the growing individual, Samoan character, as indicated in Chapter 15, has two marked sides to it, with an outer affability and respectfulness masking an inner susceptibility to choler and violence. Judge Marsack, for example, has described the Samoan as being an "odd mixture of courtesy and cantankerousness." Thomas Trood, in 1909, after an experience of Samoa extending over more than fifty years, commented on how remarkable it was that those who were "pre-eminent for kindliness of disposition and hospitality" were also a "high-spirited, turbulent people." And George Brown, in 1898, having described the Samoans as "kind, lovable and polite," at once went on to remark that they are also "extremely sensitive" to what is considered to be an insult.[11]

This touchiness is especially evident in political settings within the rank system. For example, when in 1967 a member of the Legislative Assembly of Western Samoa interjected "Alas for Samoa!" while the high-ranking prime minister was speaking, he was told, although he retracted his remark and formally apologized, that even though a nail be withdrawn from a plank the hole it has made remains. Again, during a kava ceremony at Sa'anapu in May 1966, Leaula, a talking chief from the neighboring and rival polity of Salamumu, was deliberately slighted by being lowered in the order of precedence because his village had declined to join in the rebuilding of the local hospital. His annoyed response, after gulping down his kava, was to fling the coconut shell cup back to the untitled man who had served him, instead of waiting for it to be ceremonially retrieved. At this brusque gesture the assembled chiefs of Sa'anapu visibly stiffened, and, as soon as the kava ceremony was at an end, Vole Na'oia, the officiating talking chief of Sa'anapu, turned to Leaula to ask in angry tones why he had behaved in such an unruly manner. Leaula retorted that he had wanted to hurry things up. At this the tension mounted even higher. For a time there was an ominous silence. It was broken, at last, when another talking chief from Salamumu, apprehensive at this turn of events, wryly remarked "Perhaps he was in a hurry to go to the beach to relieve himself," at which the entire fono exploded in laughter. The danger of a serious breach had passed, but Leaula, smarting at the insult to his rank, quickly hit back. There was, he said, one chief of Sa'anapu whose behavior was quite exemplary. He was Vole Na'oia, who was forever trying surreptitiously to rape his own sister. To Samoan ears this imputation is utterly outrageous, and the shock of Laula's retaliatory sally was released in further roars of cathected laughter. As these examples indicate, the Samoan ethos is far from lacking intensity in every respect as Mead reported. Rather, the pent-up antagonisms of the rank system are tenuously contained within a regime of formal etiquette in terms of which the Samoans forever contend for the upper hand, but with the saving grace of usually being able, at critical moments when open conflict threatens, to laugh uproariously at their obsessive concern with the declensions of rank.

Despite these deliverances of etiquette and laughter, the rank system and the fono, with their rivalries and punitive sanctions, do still constitute, as indeed does the wider society, a decidedly stressful psychological environment. In Chapter 15 I have dealt with some of the consequences of the stress to which children and adolescents are exposed. Comparable stress is experienced by many adults, and especially by the men whose lives are lived within the purview of the fono of their local polity. In *Leaves of the Banyan Tree,* a pungent study of the baleful consequences of chiefly ambition in twentieth-century Samoa, Albert Wendt has one of his characters remark that being a chief is "an invitation to obesity, ulcers, strokes and heart attacks." In the last three of these ailments stress is certainly a factor, as the researches of H. G. Wolff and others have shown, with the gastrointestinal tract being, in Hans Selye's words, "particularly sensitive to general stress," peptic ulcer having been described by some clinicians as "a disease of unfulfilled aggressiveness." It is thus of some pertinence that Dr. L.

Winter, a former Director of Medical Services in American Samoa, noted in 1961 that ulcers were "extremely common" there. A more recent study, directed by B. P. Maclaurin, of approximately 500 persons over the age of 18 in each of the three major health districts in Western Samoa during 1976 revealed, as compared with New Zealand, "an unusually high prevalence of peptic ulceration," with an average incidence of 7.3 percent, the approximate ratio of male to female sufferers being two to one. This incidence is appreciably higher than that found in the National Health Survey of 1957–1959 of the United States.[12]

In refuting the conclusions reached by Mead in the 1920s I have necessarily had to discuss in some detail the darker side of Samoan life, which, in constructing her negative instance, she so ignored as to turn the complexly human Samoans into characterless nonentities. The Samoans, as I have shown, do indeed have a dark side to their lives, but this, I would emphasize, is something they share with *all* human societies. And, as with all human societies, they also have their shining virtues. For John Williams, the pioneer missionary, the Samoans were a "very lively, jocose, kind people." John Erskine, a widely traveled naval officer, after visiting Samoa in 1849 declared he had never seen a people "more prepossessing in appearance and manner," and they are justly famed, in Ernest Sabatier's words, as "the most polite of Pacific peoples." Beyond these formal virtues the Samoans are also wonderfully hospitable and generous, and in their devotion to the ethics of Christianity they can display great magnanimity, as did Tupua Tamasese Lealofi III, in the most testing of situations. In fonos throughout Samoa it is common to hear mutual love extolled as an ideal, and there is perhaps no more memorable instance of the kindliness of Samoans than the road that a group of high-ranking chiefs built for Robert Louis Stevenson at Vailima, not long before his death in 1894. Tusitala, as they called him, had cared for these chiefs during their tribulation in prison, and "the road of the loving heart," which they built with their own hands, was their gesture of gratitude. It was a road, they said, that would "go on for ever," just as will, I am sure, all that is best in the fa'aSamoa.[13]

IV

MEAD AND THE BOASIAN PARADIGM

19

Mead's Misconstruing of Samoa

WHEN THEY WERE WORKING TOGETHER in 1927 on the characterization of Samoan culture, Mead and Benedict carried to its logical extreme their deeply felt belief that in human societies the traditional patterns of behavior set the mold into which the raw material of human nature flows. Thus, in *Social Organization of Manu'a,* in her discussion of dominant cultural attitudes, every detail of which had been "thrashed out" with Benedict, Mead wrote of the absolute determination of social pressure in shaping the individuals within its bounds. This notion that cultural determinism was absolute was "so obvious" to Mead that, as we have seen, she also avowed it in *Coming of Age in Samoa,* in respect of adolescent behavior.[1]

That this doctrine of the absoluteness of cultural determinism should have seemed "so obvious" to Mead is understandable. Anthropology, when she began its study in 1922, was dominated by Boas' "compelling idea," as Leslie Spier has called it, of "the complete moulding of every human expression—inner thought and external behavior—by social conditioning," and by the time she left for Samoa in 1925 she had become a fervent devotee of the notion that human behavior could be explained in purely cultural terms. Further, although by the time of Mead's recruitment to its ranks cultural anthropology had achieved its independence, it had done so at the cost of becoming an ideology that, in an actively unscientific way, sought totally to exclude biology from the explanation of human behavior. Thus as Kroeber declared, "the important thing about anthropology is not the science but an attitude of mind"—an attitude of mind, that is, committed to the doctrine of culture as a superorganic entity which incessantly shapes human behavior, "conditioning all responses." It was of this attitude of mind that Mead became a leading proponent, with (as Marvin Harris has observed) her anthropological mission, set for her by Boas, being to defeat the notion of a "panhuman hereditary human nature." She pursued this objective by tirelessly stressing, in publication after publication, "the absence of maturational regularities."[2]

In her own account of this mission, Mead describes it as a battle which she and other Boasians had had to fight with the whole battery at their command, using the most fantastic and startling examples they could muster. It is thus evident that her writings during this period, about Samoa as about other South Seas cultures, had the explicit aim of confuting biological explanations of human behavior and vindicating the doctrines of the Boasian school. By 1939 this battle, according to Mead, had been won. In retrospect, however, it is evident that her eristic approach to anthropological inquiry, which had sprung from the febrile nature-nurture controversy of the 1920s, is fundamentally at variance with the methods and values of science, and there can be no doubt that Mead's fervent desire to demonstrate the validity of the doctrines she held in common with Benedict and Boas led her, in Samoa, to overlook evidence running counter to her beliefs, and to place far too ready a credence in the notion that Manu'a could be put to anthropological use as a "negative instance."[3]

For Mead's readers in North America and elsewhere in the Western world, there could be no more plausible location for the idyllic society of which she wrote than in the South Seas, a region that since the days of Bougainville has figured in the fantasies of Europeans and Americans as a place of preternatural contentment and sensual delight. So, as Mead reports, her announcement in 1925 that she was going to Samoa caused the same breathless stir as if she had been "setting off for heaven." Indeed, there were many in the 1920s, according to Mead, who longed to go to the South Sea islands "to escape to a kind of divine nothingness in which life would be reduced to the simplest physical terms, to sunshine and the moving shadows of palm trees, to bronze-bodied girls and bronze-bodied boys, food for the asking, no work to do, no obligations to meet." Westerners with such yearnings readily succumb to the unfamiliar lushness of a tropical island, and there have been those who have described Samoa in tones of unconcealed rapture. Rupert Brooke, for example, who visited both American and Western Samoa in November 1913, wrote of experiencing there a "sheer beauty, so pure that it's difficult to breathe in it—like living in a Keats world, only . . . less syrupy." While the Samoans in this heaven on earth were "the loveliest people in the world, moving and running and dancing like gods and goddesses, very quietly and mysteriously, and utterly content," with "perfect manners and immense kindliness."[4]

It was in comparably euphoric terms that Tahiti had been described to European readers after Bougainville's visit of 1768, as though the Isles of the Blest, of which Horace and Plutarch had written so alluringly, had materialized in the far away South Seas. The New Cythera, they were told, was an earthly paradise, with no other god but love, and with inhabitants who lived in peace among themselves, knowing neither hatred, quarrels, dissension, nor civil war, constituting "perhaps the happiest society which the world knows." This account is so strikingly similar to Mead's depiction of Samoa as to make it evident that in constructing her negative instance, she was, in fundamental ways, influenced by the romantic vision that had possessed the imaginations of Westerners from the eighteenth century onward. The Samoans, she told her readers, among whom free love-making was the pastime *par excellence,* never hate enough to want to kill anyone and are "one of the most amiable, least contentious, and most peaceful peoples in the world."[5]

A romantically beguiling vision, like those of Bougainville and Brooke! Yet, as I have shown in Chapters 9 to 18, these and numerous other components of Mead's depiction of Samoa as a negative instance, on which she based her claims about Samoan adolescence and about the absolute sovereignty of nurture over nature, are fundamentally in error, so that her negative instance is no negative instance at all, and her conclusions are demonstrably invalid. How did the young Margaret Mead come so to misconstrue the ethos and ethnography of Samoa? The fervency of her belief in cultural determinism and her tendency to view the South Seas as an earthly paradise go some way in accounting for what happened, but manifestly more was involved.

The Ph.D. topic that Boas assigned to Mead was the comparative study of canoe-building, house-building, and tattooing in the Polynesian culture area. During 1924 she gathered information on these activities from the available literature on the Hawaiians, the Marquesans, the Maori, the Tahitians, and the Samoans. These doctoral studies did not have any direct relevance to the quite separate problem of adolescence in Samoa that Boas set her in 1925, and, indeed, the fact that her reading was mainly on Eastern rather than Western Polynesia concealed from her the marked extent to which the traditional culture and values of Samoa differ from those of Tahiti. Again, during the spring of 1925 she had little time for systematic preparation for her Samoan researches. Indeed, the counsel she received from Boas about these researches prior to her departure for Pago Pago lasted, she tells us, for only half an hour. During this brief meeting Boas' principal instruction was that she should concentrate on the problem he had set her and not waste time doing ethnography. Accordingly, when in the second week of November 1925 Mead reached Manu'a, she at once launched into the study of adolescence without first acquiring, either by observation or from inquiry with adult informants, a thorough understanding of the traditional values and customs of the Manu'ans. This, without doubt, was an ill-advised way to proceed, for it meant that Mead was in no position to check the statements of the girls she was studying against a well-informed knowledge of the fa'aSamoa.[6]

It is also evident that Mead greatly underestimated the complexity of the culture, society, history, and psychology of the people among whom she was to study adolescence. Samoan society, so Mead would have it, is "very simple," and Samoan culture "uncomplex." In the introduction to *Coming of Age in Samoa* she tells us that while years of study are necessary before a student can begin to understand the forces at work within "complicated civilizations like those of Europe, or the higher civilizations of the East," a "primitive people" presents a much less elaborate problem, with a trained student being able to "master the fundamental structure of a primitive society in a few months."[7]

As any one who cares to consult Augustin Krämer's *Die Samoa-Inseln,* Robert Louis Stevenson's *A Footnote to History,* or J. W. Davidson's *Samoa mo Samoa* will quickly discover, Samoan society and culture are by no means simple and uncomplex; they are marked by particularities, intricacies, and subtleties quite as daunting as those which face students of Europe and Asia. Indeed, the fa'aSamoa is so sinuously complex that, as Stevenson's step-daughter, Isobel Strong, once remarked, "one may live long in Samoa without understanding the whys and wherefores." Mead, however, spent not even a few months on the systematic study of Manu'a before launching upon the study of adolescence immediately upon her arrival in Ta'ū in accordance with Boas' instructions. Thus, she has noted that while on her later field trips she had "the more satisfactory task of learning the culture first and only afterwards working on a special problem," in Samoa this was "not necessary."[8]

For some ten weeks prior to her arrival in Manu'a, she had, it is true, been resident in the port of Pago Pago learning the vernacular, and had spent about ten days living with a Samoan

family in the village of Vaitogi. But this experience, while it did
give her a useful initial orientation, did not amount to the systematic study of the fa'aSamoa that would have enabled her to
assess adequately the statements of her adolescent informants
on the sexual and other behavior of the Manu'ans. Another
problem was that of being able to communicate adequately with
the people she was to study. Mead had arrived in Pago Pago
without any knowledge of the Samoan language, and although
she at once began its study, the ten or so weeks she gave to this
task before beginning her researches was far too brief a period
for obtaining a fluent command of the formidable Samoan
tongue, with its multiple vocabularies stemming from the distinctions of the traditional rank system. In this situation Mead
was plainly at some hazard in pursuing her inquiries in Manu'a,
for Samoans, when diverted by the stumbling efforts of outsiders to speak their demanding language, are inclined not to take
them seriously.

Mead, then, began her inquiries with her girl informants with
a far from perfect command of the vernacular, and without systematic prior investigation of Manu'an society and values.
Added to this, she elected to live not in a Samoan household but
with the handful of expatriate Americans who were the local
representatives of the naval government of American Samoa,
from which in 1925 many Manu'ans were radically disaffected.
In his introduction of September 1931 to Reo Fortune's *Sorcerers of Dobu*, Bronislaw Malinowski expressed great satisfaction
at Fortune's "ruthless avoidance" of both missionary compound
and government station in his "determination to live right
among the natives."[9] Of the immense advantage that an ethnographer gains by living among the people whose values and behavior he is intent on understanding there can be not the
slightest doubt. Mead, however, within six weeks of her arrival
in Pago Pago, and before she had spent any time actually staying in a traditional household, had come to feel that the food
she would have to eat would be too starchy, and the conditions
of living she would have to endure too nerve-racking to make
residence with a Samoan family bearable. In Ta'ū, she told
Boas, she would be able to live "in a white household" and yet

be in the midst of one of the villages from which she would be drawing her adolescent subjects. This arrangement to live not in a Samoan household but with the Holt family in their European-style house, which was also the location of the government radio station and medical dispensary, decisively determined the form her researches were to take.

According to Mead her residence in these government quarters furnished her with an absolutely essential neutral base from which she could study all of the individuals in the surrounding village while at the same time remaining "aloof from native feuds and lines of demarcation." Against this exiguous advantage she was, however, depriving herself of the close contacts that speedily develop in Samoa between an ethnographer and the members of the extended family in which he or she lives. Such contacts are essential for the gaining of a thorough understanding of the Samoan language and, most important of all, for the independent verification, by the continuous observation of actual behavior, of the statements being derived from informants. Thus, by living with the Holts, Mead was trapping herself in a situation in which she was forced to rely not on observations of the behavior of Samoans as they lived their lives beyond the precincts of the government station on Ta'ū, but on such hearsay information as she was able to extract from her adolescent subjects.[10]

That this was her situation is made clear in Mead's own account of her researches. Her living quarters, she records, were on the back verandah of the dispensary, from where she could look out across a small yard into part of the village of Lumā. This part of the government medical dispensary became her research headquarters, and soon the adolescent girls, and later the small girls whom she found she had also to study, came and filled her screen-room "day after day and night after night." When she began her researches in this artificial setting Mead was still only 23 years of age, and was smaller in stature than some of the girls she was studying. They treated her, she says, "as one of themselves."[11]

It is evident then that although, as Mead records, she could "wander freely about the village or go on fishing trips or stop at

a house where a woman was weaving" when she was away from
the dispensary, her account of adolescence in Samoa was, in the
main, derived from the young informants who came to talk with
her away from their homes in the villages of Lumā, Si'ufaga,
and Faleasao. So, as Mead states, for these three villages, from
which all her adolescent informants were drawn, she saw the
life that went on "through the eyes" of the group of girls on the
details of whose lives she was concentrating. This situation is of
crucial significance for the assessment of Mead's researches in
Manu'a, for we are clearly faced with the question of the extent
to which the lens she fashioned from what she was being told by
her adolescent informants and through which she saw Samoan
life was a true and accurate lens.[12]

As I have documented in Chapters 9 to 18, many of the assertions appearing in Mead's depiction of Samoa are fundamentally in error, and some of them preposterously false. How
are we to account for the presence of errors of this magnitude?
Some Samoans who have read *Coming of Age in Samoa* react,
as Shore reports, with anger and the insistence "that Mead
lied." This, however, is an interpretation that I have no hesita-
tion in dismissing. The succession of prefaces to *Coming of Age
in Samoa* published by Mead in 1949, 1953, 1961, and 1973 indicate clearly, in my judgment, that she did give genuine credence
to the view of Samoan life with which she returned to New York
in 1926. Moreover, in the 1969 edition of *Social Organization of
Manu'a* she freely conceded that there was a serious problem in
reconciling the "contradictions" between her own depiction of
Samoa and that contained in "other records of historical and
contemporary behavior."[13]

In Mead's view there were but two possibilities: either there
was in Manu'a at the time of her sojourn "a temporary felicitous
relaxation" of the severe ethos reported by other ethnographers, or the vantage point of the young girl from which she
"saw" Samoan society must, in some way, have been responsible. As I have documented in Chapter 8, the mid 1920s were in
no way a period of felicitous relaxation in Manu'a, being rather
a time of unusual tension during which the majority of
Manu'ans, as adherents of the Mau, were in a state of disaffec-

tion from the naval government of American Samoa. We are
thus left with Mead's second possibility, and with the problem
of the way in which her depiction of Samoa might have been affected by the vantage point of the young girls on whose testimony she relied.[14]

Mead's depiction of Samoan culture, as I have shown, is
marked by major errors, and her account of the sexual behavior
of Samoans by a mind-boggling contradiction, for she asserts
that the Samoans have a culture in which female virginity is
very highly valued, with a virginity-testing ceremony being
"theoretically observed at weddings of all ranks," while at the
same time adolescence among females is regarded as a period
"appropriate for love-making," with promiscuity before marriage being both permitted and "expected." And, indeed, she
actually describes the Samoans as making the "demand" that a
female should be "both receptive to the advances of many
lovers and yet capable of showing the tokens of virginity at
marriage." Something, it becomes plain at this juncture, is emphatically amiss, for surely no human population could be so
cognitively disoriented as to conduct their lives in such a schizo-
phrenic way. Nor are the Samoans remotely like this, for, as has
been documented in Chapter 16, they are, in fact, a people who
traditionally value virginity highly and so disapprove of premarital promiscuity as to exercise a strict surveillance over the
comings and goings of adolescent girls. That these values and
this regime were in force in Manu'a in the mid 1920s is, furthermore, clearly established by the testimony of the Manu'ans
themselves who, when I discussed this period with those who
well remembered it, confirmed that the fa'aSamoa in these
matters was operative then as it was both before and after
Mead's brief sojourn in Ta'ū. What then can have been the
source of Mead's erroneous statement that in Samoa there is
great premarital freedom, with promiscuity before marriage
among adolescent girls, being both permitted and expected?[15]

The explanation most consistently advanced by the Samoans themselves for the magnitude of the errors in her depiction of their culture and in particular of their sexual morality is,
as Gerber has reported, "that Mead's informants must have

been telling lies in order to tease her." Those Samoans who offer this explanation, which I have heard in Manu'a as well as in other parts of Samoa, are referring to the behavior called *tau fa'ase'e*, to which Samoans are much prone. *Fa'ase'e* (literally "to cause to slip") means "to dupe," as in the example given by Milner, *"e fa'ase'e gofie le teine*, the girl is easily duped"; and the phrase *tau fa'ase'e* refers to the action of deliberately duping someone, a pastime that greatly appeals to the Samoans as a respite from the severities of their authoritarian society.[16]

Because of their strict morality, Samoans show a decided reluctance to discuss sexual matters with outsiders or those in authority, a reticence that is especially marked among female adolescents. Thus, Holmes reports that when he and his wife lived in Manu'a and Tutuila in 1954 "it was never possible to obtain details of sexual experience from unmarried informants, though several of these people were constant companions and part of the household." Further, as Lauifi Ili, Holmes's principal assistant, observes, when it comes to imparting information about sexual activities, Samoan girls are "very close-mouthed and ashamed." Yet it was precisely information of this kind that Mead, a liberated young American newly arrived from New York and resident in the government station at Ta'ū, sought to extract from the adolescent girls she had been sent to study. And when she persisted in this unprecedented probing of a highly embarrassing topic, it is likely that these girls resorted, as Gerber's Samoan informants have averred, to *tau fa'ase'e*, regaling their inquisitor with counterfeit tales of casual love under the palm trees.[17]

This, then, is the explanation that Samoans give for the highly inaccurate portrayal of their sexual morality in Mead's writings. It is an explanation that accounts for how it was that this erroneous portrayal came to be made, as well as for Mead's sincere credence in the account she has given in *Coming of Age in Samoa,* for she was indeed reporting what she had been told by her adolescent informants. The Manu'ans emphasize, however, that the girls who, they claim, plied Mead with these counterfeit tales were only amusing themselves, and had no inkling that their tales would ever find their way into a book.

While we cannot, in the absence of detailed corroborative evidence, be sure about the truth of this Samoan claim that Mead was mischievously duped by her adolescent informants, we can be certain that she did return to New York in 1926 with tales running directly counter to all other ethnographic accounts of Samoa, from which she constructed her picture of Manu'a as a paradise of free love, and of Samoa as a negative instance, which, so she claimed, validated Boasian doctrine. It was this negative instance that she duly presented to Boas as the ideologically gratifying result of her inquiries in Manu'a.

For Mead, Franz Boas was a peerless intellectual leader who "saw the scientific task as one of probing into a problem now of language, now of physical type, now of art style—each a deep, sudden, intensive stab at some strategic point into an enormous, untapped and unknown mass of information." Boas continually warned his students, so Mead claims, against premature generalization, which was something he "feared like the plague." Again, in J. R. Swanton's judgment, Boas was "meticulously careful in weighing results and rigidly conservative in announcing conclusions"; while in Robert Lowie's estimation he was a scholar "concerned solely with ascertaining the truth," who controlled the ethnographic literature of the world "as well as anyone." It is pertinent then to take cognizance of Boas' response to the absolute generalization at which Mead had arrived after probing for a few months into adolescent behavior in Samoa. What can be said with certainty is that if Boas, as the instigator and supervisor of Mead's Samoan researches, had taken the elementary precaution of consulting the readily available ethnographic literature on Samoa, as, for example, the writings of Williams, Turner, Pritchard, Stuebel, and Krämer, he would have very quickly found accounts of the sexual and other behavior of the Samoans that are markedly at variance with Mead's picture of life in Manu'a; and further, that if he had done this in a thoroughgoing way, the need to check Mead's findings by an independent replication of her investigations in Samoa would have become unequivocally clear. However, when he read *Coming of Age in Samoa* in manuscript Boas voiced no doubts at all about the absoluteness of its general conclusion, and later in an enthusiastic foreword he wrote of the "painstaking investigation" on which this extreme conclusion was based. He had from the outset, as Mead reports, believed that her work in Samoa would show that culture was "very important." The response of Benedict, Mead's other mentor at Columbia University, was equally uncritical, and a few years later in *Patterns of Culture* she used Mead's conclusions, as had Boas in 1928, as apparently clinching evidence for the doctrine of cultural determinism in which she, like Boas and Mead, so fervently believed.[18]

We are thus confronted in the case of Margaret Mead's Samoan researches with an instructive example of how, as evidence is sought to substantiate a cherished doctrine, the deeply held beliefs of those involved may lead them unwittingly into error. The danger of such an outcome is inherent, it would seem, in the very process of belief formation. Thus, P. D. MacLean has suggested that the limbic system of the human brain "has the capacity to generate strong affective feelings of conviction that we attach to our beliefs regardless of whether they are true or false." In science, as Albert Einstein once remarked, "conviction is a good mainspring, but a poor regulator." In the case of Mead's Samoan researches, certainly, there is the clearest evidence that it was her deeply convinced belief in the doctrine of extreme cultural determinism, for which she was prepared to fight with the whole battery at her command, that led her to construct an account of Samoa that appeared to substantiate this very doctrine. There is, however, conclusive empirical evidence to demonstrate that Samoa, in numerous respects, is not at all as Mead depicted it to be.[19]

A crucial issue that arises from this historic case for the discipline of anthropology, which has tended to accept the reports of ethnographers as entirely empirical statements, is the extent to which other ethnographic accounts may have been distorted by doctrinal convictions, as well as the methodological question of how such distortion can best be avoided. These are no small problems. I would merely comment that as we look back on Mead's Samoan researches we are able to appreciate anew the wisdom of Karl Popper's admonition that in both science and scholarship it is, above all else, indefatigable rational criticism of our suppositions that is of decisive importance, for such criticism by "bringing out our mistakes . . . makes us understand the difficulties of the problem we are trying to solve," and so saves us from the allure of the "obvious truth" of received doctrine.[20]

20

Toward a More Scientific Anthropological Paradigm

THE NATURE-NURTURE CONTROVERSY of the 1920s has now receded into history. In the light of current scientific knowledge the exclusion of either biological or cultural variables from the etiology of adolescent or any other basic form of human behavior is unwarranted; both nature and nurture are always involved. Indeed, as Conway Zirkle has remarked, any attempt to make one more crucial than the other is "as silly as trying to determine which is the more important in deriving a product, the multiplicand or the multiplier." Yet, the significance of biology in human behavior has still to be recognized by many anthropologists. As we have seen, Mead's Samoan researches gave apparently decisive support to the movement that (in George Stocking's words) sought "an explanation of human behavior in

purely cultural terms," and so sustained the antibiological orientation of the Boasian paradigm.[1]

As I have documented in Chapter 3, the theories of the doctrine of cultural determinism were (in Melford Spiro's words)
"developed in the first instance as alternatives to and refutations of biological determinism." Thus the Boasians had an antipathy to biology, and to genetics and evolutionary biology in
particular. Boas, for example, was opposed to research in
human genetics and thought, even as late as 1939, that in respect of the human body, "a search for genes would not be ad-
visable," there being some danger that the number of genes
would "depend rather upon the number of investigators than
upon their actual existence." Again, he actively disregarded the
Darwinian theory of evolution, being, as Stocking has recorded,
"quite skeptical of natural selection." Alfred Kroeber, the most
eminent of Boas' students, was if anything even more antipa-
thetic to evolutionary biology; in his view there was "no specific
connection" between Darwinism and anthropological thought.
These were the attitudes that the young Margaret Mead came
to adopt, and which led her, when embarking on her inquiries in
Manu'a, to assume that human nature, being "the rawest, most
undifferentiated . . . raw material," could be shaped by culture
into any form.[2]

During the fifty years since Mead first avowed absolute cultural determinism, with its assumption of human nature as a
tabula rasa, biology has made unprecedented advances, so that
it is now known that what cultures have to mold is, in Vernon
Reynolds' words, "an exceedingly complex arrangement of biochemical machinery, each piece containing certain instructions
of a highly specific kind about its own development." Again,
after a period of apparent eclipse in the early 1920s, the theory
of evolution by means of natural selection, far from sinking into
oblivion, has reemerged as the unifying paradigm of all the biological sciences, from biochemistry to ethology. Indeed, with the
discovery of the way in which genetic information is stored in
nucleic acid, the molecular basis of the evolutionary process has
been revealed, and it has become apparent that the specificity

and subtlety shown by any particular enzyme is as much the result of evolution by natural selection as the clinging behavior of a newborn langur monkey or the capacity of a human infant to learn one of the modes of symbolic communication characteristic of his species. There is, then, in the ninth decade of the twentieth century a decisive summation of scientific evidence to sustain Muller's generalization that "the criterion for any material's having life is whether or not it has the potentiality . . . of evolution by Darwinian natural selection." It is thus evident that *Homo sapiens,* as a primate, is, like all other living things, a product of evolution by means of natural selection, and, further, that the coded information stored in the genes of any human individual, as also its decoding in ontogenetic development, is crucially important for the understanding of human behavior, just as is the exogenetic information that comes to be stored in an individual's memory in the course of postnatal experience and enculturation.[3]

So, as J. Z. Young states, each individual mammalian life is dependent on genetically inherited information "written in the triplets of bases of the DNA code," which produces a program embodied in the structure of the brain, the units of which are "groups of nerve cells, so organized as to produce . . . various actions at the right times." Added to this, in the case of humans, is the language and the cultural program that the growing individual learns. However, although from its earliest days the child begins to learn in a way it could not do in the womb, it is able to do this, as Young notes, "only by virtue of the neural equipment with which it is provided by heredity." This neural equipment is very far from being undifferentiated. For example, in their researches on the visual cortex of infant macaques, Hubel and Wiesal have demonstrated the presence of individual cells with highly specific characteristics, responding to features in the external environment such as orientated contours. Such specialized cells also certainly exist in the visual cortex of the human neonate. This and much other research has established that, as Young has put it, the human brain, "rather than being a general purpose computer into whose memory *any* information can be placed," is "more like one that already has a system of programs within it." Again, the researches of Prechtl, Eibl-Eibesfeldt, and others have shown that the human neonate is equipped at birth with a range of movement patterns essential for survival, as also with other behaviors and emotions—phylogenetically given in their basic structure—which unfold in the course of ontogeny in interaction with their environment.[4]

In 1955, in looking back on the history of cultural anthropology, Kroeber observed that the period when human nature was canceled out as a constant was drawing to a close, as it had become clear that cultural anthropologists could not permanently ignore the "basic genetic part" of human psychology. This was an accurate prognostication. Research since the 1950s, particularly in the field of human ethology, has shown that in significant ways human behavior is, in the words of Eibl-Eibesfeldt, "preprogrammed by phylogenetic adaptations." In this respect then there has been a quite major change since the 1920s when J. B. Watson was pontificating on there being "no such thing as any inheritance of capacity, talent, temperament, mental constitution and characteristics," and Mead and other cultural anthropologists were basing their theories about human behavior on the assumption that human nature was "the rawest, most undifferentiated . . . raw material." Indeed, so decisive has been this advance in knowledge that, as Ashley Montagu indicated in 1979, there is no longer any rational justification for belief in "the *tabula rasa* myth." We have thus reached a point at which the discipline of anthropology, if it is not to become isolated in a conceptual cul de sac, must abandon the paradigm fashioned by Kroeber and other of Boas' students, and must give full cognizance to biology, as well as to culture, in the explanation of human behavior and institutions.[5]

Since the 1920s, largely because of the writings of the Boasians, which have had the highly salutary effect of directing widespread attention to the nature of cultural phenomena, there has been a growing recognition among biologists of the significance of culture in human evolution. C. H. Waddington, for example, emphasized in 1961 that among humans there is "a second evolutionary system superimposed on top of the biological one . . . functioning by means of a different system of information transmission." Again, P. B. Medawar has referred to this method of information transmission "by the entire apparatus of culture" as exogenetic (the same term Boas used in 1924), and has noted that "the evolution of this learning process and the system of heredity that goes with it represents a fundamentally new biological stratagem—more important than any that preceded it—and totally unlike any other transaction of the organism with its environment."[6]

Another major development since the heyday of the Boasian paradigm has been the disproof of the assumption that "nothing homologous to the rudest culture" exists among even "the highest animals"—the assumption on which Kroeber based his doctrine that culture was peculiarly human, so positing a fundamental disjunction between man and all other animals. The evidence for the existence of rudimentary cultural, or exogenetic, adaptations in species other than man has now been cogently stated by J. T. Bonner in *The Evolution of Culture in Animals* (1980), in which the origins of the human cultural capacity are traced back into early biological evolution, and the error of Kroeber's doctrine that culture is without antecedents in nonhuman species clearly revealed. There is thus beginning to emerge a paradigm in which it becomes possible to view culture in an evolutionary setting and to take account of both the genetic and the exogenetic in a way that gives due regard to the crucial importance of each of these fundamental aspects of human behavior and evolution.[7]

Cultural adaptations are made possible by the evolutionary emergence of what Ernst Mayr has termed open programs of behavior, resulting from a gradual opening up of a genetic program to permit "the incorporation of personally acquired information to an ever-greater extent." In Mayr's view there are certain prerequisites if this gradual opening up of a genetic program is to occur. Thus, because personally acquired information necessitates "a far greater storage capacity than is needed for the carefully selected information of a closed genetic program," a large central nervous system is required. An open program of behavior is dependent on the brain-mediated storage and transmission of exogenetic information, and further, does not prescribe all of the steps in a behavioral sequence, but, in Karl Popper's words, "leaves open certain alternatives, certain choices, even though it may perhaps determine the probability or propensity of choosing one way or the other." Thus, as Bonner states in discussing "primitive behavioral flexibility" in nonhuman species, the distinction between "a reflex action and a brain-mediated decision is that the former has one response only, while the latter has two or more." Within an open program of behavior, then, a choice is made by the brain or in other parts of the nervous system between two or more responses to produce what Bonner calls "multiple choice behavior." The appearance of culture is thus to be viewed as "a new niche that arose from the experimentation of animals with multiple choice behavior," and it is to this evolutionary innovation that the rise of cultural adaptations in the human species is to be traced. From this kind of beginning the brain of the early hominids evolved to a point that made rudimentary traditions possible, such as have been shown to exist in populations of the Japanese macaque and the chimpanzee. There was then present a selection pressure which caused a further gradual enlargement of the cerebral hemispheres, and, in the genus *Homo,* the emergence of a dual track of inheritance characterized by the interaction of its genetic and cultural components. Further, in evolutionary perspective there is seen to be a long-existent and deep symbiosis between the genetic and the cultural, with the capacity to produce the exogenetic having arisen, by natural selection, because of its advantage to the species.[8]

We have before us then, a view of human evolution in which *the genetic and exogenetic are distinct but interacting parts of a single system.* If the working of this system is to be comprehended it is imperative, as Bonner points out, that a clear distinction be made between the genetical and the cultural, for only in this way is it possible to understand "the causes and mechanisms of change in any organism capable of both cultural and genetical change." This requirement, furthermore, holds not only for the study of the remote evolutionary history of the human species, but equally for the analysis and interpretation of cultural behavior in recent historical settings. In other words, specific cultural behaviors, to be understood adequately, need to be related to the phylogenetically given impulses in reference to which they have been evolved, and in apposition to which they survive as shared modes of socially inherited adaptation.[9]

An example of such an apposition is to be found in the respect language of the Samoans, to which brief reference has been made in Chapter 8. Of all the cultural conventions of the Samoans, none is more central to their society, with its complex rank hierarchies, than this highly developed language with its elaborate vocabulary of deferential terms for referring to the bodily parts, possessions, attributes, and actions of both titular and talking chiefs and the members of their families. Further, these terms are especially used in chiefly assemblies, which are based on rank, a form of social dominance, and within which there are always long-standing rivalries and tensions. When studying Samoan chieftainship during the years 1966 and 1967, I spent some hundreds of hours sitting cross-legged in chiefly assemblies observing in minute detail, with the gaze of a student of both culture and ethology, the behavior of the other individuals present. On some occasions the chiefs I was observing would, when contending over some burning issue, become annoyed and then angry with one another. By intently observing their physiological states, and especially their redirection and displacement activities, I was able, as their anger mounted, to monitor the behavior of these chiefs in relation to their use of respect language. From repeated observations it became evident that as chiefs became angry they tended to become *more and more polite,* with ever-increasing use of deferential words and phrases. Thus, by resort to cultural convention they could usually avoid potentially damaging situations. Occasionally, however, the conventions of culture would fail completely, and incensed chiefs, having attained to pinnacles of elaborately patterned politeness, would suddenly lapse into violent aggression, as in the attack on the titular chief Taeao that I have described in Chapter 9. In such cases there was an extremely rapid regression from conventional to impulsive behavior. For our present purpose the significance of such incidents is that when the cultural conventions that ordinarily operate within chiefly assemblies fail, activity does *not* suddenly come to an end, but rather the conventional behavior is replaced, in an instant, by highly emotional and impulsive behavior that is animal-like in its ferocity. It is thus evident that if we are to understand the Samoan respect language, which is central to their culture, we must relate it to the disruptive emotions generated by the tensions of social dominance and rank, with which this special language has been developed to deal. In this case, as in other domains of their society, impulses and emotions underlie cultural convention to make up the dual inheritance that is to be found among the Samoans, as in all human populations. It is evident, therefore, that the cultural cannot be adequately comprehended except in relation to the much older phylogenetically given structures in relation to which it has been formed by nongenetic processes. Further, it is plain that the attempt to explain human behavior in purely cultural terms, is, by the anthropological nature of things, irremediably deficient.

In retrospect, then, it is clear that the fundamental deficiency of Mead's Samoan researches was conceptual and methodological. She went to Samoa, she tells us, convinced by the doctrine of W. F. Ogburn (who made no distinction between the biological and the psychological) that one should never look for psychological explanations of social phenomena until attempts at explanation in cultural terms have been exhausted. Mead's zealous adherence to this procedural rule in her inquiries in Manu'a led her to concentrate exclusively on the domain of the cultural, and so to neglect much more deeply motivated aspects of Samoan behavior. It was also this adherence to the methods of cultural determinism that caused Mead, with Benedict's active encouragement, to depict the Samoans in Apollonian terms as the devotees of "all the decreed amenities" and of a social pattern that emphasizes "social blessedness" within an "elaborate, impersonal structure." This depiction Mead had derived directly from Benedict, who, conceiving of culture as "personality writ large," had taken from Nietzsche the designation "Apollonian" to refer to those who live by the law of measure and abjure all "disruptive psychological states." We are here dealing with a cultural ideal, and it was the beguiling conceit of the early cultural determinists that the behavior of an entire people could be adequately categorized in such unitary terms. Benedict and Mead failed to appreciate that in *The Birth of Tragedy* Nietzsche arrived at the quite explicit conclusion that the Dionysian, which symbolizes the elemental in human nature, was quite as fundamental as the Apollonian, and that Apollo had found it impossible to live without Dionysus. And so it was that Dionysus and Apollo—those archaic personifications of the two most fundamental aspects of human nature—jointly occupied the temple at Delphi, indubitably disparate, but in life inseparable, as are, as evolutionary anthropology instructs us, biology and culture.[10]

As described in Chapter 1-3, the doctrine of cultural determinism was formulated in the second decade of the twentieth century in deliberate reaction to the equally unscientific doctrine of extreme biological determinism.[11] We may thus identify biological determinism as the thesis to which cultural determinism was the antithesis. The time is now conspicuously due, in both anthropology and biology, for a synthesis in which there will be, in the study of human behavior, recognition of the radical importance of both the genetic and the exogenetic and their interaction, both in the past history of the human species and in our problematic future.

Notes

A Note on Orthography
and Pronunciation

Glossary

Acknowledgments

Index

Notes

Preface

1. K. R. Popper in B. Magee, ed., *Modern British Philosophy* (London, 1971), 73; K. R. Popper, *Conjectures and Refutations: The Growth of Scientific Knowledge* (London, 1969), 112; idem, *The Logic of Scientific Discovery* (London, 1977), 314; idem, *Objective Knowledge: An Evolutionary Approach* (Oxford, 1972), 263.

1. Galton, Eugenics, and Biological Determinism

1. "A Conversation with Margaret Mead and T. George Harris on the Anthropological Age," *Psychology Today* 4 (1970): 62.

2. N. Pastore, *The Nature-Nurture Controversy* (New York, 1949); S. A. Rice, "Biological Limits in the Development of Society," *Journal of Heredity* 15 (1924): 183; H. M. Parshley, "Heredity and

the Uplift," *American Mercury* 1 (1924): 222; J. B. Watson, "What is Behaviorism?" *Harper's Magazine* 152 (1926): 729.

3. M. Mead, *From the South Seas* (New York, 1939), ix; idem, *Coming of Age in Samoa* (New York, 1973), 197.

4. Mead, *Coming of Age,* 197; F. Boas, *Anthropology and Modern Life* (New York, 1928), 187; M. Mead, *Social Organization of Manu'a* (Honolulu, 1930), 83; F. Boas, "Eugenics," *Scientific Monthly* 3 (1916): 476.

5. Boas, "Eugenics," 472; P. Popenoe, "Nature or Nurture?" *Journal of Heredity* 6 (1915): 238; E. M. Elderton and K. Pearson, *The Relative Strength of Nurture and Nature* (London, 1915), 58; H. F. Osborn, preface (dated 13 July 1916) in M. Grant, *The Passing of the Great Race* (London, 1921, 4th rev. ed.), viii.

6. F. Boas, *Anthropology* (New York, 1908), 6, 27; C. W. Saleeby, *Parenthood and Race Culture: An Outline of Eugenics* (London, 1909); ix; Boas, "Eugenics," 472; idem, "Inventing a Great Race," *New Republic* 9 (1917): 305.

7. A. L. Kroeber, "The Superorganic," *American Anthropologist* 19 (1917): 163; R. H. Lowie, *Culture and Ethnology* (New York, 1917).

8. H. F. Osborn, preface, in Grant, *The Passing of the Great Race,* vii; A. Weismann, *Studies in the Theory of Descent* (London, 1882), I, xv; C. Darwin, *The Origin of Species by Means of Natural Selection* (Harmondsworth, 1968, orig. 1859), 458; D. W. Forrest, *Francis Galton: The Life and Work of a Victorian Genius* (London, 1974), 84.

9. K. Pearson, *The Life, Letters and Labours of Francis Galton,* I (Cambridge, 1914), plate II; II (Cambridge, 1924), 70; C. P. Blacker, *Eugenics: Galton and After* (London, 1952), 110; F. Galton, "Hereditary Talent and Character," *Macmillan's Magazine* 12 (1865): 157–166, 318–327.

10. Galton, "Hereditary Talent and Character," 322.

11. Ibid., 323; Pearson, *Life, Letters and Labours,* I, 7; II, 83ff.

12. Pearson, *Life, Letters and Labours,* II, 86: F. Galton, *Hereditary Genius* (London, 1892, orig. 1869), 325; idem, "Hereditary Talent and Character," 325.

13. Galton, "Hereditary Talent and Character," 325; idem, *Hereditary Genius,* 328.

14. F. Galton, "Hereditary Improvement," *Fraser's Magazine* 7 (1873): 116; idem, *English Men of Science: Their Nature and Nur-*

ture (London, 1874), 12. In *The Tempest,* act IV, scene 1, Prospero describes Caliban as "a devil, a born devil, on whose nature, nurture can never stick."

15. F. Galton, *Inquiries into Human Faculty and Its Development* (London, 1907, orig. 1883), 217; R. H. Lowie, "Applied Psychology," *The Freeman* 1 (1920): 92.

16. Galton, "Hereditary Talent and Character," 165; idem, "Hereditary Improvement," 120; idem, *Inquiries into Human Faculty,* 220. The name Galton first gave to his scheme for hereditary improvement was *viriculture.* In 1883 he replaced viriculture with the term *eugenics,* derived from the Greek *eugenes,* meaning good in stock, hereditarily endowed with noble qualities, which was, he thought, a "neater" word.

17. Pearson, *Life, Letters, and Labours,* I, 6; idem, "Some Recent Misinterpretations of the Problem of Nurture and Nature," in E. M. Elderton and K. Pearson, *The Relative Strength of Nature and Nurture* (London, 1915) 30; C. Darwin, *The Descent of Man* (London, 1901, orig. 1871), 945.

18. For a fuller account of these events see D. Freeman, "The Evolutionary Theories of Charles Darwin and Herbert Spencer," *Current Anthropology* 15 (1974): 216.

19. E. Romanes, ed., *The Life and Letters of George John Romanes* (London, 1896), 238 ff.; G. J. Romanes, "Mr. Wallace on Darwinism," *Contemporary Review* 63 (1889): 248.

20. T. H. Huxley, *Evolution and Ethics and Other Essays* (London, 1894), 37.

21. B. Kidd, *Social Evolution* (London, 1898, 3rd ed.), 339; A. R. Wallace, "Human Selection," *Fortnightly Review* 48 (1890): 325.

22. F. Galton, "The Possible Improvement of the Human Breed under the Existing Conditions of Law and Sentiment," *Annual Report of Smithsonian Institution for 1901* (1902), 538; cf. *Nature,* 1 November 1901.

23. Huxley, *Evolution and Ethics,* 37, 83.

24. E. R. Lankester, "The Significance of the Increased Size of the Cerebrum in Recent as Compared with Extinct Mammalia," *Nature* 61 (1901): 624; idem, *Science from an Easy Chair* (London, 1908), 101.

25. Pearson, *Life, Letters and Labours,* IIIA (1930), 217, 412, 435; Galton, "The Possible Improvement of the Human Breed," 534, 538.

26. F. Galton, *Probability, The Foundation of Eugenics* (Oxford, 1907), 7.

27. K. Pearson, *The Scope and Importance to the State of the Science of National Eugenics* (London, 1909), 44 ff.; Galton, *Probability*, 30; C. W. Saleeby, *Parenthood and Race Culture: An Outline of Eugenics* (London, 1909), ix.

28. Pearson, *Life, Letters and Labours*, IIIA, 235; "Francis Galton," *American Breeders Magazine* 2 (1911): 62; M. H. Haller, *Eugenics: Hereditarian Attitudes in American Thought* (New Brunswick, 1963), 62.

29. C. B. Davenport, "Report of Committee on Eugenics," *American Breeders Magazine* 1 (1910): 129; idem, *Heredity in Relation to Eugenics* (New York, 1911), 271.

30. E. Radl, *The History of Biological Theories* (London, 1930, orig. 1909), 388; R. Pearl, "Recent Discussions of Heredity," *The Dial* 52 (1912): 397; J. A. Thomson, review of *The Methods and Scope of Genetics* by W. Bateson, *Eugenics Review* 1 (1910): 60.

31. R. Pearl, "Controlling Man's Evolution," *The Dial* 53 (1912): 49; Haller, *Eugenics*, 94.

32. K. Pearson, *Francis Galton, 1822–1911: A Centenary Appreciation* (Cambridge, 1922), 17; idem, *Nature and Nurture: The Problem of the Future* (London, 1913, orig. 1910), 27.

33. F. Boas, *The Mind of Primitive Man* (New York, 1938, orig. 1911), 41; M. Crackenthorpe, "Sir Francis Galton, F.R.S.: A Memoir," *Eugenics Review* 3 (1911): 8.

2. Boas and the Distinction between Culture and Heredity

1. A. L. Kroeber, "Franz Boas: The Man," *Memoirs, American Anthropological Association* 61 (1943): 21; R. H. Lowie, "Science," in H. E. Stearns, ed., *Civilization in the United States* (New York, 1922), 154; idem, review of *Race, Language and Culture* by F. Boas, *Science* 91 (1940): 599; A. Goldenweiser, "Recent Trends in American Anthropology," *American Anthropologist* 43 (1941): 153.

2. F. Boas, "The Mind of Primitive Man," *Journal of American Folk-Lore* 14 (1901): 3; L. Spier, "Some Central Elements in the Legacy," in W. Goldschmidt, ed., *The Anthropology of Franz Boas, Memoirs, American Anthropological Association* 89 (1959): 147.

3. E. Haeckel, "Professor Haeckel on Darwin, Goethe and La-

marck," *Nature* 26 (1882): 534, 541; "Haeckel's History of Creation," *Nature* 13 (1875): 122; A. Lane-Fox Pitt-Rivers, "On the Evolution of Culture," in J. L. Myres, ed., *The Evolution of Culture and Other Essays* (Oxford, 1906; orig. 1875), 24.

4. F. Boas, "The Methods of Ethnology" (1920), in F. Boas, *Race, Language and Culture* (New York, 1940), 281; E. B. Tylor, *Primitive Culture* (London, 1929; orig. 1871), I, 2; F. Boas, "The Aims of Ethnology" (1889), in *Race, Language and Culture,* 637.

5. F. Galton, "Hereditary Improvement," *Fraser's Magazine* 7 (1873): 128; F. Boas, "An Anthropologist's Credo," *The Nation* 147 (1938): 201; C. Wittke, *Refugees of Revolution: The Germany Forty-Eighters in America* (Philadelphia, (1952), 18.

6. Boas is quoted in G. W. Stocking, *Race, Culture and Evolution* (New York, 1968), 149, 143; C. Kluckhohn and O. Prufer, "Influences During the Formative Years," in W. Goldschmidt, ed., *The Anthropology of Franz Boas, Memoirs, American Anthropological Association* 89 (1959): 6.

7. J. E. Smith, "The Question of Man" in C. Hendel, ed., *The Philosophy of Kant and Our Modern World* (New York, 1957), 20.

8. H. A. Hodges, *Wilhelm Dilthey* (London, 1944), 82.

9. Stocking, *Race, Culture, and Evolution,* 138 (Stocking suggests that it may have been during this year at Berlin that Boas read, or perhaps even heard, Dilthey); Boas, "An Anthropologist's Credo," 201.

10. Boas, "An Anthropologist's Credo," 201; idem, "The Aims of Ethnology," 638.

11. Boas, "An Anthropologist's Credo," 202; idem, "A Journey in Cumberland Sound and on the West Side of Davis Strait in 1883 and 1884," *American Geographical Society Bulletin* 16 (1884): 271; Stocking, *Race, Culture, and Evolution,* 148.

12. The use of "exogenetic" in this context as a synonym for "cultural" is warranted in that Boas later used the term "exogene" to refer to cultural processes: cf. F. Boas, "The Question of Racial Purity," *American Mercury* 3 (1924): 164. For further information on the term exogenetic see D. Freeman, "Sociobiology: The 'Antidiscipline' of Anthropology," in A. Montagu, ed., *Sociobiology Examined* (New York, 1980), 216.

13. R. Virchow, "The Liberty of Science in the Modern State," *Nature* 17 (1877): 72; E. Haeckel, *Freedom in Science and Teaching* (London, 1879), 7.

14. F. Boas, "Rudolf Virchow's Anthropological Work," *Science* 16 (1902): 441; Kroeber, "Franz Boas: The Man," 10; P. Radin, "The Mind of Primitive Man," *New Republic* 98 (1939): 303.

15. F. Boas, "Race," *Encyclopaedia of the Social Sciences* 13, (1934): 34; idem, "Psychological Problems in Anthropology," *American Journal of Psychology* 21 (1910): 373.

16. T. Waitz, *Introduction to Anthropology* (London, 1863), 3.

17. Ibid., 74; E. Becker, *The Lost Science of Man* (New York, 1971), 113.

18. Stocking, *Race, Culture and Evolution,* 184; Kroeber, "Franz Boas: The Man," 7; Kluckhohn and Prufer, "Influences During the Formative Years," 22; F. Boas, "The Aims of Anthropological Research" (1932), in *Race, Language and Culture,* 246; idem, *The Mind of Primitive Man* (New York, 1911), 64, 75; idem, "The Aims of Ethnology," 633; idem, *Changes in the Bodily form of Descendants of Immigrants* (Washington, D. C., 1911), 39.

19. Boas, "The Mind of Primitive Man," 3; idem, "Human Faculty as Determined by Race," *Proceedings, American Association for the Advancement of Science* 43 (1894): 318.

20. Boas, *The Mind of Primitive Man,* 43; idem, "The Question of Racial Purity," 163.

21. F. Boas, "The Coast Tribes of British Columbia," *Science* 9 (1887): 289; idem, "The Aims of Ethnology," 627; idem, "The Growth of Indian Mythologies," *Journal of American Folk-Lore* 9 (1896): 11; idem, "On Alternating Sounds," *American Anthropologist* 2 (1889): 47; Stocking, *Race, Culture, and Evolution,* 159.

22. F. Boas, "The Limitations of the Comparative Method in Anthropology," *Science* 4 (1896): 908; idem, "The Mind of Primitive Man," 5.

23. Boas, "The Mind of Primitive Man," 3; W. K. C. Guthrie, *The Sophists* (Cambridge, 1971), 21; C. Lévi-Strauss, "Rousseau, Father of Anthropology," *UNESCO Courier* 3 (1963): 11.

24. R. H. Lowie, *The History of Ethnological Theory* (New York, 1937), 17; F. Boas, *The Mind of Primitive Man,* 42.

25. Boas, *The Mind of Primitive Man,* 231; Stocking, *Race, Culture, and Evolution,* 264.

26. C. B. Davenport, *Heredity in Relation to Eugenics* (New York, 1911), iv; idem, "Euthenics and Eugenics," *Popular Science Monthly* 78 (1911): 20.

27. Davenport, "Euthenics and Eugenics," 18.

3. The Launching of Cultural Determinism

1. R. Pearl, "Genetics and Eugenics," *Eugenics Review* 3 (1911): 335; idem, "Controlling Man's Evolution," *The Dial,* 53 (1912): 49; K. Pearson, *The Groundwork of Eugenics* (London, 1912), 49.

2. L. S. Hearnshaw, *Cyril Burt, Psychologist* (London, 1979), 23; C. Burt, "The Inheritance of Mental Character," *Eugenics Review* 4 (1912): 200; M. Mead, "1925–1939," in M. Mead, *From the South Seas* (New York, 1939), x.

3. Pearl, "Controlling Man's Evolution," 49; C. B. Davenport, "Euthenics and Eugenics," *Popular Science Monthly* 78 (1911): 20; "The Eugenics Record Office," *Science* 39 (1913): 553; C. E. Rosenberg, "Charles Benedict Davenport and the Beginning of Human Genetics," *Bulletin of the History of Medicine* 35 (1961): 270, 217; C. B. Davenport, "Heredity of Some Emotional Traits," *Report, Eighty-Fourth Meeting, British Association for the Advancement of Science, Australia, 1914* (London, 1915), 419; idem, "Heredity, Culpability, Praiseworthiness, Punishment and Reward," *Popular Science Monthly* 83 (1913): 36.

4. L. Darwin, review of *Hereditary Genius* by Sir Francis Galton, *Eugenics Review* 6 (1914): 251; E. M. Elderton and K. Pearson, *The Relative Strength of Nature and Nurture* (London, 1915), 30; Rosenberg, "Charles Benedict Davenport," 273.

5. H. F. Osborn, preface in M. Grant, *The Passing of the Great Race* (London, 1921; orig. 1916), viii; R. D. Kingham, review of *Race Improvement or Eugenics* by H. Baker, *Eugenics Review* 5 (1913): 178; J. A. Lindsay, review of *Principles of Eugenics* by B. Eames, *Eugenics Review* 6 (1915): 318; "Eugenics in the Colleges," *Journal of Heredity* 5 (1914): 186; G. H. Parker, "The Eugenics Movement as a Public Service," *Science* 41 (1915): 345; W. C. Rucker, "More 'Eugenic Laws,'" *Journal of Heredity* 6 (1915): 219; M. H. Haller, *Eugenics: Hereditarian Attitudes in American Thought* (New Brunswick, 1963), 150; review of *The Passing of the Great Race* by M. Grant, *Journal of Heredity* 8 (1917): 40; M. Mead, preface, 1973 edition, *Coming of Age in Samoa* (New York, 1973); review of *The Progress of Eugenics* by C. M. Saleeby, *The Nation* 100 (1915): 606; P. Popenoe, "Nature or Nurture?" *Journal of Heredity* 6 (1915): 227; W. E. Castle et al., *Heredity and Eugenics* (Chicago, 1912), 309.

6. R. H. Lowie, "Alfred Russel Wallace," *New Republic* 9 (1916): 16; A. R. Wallace, "The Origin of Human Races and the Antiquity of Man Deduced from the Theory of Natural Selection," *Journal of the Anthropological Society of London* 2 (1864): 187.

7. F. Boas, "Eugenics," *Scientific Monthly* 3 (1916): 417; K. M. Ludmerer, *Genetics and American Society: An Historical Appraisal* (Baltimore, 1972), 116.

8. A. L. Kroeber, "Inheritance by Magic," *American Anthropologist* 18 (1916): 34; "Anthropology," in *The New International Year Book* (New York, 1918), 32; A. L. Kroeber, "The Superorganic," *American Anthropologist* 19 (1917): 176, 189.

9. A. L. Kroeber, *The Nature of Culture* (Chicago, 1952); idem, "Decorative Symbolism of the Arapaho," *American Anthropologist* 3 (1901): 332.

10. A. L. Kroeber, "The Morals of Uncivilized People," *American Anthropologist* 12 (1910): 437.

11. G. de Beer, *Charles Darwin* (Melbourne, 1963), 183; Ludmerer, *Genetics and American Society,* 45; A. R. Wallace, "The Present Position of Darwinism," *Contemporary Review* 94 (1908): 129; H. De Vries, "The Principles of the Theory of Mutation," *Science* 40 (1914): 77; W. Bateson, "Address of the President of the British Association for the Advancement of Science, Melbourne, 14 August, Sydney, 20 August," *Science* 40 (1914): 287, 319; Kroeber, "Inheritance by Magic," 27.

12. R. H. Lowie, "Theoretical Ethnology," *Psychological Bulletin* 13 (1916): 398; idem, *The History of Ethnological Theory* (New York, 1937), 200. In 1910, in "The Morals of Uncivilized People," Kroeber equated the terms "culture" and "civilization." In his papers published during World War I (as Stocking has noted), "Kroeber's sensitivity to its Germanic associations ... prevented him from using the term 'culture,'" and he spoke instead of "history," "civilization" and "the social." G. W. Stocking, *Race, Culture and Evolution* (New York, 1968), 267.

13. T. Kroeber, *Alfred Kroeber: A Personal Configuration* (Berkeley, 1970), 90; H. K. Haeberlin, "Anti-Professions," *American Anthropologist* 17 (1915): 768; R. H. Lowie, "Psychology and Sociology," *American Journal of Sociology* 21 (1915): 218; Kroeber, "Inheritance by Magic," 29; idem, 'Heredity without Magic,' *American Anthropologist* 18 (1916): 294.

14. Kroeber, "Heredity without Magic," 295; idem, *The Nature of Culture,* 9.

15. Kroeber, "Inheritance by Magic," 26; G. H. Parker, *What is Evolution?* (Cambridge, Mass., 1926, orig. 1925), 97.

16. A. G. Webster, "Annual Meeting of the National Academy of Sciences," *The Nation* 100 (1915): 475; T. H. Morgan, A. H. Sturtevant, H. J. Muller, and C. B. Bridges, *The Mechanism of Mendelian Heredity* (New York, 1915); E. Huntington, "Heredity and Human Responsibility," *Yale Review* 6 (1917): 668; K. M. Ludmerer, *Genetics and American Society* (Baltimore, 1972), 34.

17. E. G. Conklin, *Heredity and Environment in the Development of Man* (Princeton, 1930, orig. 1915), 125.

18. R. H. Lowie, "The Universalist Fallacy," *New Republic* 13 (1917): 4. Ernst Haeckel had from the 1870s vehemently advocated a "monistic explanation of the whole," and for Lowie Haeckel was "the Hotspur prophet of the evolutionary faith." A. L. Kroeber, "The Superorganic," *American Anthropologist* 19 (1917): 163: idem, *The Nature of Culture,* 22.

19. Kroeber, "The Superorganic," 177.

20. Ibid., 209, 213; H. De Vries, "The Principles of the Theory of Mutation," *Science* 40 (1914): 77; Kroeber, *The Nature of Culture,* 9.

21. R. H. Lowie, *Culture and Ethnology* (New York, 1919, orig. 1917), 66; "Anthropology," *The New International Year Book,* 32; R. H. Lowie, "The Universalist Fallacy," *New Republic* 13 (1917): 4.

22. A. L. Kroeber, "On the Principle of Order in Civilization as Exemplified by Changes in Fashion," *American Anthropologist* 21 (1919): 263.

23. Kroeber, "The Superorganic," 193; R. H. Lowie, *The History of Ethnological Theory,* 200; E. Leach, *Social Anthropology* (London, 1982), 31. Inasmuch as it has, in accordance with Durkheimian precept, totally excluded biological variables, social anthropology in Great Britain and elsewhere, despite various differences in emphasis, has operated within the same basic paradigm as American cultural anthropology. E. Sapir, "Do We Need a 'Superorganic?'" *American Anthropologist* 19 (1917): 441; idem, letter to Lowie, Ottawa, 10 July 1917, in *Letters from Edward Sapir to Robert H. Lowie* (n.p., 1965), 25.

24. Stocking, *Race, Culture and Evolution,* 302, 303; R. Darnell, "The Development of American Anthropology, 1879–1920" (Ph.D. diss., University of Pennsylvania, 1969), 421; Kroeber, "The Superorganic," 183; T. S. Kuhn, *The Essential Tension* (Chicago, 1978), 297; L. J. Halle, *The Ideological Imagination,* (London, 1972), 5.

25. F. Boas, "The Mind of Primitive Man," *Journal of American Folk-Lore* 14 (1901): 11; R. Bunzel, in M. Mead and R. Bunzel, eds., *The Golden Age of American Anthropology* (New York, 1960), 400; A. Lesser, "Franz Boas," in S. Silverman, ed., *Totems and Teachers: Perspectives on the History of Anthropology* (New York, 1981), 3.

26. W. K. Gregory, "The Galton Society for the Study of the Origin and Evolution of Man," *Science* 49 (1919): 267.

4. Boas Poses an Intractable Problem

1. E. Sapir, "Primitive Society," *The Freeman* 1 (1920): 377; R. Darnell, "The Development of American Anthropology, 1879–1920" (Ph.D. diss., University of Pennsylvania, 1969), xxxxii.

2. Sapir, "Primitive Society," 377; idem, "Primitive Humanity and Anthropology," *The Dial* 69 (1920): 532; cf. Mead's remark of 2 June 1975 in her foreword to D. F. Tuzin, *The Ilahita Arapesh* (Berkeley, 1976), xvii, that she was "suckled on Lowie's *Primitive Society*"; F. Boas, "Eugenics," *Scientific Monthly* 3 (1916): 476.

3. H. L. Laughlin, "The Relation of Eugenics to Other Sciences," *Eugenics Review* 11 (1919): 53; R. H. Lowie, "The Father of Eugenics," *The Freeman* 1 (1920): 471; "The Second International Congress of Eugenics," *Journal of Heredity* 12 (1921): 219.

4. L. Stoddard, *The Rising Tide of Color* (New York, 1920); F. Boas, "Inventing a Great Race," *New Republic* 9 (1917): 305; idem, "Peoples at War," *American Journal of Physical Anthropology* 1 (1918): 363; M. Grant, "Discussion of Article on Democracy and Heredity," *Journal of Heredity* 10 (1919): 165; idem, *The Passing of the Great Race,* 4th rev. ed. (London, 1921), 17; H. F. Osborn, "The Second International Congress of Eugenics: Address of Welcome," *Science* 54 (1921): 312; C. B. Davenport, "Research in Eugenics," *Science* 54 (1921): 394.

5. Osborn, "The Second International Congress," 313; G. Adami, "The True Aristocracy," *Eugenics Review* 14 (1922): 185.

6. F. Boas, review of *The Rising Tide of Color* by L. Stoddard, *The Nation* 111 (1920): 656; Lowie, "The Father of Eugenics," 473; Grant, *The Passing of the Great Race,* 16; Lowie, "Mr. Grant's Apologia," *The Freeman* 4 (1922): 476.

7. F. Boas, review of *The Rising Tide of Color,* 656; Lowie, "The Father of Eugenics," 472.

8. J. B. Watson, "Psychology as the Behaviorist Views It," *Psychological Review* 20 (1913): 158; M. E. Haggerty, review of *Behavior* by J. B. Watson, *Journal of Philosophy* 13 (1916): 470; W. R.

Wells, "The Anti-Instinct Fallacy," *Psychological Review* 30 (1923): 229.

9. R. S. Woodworth, "John Broadus Watson, 1873–1958," *American Journal of Psychology* 72 (1959): 305; J. R. Kantor, "A Functional Interpretation of Human Instincts," *Psychological Review* 27 (1920): 52; Z. Y. Kuo, "Giving up Instincts in Psychology," *Journal of Philosophy* 18 (1921): 658; J. R. Kantor, *Principles of Psychology* (New York, 1924), 172; J. B. Watson, *Behaviorism* (New York, 1924), 74.

10. Z. Y. Kuo, "A Psychology without Heredity," *Psychological Review* 31 (1924): 438; L. L. Bernard, *Instinct: A Study in Social Psychology* (London, 1924), 524; J. Dewey, *Human Nature and Conduct: An Introduction to Social Psychology* (New York, 1922), 95.

11. H. M. Parshley, "Heredity and the Uplift," *American Mercury* 1 (1924): 222.

12. F. Boas, "The Question of Racial Purity," *American Mercury* 3 (1924): 163.

13. M. Mead, *Blackberry Winter* (New York, 1972), 111; A. L. Kroeber, "Franz Boas: The Man," *Memoirs, American Anthropological Association* 61 (1943): 15; M. Mead, *Anthropologists and What They Do* (New York, 1965), 157; idem, *An Anthropologist at Work* (London, 1959), 4; idem, *Ruth Benedict* (New York, 1974), 3; idem, "Ruth Benedict," *International Encyclopedia of the Social Sciences* 2 (1968): 48. Mead has recorded that from February 1923 she began to know Ruth Benedict not only as a teacher but also as a friend. However, she continued to call her Mrs. Benedict until she got her degree later in 1923 after which "almost imperceptibly" their relationship became one of colleagues and close friends (*Blackberry Winter,* p. 115).

14. A. A. Goldenweiser, "The Autonomy of the Social," *American Anthropologist* 19 (1917): 448; E. Sapir, letter to Benedict, Ottawa, 25 June 1922, in Mead, *An Anthropologist at Work,* 49.

15. R. Benedict, "Nature and Nurture," *The Nation* 118 (1924): 118; idem, "Toward a Social Psychology," *The Nation* 119 (1924): 51; A. L. Kroeber, *Anthropology* (London, 1923), 3.

16. Mead, *Blackberry Winter,* 113; idem, *An Anthropologist at Work,* 67; cf. Benedict's entry in her diary on 7 March 1923, after talking with Mead: "she rests me like a padded chair and a fire place."

17. Mead, *Blackberry Winter,* 111; W. F. Ogburn, *Social Change*

with Respect to Culture and Original Nature (New York, 1950; orig. 1922), 11; M. Mead, "Retrospects and Prospects," in T. Gladwin and W. C. Sturtevant, eds., *Anthropology and Human Behavior* (Washington, D.C., 1962), 121.

18. Mead, *An Anthropologist at Work,* 68, 69, 121, 286; idem, *Blackberry Winter,* 114; idem, "Rank in Polynesia," *Report, Ninety-Second Meeting, British Association for the Advancement of Science* (London, 1924), 421.

19. M. Mead, "Apprenticeship under Boas," *Memoirs, American Anthropological Association* 89 (1959): 42; idem; "Retrospects and Prospects," 122; G. S. Hall, *Adolescence* (New York, 1904), 2 vols.; F. P. Rice, *The Adolescent: Development, Relationships and Culture* (Boston, 1975), 12; H. L. Mencken, "The Sex Uproar," *The Nation* 119 (1924): 91; M. Mead, *Letters from the Field, 1925–1975* (New York, 1977), 19: "I imagine that my age and physique—at about 23 years old I was 5 feet 2½ inches tall and weighed 98 pounds—had something to do with his choice." It would seem, as Mead has suggested, that Boas chose adolescence as a problem for investigation from his knowledge of, and disagreement with, the writings of G. Stanley Hall. Boas had been associated with Hall at Clark University in 1889–1892. M. Herskovits, *Franz Boas* (New York, 1953), 13.

20. M. Mead, *Letters from the Field,* 19; idem, "Apprenticeship under Boas," 42; "A Conversation with Margaret Mead and T. George Harris on the Anthropological Age," *Psychology Today* 4 (1970): 62; Mead, *Blackberry Winter,* 129.

21. Mead, *Blackberry Winter,* 132.

22. Mead, *Letters from the Field,* 23; W. Somerset Maugham, *The Trembling of a Leaf* (London, 1921), 250.

5. Mead Presents Boas with an Absolute Answer

1. M. Mead, *Blackberry Winter* (New York, 1972), 137; idem, *Social Organization of Manu'a* (Honolulu, 1969), xviii.

2. M. Mead, *Letters from the Field 1925–1975* (New York, 1977), 26.

3. Ibid., 29. R. P. Rohner records in his "Franz Boas: Ethnographer on the Northwest Coast," in J. Helm, ed., *Pioneers of American Anthropology* (Seattle, 1966), 210, that Boas, during his field work on the Northwest Coast of America, rarely lived in an Indian household or community preferring instead to stay "in a hotel or

some other public accommodation within walking distance from the village where he wanted to work."

4. Mead, *Letters from the Field,* 28.

5. This close chaperoning would have been, although Mead seems to have had no inkling of this, a safeguard against *moetotolo,* or surreptitious rape, which is always a possibility in a Samoan village; see Chapter 16.

6. Mead, *Letters from the Field,* 30ff.; idem, *Blackberry Winter,* 148 ff.; idem, "Field Work in the Pacific Islands, 1925-1967," in P. Golde, ed., *Women in the Field* (Chicago, 1970), 318.

7. Mead, *Letters from the Field,* 30; idem, *Blackberry Winter,* 150.

8. H. F. Bryan, *American Samoa: A General Report by the Governor* (Washington, D.C., 1927), 47 ff.; A. H. Leibowitz, "American Samoa: Decline of a Culture," *California Western International Law Journal* 10 (1980): 220.

9. Bryan, *American Samoa,* 4 ff.; J. A. C. Gray, *Amerika Samoa: A History of American Samoa and Its United States Naval Administration* (Annapolis, 1960), 187; Mead, *Letters from the Field,* 55; A. F. Judd, Expanded notes, ethnology, etc., American Samoa, February 15-April 2, 1926; Islands of Tutuila, Ofu, and Ta'ū, Mss, Bernice P. Bishop Museum Library, p. 29. In *Coming of Age in Samoa* (New York, 1973), 266, Mead states that Manu'a, in 1926, was "the most primitive part of Samoa." This was not the case. At that time, and up to the advent of the Pacific war of 1941-1946, there were numerous villages in Western Samoa that had had less contact with Western institutions and values than those of Lumā, Si'ufaga, and Faleasao, in Manu'a, in which Mead worked.

10. When Mead reached Ta'ū in November 1925, she had been learning Samoan for only ten weeks; thenceforward she lived as a member of the Holts' English-speaking household, and her command of the formidable Samoan language, with its complex terminologies derived from rank and ancient tradition, remained far from perfect. For example, in the fifteen words of Mead's Samoan dedication in the first edition of *Coming of Age in Samoa* in 1928 (which are reprinted in the 1973 Morrow paperback edition) there are no fewer than seven errors, several of them egregious. For a detailed account of the quality of Mead's use of the Samoan language, see D. Freeman, "*Social Organization of Manu'a* (1930 and 1969) by Margaret Mead: Some Errata," *Journal of the Polynesian Society* 81 (1972): 70-78.

11. In *Coming of Age in Samoa* Mead used the term "puberty" as we would now use "menarche."

12. Mead, *Coming of Age,* 282.

13. Mead, *Blackberry Winter,* 151; idem, "Return to Samoa," *Redbook* 139 (1972): 29; A. M. Noble, *Regulations and Orders for the Government of American Samoa* (San Francisco, 1921), 53; Mead, *Letters from the Field,* 45 ff.

14. Judd, Expanded notes, etc.; Mead, *Letters from the Field,* 55.

15. In the late nineteenth century, in an abrupt departure from ancient tradition, Margaret Young, who was of part British and part Samoan descent and whose family had acquired local influence, was installed as the Tui, or Queen of Manu'a. Stevenson (*The Letters of Robert Louis Stevenson,* ed. S. Colvin, London, 1899, II, 338), after a visit to Manu'a in 1894, described her, in a letter to Henry James, as a little slip of a half-caste girl about twenty who sat "all day in a pink gown, in a little white European house with about a quarter of an acre of roses in front of it, looking at the palm-trees on the village street, and listening to the surf." The following year, aged only twenty-three, Margaret Young met a tragic death when an over-turned kerosene lamp set fire to the mosquito net in which she was sleeping. After this dire event the chiefs of Manu'a ruled that hence-forward women would be forbidden from holding chiefly titles and from participating in fono. Mead, like Margaret Young, was given the Samoan name of Makelita, and may well have been identified with her by the Manu'ans; there exists a photograph of Mead in Ta'ū, wearing a ceremonial dress woven by Margaret Young, and sitting, in contravention of Samoan custom, on a bonito canoe; cf. M. Mead, "A Lapse of Animism among a Primitive People," *Psyche* 9 (1929): 74: "No woman is permitted to touch a bonito canoe."

16. Mead, *Blackberry Winter,* 151; idem, *Social Organization of Manu'a,* xviii.

17. Mead, *Social Organization of Manua,* 224 ff.; idem, *Black-berry Winter,* 156.

18. M. Mead, *An Anthropologist at Work: Writings of Ruth Benedict* (London, 1959), 292.

19. R. Benedict, "Toward a Social Psychology," *The Nation* 119 (1924): 51; Mead, *An Anthropologist at Work,* 202. Mead reports that when Reo Fortune was shown the anthology compiled by Benedict he looked up from Amy Lowell's poem to inquire, "Is that why you are always talking about patterns?"

20. Mead, *An Anthropologist at Work,* 301; idem, *Ruth Benedict* (New York, 1974), 34.

21. M. Mead, *Anthropologists and What They Do* (New York, 1965), 121; idem, *An Anthropologist at Work,* 208.

22. Mead, *Anthropologists and What They Do,* 121 ff.

23. Mead, *An Anthropologist at Work,* 206 ff.; idem, *Blackberry Winter,* 195; R. Benedict, "Psychological Types in the Cultures of the Southwest" (1928), in Mead, *An Anthropologist at Work,* 248 ff.

24. R. Benedict, "The Science of Custom," (1929), in V. F. Calverton, ed., *The Making of Man* (New York, 1931), 815; Mead, *An Anthropologist at Work,* 206 ff.; idem, *Blackberry Winter,* 195.

25. Benedict, "Psychological Types in the Southwest," 261; Mead, *Social Organization of Manu'a,* 80 ff.; idem, *Sex and Temperament in Three Primitive Societies* (1935), in *From the South Seas* (New York, 1939), 292.

26. M. Mead, *New Lives for Old* (New York, 1966), 107; idem, *An Anthropologist at Work,* 305; idem, *Social Organization of Manu'a,* 83.

27. M. Mead, "Preface to the 1949 Edition," *Coming of Age in Samoa* (Mentor Books, New York, 1949), ix.

28. Mead, *An Anthropologist at Work,* 289; idem, "South Sea Hints on Bringing up Children," *Parents' Magazine* 4 (1929): 22.

29. "A Conversation with Margaret Mead and T. George Harris on the Anthropological Age," *Psychology Today* 4 (1970): 66.

30. M. Mead, Interview with A. Kuper, B.B.C., 1976.

31. Mead, *Coming of Age,* 197.

32. "A Conversation with Margaret Mead," *Psychology Today,* 66; Mead, *Blackberry Winter, 121.*

33. J. Epstein, *Epstein: An Autobiography* (London, 1963), 131.

34. Mead, *An Anthropologist at Work,* 309; idem, *Anthropologists and What They Do,* 125.

35. F. Boas, foreword, in Mead, *Coming of Age,* ix; idem, *Anthropology and Modern Life* (New York, 1928), 186.

36. Mead, *An Anthropologist at Work,* 310.

37. J. B. Watson, *The Ways of Behaviorism* (New York, 1928). In Watson's view Freud's theory of the unconscious was "voodooism" and "a substitution of demonology for science"; idem, "The Myth of the Unconscious," *Harper's Magazine* 155 (1927): 729. Rather similar views were held by the Boasians during the 1920s. In March 1926 Benedict (*An Anthropologist at Work,* 305) wrote to

Mead telling her that Malinowski, who had been visiting New York, felt that psychoanalysis, about which he was as skeptical as was Boas, was only for extremists. This same stance is reflected in Mead's writings on Samoa. In *Coming of Age* (212), she reports that the larger family community seemed to ensure the child "against the development of the crippling attitudes which have been labelled Oedipus complexes, Electra complexes, and so on." And in *Male and Female* (Harmondsworth, 1962), 124, she asserted that "perhaps more sharply than in any known society, Samoan culture demonstrates how much the tragic or easy solution of the Oedipus situation depends upon the inner-relationship between parents and children and is not created out of whole cloth by the young child's biological impulses." My own researches in Samoa, during the years 1966–1967, revealed the Oedipus situation to be decidedly present.

38. V. F. Calverton, "The Analysis of Behavior," *Modern Quarterly* 4 (1927): 302.

39. R. L. Finney, "Culture and the Original Nature of Man," *Journal of Applied Sociology* 11 (1927): 343.

40. R. Benedict, "Nature and Nurture," *The Nation* 118 (1924): 118; idem, review of *Coming of Age in Samoa, Journal of Philosophy* 26 (1929); 110.

6. Mead's Depiction of the Samoans

1. M. Mead, *Coming of Age in Samoa* (New York, 1973), 8, 11; idem, *Social Organization of Manu'a* (Honolulu, 1930), 55.

2. Mead, *Coming of Age,* 198; Mead's statement that no great disasters threaten the lives of Samoans is scarcely true, for the Samoan islands are regularly stricken by severe hurricanes. In the hurricane of 10 January 1915, for example, as is recorded by H. F. Bryan in *American Samoa* (Washington, 1927), 4, the churches, schoolhouses, stores, and most of the houses of Manu'a were blown down and the greater part of the crops destroyed. Indeed, so severe were the food shortages following this hurricane that over half the population of Manu'a had to be transported to Tutuila and maintained there for several months. Again, on 1 January 1926, during the course of Mead's own stay in Manu'a, there was a severe hurricane which, so she states in *Blackberry Winter* (New York, 1972), 150, "destroyed every house in the village and ruined the crops."

3. M. Mead, *Male and Female* (Harmondsworth, 1962), 100, 201; idem, *Coming of Age,* 122, 170; idem, "The Role of the Individual in Samoan Culture," *Journal of the Royal Anthropological Institute* 58 (1928): 418; idem, "The Samoans," in M. Mead, ed., *Cooperation and Competition among Primitive Peoples* (New York, 1937), 308; idem, "1925–1939," in *From the South Seas* (New York, 1939), xxvi.

4. M. Mead, *An Anthropologist at Work* (London, 1959), 547; idem, *Anthropologists and What They Do* (New York, 1965), 141.

5. M. Mead, *Growing Up in New Guinea* (1930), in *From the South Seas* (New York, 1939), 219, 234; idem, "The Samoans," 309, 502; idem, "1925–1939," xxvi; idem, "Two South Sea Educational Experiments and Their American Implications," *University of Pennsylvania School of Education Bulletin* 31 (1931): 495; idem, *Coming of Age,* 151, 157, 158, 200, 207; idem, "The Role of the Individual in Samoan Culture," *Journal of the Royal Anthropological Institute* 58 (1928): 494.

6. M. Mead, "Creativity in Cross-Cultural Perspective," in H. H. Anderson, ed., *Creativity and Its Cultivation* (New York, 1959), 225, 231; idem, *Male and Female,* 123; idem, "The Human Condition," in R. Metraux, ed., *Some Personal Views* (New York, 1979), 211.

7. Mead, *Male and Female,* 120, 201; idem, "The Sex Life of the Unmarried Adult in Primitive Society," in I. S. Wile, ed., *The Sex Life of the Unmarried Adult* (London, 1935), 62; idem, "Back of Adolescence Lies Early Childhood," *Childhood Education* 18 (1941): 58; idem, "Broken Homes," *The Nation* 128 (1929): 254; idem, "Parents and Children in Samoa," *Child Study* 9 (1932): 232; idem, *Growing Up in New Guinea,* 239; idem, "South Sea Hints on Bringing Up Children," *Parents' Magazine* 4 (1929): 22; idem, *Coming of Age,* 213; idem, "Social Change and Cultural Surrogates," *Journal of Educational Sociology* 14 (1940): 96.

8. Mead, "South Sea Hints on Bringing Up Children," 50; idem, "Back of Adolescence Lies Early Childhood," *Childhood Education* 18 (1941): 59.

9. Mead, *Social Organization of Manu'a,* 91; idem, "Samoan Children at Work and Play," *Natural History* 28 (1928): 632; idem, "The Role of the Individual in Samoan Culture," 487, 494; idem, *Coming of Age,* 161.

10. Mead, *Male and Female,* 99, 124, 202.

11. Mead, "Samoan Children at Work and Play," 633; idem, *Coming of Age*, 23, 25, 159; idem, "The Role of the Individual in Samoan Culture," 487.

12. Mead, "The Samoans," 302, 308; idem, *Male and Female*, 201; idem, *Coming of Age*, 35.

13. M. Mead, "Jealousy: Primitive and Civilized," in S. D. Schmalhausen and V. F. Calverton, eds, *Woman's Coming of Age: A Symposium* (New York, 1931), 43; idem, "The Samoans," 304; idem, "Life as a Samoan Girl," in *All True! The Record of Actual Adventures that Have Happened to Ten Women of Today* (New York, 1931), 106; idem, "The Role of the Individual in Samoan Culture," 492.

14. Mead, *Social Organization of Manu'a*, 7; idem, "The Role of the Individual in Samoan Culture," 493, 495; idem, "The Samoans," 287.

15. Mead, "The Samoans," 302, 474; idem, *Male and Female*, 360; idem, "The Role of the Individual in Samoan Culture," 484; idem, *Social Organization of Manu'a*, 168.

16. M. Mead, *Sex and Temperament in Three Primitive Societies* (1935), in *From the South Seas*, 285; idem, *Male and Female*, 361; idem, "The Role of the Individual in Samoan Culture," 494; idem, "Life as a Samoan Girl," 99; idem, review of *Samoa Under the Sailing Gods* by N. A. Rowe, *The Nation* 133 (1931): 138; idem, *Anthropologists and What They Do*, 141; idem, *Coming of Age*, 198.

17. Mead, "The Samoans," 304; idem, "The Role of the Individual in Samoan Culture," 495; idem, "A Lapse of Animism among a Primitive People," *Psyche* 9 (1928): 77; idem, "Social Change and Cultural Surrogates," *Journal of Educational Sociology* 14 (1940): 96.

18. Mead, *Coming of Age*, 126, 161, 164, 277; idem, "Americanization in Samoa," *American Mercury* 16 (1929): 269; idem, *Social Organization of Manu'a*, 80 and 86; idem, *Male and Female*, 100, 124.

19. Mead, "Americanization in Samoa," 269; idem, "The Sex Life of the Unmarried Adult in Primitive Society," 62; idem, *Male and Female*, 119, 123, 201; idem, *Coming of Age*, 105, 108, 223; idem, "Jealousy: Primitive and Civilized," 43, 46; idem, *Social Organization of Manu'a*, 84.

20. Mead, "The Samoans," 310; idem, "The Sex Life of the Unmarried Adult in Primitive Society," 61 ff.; idem, *Male and Female*, 192; idem, *Social Organization of Manu'a*, 84; idem, "Cultural Con-

texts of Puberty and Adolescence," *Bulletin of the Philadelphia Association for Psychoanalysis* 9 (1959): 62; idem, *Coming of Age,* 33, 153, 157.

21. Mead, *Male and Female,* 201, 220; idem, "The Role of the Individual in Samoan Culture," 487.

22. M. Mead, "The Primitive Child," in C. Murchison, ed., *A Handbook of Child Psychology* (New York, 1967, orig. 1933), 914; idem, "Adolescence in Primitive and Modern Society," in V. F. Calverton and S. D. Schmalhausen, eds, *The New Generation* (London, 1930), 179.

23. M. Mead, "Cultural Contexts of Puberty and Adolescence," 62; idem, "The Samoans," 308; idem, "Adolescence in Primitive and Modern Society," 174; idem, "South Sea Hints on Bringing Up Children," 22.

7. The Myth Takes Shape

1. D. Hume, *An Inquiry Concerning Human Understanding* (London, 1809, orig. 1748), II, 86.

2. S. D. Schmalhausen, *Our Changing Human Nature* (New York, 1929), 481; J. B. Watson and R. Watson, *Psychological Care of Infant and Child* (London, 1928), 18.

3. *The Nation,* 6 February 1929; S. Nearing, "The Child in Soviet Russia," in V. F. Calverton and S. D. Schmalhausen, eds., *The New Generation* (London, 1930), 233; E. C. Lindeman, "Is Human Nature changing in Russia?" *Survey Graphic* 12 (1933): 142; V. F. Calverton, "Red Love in Soviet Russia," *Modern Quarterly* 4 (1927): 188.

4. V. F. Calverton, *The Bankruptcy of Marriage* (London, 1928), 21; Mrs. B. Russell, introduction, in B. Lindsey, *The Companionate Marriage* (New York, 1928), xix; S. D. Schmalhausen, *Why We Misbehave* (New York, 1928), 14 ff.; idem, "The Sexual Revolution," in V. F. Calverton and S. D. Schmalhausen, eds., *Sex in Civilization* (London, 1929), 354 ff.

5. Schmalhausen, "The Sexual Revolution," 391; E. Sapir, "The Discipline of Sex," *American Mercury* 16 (1929): 413.

6. F. Kirchwey, "Sex in the South Seas," *The Nation* 127 (1928): 427; Schmalhausen, *Our Changing Human Nature,* 8.

7. B. Russell, *Marriage and Morals* (London, 1958, orig. 1929), 107; H. Ellis, introduction in V. F. Calverton and S. D. Schmalhausen, eds., *Sex in Civilization* (London, 1929), 25; idem, "Perversion

in Childhood and Adolescence," in Calverton and Schmalhausen, eds., *The New Generation,* 543.

8. Calverton and Schmalhausen, eds., *The New Generation,* 18, 13.

9. J. B. Watson, *Behaviorism* (New York, 1924), 74; " 'Physiological Psychology"—A New Variety," *Journal of Heredity* 17 (1926): 362.

10. M. Mead, "Adolescence in Primitive and Modern Society," in Calverton and Schmalhausen, eds., *The New Generation,* 174; R. H. Lowie, review of *Coming of Age in Samoa, American Anthropologist* 31 (1929): 532; J. H. Driberg, review of *Coming of Age in Samoa, Man* 29 (1929): 179; B. Malinowski, in *The Nation* 127 (1928): 402.

11. G. W. Stocking, *Race, Culture and Evolution* (New York, 1968), 267.

12. E. Erikson, *Childhood and Society* (Harmondsworth, 1965), 318; G. Dorsey, in *The Nation* 127 (1928): ii; H. L. Mencken, "Adolescence," *American Mercury* 15 (1928): 379; R. Benedict, "The Younger Generation with a Difference," *New Republic* 57 (1928): 50; idem, review of *Coming of Age in Samoa, Journal of Philosophy* 26 (1929): 110.

13. R. Benedict, *Patterns of Culture* (London, 1945, orig, 1934), 21; F. Boas, "Race," *Encyclopaedia of the Social Sciences* 13 (1934): 34.

14. From the 1920s onward it was common for the Boasians and others to think of culture as being, in the words of Ruth Bunzel, "some kind of mechanical press into which most individuals were poured to be moulded." M. Mead and R. Bunzel, eds., *The Golden Age of American Anthropology* (New York, 1960), 576. In *We, the Tikopia* (London, 1936, 418), Firth wrote of how "like raw material in a factory" the members of a society "come from the furnace, are gripped by different pieces of complicated machinery, are beaten, cut, rolled, twisted, reheated to make an implement fit for social use."

15. M. Mead, *Growing Up in New Guinea,* in *From the South Seas* (New York, 1939), 212; idem, "More Comprehensive Field Methods," *American Anthropologist* 35 (1933): 15; idem, "1925–1939," in *From the South Seas,* x; O. Klineberg, *Social Psychology* (New York, 1940), 492. Further, as F. L. K. Hsu has noted in "Margaret Mead and Psychological Anthropology," *American Anthropologist* 82 (1980): 349, it was Mead's trilogy of *Coming of Age*

in Samoa, Growing Up in New Guinea, and *Sex and Temperament in Three Primitive Societies,* together with Benedict's *Patterns of Culture,* that "ushered in and firmly established the national-character approaches in psychological anthropology."

16. L. J. Russell, "Is Anthropology Relevant to Ethics?" *Aristotelian Society,* Supplementary Volume, XX (1946): 62; L. A. White, *The Science of Culture* (New York, 1949), 154.

17. M. Mead, *Male and Female* (Harmondsworth, 1962), 68; idem, "Preface 1961 Edition," *Coming of Age in Samoa* (New York, 1961), 3.

18. "Margaret Mead," *The Observer,* 29 January 1950; E. E. Evans-Pritchard, *Social Anthropology* (London, 1951), 96; M. J. Herskovits, *Man and His Works: The Science of Cultural Anthropology* (New York, 1950), 44.

19. F. M. Keesing, *Modern Samoa: Its Government and Changing Life* (London, 1934), 497; W. E. H. Stanner, *The South Seas in Transition* (Sydney, 1953), 313; L. Trilling, *Beyond Culture* (London, 1966, orig. 1955), 116.

20. L. D. Holmes, "A Restudy of Manu'an Culture: A Problem in Methodology" (Ph.D. diss., Northwestern University, 1957).

21. Ibid., 224, 226, 227, 228; L. D. Holmes, *Ta'ū: Stability and Change in a Samoan Village* (Wellington, 1958), 32, 41, 44, 54, 56.

22. Holmes, "A Restudy of Manu'an Culture," 232.

23. D. T. Campbell, "The Mutual Methological Relevance of Anthropology and Psychology," in F. L. K. Hsu, ed., *Psychological Anthropology* (Homewood, Ill., 1961), 340.

24. M. Mead, "Preface to the 1949 Edition," *Coming of Age in Samoa* (Mentor Books, New York, 1949), x; idem, Preface, *Coming of Age in Samoa* (Modern Library, New York, 1953), 3; idem, "Preface, 1961 Edition," *Coming of Age in Samoa* (Apollo Edition, New York, 1961), 4.

25. J. J. Honigmann, *Understanding Culture* (New York, 1963), 273; G. M. Carstairs, *This Island Now: The B.B.C. Reith Lectures, 1962* (Harmondsworth, 1963), 49; G. Devereux, *From Anxiety to Method in the Behavioral Sciences* (The Hague, 1967), 196; D. Price-Williams, "Cross-Cultural Studies," in B. M. Foss, ed., *New Horizons in Psychology* (Harmondsworth, 1966), 409; E. L. Schusky and T. P. Culbert, *Introducing Culture* (Englewood Cliffs, N.J., 1967), iii, 68; "Margaret Mead Today: Mother to the World," *Time,* 21 March 1969, p. 60.

26. M. Mead, "Conclusion, 1969: Reflections on Later Theoretical Work on the Samoans," in *Social Organization of Manu'a* (Honolulu, 1969), 227.

27. In November 1971, en route from New Guinea to New York, Mead made what the *Pacific Islands Monthly* (December 1971, p. 27) called "a sentimental five day visit" to American Samoa. During her stay in Ta'ū, she dedicated a power plant, and she met many Manu'ans who remembered her as a young researcher. Despite the central importance of Samoa in Mead's anthropological career, she at no time visited the islands of western Samoa.

28. This evidence was conspicuously present in N. A. Rowe, *Samoa Under the Sailing Gods* (London and New York, 1930); J. Copp and Fa'afouina I. Pula, *The Samoan Dance of Life* (Boston, 1950); L. H. Holmes, *Ta'ū: Stability and Change in a Samoan Village* (Wellington, 1958); and J. A. C. Gray, *Amerika Samoa: A History of American Samoa and Its United States Naval Administration* (Annapolis, 1960)—all of which were well known to Mead, for she had reviewed Rowe, Holmes, and Gray, and had written a preface to the account of the realities of Samoan behavior recorded, with the editorial assistance of Copp, by Fa'afouina Pula. Further, when Mead visited the Research School of Pacific Studies of the Australian National University in 1964, I communicated to her, during a private interview of two and a half hours, on 10 November 1964 (not 1965, as she has it on p. 227 of the 1969 edition of *Social Organization of Manu'a*), a wide range of ethnographic and historical facts at variance with her own account of Samoa.

29. Various literal inaccuracies in the 1928 text of *Coming of Age in Samoa* have been repeated in all of the subsequent editions I have inspected.

30. M. H. Fried, *The Study of Anthropology* (New York, 1972), 5; *Anthropology Today* (Del Mar, Calif., 1971), 354; E. A. Hoebel, *Anthropology: The Study of Man* (New York, 1972), 8, 44.

31. E. R. Gerber, "The Cultural Patterning of Emotions in Samoa" (Ph.D. diss., University of California, San Diego, 1975), 126; I would add that I have a high regard for the excellent ethnography of Gerber's dissertation.

32. V. Rubin, "Margaret Mead: An Appreciation," *Human Organization* 38 (1979): 194; Robert A. LeVine, foreword to G. H. Herdt, *Guardians of the Flutes* (New York, 1981), ix.

8. The Historical Setting of Mead's Research

1. M. Mead, "Preface to the 1949 Edition," in *Coming of Age in Samoa* (Mentor Books, New York, 1949), x; idem, "Preface 1961 Edition," in *Coming of Age in Samoa* (New York, 1961), 4; idem, "Preface 1973 Edition," in *Coming of Age in Samoa* (New York, 1973), 2. In her Preface of 1973 Mead described the 1969 edition of *Social Organization of Manu'a* as having been "revised in the light of contemporary ethnographic theory." In fact the original text of 1930 was reprinted without revision of any kind; see D. Freeman, *"Social Organization of Manu'a* (1930 and 1969) by Margaret Mead: Some Errata," *Journal of the Polynesian Society* 81 (1972): 70–78. The 1969 edition did however include a new introduction by Mead as well as a conclusion entitled "Reflections on Later Theoretical Work on the Samoans" in which she dealt with criticisms of her depiction of Samoa.

2. M. Mead, review of *Elite Communication in Samoa*, by F. M. Keesing and M. M. Keesing, *American Anthropologist* 60 (1958): 1233.

3. J. Williams, "Narrative of a Voyage Performed in the Missionary Schooner 'Olive Branch,' 1832," L.M.S. Archives. (The archives of the London Missionary Society are held in the library of the School of Oriental and African Studies, University of London).

4. E. Behrens, *Reise durch die Südländer und um die Welt* (Frankfurt, 1737); L. A. de Bougainville, *A Voyage round the World performed in the years 1766, 1767, 1768 and 1769* (London, 1772), 278 ff.; J. F. G. de La Pérouse, *A Voyage round the World in the Years 1785, 1786, 1787 and 1788* (London, 1798), III, 61 ff.; E. Edwards and G. Hamilton, *Voyage of H.M.S. Pandora Dispatched to Arrest the Mutineers of the Bounty in the South Seas, 1790–1791* (London, 1915), 48 ff.; O. Von Kotzebue, *A New Voyage Around the World in the Years 1823, 1824, 1825 and 1826* (London, 1830), I, 256 ff.; J. Williams, *A Narrative of Missionary Enterprises in the South Sea Islands* (London, 1837), 324 ff.; G. Turner, *Nineteen Years in Polynesia* (London, 1861); A. M. Murray, *Forty Years' Mission Work in Polynesia and New Guinea from 1835 to 1875* (London, 1876); G. Turner, *Samoa A Hundred Years Ago and Long Before* (London, 1884); T. Powell, "A Samoan Tradition of the Creation and the Deluge," *Journal of the Transactions of the Victoria Institute* 20 (1887): 145–175; T. Powell and G. Pratt, "Some Folk-Songs and Myths from Samoa," *Journal and Proceedings of the Royal Society*

of New South Wales 24–26 (1890–1892); G. Pratt, "The Genealogy of the Kings and Princes of Samoa," *Report, Australasian Association for the Advancement of Science* 2 (1890): 655–663; S. Ella, "The Ancient Government of Samoa," *Report, Australasian Association for the Advancement of Science* 6 (1895): 596–603; J. B. Stair, *Old Samoa* (London, 1897); G. Brown, *Melanesians and Polynesians* (London, 1910); R. P. A. Monfat, *Les Premiers Missionnaires des Samoa* (Lyon, 1923); C. Wilkes, *Narrative of the United States Exploring Expedition during the Years 1838–1842* (London, 1845), 5 vols; H. Hale, *Ethnography and Philology* (Philadelphia, 1846); J. E. Erskine, *Journal of a Cruise among the Islands of the Western Pacific* (London, 1853); W. T. Pritchard, *Polynesian Reminiscences, or Life in the South Pacific Islands* (London, 1866); T. Trood, *Island Reminiscences* (Sydney, 1912); A. P. Maudsley, *Life in the Pacific Fifty Years Ago* (London, 1930); W. B. Churchward, *My Consulate in Samoa* (London, 1887); R. L. Stevenson, *A Footnote to History: Eight Years of Trouble in Samoa* (London, 1892); O. Stuebel, *Samoanische Texte* (Berlin, 1895); E. Schultz, "The Most Important Principles of Samoan Family Law, and the Laws of Inheritance," *Journal of the Polynesian Society* 20 (1911): 43–53; A. Krämer, *Die Samoa-Inseln* (Stuttgart, 1902–1903), 2 vols.

5. R. B. Dixon, review of *Melanesians and Polynesians* by G. Brown, *American Anthropologist* 13 (1911): 140; M. Mead, "Conclusion 1969: Reflections on Later Theoretical Work on the Samoans," in *Social Organization of Manu'a* (Honolulu, 1969), 228.

6. M. Mead, "The Samoans," in M. Mead, ed., *Cooperation and Competition among Primitive Peoples* (New York, 1937), 282; Turner, *Nineteen Years in Polynesia,* 279; B. Shore, "A Samoan Theory of Action: Social Control and Social Order in a Polynesian Paradox (Ph.D. diss., University of Chicago, 1977), ix.

7. In etymological terms *fa'aSamoa* means "in the manner of the family of the Tui Manu'a," *Sā* being a particle which is used as a prefix to refer to a family, while Moa is the family name of the Tui Manu'a.

8. *American Samoa: Hearings before the Commission Appointed by the President of the United States in Accordance with Public Resolution no. 89, 70th Congress* (Washington, D.C., 1931), 26.

9. H. F. Bryan, *American Samoa: A General Report by the Governor* (Washington, D.C., 1927), 58. For a fuller account of the Mau in Western Samoa, see J. W. Davidson, *Samoa mo Samoa: The*

Emergence of the Independent State of Western Samoa (Melbourne, 1967), 114 ff.

10. M. A. Ripley, "Samoa: Shall we Navalize or Civilize It?" *The Nation* 122 (1926): 393; F. J. West, *Political Advancement in the South Pacific* (Melbourne, 1961), 135.

11. J. A. C. Gray, *Amerika Samoa: A History of American Samoa and Its United States Naval Administration* (Annapolis, 1960), 207 ff.

12. A. F. Judd, Expanded notes, ethnology, etc., American Samoa, February 15–April 2, 1926; Islands of Tutuila, Ofu and Ta'ū," p. 9, Bernice P. Bishop Library, Honolulu. Judd subsequently became the legal adviser to the congressional commission that visited American Samoa in 1930 to inquire into the period of unrest that had begun there in 1920.

13. West, *Political Advancement,* 135. *American Samoa: Hearings before the Commission,* 26; *Western Samoa (Report of the Royal Commission Concerning the Administration of),* (Wellington, 1927); Mead, *Coming of Age,* 198.

14. F. M. Keesing, *Modern Samoa* (London, 1934), 476; Gray, *Amerika Samoa,* 236. Mead herself, in a survey of "Samoan civilization" as it existed in 1926, gave it as her opinion that "given no additional outside stimulus or attempt to modify conditions Samoan culture might remain very much the same for two hundred years" (*Coming of Age,* 273).

15. Krämer, *Die Samoa-Inseln;* R. P. Gilson, *Samoa 1830 to 1900: The Politics of a Multi-Cultural Community* (Melbourne, 1970).

16. Buzacott and Barff, when they visited Samoa in 1834 (Journal, L.M.S. Archives), remarked on the "singular government," of Samoa with every settlement, or local polity, having its own chiefs. D. Freeman, "The Social Structure of a Samoan Village Community" (Academic Postgraduate Diploma in Anthropology diss., University of London, 1948); idem, "Some Observations on Kinship and Political Authority in Samoa," *American Anthropologist* 66 (1964): 554.

17. For example (as reported in the *Samoa Times* of 7 December 1918), Tasea was found guilty by the High Court of Western Samoa of having clubbed another man for having made statements in public about the genealogy of Tasea's family. See also a letter from G. Fa'alava'au (Member of the Legislative Council of Western Samoa) in the *Western Samoan Mail* of 10 May 1941: "The publication of an

adverse version of the genealogy of a rival chief much more than affecting a whole village and involving its highest chiefs was, and is, to
the Samoans, an offence the cost of the correction of which is dearer
than life." Ella, "The Ancient Government of Samoa," 598. A number of the genealogies published by Krämer in 1902 contained, at
that time, some thirty-two generations.

18. P. H. Buck, in a letter to Sir Apirana Ngata, cited in J. B.
Conliffe, *Te Rangi Hiroa: The Life of Sir Peter Buck* (Christchurch,
1971), 156. Fa'afouina Pula, in *The Samoan Dance of Life* (Boston,
1950), 112, describes the fa'alupega of Samoan villages as "very, very
important" and adds that "if they are not given perfectly, it will
mean a great trouble." In pagan times such trouble often meant war.

19. R. L. Stevenson, *A Footnote to History* (London, 1892), 14; G.
Pratt, letter dated Matautu, Savai'i, 18 June 1847, L.M.S. Archives;
J. Fraser, "Six Solos about the Kava (Plant and Drink)," *Journal
and Proceedings of the Royal Society of New South Wales* 25
(1891): 96.

20. G. B. Milner, "The Samoan Vocabulary of Respect," *Journal
of the Royal Anthropological Institute* 91 (1961): 304. Cf. F. Stevenson, *Our Samoan Adventure* (London, 1956), 182: when Robert
Louis Stevenson called on the paramount chief Mata'afa, he was
obliged to use as an interpreter his Samoan cook, Talolo, who
"nearly expired with fright and misery for he could not speak the
high-chief language and felt every word he uttered to be an insult to
Mata'afa." Schultz, in his *Proverbial Expressions of the Samoans*
(Wellington, 1965), 92, recounts that a titular chief, when his servants persisted in using the common word *fepulafi,* meaning to stare,
instead of the respectful *sisila,* became so incensed that he killed
them.

21. G. Brown, *An Autobiography* (London, 1898), 32 ff.

22. Cf. G. Turner, *Samoa A Hundred Years Ago and Long Before* (London, 1884), 175: "The turtle . . . the best joint, and anything
choice is sure to be laid before the chief."

23. Davidson, *Samoa mo Samoa,* 19; G. Pratt, letter dated Matautu, Savai'i, 1 Dec. 1842, L.M.S. Archives; J. Williams, *A Narrative of Missionary Enterprises in the South Sea Islands* (London,
1837), 334. In September 1966 I attended a fono of the Va'a-Nofoa-
Tolu, comprising the highest-ranking titular chiefs of the 'āiga Tau-
lagi, Taua'ana, and Satunumafono, of A'ana and Safata, and their
talking chiefs. The talking chiefs, although they were served their
food immediately after their titular chiefs, were required to wait to

begin eating until all of the titular chiefs had completed their repasts.

24. G. Pratt, "Silia-i-Vao—a Tala," *Journal of the Polynesian Society* 6 (1897): 76.

25. Marsack, *Notes,* 19.

26. Davidson, *Samoa mo Samoa,* 19; Schultz, 46.

27. Schultz, "Principles of Samoan Family Law," 46; Shore, "A Samoan Theory of Action," 180.

28. Cf. Brother Herman, trans., *Institutions and Customs of the Samoans* (Tutuila, 1954), 4: "The seat of the high chief is known to all and strictly forbidden to anyone else."

29. Fraser and Pratt, "Six Solos about the Kava," 105.

30. Cf. J. Fraser, "Ia le Malaga," *Journal and Proceedings of the Royal Society of New South Wales* 26 (1892): 293: "In Samoa it is a grievous insult to a chief to omit his name from a list" (when kava is being distributed).

31. L. D. Holmes, "A Restudy of Manu'an Culture" (Ph.D. diss., Northwestern University, 1957), 227.

32. Cf. F. A. Young, "Stability and Change in Samoa" (Ph.D. diss., University of Oregon, 1976), 38: "From their early years Samoan children are taught the principle of obedience to parents"; E. R. Gerber, "The Cultural Patterning of Emotions in Samoa" (Ph.D. diss., University of California, San Diego, 1975), 37: "Samoans believe that deference and obedience are due to anyone older than oneself"; Shore, "A Samoan Theory of Action," 176: "obedience is . . . a central and explicit Samoan value, especially for children."

9. Rank

1. M. Mead, *Blackberry Winter* (New York, 1972), 151. The fact that Mead was denied entry to chiefly fonos (as distinct from the social ceremonies associated with the reception of a traveling party), was confirmed during my inquiries in Ta'ū in 1967. M. Mead, *Letters from the Field, 1925-1975* (New York, 1977), 51; idem, "The Role of the Individual in Samoan Culture," *Journal of the Royal Anthropological Institute* 58 (1928): 492. In her chapter on the Samoans in *Cooperation and Competition among Primitive Peoples* (New York, 1937), 305, Mead went even further, asserting that if a high-ranking chief were to make his own speeches in the fono he would be committing "the great Samoan sin" of *tautalaitiiti,* by talking above his rank.

2. J. Williams, "Narrative of a Voyage Performed in the Missionary Schooner 'Olive Branch,' 1832," L.M.S. Archives. In some polities, such as Salai'ilua in Savai'i, there is, in Shore's words, an "inversion in *ali'i* and *tulafale* relations" with the talking chiefs having the main voice in juridicial fono; B. Shore, "A Samoan Theory of Action: Social Control and Social Order in a Polynesian Paradox" (Ph.D. diss., University of Chicago, 1977), 180.

3. R. L. Stevenson, *A Footnote to History* (Leipzig, 1892), 130.

4. Mead, *Cooperation and Competition,* 304; T. Powell, "A Samoan Tradition of the Creation and the Deluge," *Journal of the Transactions of the Victoria Institute or Philosophical Society of Great Britain* 20 (1887): 147; J. Fraser, "Some Folk-Songs and Myths from Samoa," *Journal and Proceedings of the Royal Society of New South Wales* 24 (1890): 196.

5. Fraser, "Some Folk-Songs and Myths," 213; Powell, "A Samoan Tradition of the Creation and the Deluge," 157; cf. T. Powell, Report dated Ta'ū, Manu'a, 24 July 1871, L.M.S. Archives: "Tui Manu'a is the acknowledged source of all the surrounding Tui."

6. M. Mead, *Social Organization of Manu'a* (Honolulu, 1930), 180; T. Nightingale, *Oceanic Sketches* (London, 1835), 86; T. H. Hood, *Notes of a Cruise in H.M.S. 'Fawn' in the Western Pacific in the Year 1862* (Edinburgh, 1863), 107.

7. M. Mead, "Jealousy: Primitive and Civilized," in S. D. Schmalhausen and V. F. Calverton, eds., *Woman's Coming of Age: A Symposium* (London, 1931), 43; J. Fraser, "The History of Tagaloa-a-Ui, Ali'a-Matua and Ali'a-Tama, Kings of Manu'a," *Journal and Proceedings of the Royal Society of New South Wales* 26 (1892): 299.

8. W. T. Pritchard, *Polynesian Reminiscences* (London, 1866), 55; J. A. C. Gray, *Amerika Samoa: A History of American Samoa and Its United States Naval Administration* (Annapolis, 1960), 71.

9. A. Krämer, *Die Samoa-Inseln* (Stuttgart, 1902), I, 15; S. Ella, " 'O le Tala ia Taema ma Nafanua," *Journal of the Polynesian Society* 6 (1897): 154; T. Heath, "The War in A'ana—a Samoan Tale" (1838), L.M.S. Archives; J. Williams, *A Narrative of Missionary Enterprises in the South Sea Islands* (London, 1837), 533.

10. M. Mead, "The Role of the Individual in Samoan Culture," *Journal of the Royal Anthropological Institute* 58 (1928): 493; Pritchard, *Polynesian Reminiscences,* 126; W. B. Churchward, *My Consulate in Samoa* (London, 1887), 55.

11. Gray, *Amerika Samoa,* 140 ff.

12. Ibid., 147.

13. Ibid., 146.

14. Mead, "The Role of the Individual," 495; Krämer, *Die Samoa-Inseln,* I, 1 ff.

10. Cooperation and Competition

1. M. Mead, ed., *Cooperation and Competition among Primitive Peoples* (New York, 1937).

2. M. Mead, *Coming of Age in Samoa* (New York, 1973), 35; idem, *Cooperation and Competition,* 8, 301 ff. For a discussion of sexual jealousy see Chapter 16.

3. J. Williams, "Narrative of a Voyage in the Missionary Schooner 'Olive Branch,' 1832," L.M.S. Archives.

4. T. Nightingale, *Oceanic Sketches* (London, 1835), 75. For other accounts of club fighting see C. Wilkes, *Narrative of the United States Exploring Expedition during the Years 1838-1842* (London, 1845), II, 137; A. Krämer, *Die Samoa-Inseln* (Stuttgart, 1903), II, 335; G. Brown, *Melanesians and Polynesians* (London, 1910), 340.

5. C. Hardie, letter dated Manono, 1 December 1837, L.M.S. Archives.

6. J. B. Stair, "Jottings on the Mythology and Spirit-Lore of Old Samoa," *Journal of the Polynesian Society* 5 (1896): 55.

7. W. T. Pritchard, *Polynesian Reminiscences* (London, 1866), 162; Krämer, *Die Samoa-Inseln,* II, 334; E. Schultz, *Proverbial Expressions of the Samoans* (Wellington, 1965), 139.

8. G. Turner, *Nineteen Years in Polynesia* (London, 1861), 210 ff.; J. B. Stair, *Old Samoa* (London, 1897), 132 ff.

9. L. B. Wright and M. I. Fry, *Puritans in the South Seas* (New York, 1936), 227; W. B. Churchward, *My Consulate in Samoa* (London, 1887), 142. Aletta Lewis, who was in American Samoa in 1929, reports a "passionate craze for playing cricket on village *malaes*"; A. Lewis, *They Call Them Savages* (London, 1938), 106. Rugby arouses passionate competitiveness; for example, in April 1967 in Apia, the players and supporters of a defeated team "viciously assaulted" the referee with rocks, sticks, and fists injuring him extensively about the face and head, according to the *Samoa Bulletin* of 26 April 1967.

10. Police Records, Western Samoa, P.C. 66/2095, 1966.

11. Brother Herman, *Tales of Ancient Samoa* (Apia, 1966), 85; P. H. Buck, Field Notebook III, p. 53, 11 October 1927, Bernice P.

Bishop Museum Library, Honolulu; J. D. Freeman, "The Tradition of Sanalala," *Journal of the Polynesian Society* 56 (1947): 297; Krämer, *Die Samoa-Inseln* I, 153; S. Osborn, *Samoanische Zeitung,* Apia, 28 September 1901; B. Shore, "A Samoan Theory of Action: Social Control and Social Order in a Polynesian Paradox" (Ph.D. diss., University of Chicago, 1977), 144.

12. L. D. Holmes, "A Restudy of Manu'an Culture," (Ph.D. diss., Northwestern University, 1957), 226; G. B. Milner, *Samoan Dictionary* (London, 1966), 247; Brother Herman, trans., *Institutions and Customs of the Samoans* (Tutuila, 1954), 4; Stair, *Old Samoa,* 85.

13. G. Platt, Journal, 1835, L.M.S. Archives; R. L. Stevenson, *A Footnote to History* (Leipzig, 1892), 16; T. H. Hood, *Notes on a Cruise of the H. M. S. 'Fawn' in the Western Pacific in the Year 1862* (Edinburgh, 1863), 77; F. A. Young, "Stability and Change in Samoa," (Ph.D. diss., University of Oregon, 1976), 10; M. MacKenzie, "More North American than the North Americans: Medical Consequences of Migrant Enthusiasm, Willing and Unwilled" (Department of Anthropology, University of California, Berkeley, n.d.), 4.

14. Police Records, Western Samoa, P.C. 2811, 1961.

15. *American Samoa: Hearings before the Commission Appointed by the President of the United States* (Washington, D.C., 1931), 24; Mead, *Cooperation and Competition,* 299; F. H. Flaherty, "Behind the Scenes with Our Samoan Stars," *Asia* 25 (1925): 747 (the Flahertys' film, *Moana,* opened in New York on 7 February 1926, when Mead was in Manu'a); M. Mead, letter dated Ta'ū, 16 January 1926, in *Letters from the Field, 1925–1975* (New York, 1977), 47; G. Drummond, letter dated Falealupo, Savai'i, 26 October 1842, L.M.S. Archives.

16. A. Murray, letter dated Tutuila, 10 June 1839, L.M.S. Archives; Churchward, *My Consulate in Samoa,* 348; Osborn, *Samoanische Zeitung* 9.

17. *Western Samoa (Report of the Royal Commission Concerning the Administration of)* (Wellington, 1927), 267; *O le Savali,* 1 September 1916, Apia, Western Samoa.

18. Williams, "Narrative of a Voyage"; A. Macdonald, letter dated Palauli, Savai'i, 13 September 1843, L.M.S. Archives.

19. G. Pratt, letter dated Matautu, Savai'i, 19 September 1868, L.M.S. Archives.

20. A. Lewis, *They Call Them Savages* (London, 1938), 48.

21. M. Mead, "Two South Seas Educational Experiments and Their American Implications," *University of Pennsylvania School*

of Education Bulletin 31 (1931): 494; idem, *Cooperation and Competition,* 308.

22. F. M. Keesing, *Modern Samoa* (London, 1934), 414 ff.; Milner, *Samoan Dictionary,* 112.

23. J. Williams, *A Narrative of Missionary Enterprises in the South Sea Islands* (London, 1837), 355; Minutes of meeting held at Saliemoa, western Samoa on 17 May 1842; L.M.S. Archives; C. Pickering, *The Races of Man* (London, 1849), 76.

24. Holmes, "A Restudy of Samoan Culture," 225; cf. L. D. Holmes, *Ta'ū* (Wellington, 1958), 35: "Great pride is taken by parents in the achievements of the children in church school, and special awards are given to outstanding students from time to time."

25. D. Pitt and C. Macpherson, *Emerging Pluralism: The Samoan Community in New Zealand* (Auckland, 1974), 91.

11. Aggressive Behavior and Warfare

1. M. Mead, *Sex and Temperament in Three Primitive Societies,* in *From the South Seas* (New York, 1939), 285; idem, review of *Samoa under the Sailing Gods* by N. A. Rowe, *The Nation* 133 (1931): 138; idem, *Male and Female* (Harmondsworth, 1962, orig. 1950), 220, 360.

2. J. F. G. de La Pérouse, *A Voyage Round the World in the Years 1785, 1786, 1787 and 1788* (London, 1798), III, 100, 103, 407; O. Von Kotzebue, *A New Voyage Round the World in the Years 1823, 1824, 1825, and 1826* (London, 1830), 258.

3. J. Williams, *A Narrative of Missionary Enterprises in the South Sea Islands* (London, 1837), 333, 533; C. Barff, Journal, 1830, Mitchell Library, Sydney; J. Williams, "Narrative of a Voyage in the Missionary Schooner 'Olive Branch,' 1832," L.M.S. Archives; T. Heath, "The War in A'ana: A Samoan Tale," 1838, L.M.S. Archives.

4. Williams, *Narrative of Missionary Enterprises,* 533; idem, "Narrative of a Voyage"; J. B. Stair, *Old Samoa* (London, 1897), 243.

5. Williams, "Narrative of a Voyage"; idem, letter to Rev. W. Ellis dated Rarotonga, 6 January 1833. In 1846 the total population of the polity of Ta'ū (including Faleasao), was 595 (M. Hunkin, letter dated Manu'a, 9 October 1846). If one assumes a population in 1832 of say 700, this would mean (about 40 percent of the male population being boys) a total of some 210 adult males. The death of 35 of this number represents a loss of approximately 16 percent of the adult male population.

6. L. D. Holmes, "A Restudy of Manu'an Culture" (Ph.D. diss., Northwestern University, 1957); 225; *Annual Report, 1965,* Police and Prisons Department, Government of Western Samoa.

7. G. Platt, Journal, 1836, L.M.S. Archives.

8. Police Records, Western Samoa, P.C. 493, 1961.

9. Police Records, Western Samoa, P.C. 203–204, 1963.

10. Police Records, Western Samoa, P.C. 3322–3331, 1962.

11. *Samoa Times,* 3 November 1967.

12. Mead, *Male and Female,* 361; idem, "Life as a Samoan Girl," in *All True! The Record of Actual Adventures that Have Happened to Ten Women of Today* (New York, 1931), 99.

13. Police Records, Western Samoa, P.C. 3402, 1963.

14. Police Records, Western Samoa, P.C. 5092, 1964.

15. One measure of the contentiousness of Samoans is the fact that (according to the Registrar of the Land and Titles Court Mulinu'u, Western Samoa) during the period 1966–1967, when the population of Western Samoa was about 130,000, some 1,400 statements of intention to proceed to litigation were received each year: a rate of 1,077 such actions per 100,000 of population per annum.

16. Sir Angus Sharp, interview, *New Zealand Herald,* 22 July 1978; American Samoa's Annual Report, Fiscal Year 1980, 111, 129. L. S. W. Duncan, in "Crime by Polynesians in Auckland" (M.A. thesis, University of Auckland, 1970), 122 ff., showed that in 1966 Samoans were charged with more crimes of violence than other Pacific migrants. *Annual Report,* 1966, Police and Prisons Department, Government of Western Samoa.

17. M. E. Wolfgang, ed., *Studies in Homicide* (New York, 1967), 285.

18. *Annual Reports,* 1965 and 1966, Police and Prisons Department, Government of Western Samoa; *Crime in New Zealand* (Wellington, 1968), 211; D. Biles, ed., *Crime and Justice in Australia* (Melbourne, 1977), 18; Federal Bureau of Investigation, U.S. Department of Justice, *Uniform Crime Reports for the United States* (Washington, D.C., 1965), 108.

19. M. Mead, *Social Organization of Manu'a* (Honolulu, 1930), 157, 168; idem, "The Role of the Individual in Samoan Culture," *Journal of the Royal Anthropological Institute* 58 (1928): 484; idem, "The Samoans," in M. Mead, ed., *Cooperation and Competition among Primitive Peoples* (New York, 1937), 481 ff.

20. *American Samoa. Hearings Before the Commission Appointed by the President of the United States* (Washington, D.C.,

1931), 98, 307; *Western Samoa (Report of the Royal Commission Concerning the Administration of)*, (Wellington, 1927), 361.

21. A. W. Murray, *Forty Years' Mission Work in Polynesia and New Guinea from 1835 to 1875* (London, 1876), 40; J. B. Stair, *Old Samoa* (London, 1897), 242; C. Wilkes, *Narrative of the United States Exploring Expedition during the Years 1838–1842* (London, 1845), II, 65, 150; J. King, letter dated Falealupo, Savai'i, 30 September 1864, L.M.S. Archives; S. J. Whitmee, "Mr. Wallace on the Ethnology of Polynesia," *Contemporary Review* 21 (1873): 397; A. Krämer, *Die Samoa-Inseln* (Stuttgart, 1903), II, 341.

22. Krämer, *Die Samoa-Inseln,* II, 340; T. Powell, letter dated Pago Pago, Tutuila, 1 July 1859, L.M.S. Archives; C. Hardie, letter dated Sapapali'i, Savai'i, 11 March 1844, L.M.S. Archives.

23. J. Frazer, *The Belief in Immortality* (London, 1922), II, 162; W. T. Pritchard, *Polynesian Reminiscences* (London, 1866), 57; R. L. Stevenson, in his letter to the editor of the *Pall Mall Gazette* of 4 September 1893 (*Collected Works,* XVII, 385), gives an account of fifteen heads being paraded before Malietoa at Mulinu'u, where the "king" received them and complimented each successful warrior.

24. Josia, "The Autobiography of Josia: A Samoan Native Pastor," translated from the Samoan, *L.M.S. Chronicle,* May 1866, p. 200; J. Williams, "Narrative of a Voyage"; M. Hunkin, report dated Manu'a, February 1845, L.M.S. Archives; Heath, "The War in A'ana."

25. Heath, "The War in A'ana"; C. Hardie, letter dated Malua, Upolu, 5 August 1848, L.M.S. Archives.

26. A. Murray, letter dated Pago Pago, Tutuila, 2 November 1842, L.M.S. Archives; F. A. Young, "Stability and Change in Samoa" (Ph.D. diss., University of Oregon, 1972), 14; T. Powell, report dated Ta'ū, 24 July 1871, L.M.S. Archives.

27. Dr. Peter Buck, during his visit to Manu'a in October 1927, was told of the heavy defeat that Ta'ū inflicted on Olosega in 1867 and was taken to the site of the main battle; Field Notebook IV, p. 20, 24 October 1927, Bernice P. Bishop Museum, Honolulu; cf. Powell, report dated Ta'ū, 24 July 1871. In 1871 boys made up 43.5 percent of the male population of Manu'a.

28. S. Ella, " 'O le Tala ia Taema ma Nafanua," *Journal of the Polynesian Society* 6 (1897): 154; J. E. Erskine, *Journal of a Cruise among the Islands of the Western Pacific* (London, 1853), 63; G. Turner, letter dated Malua, Upolu, 30 September 1853, L.M.S. Archives; Williams, "Narrative of a Voyage."

29. A. Wendt, *Pouliuli* (Auckland, 1977), 80; Krämer, *Die Samoa-Inseln,* II, 342.

30. Williams, "Narrative of a Voyage"; Krämer, *Die Samoa-Inseln,* I, 259.

31. R. S. Moore and J. R. Farrington, *The American Samoan Commission's Visit to Samoa, September–October, 1930* (Washington, D.C., 1931), 58; Stair, *Old Samoa,* 21; J. Fraser, "Some Folk-Songs and Myths from Samoa," *Journal and Proceedings of the Royal Society of New South Wales* 25 (1891): 141; Pritchard, *Polynesian Reminiscences,* 151; G. Turner, *Samoa a Hundred Years Ago and Long Before* (London, 1884), 190.

32. Turner, *Samoa a Hundred Years Ago,* ch. 4.

33. Mead, *Social Organization of Manu'a,* 167, 168, 177, 208. In "Le 'Ava: A Solo," a text collected by Thomas Powell from Tauanu'u, "the legend keeper of Manu'a," around 1870, Le Fanoga is specifically mentioned as a war god. Although Mead listed this source, which is contained in Fraser, "Folk-Songs and Myths from Samoa," *Journal of the Polynesian Society* 6 (1897): 119, in the bibliography of *Social Organization of Manu'a,* she does not seem to have taken cognizance of its contents.

34. C. Hardie, diary, Mitchell Library, Sydney.

35. Williams, "Narrative of a Voyage"; Williams also lists Foilagi and Toatoa as being war gods of Manu'a. Neither is mentioned by Mead.

12. Religion: Pagan and Christian

1. M. Mead, *An Inquiry into the Question of Cultural Stability in Polynesia* (New York, 1928); idem, "The Role of the Individual in Samoan Culture," *Journal of the Royal Anthropological Institute* 53 (1928): 491, 494; idem, "The Samoans," in M. Mead, ed., *Cooperation and Competition among Primitive Peoples* (New York, 1937), 304; idem, "A Lapse of Animism among a Primitive People," *Psyche* 9 (1928): 77; idem, *Social Organization of Manu'a* (Honolulu, 1930), 84, 86.

2. R. Firth, *The Work of the Gods in Tikopia* (London, 1940), 2 vols.; idem, *Rank and Religion in Tikopia* (London, 1970), 313.

3. J. Williams, "Narrative of a Voyage in the Missionary Schooner 'Olive Branch,' 1832," L.M.S. Archives; idem, *A Narrative of Missionary Enterprises in the South Sea Islands* (London, 1837), 540; A. Buzacott, journal, 1836, L.M.S. Archives.

4. H. Hale, Notes, Mitchell Library, Sydney; G. Turner, "Fifty-five Years Mission Work in Samoa" (1891), L.M.S. Archives; idem, *Samoa a Hundred Years Ago and Long Before* (London, 1884), 23–77, 156; W. T. Pritchard, *Polynesian Reminiscences* (London, 1866), 108, 122. The individual gods of ali'i were particularly associated with sacred stones, that of the paramount chief of Sa'anapu being a stone (which I was shown in 1942) shaped like the shell of a turtle and situated in a fresh-water spring named Tui Atua. Some of the more important gods and spirits of pagan times were also well remembered in Sa'anapu in the early 1940s. Thus in 1942 I had pointed out to me several times a moving light in the bay beyond Lotofagā in Safata which was said to be Putepute, an ancestral ghost of the 'Āiga Satunumafono, one of the major families of western Samoa.

5. Williams, "Narrative of a Voyage"; for an account of spirit possession, see J. D. Freeman, "The Joe Gimlet or Siovili Cult: An Episode in the Religious History of Early Samoa," in J. D. Freeman and W. R. Geddes, eds., *Anthropology in the South Seas* (New Plymouth, New Zealand, 1959), 191; cf. Firth's account, in *The Work of the Gods,* II, 224, of the possession of a Tikopian man: "His trembling became more violent, and his locked hands rattled on the coconut matting. Suddenly he emitted a shriek, then with head swinging rapidly from side to side he began to speak in loud, metallic, curiously prolonged tones. This was regarded by the natives as the voice of the deity."

6. G. Brown, *Melanesians and Polynesians* (London, 1910), 224. A spirit medium was also called a *va'a atua,* or vessel of the gods, and, in Manu'a, a *va'a Tagaloa,* or vessel of Tagaloa; cf. Mead, *Social Organization of Manu'a,* 160.

7. J. B. Stair, "Jottings on the Mythology and Spirit-Lore of Old Samoa," *Journal of the Polynesian Society* 5 (1896): 42; Pritchard, *Polynesian Reminiscences,* 110.

8. T. Powell, "Some Folk-Songs and Myths from Samoa," *Journal and Proceedings of the Royal Society of New South Wales* 25 (1891): 133; Williams, "Narrative of a Voyage."

9. S. Ella, "Samoa, &c.," *Report, Australasian Association for the Advancement of Science* 4 (1892): 638; Brown, *Melanesians and Polynesians,* 228; S. Ella, "The Ancient Samoan Government," *Report of the Sixth Meeting of the Australasian Association for the Advancement of Science* 6 (1895): 602.

10. Mead, "A Lapse of Animism," 77.

11. G. Pratt, *Grammar and Dictionary of the Samoan Language*, 4th ed. (Malua, 1911), 203; idem, "Some Folk-Songs and Myths from Samoa," 146; Turner, *Samoa a Hundred Years Ago*, 204 ff.

12. Firth, *Rank and Religion*, 313. The linguistic relationship between Samoa and Tikopia is close, and Firth, in his *History and Traditions of Tikopia* (Wellington, 1961), 166, has suggested that "an early settlement from Samoa could have provided many of the basic components of Tikopia society, into which the contibutions of various immigrant elements were continually built, and which in time constituted an individual social entity." Mead, *Social Organization of Manu'a*, 157. Mead's study of the history of pagan Samoa was perfunctory. In Manu'a in 1926 she told A. F. Judd, in answer to his specific questioning, that she could find no trace of an early religion except "belief in devils" (Expanded notes, ethnology, etc., American Samoa, February 15–April 2, 1926, Islands of Tutuila, Ofu and Ta'ū, Bernice P. Bishop Museum Library, p. 77). Williams' *Narrative of Missionary Enterprises in the South Sea Islands* (1837), a crucially important source on pagan Samoa, is not listed in the bibliography of Mead's *Social Organization of Manu'a,* and at no stage in her anthropological career did she consult the information available in the archives of the London Missionary Society, which is indispensable to any scholarly study of early Samoa.

13. Williams, "Narrative of a Voyage"; idem, *Narrative of Missionary Enterprises,* 546; idem, letter dated "On board the Missionary Ship 'Camden,' in sight of Rotuma," 12 November 1839, L.M.S. Archives; T. Powell, in his "A Samoan Tradition of the Creation and the Deluge," *Journal of the Transactions of the Victoria Institute, or Philosophical Society of Great Britain* 20 (1887): 148, gives as the meaning of the word *Tagaloa* "the Unrestrained or Illimitable," from *taga,* unrestrained by *tabu,* and *loa,* continuously.

14. Powell, "A Samoan Tradition of the Creation and the Deluge," 148, 155; Fraser, "Some Folk-Songs and Myths from Samoa," 102; J. Dowson, *A Classical Dictionary of Hindu Mythology and Religion, Geography, History and Literature,* 7th ed. (London, 1950), 56; J. Fraser, "The Samoan Story of Creation," *Journal of the Polynesian Society* 1 (1892): 164.

15. Fraser, "The Samoan Story of Creation"; idem, "Folk-Songs and Myths from Samoa," *Journal of the Polynesian Society* 6 (1897): 67; idem, "Some Folk-Songs and Myths from Samoa," 96, 138.

16. Fraser, "Some Folk-Songs and Myths from Samoa," 102; idem, "Folk-Songs and Myths from Samoa," 67; Powell, "A Samoan Tradition of the Creation and the Deluge," 152.

17. Turner, *Samoa a Hundred Years Ago,* 53; Fraser, "Folk-Songs and Myths from Samoa," 31.

18. Fraser, "Folk-Songs and Myths from Samoa," 34, 27; Turner, *Samoa a Hundred Years Ago,* 43; Fraser, "Some Folk-Songs and Myths from Samoa," 74, 99, 116; O. Stuebel, *Selections from Samoan Texts,* trans. Brother Herman (Tutuila, n.d.), 5; E. Schultz, *Proverbial Expressions of the Samoans* (Wellington, 1965), 100.

19. Williams, "Narrative of a Voyage"; T. Heath, letter dated Apia, 30 March 1840, L.M.S. Archives; M. Hunkin, letter dated Manu'a, 9 October 1846, L.M.S. Archives; C. Wilkes, *Narrative of the United States Exploring Expedition during the Years 1838–1842* (London, 1845), II, 75, 79.

20. L. D. Holmes, *Ta'ū* (Wellington, 1958), 32; H. F. Bryan, *American Samoa: A General Report by the Governor* (Washington, D.C., 1927), 6; A. F. Judd, Expanded notes, ethnology, etc., p. 95; B. Cartwright, Field Notebook I, p. 37, 11 September 1927, Bernice P. Bishop Museum, Honolulu; P.H. Buck, "Samoan Education," *The Friend* 151 (1932): 404; *American Samoa: Hearings before the Commission Appointed by the President of the United States* (Washington, D.C., 1931), 286. Tufele Iosefa's statement also holds for the Samoans of the western islands. In 1954 at the constitutional convention of Western Samoa it was averred that above all Samoans are God-fearing, and when Western Samoa was established as an independent state, it was with arms bearing the words "Samoa is Founded on God"; cf. the statement of a citizen of Western Samoa reported by M. Shadbolt in "Western Samoa," *National Geographic Magazine* 122 (1962): 576: "To understand Samoa, you must understand our passion for religion."

21. M. Mead, *Male and Female* (Harmondsworth, 1962, orig. 1950), 100, 125; idem, *Coming of Age in Samoa* (New York, 1973), 161; idem, "Americanization in Samoa," *American Mercury* 16 (1929): 269; idem, "Stevenson's Samoa Today," *The World Today* 58 (1931): 349. Mead's failure to comprehend the significance of the Christian religion in the lives of twentieth-century Samoans is also revealed in her remark to Aletta Lewis in October 1928: "They are Christians, but they've been Christian so long they've almost gotten over it"; A. Lewis, *They Call Them Savages* (London, 1938), 21.

22. Mead, *Coming of Age,* 165, 285.

23. *A Few Lessons in English and Tahitian* (Tahiti: Mission Press, 1832); J. Fraser, "Some Folk-Songs and Myths from Samoa," *Journal and Proceedings of the Royal Society of New South Wales* 25 (1891): 102; *'O le Fesili* (Samoa, 1842), 6.

24. G. Turner, *Nineteen Years in Polynesia* (London, 1861), 293; *'O Pese ma Vi'iga i le Atua* (Malua, n.d.), 5.

25. Mead, *Coming of Age,* 126, 193, 277.

26. G. Pratt, *Grammar and Dictionary of the Samoan Language,* 4th ed. (Malua, 1911), 22; *'O le Fesili,* 6; *'O Pese ma Vi'iga i le Atua,* 94.

27. *'O Pese ma Vi'iga i le Atua,* 119; *'O le Tusi Paia* (London, 1938), 1029.

28. J. Ablen, in "Samoan Family and Community in Crisis: The All Hallows Fire," *Program Information Series* 3 (1972): 33, notes that the All Hallows fire in San Francisco of 1946, in which seventeen Samoans were killed and forty-two seriously burned, was said by some Samoan informants to be God's punishment for people's sins.

29. M. Mead, "Social Change and Cultural Surrogates," in C. Kluckhohn and H. A. Murray, eds, *Personality in Nature, Society and Culture* (New York, 1950), 515; D. Freeman, "A Happening Frightening to both Ghosts and Men: A Case Study from Western Samoa," in N. Gunson, ed., *The Changing Pacific* (Melbourne, 1978), 163–173; Brown, *Melanesians and Polynesians,* 230.

30. Brown, *Melanesians and Polynesians,* 382.

13. Punishment

1. M. Mead, *Social Organization of Manu'a* (Honolulu, 1930), 70, 82; idem, "The Role of the Individual in Samoan Culture," *Journal of the Royal Anthropological Institute* 58 (1928): 494; J. Fraser, "Some Folk-Songs and Myths from Samoa," *Journal and Proceedings of the Royal Society of New South Wales* 25 (1891): 74.

2. *Western Samoan Mail,* 3 May 1941.

3. Ibid.; A. Krämer, *Die Samoa-Inseln* (Stuttgart, 1902), I, 200; O. Stuebel, *Selections from Samoan Texts,* trans. Brother Herman (Tutuila, n.d.), 50.

4. *Western Samoan Mail,* 3 May 1941.

5. G. Turner, *Nineteen Years in Polynesia* (London, 1861), 286; G. Brown, *Melanesians and Polynesians* (London, 1910), 289; Mead, *Social Organization of Manu'a,* 43; F. H. Flaherty, "Fa'aSa-

moa," *Asia* 25 (1925): 1,090; *Canberra Times,* 14 January 1981. As Brown notes, the punishment of saisai, as well as the form of the ifoga (see Chapter 12), indicates that cannibalism was once customary in Samoa, and this accounts for the terrible disgrace associated with saisai as a form of punishment.

6. *Report of the Commission to Inquire into and Report upon the Organization of District and Village Government in Western Samoa* (Wellington, 1950), 33; Brother Herman, trans., *Institutions and Customs of the Samoans* (Tutuila, 1954, orig. 1944), 3; R. G. Crocombe and M. Crocombe, *The Works of Ta'unga* (Canberra, 1968), 129.

7. J. B. Stair, *Old Samoa* (London, 1897), 91. For an account of a juridical fono see D. Freeman, "A Happening Frightening to Both Ghosts and Men: A Case Study from Western Samoa," in N. Gunson, ed., *The Changing Pacific* (Melbourne, 1978), 163–173; *Western Samoa (Report of Royal Commission Concerning the Administration of)* (Wellington, 1927), 269. Shore reports banishment and a fine of fifteen large sows being imposed on a talking chief in Sala'ilua in the early 1970s, though this banishment order, as sometimes happens, was later rescinded and the fine reduced to five pigs; B. Shore, "A Samoan Theory of Action: Social Control and Social Order in a Polynesian Paradox" (Ph.D. diss., University of Chicago, 1977), 144.

8. Krämer, *Die Samoa-Inseln,* II, 101, 384; C. Wilkes, *Narrative of the United States Exploring Expedition during the Years 1838–1842* (London, 1845), II, 150; Stair, *Old Samoa,* 95; Turner, *Nineteen Years in Polynesia,* 286; Brown, *Melanesians and Polynesians,* 291; *Institutions and Customs of the Samoans,* 4.

9. Turner, *Nineteen Years in Polynesia,* 285; Brown, *Melanesians and Polynesians,* 289.

10. J. B. Stair, "Jottings on the Mythology and the Spirit-Lore of Old Samoa," *Journal of the Polynesian Society* 5 (1896): 38; R. S. Moore and J. R. Farrington, *The American Samoan Commission's Visit to Samoa: September–October, 1930* (Washington, D.C., 1931), 30.

14. Childrearing

1. M. Mead, *Male and Female* (Harmondsworth, 1962), 201; idem, "South Sea Hints on Bringing Up Children," *Parents' Magazine* 4 (1929): 22, 50; idem, "Back of Adolescence Lies Early Childhood," *Childhood Education* 18 (1941): 58; idem, "Broken Homes,"

The Nation 128 (1929): 254; idem, *Growing up in New Guinea,* in *From the South Seas* (New York, 1939), 239; idem, "Parents and Children in Samoa," *Child Study* 9 (1932): 232.

2. M. Mead, *Continuities in Cultural Evolution* (New Haven, 1964), 9; J. B. Watson, *Psychological Care of Infant and Child* (London, 1928), 14, 28; idem, "Should a Child Have More Than One Mother? A Psychologist's Notion of a Better Way to Grow Up," *Liberty,* 29 June 1929, p. 33.

3. K. Lorenz, "Der Kumpan in der Umwelt des Vogels," *Journal of Ornithology* 83 (1935): 137; J. P. Scott and J. L. Fuller, *The Genetics and Social Behavior of the Dog* (Chicago, (1965); H. F. Harlow, "The Nature of Love," *American Psychologist* 13 (1958): 673; J. Bowlby, *Attachment and Loss,* vol. I *Attachment* (London, 1969), 179, vol. II, *Separation, Anxiety and Anger* (London, 1973); R. A. Spitz and K. M. Wolf, "The Smiling Response: a Contribution to the Ontogenesis of Social Relations," *Genetic Psychology Monographs* 34 (1946): 57. Our observation of a Samoan infant (born on 20 January 1966) showed that nonselective smiling was at its peak during his fourth month, when he would smile at complete strangers and respond with a marked smile even when approached by someone wearing a mask with a highly threatening expression. At the end of the third quarter of his first year, however, this infant did not respond when smiled at by a stranger, and when confronted by the same threatening mask would turn away in alarm to cling closely to his mother, to whom he had by then become behaviorally attached.

4. D. Freeman, "Kinship, Attachment Behavior and the Primary Bond," in J. Goody, ed., *The Character of Kinship* (Cambridge, 1973), 109 ff.

5. M. Mead, *Coming of Age in Samoa* (New York, 1973), 22.

6. Mead, "Broken Homes," 254; idem, *Social Organization of Manu'a* (Honolulu, 1930), 91; idem, "Samoan Children at Work and Play," *Natural History* 28 (1928): 632; idem, *Coming of Age,* 42; idem, "The Role of the Individual in Samoan Culture," *Journal of the Royal Anthropological Institute* 58 (1928): 487.

7. E. R. Gerber, "The Cultural Patterning of Emotions in Samoa" (Ph.D. diss., University of California, San Diego, 1975), 76.

8. M. Mead, "Psychologic Weaning: Childhood and Adolescence," in M. Mead, *Anthropology: A Human Science: Selected Papers, 1939–1960* (New York, 1964), 43; idem, "Samoan Children at Work and Play," 633; idem, *Coming of Age,* 159; idem, *Male and Female,* 99, 124; idem, *Anthropologists and What They Do,* 124.

9. C. Wilkes, *Narrative of the United States Exploring Expedition during the Years 1838–1842* (London, 1845), II, 73; J. B. Stair, *Old Samoa* (London, 1897), 178; L. D. Holmes, *Samoan Village* (New York, 1974), 78; S. Hirsh, "The Social Organization of an Urban Village in Samoa," *Journal of the Polynesian Society* 67 (1958): 281; Mead, *Social Organization of Manu'a,* 226 ff.; Gerber, "The Cultural Patterning of Emotions in Samoa," 57 ff.

10. Gerber, "The Cultural Patterning of Emotions in Samoa," 55; Proverbs 13: 24, 22: 6.

11. Gerber, "The Cultural Patterning of Emotions in Samoa," 72.

12. L. D. Holmes, *Ta'ū: Stability and Change in a Samoan Village* (Wellington, 1958), 44.

13. Police Records, Western Samoa, P.C. 3487, 1958, and P.C. 3611, 1963.

14. For a reproduction of a drawing by a 6-year-old Samoan girl, see D. Freeman, "Functional Aspects of Aggression, Fear and Attachment in Anthropological Perspective," in M. von Cranach et al., eds., *Human Ethology: Claims and Limits of a New Discipline* (Cambridge, 1979), 292.

15. *Samoa Times,* 29 June 1918; R. A. Goodman, "Some Aitu Beliefs of Modern Samoans," *Journal of the Polynesian Society* 80 (1971): 471.

15. Samoan Character

1. M. Mead, *Growing Up in New Guinea,* in M. Mead, *From the South Seas* (New York, 1939), 234; idem, "Jealousy: Primitive and Civilized," in S. D. Schmalhausen and V. F. Calverton, eds., *Woman's Coming of Age: A Symposium* (New York, 1931), 46; idem, *Coming of Age in Samoa* (New York, 1973), 199; idem, *Social Organization of Manu'a* (Honolulu, 1930), 84.

2. M. Mead, *Male and Female* (Harmondsworth, 1962), 100; idem, *Social Organization of Manu'a,* 43, 100; idem, *Coming of Age,* 155 ff.

3. W. Harbutt, in a letter dated Lepā, Upolu, 28 January 1841, L.M.S. Archives; G. A. Lundie, *Missionary Life in Samoa* (Edinburgh, 1846), 105, 117; A. W. Murray, Journal, 6 June 1840, L.M.S. Archives.

4. Mead, *Coming of Age,* 160; T. Powell, letter dated Pago Pago, 23 October 1869, L.M.S. Archives; *'O le Savali,* Apia, Western Samoa, 21 March 1967.

5. G. Pratt, *Grammar and Dictionary of the Samoan Language* (Malua, 1911) 224, 327; J. Williams, *A Narrative of Missionary Enterprises in the South Sea Islands* (London, 1837), 442; G. Turner, *Nineteen Years in Polynesia* (London, 1861), 227; W. T. Pritchard, *Polynesian Reminiscences* (London, 1866), 148.

6. G. Brown, *Pioneer Missionary and Explorer: An Autobiography* (London, 1908), 34; Turner, *Nineteen Years in Polynesia,* 343; Pratt, *Grammar and Dictionary,* 157, 188.

7. Mead, *Coming of Age,* 206 ff.

8. R. L. Stevenson, *A Footnote to History* (Leipzig, 1892), 48; A. Wendt, *Pouliuli* (Wellington, 1977), 116.

9. C. Wilkes, *Narrative of the United States Exploring Expedition during the Years 1838–1842* (London, 1845), V, 23; B. Cartwright, Field Notebook II, p. 66, Bernice P. Bishop Museum, Honolulu.

10. J. Williams, "Narrative of a Voyage Performed in the Missionary Schooner 'Olive Branch,' 1832," L.M.S. Archives; Pratt, *Grammar and Dictionary,* 229; R. L. Stevenson, *Vailima Letters* (London, 1912), 115; C. C. Marsack, *Samoan Medley* (London, 1964), 29.

11. Mead, *Male and Female,* 100; idem, *Coming of Age,* 123.

12. O. Fenichal, *The Psychoanalytic Theory of Neurosis* (London, 1946), 279; M. Mackenzie, "More North American than the North Americans: Medical Consequences of Migrant Enthusiasm, Willing and Unwilled" (Department of Anthropology, University of California, Berkeley, n.d.), 3; R. Rose, *South Seas Magic* (London, 1959), 102.

13. Turner, *Nineteen Years in Polynesia,* 340.

14. M. Mead, "The Role of the Individual in Samoan Culture," *Journal of the Royal Anthropological Institute* 58 (1928): 494.

15. Of the twenty-two cases of suicide, eight were by hanging, six by shooting, four by poisoning, three by leaping from a height, and one by cutting the throat.

16. G. Pratt, Note, Papers of G. Brown, Mitchell Library, Sydney.

17. L. D. Holmes, in "The Restudy of Manu'an Culture: A Problem of Methodology" (Ph.D. diss., Northwestern University, 1957), 222, reports a comparable case of a girl of Ta'ū who, because she could not marry the man she desired, ate poisonous seaweed.

18. Information supplied by the Chief Statistician, Commonwealth Department of Health, Canberra, A.C.T.; *Crime in New*

Zealand (Wellington, 1968), 84 ff.; J. King, in an article in *The New Pacific Magazine* 6 (1981): 28, estimates the suicide rate in Western Samoa at 20 per 100,000, and that of American Samoa (since 1968) at 7.6 per 100,000 per annum. As M. B. Clinard reports in *Sociology of Deviant Behavior* (New York, 1974), 635, "the older a person is, in the United States and generally throughout Western European countries, the more likely he is to take his own life." The rates in the United States for 1970 were about three times as great for those between 45 and 54 as for those between 15 and 24. In contrast, in Samoa it is the young who tend to commit suicide: of the twenty-two cases I investigated, only one was over 45 years of age, while fifteen, or 68 percent, were in the age group 15–24, and one was a girl of 14.

19. Mead, *Social Organization of Manu'a,* 98, 161.

20. T. K. Oesterreich, *Possession, Demoniacal and Other Among Primitive Races in Antiquity, the Middle Ages and Modern Times* (New York, 1966), 39; W. Sargant, *The Mind Possessed* (London, 1973), 12; I. P. Pavlov, *Lectures on Conditional Reflexes, II: Conditioned Reflexes and Psychiatry* (London, 1941); B. Shore, "A Samoan Theory of Action: Social Control and Social Order in a Polynesian Paradox" (Ph.D. diss., University of Chicago, 1977), 147.

21. A Buzacott, Journal, 1836, L.M.S. Archives; L. D. Holmes, *Ta'ū: Stability and Change in a Samoan Village* (Wellington, 1958), 33; R. A. Goodman, "Some Aitu Beliefs of Modern Samoans," *Journal of the Polynesian Society* 80 (1971): 468.

22. Buzacott, Journal, 1836.

23. When I returned to Western Samoa in 1981 I learned that Mu, when 27 years of age, had killed himself with a shotgun after a disagreement with his natal mother.

24. According to information provided in 1967 by the Records Section of the Apia Hospital, during the years 1955–1967 a total of sixty-three psychiatrically ill individuals were institutionalized. The population of Western Samoa was 91,833 in 1956 and 131,552 in 1966.

16. Sexual Mores and Behavior

1. M. Mead, *Blackberry Winter* (New York, 1972), 167; *American Mercury* 15 (1928): xxii; F. O'Brien, cited on the back cover of the Mentor edition of *Coming of Age in Samoa* (New York, 1962); M. Mead, "The Samoans," in M. Mead, ed., *Cooperation and Competition among Primitive Peoples* (New York, 1937), 123, 310; idem, "Americanization in Samoa," *American Mercury* 16 (1929):

269; idem, *Coming of Age in Samoa* (New York, 1973), 195; J. J. Honigmann, *Understanding Culture* (New York, 1963), 273; R. H. Lowie, review of *Coming of Age in Samoa, American Anthropologist* 31 (1929): 532.

2. R. H. Lowie, *Robert H. Lowie, Ethnologist: A Personal Record* (Berkeley, 1959), 110; E. G. Burrows, "Western Polynesia, A Study in Cultural Differentiation," *Etnologiska Studier* 7 (1938): 5; C. Wilkes, *Narrative of the United States Exploring Expedition during the Years 1838-1842* (London, 1845), II, 73; R. G. Crocombe and M. Crocombe, *The Works of Ta'unga: Records of a Polynesian Traveller in the South Seas 1833-1896* (Canberra, 1968), 132; W. T. Pritchard, *Polynesian Reminiscences* (London, 1866), 138; A. Krämer, *Die Samoa-Inseln* (Stuttgart, 1902), I, 39; Constitutional Convention of Western Samoa (1954), Papers and Proceedings (Nelson Memorial Library, Apia, Western Samoa).

3. Mead, *Coming of Age,* 98; idem, "The Sex Life of the Unmarried Adult in Primitive Society," in I. S. Wile, ed., *The Sex Life of the Unmarried Adult* (London, 1953), 61; idem, *Male and Female* (Harmondsworth, 1962), 119. In all of the editions of *Coming of Age in Samoa* that I have inspected, Mead spells the Samoan term for a ceremonial virgin incorrectly as *taupo,* instead of *tāupou* (as in the dictionaries of Pratt and Milner). This is a major solecism, for, as Krämer notes in *Die Samoa-Inseln,* I, 32, *taupo* literally means "to indulge in love affairs at night," a connotation totally alien to the culturally defined role of a ceremonial virgin.

4. 'Aiono Ma'ia'i, *Tama Samoa Ala Mai* (Apia, 1964), 10; R. L. Stevenson, *Vailima Papers* (London, 1924), 278. S. Ella, "Samoa, etc.," *Report, Australasian Association for the Advancement of Science* 4 (1892): 623; J. Lefarge, *Reminiscences of the South Seas* (London, 1914), 120.

5. J. Bugge, *Virginitas: An Essay in the History of a Medieval Ideal* (The Hague, 1975), 17.

6. G. Brown, *Melanesians and Polynesians* (London, 1910), 56; for a photograph of virgin locks of the kind once affected by virgins in Samoa, see Laura Thompson's photograph, taken in the 1930s, of a girl of the Lau Islands (to the west of Samoa), in her *Fijian Frontier* (New York, 1940), 58; J. Williams, "Narrative of a Voyage Performed in the Missionary Schooner 'Olive Branch,' 1832," L.M.S. Archives.

7. G. Turner, *Nineteen Years in Polynesia* (London, 1861), 321; 'Aiono Ma'ia'i, *Tama Samoa Ala Mai,* 11.

8. G. Turner, *Samoa a Hundred Years Ago and Long Before* (London, 1884), 94; Williams, "Narrative of a Voyage"; R. W. Williamson, *Essays in Polynesian Ethnology* (Cambridge, 1939), 321.

9. Williams, "Narrative of a Voyage"; both Turner, *Samoa a Hundred Years Ago,* 94 and Pritchard, *Polynesian Reminiscences,* 138, also report wild enthusiasm on the part of the immediate relations of a taupou, when at her ceremonial defloration she proved to be a virgin, with the cutting of heads with stones until the blood flowed freely.

10. Williams, "Narrative of a Voyage"; Pritchard, *Polynesian Reminiscences,* 139.

11. J. E. Erskine, *Journal of a Cruise among the Islands of the Western Pacific* (London, 1853), 411.

12. Ibid., 414.

13. A. Krämer, *Salamasina,* trans. Brother Herman (Pago Pago, 1958; orig, 1923), 24; W. Harbutt, letter dated Upolu, 21 April 1856, L.M.S. Archives; Pritchard, *Polynesian Reminiscences,* 53.

14. R. M. Moyle, "Sexuality in Samoan Art Forms," *Archives of Sexual Behavior* 3 (1975): 231; the translation is my own.

15. E. Tregear, *The Maori-Polynesian Comparative Dictionary* (Wellington, 1891), 113; G. B. Milner, *Samoan Dictionary* (London, 1966), 6.

16. Police Records, Western Samoa, P.C. 208, 1963; P. H. Buck, Field Notebook V, p. 54, 17 December 1927, Bernice P. Bishop Museum, Honolulu.

17. E. W. Gifford, *Tongan Society* (Honolulu, 1929), 186; L. Thompson, *Fijian Frontier* (New York, 1940), 48; R. Firth, *We, the Tikopia* (London, 1936), 514 and 559.

18. Turner, *Nineteen Years in Polynesia,* 188; O. Stuebel, *Selections from Samoan Texts,* trans. Brother Herman (Pago Pago, n.d.), 40 ff.; B. Shore, "A Samoan Theory of Action: Social Control and Social Order in a Polynesian Paradox" (Ph.D. diss., University of Chicago, 1977), 422.

19. E. R. Gerber, "The Cultural Patterning of Emotions in Samoa" (Ph.D. diss., University of California, San Diego, 1975), 97; F. A. Young, "Stability and Change in Samoa" (Ph.D. diss., University of Oregon, 1976), 39; Police Records, Western Samoa, P.C. 1804, 1959; P.C. 694, 1964.

20. L. D. Holmes, *Ta'ū: Stability and Change in a Samoan Village* (Wellington, 1958), 47, records that "when Mead resided in Ta'ū village there was a pastor's boarding school for girls aged

twelve to eighteen"; cf. F. G. Calkins, *My Samoan Chief* (Honolulu, 1975), 18, who records the statement of her Samoan husband, Vaiao J. Ala'ilima, that "respectable young Samoan ladies at a critical age usually lived with the village pastor for safekeeping." Under Samoan custom a girl was required to be a virgin to qualify for residence in a pastor's household. It is unlikely, therefore, that as claimed in table 1 in *Coming of Age in Samoa,* two girls were still resident in the pastor's household after having had heterosexual experience. If the two girls had, in fact, not had heterosexual experience, the proportion of virgins in Mead's sample is then 60 percent; Mead, *Coming of Age,* 168, 282, 285.

21. Shore, "A Samoan Theory of Action," 422; Mead, *Coming of Age,* 98; Archives, High Court of American Samoa, Fagatogo, Tutuila, American Samoa.

22. Of the twenty-two girls in the age-group 16–18 in Sa'anapu in August 1967, eighteen, or 82 percent, were members of the Ekalesia. Membership in the Ekalesia by an unmarried adolescent girl is based on acceptance by other members, who exercise a very strict surveillance in this matter, that she is a virgin. The classing of a girl as a virgin is based on this and all other available relevant evidence. In contrast, only one of the twenty-five adolescent males in the age-group 16–18 was a communicant member of the Ekalesia.

23. Shore, "A Samoan Theory of Action," 422. Although the ideal of chastity for women before marriage is still of great importance in Samoa, changes in sexual mores have occurred and are still occurring following the large-scale migration, from the 1950s onward, of American Samoans to the United States and of Western Samoans to New Zealand, which has led to acquaintance with the sexual permissiveness of Western societies. Some of these migrants have returned to Samoa, and in consequence sexual behavior has, since the 1960s, begun to depart from the traditional system.

24. M. Mead, "Cultural Contexts of Puberty and Adolescence," *Bulletin of the Philadelphia Association for Psychoanalysis* 9 (1959): 62; J. J. Honigmann, *Understanding Culture* (New York, 1963), 273.

25. Pritchard, *Polynesian Reminiscences,* 134. Mead is in error in claiming, in *Coming of Age in Samoa,* 152, that in Samoa illegitimate children are "enthusiastically welcomed"; cf. L. D. Holmes's statement, in *Samoan Village* (New York, 1974), 82, that the village council of Fitiuta, Manu'a "imposes heavy fines on any family wherein a member gives birth to a child out of wedlock."

26. N. A. Rowe, *Samoa under the Sailing Gods* (New York and London, 1930), 271; in a footnote to his description of "a Samoan girl's moral code," Rowe adds the comment, "they are singularly chaste compared to most Polynesians."

27. A. Wendt, *Pouliuli* (Auckland, 1977), 121.

28. Mead, "The Sex Life of the Unmarried Adult in Primitive Society," 62; idem, *Coming of Age,* 90; idem, *Social Organization of Manu'a* (Honolulu, 1930), 84; idem, "Jealousy: Primitive and Civilized," in S. D. Schmalhausen and V. F. Calverton, eds., *Woman's Coming of Age: A Symposium* (New York, 1931), 44, 46.

29. Pritchard, *Polynesian Reminiscences,* 393; Wilkes, *Narrative of the United States Exploring Expedition,* II, 138; Turner, *Nineteen Years in Polynesia,* 285, 336; Stuebel, *Selections from Samoan Texts,* 47 ff.; Brown, *Melanesians and Polynesians,* 266.

30. A. M. Noble and W. Evans, *Codification of the Regulations and Orders for the Government of American Samoa* (San Francisco, 1921), 25. For example, in 1927 a man named Peresetene, having been charged that he "did sleep with Ta'e, the wife of Patolo, in violation of Section 23," was fined $25, while Ta'e was fined $15; Archives, High Court of American Samoa, Fagatogo, Tutuila.

31. A. Calder-Marshall, *The Innocent Eye: The Life of Robert J. Flaherty* (London, 1963), 114; F. H. Flaherty, "Fa'aSamoa," *Asia* 25 (1925): 1098; F. G. Calkins, *My Samoan Chief* (Honolulu, 1975), 82.

32. L. A. White, *The Science of Culture* (New York, 1949), 154; C. C. Marsack, letter to D. Freeman dated 1 April 1969; J. L. Brenchley, *Jottings during the Cruise of H.M.S. 'Curacoa,' among the South Sea Islands in 1865* (London, 1873), 58. Mead's inaccurate portrayal of Samoan attitudes about adultery had misled a number of writers. As already noted, Bertrand Russell, in his still widely read *Marriage and Morals* (London, 1958; orig. 1929), 107, citing Mead, states quite erroneously that the Samoans, "when they have to go on a journey, fully expect their wives to console themselves for their absence"; while L. Malson, a French professor of social psychiatry, in L. Malson and J. Itard, *Wolf Children: The Wild Boy of Aveyron* (London, 1972), 25, has published the preposterous statement that the Samoans practice "conjugal hospitality."

33. Police Records, Western Samoa, P.C. 947, 1956 and P.C. 674, 1964.

34. Gerber, "The Cultural Patterning of Emotions in Samoa," 150; Police Records, Western Samoa, P.C. 3863, 1964; G. P. Murdock, *Our Primitive Contemporaries* (New York, 1934), 72.

35. Mead, *Male and Female,* 202; idem, "The Role of the Individual in Samoan Culture," *Journal of the Royal Anthropological Institute* 58 (1928): 487.

36. Mead, *Social Organization of Manu'a,* 227; idem, "The Samoans," in M. Mead, ed., *Cooperation and Competition among Primitive Peoples* (New York, 1937), 302; idem, *Coming of Age,* 93.

37. Fa'afouina Pula, *The Samoan Dance of Life,* 125; Archives, High Court of American Samoa, Fagatogo, Tutuila, American Samoa.

38. G. Platt, Journal, 15 May 1836, L.M.S. Archives; Mead, *Coming of Age,* 95; *Samoa Times,* 29 December 1967.

39. Police Records, Western Samoa, P.C. 2197, 1960.

40. J. M. Macdonald, *Rape: Offenders and Their Victims* (Springfield, Ill., 1975), 25 ff.; Annual Report, Police and Prisons Department, Government of Western Samoa, 1966, Appendix A. According to American Samoa's Annual Report, Fiscal Year 1980, p. 129, the average number of forcible rapes per year during the years 1975–1980 was 14, which is equal to a rate of approximately 45 per 100,000.

41. In *Coming of Age in Samoa,* 151, Mead states categorically that there is no frigidity in Samoa. In fact, because of anxiety over rape, which in some cases results in phobic states, frigidity is indeed found among Samoan women, and as Holmes, *Ta'ū* (Wellington, 1958), 55, correctly reports it, "often produces family tensions."

42. G. Pratt, in a letter dated Matautu, Savai'i, 11 June 1845, L.M.S. Archives; Archives, High Court of American Samoa, Fagatogo, Tutuila, American Samoa; *American Samoa. Hearings Before the Commission Appointed by the President of the United States* (Washington, D.C., 1931), 391; A. M. Noble and E. Evans, *Codification of the Regulations and Orders for the Government of American Samoa* (San Francisco, 1921), 31.

43. In *Male and Female,* 193, Mead asserts that "we have no evidence that suggests that rape within the meaning of the act—that is, rape of a totally unwilling female—has ever become recognized social practice." Ironically, recognized social practice is exactly what rape, both surreptitious and forcible, has long been among the men of one of the societies Mead herself had studied—that of the Samoans.

44. Mead, *Male and Female,* 119; idem, "Cultural Contexts of Puberty and Adolescence," 62; idem, *Coming of Age,* 98.

45. J. Williams, "Narrative of a Voyage"; J. S. C. Dumont D'Ur-

ville, *Voyage au Pole Sud et dans l'Océanie sur les Corvettes l'Astrolabe et la Zéleé pendant les Années 1837–1840* (Paris, 1842), IV, 338; Turner, *Nineteen Years in Polynesia,* 188; Pritchard, *Polynesian Reminiscences,* 139; Brenchley, *Jottings During the Cruise of H.M.S. 'Curacoa,'* 58 ff.; G. B. Rieman, *Papalangee, or Uncle Sam in Samoa* (Oakland, 1874); Brown, *Melanesians and Polynesians,* 122; Mead, *Social Organization of Manu'a,* 96.

46. M. Mead, "Weaver of the Border," in J. Casagrande, ed., *In the Company of Man* (New York, 1960), 189.

47. R. W. Robson, *Queen Emma* (Sydney, 1965), 220 ff.; Mead, "Weaver of the Border," 188.

48. Mead, "The Sex Life of the Unmarried Adult in Primitive Society," 63; idem, *Male and Female,* 120. Holmes in his *Ta'ū,* 53, echoing Mead, stated that "many a girl has been saved embarrassment by the substitution of a chicken bladder full of blood for that normally produced by a broken hymen." This, to the ornithologically uninformed, may seem circumstantially convincing. However, as O. C. Bradley, in *The Structure of the Fowl* (Edinburgh, 1960), 56, records, "the urinary organs of the fowl consist of two kidneys, each with a ureter, by which the semi-solid urine is conveyed to the cloaca." And so the chicken is without a bladder into which its blood might conveniently be put to solve an unreal enigma of Mead's own making.

17. Adolescence

1. R. Benedict, review of *Coming of Age in Samoa, Journal of Philosophy* 26 (1929): 110; M. Mead, "On the Implications for Anthropology of the Gesell-Ilg Approach to Maturation," *American Anthropologist* 49 (1947): 74; idem, "Cultural Contexts of Puberty and Adolescence," *Bulletin of the Philadelphia Association for Psychoanalysis* 9 (1959): 62; idem, "The Samoans," in M. Mead, ed., *Cooperation and Competition among Primitive Peoples* (New York, 1937), 308; idem, "Adolescence in Primitive and Modern Society," in V. F. Calverton and S. D. Schmalhausen, eds., *The New Generation* (London, 1930), 174; idem, "South Sea Hints on Bringing Up Children," *Parents' Magazine* 4 (1929): 20.

2. H. Katchadourian, *The Biology of Adolescence* (San Francisco, 1977), 11; W. A. Lunden, *Statistics on Delinquents and Delinquency* (Springfield, 1964), 60; M. R. Haskell and L. Yablonsky, *Juvenile Delinquency* (Chicago, 1974), 63.

3. M. Mead, *Blackberry Winter* (New York, 1972), 196; idem, *Growing Up in New Guinea,* in M. Mead, *From the South Seas* (New York, 1939), 212; idem, *Sex and Temperament in Three Primitive Societies,* in Mead, *From the South Seas,* 282.

4. M. Mead, *Coming of Age in Samoa* (New York, 1973), 169 ff.

5. Ibid., 171 ff.

6. Ibid., 155 ff.; E. Schultz, *Proverbial Expressions of the Samoans* (Wellington, 1965), 101.

7. H. S. Sandhu, *Juvenile Delinquency* (New York, 1977), 2; P. W. Tappan, *Juvenile Delinquency* (New York, 1949); D. J. West, *The Young Offender* (Harmondsworth, 1967), 15.

8. Mead, "The Samoans," 308; idem, *Male and Female* (Harmondsworth, 1962; orig. 1950), 99; H. A. Bloch and F. T. Flynn, *Delinquency* (New York, 1956), 37.

9. F. G. Calkins, *My Samoan Chief* (Honolulu, 1975), 18; F. Larkin, *The Australian,* 7 September 1971.

10. Katchadourian, *The Biology of Adolescence,* 43.

11. Police Records, Western Samoa, P.C. 1935, 1965.

12. M. Amir, "Forcible Rape," in L. G. Schultz, ed., *Rape Victimology* (Springfield, 1975), 52; J. P. Bush, *Rape in Australia* (Melbourne, 1977), 145.

13. W. Healy and A. F. Bronner, *Delinquents and Criminals* (New York, 1926), 256; H. Adler, F. Cahn, and J. Stuart, *The Incidence of Delinquency in Berkeley, 1928–1932* (Berkeley, 1934); H. A. Bloch and F. T. Flynn, *Delinquency* (New York, 1956), 50; M. R. Haskell and L. Yablonsky, *Juvenile Delinquency* (Chicago, 1974), 63; D. Challinger, *Young Offenders* (Melbourne, 1977), 45.

14. C. Burt, *The Young Delinquent* (London, 1969; orig. 1925), 218; W. A. Lunden, *Crimes and Criminals,* (Ames, Ia., 1967), 117.

18. The Samoan Ethos

1. M. Mead, "Weaver of the Border," in J. Casagrande, ed., *In the Company of Man* (New York, 1960), 189; idem, *Growing Up in New Guinea,* in *From the South Seas* (New York, 1939), 219, 234; idem, *Coming of Age in Samoa,* (New York, 1973), 198. Mead's assertion that in Samoa "strong allegiances are disallowed" is untrue; cf. L. D. Holmes, *Ta'ū* (Wellington, 1958), 36, for an account of the intensity of sectarian intolerance in Manu'a.

2. Soloi's phrase was *le 'o ni tagata ola;* A. Wendt, *Leaves of the Banyan Tree* (London, 1980), 94.

3. J. A. C. Gray, *Amerika Samoa* (Annapolis, 1960), 208. Although Mead makes no direct reference to these historic happenings, she certainly knew of them. In *Social Organization of Manu'a* (Honolulu, 1930), 167, for example, she mentions a dream of "the high chief of Lumā," Sotoa (she spells it Soatoa), which he had had "before the political trouble resulting from the attempt to reinstate the Tui Manu'a." Nowhere does she discuss the relevance of these crucial events to her depiction of the Samoan ethos.

4. D. Freeman, "A Happening Frightening to Both Ghosts and Men: A Case Study from Western Samoa," in N. Gunson, ed., *The Changing Pacific* (Melbourne, 1978), 163–173; N. A. Rowe, *Samoa under the Sailing Gods* (New York and London, 1930), 267.

5. B. Tripp, *My Trip to Samoa* (Cedar Rapids, Ia., 1911), 73; Gray, *Amerika Samoa,* 149; *American Samoa. Hearings Before the Commission Appointed by the President of the United States* (Washington, D.C., 1931), 76; *Western Samoa (Report of the Royal Commission Concerning the Administration of)* (Wellington, 1927).

6. *Western Samoa,* 354, 427; J. W. Davidson, *Samoa mo Samoa: The Emergence of the Independent State of Western Samoa* (Melbourne, 1967), 125.

7. *Western Samoa,* xliv; Rowe, *Samoa under the Sailing Gods,* 252, 278; *Samoa Times,* 18 January 1929; Davidson, *Samoa mo Samoa,* 138.

8. Rowe, *Samoa under the Sailing Gods,* 274; for an account of the emergence of the independent state of Western Samoa see Davidson, *Samoa mo Samoa;* for an account of reconciliation see Freeman, "A Happening Frightening to Both Ghosts and Men," 172.

9. Thucydides, *The Peloponnesian War,* bk. III, LXII, cited in E. Sagan, *The Lust to Annihilate: A Psychoanalytic Study of Violence in Ancient Greek Culture* (New York, 1979), 173; R. L. Stevenson, *Vailima Papers* (London, 1924), 71; A. Wendt, *Pouliuli* (Auckland, 1977), 17.

10. M. M. Lefkowitz, L. O. Walden, and L. D. Eron, "Punishment, Identification and Aggression," in R. H. Walters et al., eds., *Punishment: Selected Readings* (Harmondsworth, 1972), 378; D. D. Woodman, "What Makes a Psychopath?" *New Society* 53 (1980): 447; M. Mackenzie, "More North American than the North Americans: Medical Consequences of Migrant Enthusiasm, Willing and Unwilled" (Department of Anthropology, University of California, Berkeley, n.d.), 3.

11. C. C. Marsack, *Samoan Medley* (London, 1964), 25; T. Trood,

letter to W. Solf dated 6 February 1909, in C. G. R. McKay, *A Chronology of Western Samoa* (Apia, 1937), 33; G. Brown, *An Autobiography* (London, 1898), 34.

12. Wendt, *Leaves of the Banyan Tree,* 331; H. G. Wolff, *Stress and Disease,* 2nd ed. (Springfield, 1968), 218; H. Selye, *The Stress of Life* (New York, 1978), 259; S. S. Miller, ed., *Symptoms* (London, 1979), 322; L. Winter in *The Milwaukee Journal,* 13 March 1961, p. 11; B. P. Maclaurin, T. E. M. Wardill, S. T. Fa'aiuaso, and M. McKinnon, "Geographic Distribution of Peptic Ulcer Disease in Western Samoa," *New Zealand Medical Journal* 89 (1979): 341. As Wolff notes, the U.S. National Health Survey of 230,000 persons in 73,000 households during the years 1957–1969 revealed an average incidence of peptic ulcer of 5 percent in persons 25 and older.

13. J. Williams, "Narrative of a Voyage Performed in the Missionary Schooner 'Olive Branch,' 1832," L.M.S. Archives; J. E. Erskine, *Journal of a Cruise among the Islands of the Western Pacific* (London, 1853), 36; E. Sabatier, *Astride the Equator: An Account of the Gilbert Islands* (Melbourne, 1977), 92; R. L. Stevenson, in S. Colvin, ed., *The Letters of Robert Louis Stevenson* (London, 1899, II, 360.

19. Mead's Misconstruing of Samoa

1. R. Benedict, "The Science of Custom," (1929), in V. F. Calverton, ed., *The Making of Man* (New York, 1931), 815; M. Mead, *Social Organization of Manu'a* (Honolulu, 1930), 83; idem, *An Anthropologist at Work* (New York, 1959), 212; idem, *Coming of Age in Samoa* (New York, 1973), 197.

2. L. Spier, "Some Central Elements in the Legacy," in W. Goldschmidt, ed., *The Anthropology of Franz Boas, Memoirs, American Anthropological Association* 89 (1959): 146; G. W. Stocking, *Race, Culture and Evolution* (New York, 1968), 303; A. L. Kroeber, "The Anthropological Attitude," *American Mercury* 13 (1928): 490; M. Harris, *The Rise of Anthropological Theory* (London, 1969), 427.

3. M. Mead, *From the South Seas* (New York, 1939), x.

4. M. Mead, "The Arts in Bali," *Yale Review* 30 (1940): 336; G. Keynes, ed., *The Letters of Rupert Brooke* (London, 1968) 525, 542.

5. J. Ferguson, *Utopias of the Classical World* (London, 1975), 14, 16; G. Daws, *A Dream of Islands* (Milton, Queensland, 1980), 4;

L. D. Hammond, ed., *News from New Cythera: A Report of Bougainville's Voyage, 1766-1769* (Minneapolis, 1970), 27, 44; M. Mead, "Americanization in Samoa," *American Mercury* 16 (1929): 269; idem, "Life as a Samoan Girl," in *All True! The Record of Actual Adventures that Have Happened to Ten Women of Today* (New York, 1931), 99; idem, review of *Samoa under the Sailing Gods* by N. Rowe, *The Nation* 133 (1931): 138.

6. M. Mead, *An Inquiry into the Question of Cultural Stability in Polynesia* (New York, 1928), 7; idem, *Blackberry Winter* (New York, 1972), 132, 138.

7. Mead, *Social Organization of Manu'a*, 55; idem, *Coming of Age*, 8, 11.

8. A. Krämer, *Die Samoa-Inseln* (Stuttgart, 1902–1903); R. L. Stevenson, *A Footnote to History*, in *Vailima Papers* (London, 1924); J. W. Davidson, *Samoa mo Samoa* (Melbourne, 1967); I. Strong and L. Osbourne, *Memories of Vailima* (New York, 1902), 169; M. Mead, *Blackberry Winter* (New York, 1972), 154.

9. B. Malinowski, in R. F. Fortune, *Sorcerers of Dobu* (London, 1932), xix.

10. Mead, *Social Organization of Manu'a*, 4; idem, *Coming of Age*, vi; cf. P. J. Pelto and G. H. Pelto, *Anthropological Research: The Structure of Inquiry*, 2nd ed. (Cambridge, 1978), 75: "Participant observation is essential for checking and evaluating key-informant data."

11. Mead, *Blackberry Winter*, 150 ff.; idem, *Letters from the Field, 1925-1975* (New York, 1977), 55.

12. Mead, *Blackberry Winter*, 151; idem, *Social Organization of Manu'a* (Honolulu, 1969), xvii, 224.

13. B. Shore, "Sexuality and Gender in Samoa: Conceptions and Missed Conceptions," in S. Ortner and H. Whitehead, eds., *Sexual Meanings* (Cambridge, 1982), 213, n. 2; Mead, *Social Organization of Manu'a* (1969), 227.

14. Mead, *Social Organization of Manu'a* (1969), 228.

15. Mead, *Coming of Age*, 98; 160; idem, "Cultural Contexts of Puberty and Adolescence," *Bulletin of the Philadelphia Association for Psychoanalysis* 9 (1959): 62; idem, "The Sex Life of the Unmarried Adult in Primitive Society," in I. S. Wile, ed., *The Sex Life of the Unmarried Adult* (London, 1935), 61; idem, *Male and Female* (Harmondsworth, 1962), 119; idem, "Anthropology," in V. Robinson, ed., *Encyclopedia Sexualis* (New York, 1936), 23.

16. E. R. Gerber, "The Cultural Patterning of Emotions in Samoa" (Ph.D. diss., University of California, San Diego, 1975), 126; G. B. Milner, *Samoan Dictionary* (London, 1966), 205.

17. L. D. Holmes, "A Restudy of Manu'an Culture," (Ph.D. diss., Northwestern University, 1957), vii. The view advanced by Gerber's informants is commonplace among Samoans, as Nicholas von Hoffman recounts in his rumbustious account of American Samoa, *Tales from the Margaret Mead Taproom* (Kansas City, 1976), 97 ff. Having cited a paragraph from Mead's *Coming of Age in Samoa* ending with a reference to "the whisper of lovers, until the village rests till dawn," von Hoffman comments: "It's passages like that which have given the South Seas their dishy reputation, although you can find a lot of Samoans who'll tell you that Maggy is a crock. There are supposed to be a bunch of old ladies on the island who claim to be the little girls in Mead's book and who say that they just made up every kind of sexy story for the funny *palagi* lady because she dug dirt."

18. M. Mead, "Apprenticeship Under Boas," in W. Goldschmidt, ed., *The Anthropology of Franz Boas, Memoirs, American Anthropological Association* 89 (1959): 29; J. R. Swanton, "The President Elect," *Science* 73 (1931): 148; R. H. Lowie, review of *Race, Language and Culture* by Franz Boas, *Science* 91 (1940): 599; idem, *The History of Ethnological Theory* (New York, 1937), 151; R. Benedict, *Patterns of Culture* (London, 1945; orig. 1934), 21.

19. P. D. MacLean, "The Evolution of Three Mentalities," in S. L. Washburn and E. R. McCown, eds., *Human Evolution: Biosocial Perspectives* (Menlo Park, Calif., 1978), 47; A. Einstein, quoted in A. P. French, ed., *Einstein: A Centenary Volume* (London, 1979), 209.

20. K. R. Popper, *Conjectures and Refutations: The Growth of Scientific Knowledge* (London, 1969), vii, 16; cf. E. Gellner, *Legitimation of Belief* (Cambridge, 1974), 171: "Popper's theory is not a descriptive account of humanity's actual cognitive practice but rather a prescription, an ethic, which at the same time also singles out *science* from the rest of putative cognition and explains the secret of its success."

20. Toward a More Scientific Anthropological Paradigm

1. C. Zirkle, *Evolution, Marxian Biology and the Social Scene* (Philadelphia, 1959), 447; G. W. Stocking, *Race, Culture and Evolution* (New York, 1968), 303. In using *paradigm* as a convenient term to refer to the disciplinary matrix of a science I do not accept

Kuhn's notion that paradigms are incommensurable. Rather I consider that a paradigm may be actively improved by the employment of what Popper has called "the critical method of error elimination"; cf. P. B. Medawar's comments on this issue in his *Advice to a Young Scientist* (London, 1981), 92: "As for revolutions, they are constantly in progress; a scientist does not hold exactly the same opinions about his research from one day to the next, for reading, reflection, and discussions with colleagues cause a change in emphasis here or there and possible even a radical appraisal of his way of thinking."

2. M. E. Spiro, "Culture and Human Nature," in G. D. Spindler, ed., *The Making of Psychological Anthropology* (Berkeley, 1978), 350; F. Boas, "Genetic and Environmental Factors in Anthropology," *The Teaching Biologist* 9 (1939): 17; idem, "The Tempo of Growth in Fraternities" (1935), in *Race, Language and Culture* (New York, 1940), 88; Stocking, *Race, Culture, and Evolution,* 184; F. Boas, *Anthropology and Modern Life* (New York, 1928), 201; A. L. Kroeber, "The Anthropological Attitude," *American Mercury* 13 (1928): 495; M. Mead, *Growing Up in New Guinea,* in *From the South Seas* (New York, 1939), 212.

3. V. Reynolds, *The Biology of Human Action* (San Francisco, 1980), 89. In 1922, in the course of a British Association symposium on Darwinism, as part of a chorus of criticism by J. C. Willis and others, J. T. Cunningham gave it as his opinion that natural selection was "as extinct as the dodo"; *Nature* 110 (1922): 752. E. Mayr, *Animal Species and Evolution* (Cambridge, Mass., 1963), 1; F. Crick, *Of Molecules and Men* (Seattle and London, 1966), 52; P. Jay, "Mother-Infant Relations in Langurs," in H. Rheingold, ed., *Maternal Behavior in Mammals* (New York, 1963), 286; E. H. Lenneberg, *Biological Foundations of Language* (New York, 1967), 28, 128 ff.; H. J. Muller, "The Gene Material as the Initiator and Organizing Basis of Life," in R. A. Brink, ed., *Heritage from Mendel* (Madison, Wis., 1967), 443.

4. J. Z. Young, *Programs of the Brain* (London, 1978), 10 ff.; D. H. Hubel and T. N. Wiesel, "Functional Architecture of Macaque Monkey Visual Cortex," *Proceedings of the Royal Society of London, B* 198 (1977): 1; for a summary of H. F. R. Prechtl's researches see I. Eibl-Eibesfeldt, *Ethology: The Biology of Behavior* (New York, 1975), 445 ff.; idem, "Human Ethology: Concepts and Implications for the Sciences of Man," *The Behavioral and Brain Sciences* 2 (1979): 1.

5. A. L. Kroeber, "On Human Nature" (1955), in *An Anthropol-*

ogist Looks at History (Berkeley and Los Angeles, 1963), 204; M. von Cranach et al., eds., *Human Ethology: Claims and Limits of a New Discipline* (Cambridge, 1979); I. Eibl-Eibesfeldt, *The Biology of Peace and War* (London, 1979), 15 (as Eibl-Eibesfeldt notes, the ethologist's recognition of phylogenetically programmed behavior does not deny the influence of experience on such behavior, for "both reinforcing and inhibitory influences can be exercised"); A. Montagu, in *The Behavioral and Brain Sciences* 2 (1979): 43.

6. C. H. Waddington, "The Human Evolutionary System," in M. Banton, ed., *Darwinism and the Study of Society* (London, 1961), 70; P. B. Medawar, "Unnatural Science," *The New York Review of Books* 24 (1977): 14; idem, "Technology and Evolution," in *Frontiers of Knowledge* (New York, 1975), 109.

7. J. T. Bonner, *The Evolution of Culture in Animals* (Princeton, 1980).

8. E. Mayr, "Behavior Programs and Evolutionary Strategies" (1974), in *Evolution and the Diversity of Life: Selected Essays* (Cambridge, Mass., 1976), 694 ff.; K. R. Popper, "Natural Selection and the Emergence of Mind" (First Darwin Lecture, delivered at Darwin College, Cambridge, 8 November 1977); Bonner, *The Evolution of Culture in Animals,* 144 ff.; K. Lorenz, *Behind the Mirror* (London, 1977), 175. For further discussion of the anthropological significance of multiple choice behavior, cf. D. Freeman, "The Anthropology of Choice," *Canberra Anthropology* 4 (1981): 82.

9. Bonner, *The Evolution of Culture in Animals,* 19.

10. M. Mead, "Retrospects and Prospects," in T. Gladwin and W. C. Sturtevant, eds., *Anthropology and Human Behavior* (Washington, D.C., 1962), 121; R. Benedict, *Patterns of Culture* (London, 1945; orig. 1934), 57; F. Nietzsche, *The Birth of Tragedy* (New York, 1956; orig. 1872), 34; J. E. Harrison, *Themis* (London, 1963), 443.

11. Extreme biological determinism, or geneticism, has also survived into the 1980s; cf. the characterization of geneticism as "the enthusiastic misapplication of not fully understood genetic principles in situations to which they do not apply," in P. B. and J. S. Medawar, *The Life Science: Current Ideas of Biology* (London, 1977), 38.

A Note on
Orthography
and Pronunciation

Fourteen letters only are used in the writing of classical Samoan (other than in loan-words recently introduced into the language): *a, e, f, g, i, l, m, n, o, p, s, t, u, v.* The letters *h, k,* and *r,* are used in writing some words of foreign origin.

In contemporary Samoa there are two distinct forms of pronunciation, one formal and the other colloquial. As G. B. Milner notes in his *Samoan Dictionary* (London, 1966), xiv, formal pronunciation "is held out to children, students and foreign visitors as a model to follow and is regarded by an overwhelming majority of Samoans as representing an earlier and purer state of the language than that which . . . exists today," while the colloquial pronunciation (in which the *t* of the classical language becomes a *k*) is "used by the great majority of Samoans both in their private and public relations." In his dictionary, Milner adopts the formal pronunciation as his standard of description, as did Pratt before him, and it is this standard that I have also chosen to follow.

It is worthy of special mention that the five vowels, *a, e, i, o, u* (each of which is distinctly pronounced) may be phonetically either long or short; long vowels may be marked with a macron. In this book macrons have been used only where strictly necessary as a guide to pronunciation. Again the letter *g* represents a nasal sound, as in the English word *singer,* which in other Polynesian languages is written *ng*. Finally, I have used an apostrophe to mark the glottal stop that occurs in many Samoan words. This represents a break, or catch in the voice similar to that found in the Cockney pronunciation of English, in which, for example, the word *letter* is pronounced *le'er*. Those wanting further information on the phonology and pronunciation of Samoan should consult either Chapter 1 of G. Pratt's *Grammar and Dictionary of the Samoan Language* (Malua, 1960), or the preface to Milner's *Samoan Dictionary*.

Glossary

aganu'u   custom
agasala   sin, conduct deserving of punishment
'āiga   family, relative
aitu   a ghost or spirit
ali'i   a titular chief
ali'i pa'ia   a sacred chief
Atua   God
aualuma   a group consisting of women (including widows) who are
    resident members, by birth or adoption, of a local polity
'aumaga   a group consisting of the untitled men of a local polity
'ava   kava, a ceremonial beverage made from the root of the shrub
    Piper methysticum
avaga   an elopement
Ekalesia   the communicant body of the church
fa'ali'i   to throw a tantrum

fa'alupega   a set of traditional phrases that name in order of rank the principal titles and family connections of a local polity, district, and so on

fa'aSamoa   the customs and traditions of the Samoan people

fa'avae   foundation, or constitution

fale tele   a round house traditionally used for the reception of guests and the holding of meetings

fono   chiefly assembly, any formal meeting

fono manu   a juridical fono

gafa   a genealogy

ifoga   a ceremonial apology or request for forgiveness

ma'i aitu   an illness caused, according to Samoans, by an individual being possessed by a ghost

malae   an open space, usually in the center of a nu'u, where ceremonies and other activities are held

malaga   journey, traveling party

mālō   the dominant part or faction, victorious in war; in modern times, the government

mamalu   honor, dignity

manaia   the son of a titular chief possessing a title with certain ceremonial duties and privileges

matai   the titled head of an 'aiga, who may be either an ali'i or a tulafale

moetotolo   surreptitious rape

musu   utterly uncooperative, sullen, and obdurate

nu'u   a local polity, or village

papalagi or **palagi**   a European

pa'umutu   a sexually promiscuous female

pule   power, authority, control

saisai   a humiliating form of punishment in which an individual is tied up like a pig about to be baked

ta'alolo   a ceremonial presentation of food and other gifts offered to a distinguished visitor

tafa'ifa   in western Samoa, the four titles Tui A'ana, Tui Atua, Gatoaitele, and Tamasoāli'i, which conferred titular supremacy or "kingship"

tama'āiga   "royal son," applied in western Samoa to the high-ranking titles Malietoa, Mata'afa, Tamasese, and Tuimaleali'ifano

taula aitu   a spirit medium

taule'ale'a (pl. **taulele'a**)   an untitled man

taupou   a ceremonial virgin

tautalaitiiti   impudent, cheeky; lit. to speak up while still young

teine muli   a virgin

toa   a warrior

to'ilalo   the defeated party or faction in a war or other contest

tosogafafine   forcible rape

tuiga   an ornamented headdress of human hair bleached to a golden color, the wearing of which is the prerogative of certain titular chiefs and their families

tulafale   a talking chief, or orator

tulafono   law, a rule enacted by a fono

tupu   the term formerly used to refer to the paramount chief of western Samoa

Acknowledgments

THE RESEARCHES on which this book are based have extended over several decades, and I wish to express my deep gratitude to all those individuals who, over the years, have helped me in my work. Among those who introduced me to the study of anthropology I would particularly mention H. D. Skinner and Ernest Beaglehole, who guided my early researches in Samoa; Sir Raymond Firth and S. F. Nadel, whose student I was at the University of London, and Meyer Fortes, who supervised my studies at King's College, Cambridge. Again, I have derived great benefit and encouragement from Sir Karl Popper's interest in the long-term research project of which this book is the summation.

During my work in Samoa in the 1960s I was given vital support by Sir John Crawford, at that time director of the Research School of Pacific Studies at the Australian National University, and by Paul Gabites, then New Zealand High Commissioner in Western Samoa. In both Upolu and Savai'i in 1967 I learned much from collaborative research with Irenäus Eibl-Eibesfeldt, and over many years I was fortunate in being able to discuss our common interest in Samoa with J. W. Davidson, the Foundation Professor of Pacific History at the Australian National University and my friend from the time of our undergraduate days together at Victoria University College in Wellington, New Zealand. Similarly, I have benefited from my correspondence about things Samoan with Sir Charles Marsack, who for many years was president of the Land and Titles Court in Western Samoa.

It is to the people of Samoa themselves, however, that I am most deeply indebted. During my visits to their islands I have been treated with the greatest civility and kindness, and after an association over many years, particularly with the village of Sa'anapu, my regard for the Samoan people is profound. Robert Louis Stevenson, not long before his death at Vailima in 1894, told the chiefs who had become his friends that he had come to "love Samoa and her people" and had chosen them "to live and die with." Anyone who has really come to know the Samoans and the *fa'aSamoa* will apprehend and share the spirit and intent of these heartfelt words.

My researches in Western Samoa during 1966–1967 were supported by its then prime minister, Mata'afa Fiame Faumuina Mulinu'u II, and by the Masiofo Fetaui Mata'afa, whose father, Le Mamea Matatumua, was my first mentor in the *fa'aSamoa*. I remain most grateful for their hospitality and their interest in my work. I also wish to acknowledge my indebtedness to my friend and principal tutor in the Samoan language, Lefau So'onalole Masina, and to all members of his family. On several occasions in my study of Samoan values I have been privileged to have the counsel of that nonpareil among Samoan ladies of rank, To'oa Salamasina Malietoa, and in 1981 I was exceptionally fortunate in having a draft of this book subjected to the critical scrutiny of Le Tagaloa Leota Pita of the University of Samoa, and in being able to discuss the results of my researches with his wife, Aiono Fanaafi, the vice-chancellor of that university. To these eminent Samoans I am especially grateful.

To the *ali'i* and *tulafale* and all the people of Sa'anapu I am thankful for an association that has extended over four decades, during the chieftainships of both 'Anapu Solofa and his son 'Anapu 'Aiali'i. It was Lauvi Vainu'u, who, in 1942, by taking me into his *'āiga,* enabled me to appreciate at first hand the realities of the *fa'aSamoa,* and, since that time, I have been helped in innumerable ways by many others of Sa'anapu, to all of whom I now say *fa'afetai, tele tele lava.* In particular, my thanks are due for assistance during the years 1966–1967 to Lea'ana Fa'alolo and all the members of his *'āiga,* as also to the talking chiefs Tuigale'ava Tiuga and Le Sa Vai, who, in 1967, accompanied me on a memorable *malaga* to Tutuila and Manu'a.

In Manu'a in 1967, I was especially helped by the Reverend John Soloi, then pastor at Fitiuta, and by Pese Olioli and his family, of Si'ufaga. For most valuable assistance during my visit to Tutuila in 1981 my thanks are due to Robert L. Gornick, Clerk of Courts in the High Court of American Samoa, and to Tuiteleleapaga Napoleone, who was a young man in Manu'a at the time of Margaret Mead's sojourn there.

Many librarians have assisted me in my researches. I am especially thankful to Mataina Te'o and others of the Nelson Memorial Library, Apia, Western Samoa; Miss I. Fletcher, formerly Librarian at Livingstone House, London; Cynthia Timberlake and Marguerite Ashford of the Library of the Bernice P. Bishop Museum, Honolulu, Hawai'i; and the staffs of the Alexander Turnbull Library, Wellington, New Zealand; the Mitchell Library, Sydney, Australia; and the Menzies Library of the Australian National University, Canberra. For research assistance over many years, I am indebted to Henny Fokker-Bakker and Judith Wilson. For the map I am grateful to Theo Baumann.

To G. N. Appell, John Bowles, James Fox, Robert Hunt, Michael Jackson, H. E. Maude, Michael Moerman, H. Neumann, Uili F. Nokise, Vernon Reynolds, Bradd Shore, O. H. K. Spate, D. F. Tuzin, Gerard Ward, and Albert Wendt, I am grateful for insightfully critical comments on earlier drafts of this book; and to Ann Buller, Ita Pead, and Ria van de Zandt for having so cheerfully and efficiently typed these various drafts. I am deeply appreciative of the exceptional editorial skills of Camille Smith, of Harvard University Press.

Finally, my very special thanks are due to my daughters Jennifer and Hilary, who, through their friendships with Samoan girls of their own ages, provided me with information and insights of a particularly valuable kind; and, beyond all others, to my wife, Monica, who was with me in Samoa in 1966–1967 and again in 1981, and who has contributed, as only she could, to my work on this book.

Index